PENGUIN REFERENCE BOOKS

# THE PENGUIN DICTIONARY
# OF PROVERBS

Rosalind Fergusson was born in Liverpool in 1953 and obtained her degree in French from Exeter University. From there she took a teaching certificate and became an assistant teacher at a school in West Sussex. From 1978 to 1984 she worked for Market House Books where she trained as an assistant editor and lexicographer and rose to the position of Senior Editor. During this time she worked on a range of books, particularly dictionaries. Since leaving Market House Books she has worked as a freelance editor.

Her other publications include *The Mr Men Word Books* (1979), *Pan's English–French Dictionary* (1982), *The Penguin Rhyming Dictionary* (1985) and *Choose Your Baby's Name* (1987). Rosalind Fergusson has also edited and co-edited a number of dictionaries and reference books and has contributed to Secker & Warburg's *Dictionary of British History* (1981) and Longman's *Dictionary of Twentieth Century Biography* (1985) among others.

Rosalind Fergusson is married and lives in Southbourne. Her leisure interests include walking, photography and music.

# THE PENGUIN DICTIONARY OF
# PROVERBS

ROSALIND FERGUSSON

MARKET HOUSE BOOKS LTD

Bloomsbury Books
London

PENGUIN BOOKS

Published by the Penguin Group
Penguin Books Ltd, 27 Wrights Lane, London W8 5TZ, England
Penguin Books USA Inc., 375 Hudson Street, New York, New York 10014, USA
Penguin Books Australia Ltd, Ringwood, Victoria, Australia
Penguin Books Canada Ltd, 10 Alcorn Avenue, Toronto, Ontario, Canada M4V 3B2
Penguin Books (NZ) Ltd, 182-190 Wairau Road, Auckland 10, New Zealand

Penguin Books Ltd, Registered Offices: Harmondsworth, Middlesex, England

First published by Penguin Books 1983
Published simultaneously by Allen Lane
This edition published by Bloomsbury Books, an imprint of
Godfrey Cave Associates Ltd, 42 Bloomsbury Street, London WC1B 3QJ,
under licence from Penguin Books Ltd, 1991
1 3 5 7 9 10 8 6 4 2

Copyright © Market House Books Ltd, 1983

Printed in England by
BPCC Hazell Books
Aylesbury, Bucks, England
Member of BPCC Ltd

ISBN 1 85471 095 8

# PREFACE

This collection of over 6,000 proverbs, from all nations and all ages, ranges from the classical wisdom of *Familiarity breeds contempt* to the twentieth-century cynicism of *Those who can, do; those who can't, teach.* For the purposes of this dictionary a proverb is defined as a succinct and memorable statement that contains advice (*First thrive and then wive*), a warning or prediction (*Marry in haste and repent at leisure*), or an analytical observation (*A maid marries to please her parents, a widow to please herself*). Idiomatic phrases, such as *between the devil and the deep blue sea*, and similes, such as *like a bat out of hell*, are not included.

The proverbs are arranged in the book in categories, such as ABSENCE, LOVE, and WEATHER, and are divided within each category into groups that express various aspects of the main theme. This arrangement draws attention to the less common variants of familiar proverbs, and also reveals some interesting contradictions. The categories themselves are arranged throughout the text in alphabetical order.

Some proverbs are simple folk sayings (*An apple a day keeps the doctor away*); these have only their literal meaning. Some, broader and more philosophical, aspire to deal with the great mysteries and paradoxes of life. (*Opportunity seldom knocks twice*). Others are metaphorical; while apparently belonging to the first class they really belong to the second. *There is more than one way to skin a cat* has no more to do with cats than *Don't count your chickens before they are hatched* has to do with chickens. In this book these metaphorical proverbs are sorted into categories that refer to their metaphorical rather than their literal meanings; thus *Every cloud has a silver lining* appears under OPTIMISM (not WEATHER). This system greatly reduces the need to explain the meaning of the proverbs; however, a short explanation is provided where the meaning is obscure or ambiguous. Archaic and dialect words are also explained or translated if their meaning is not apparent from the context.

As many of the proverbs in this collection have been handed down by word of mouth from generation to generation, it is inevitable that slight variations in the wording will exist. In general, the proverbs have been entered in their most familiar form, but the most common variants are also mentioned. In most cases the origins are obscure, but proverbs that are direct quotations from the Bible, from Shakespeare, or from some other literary source are labelled accordingly. However, many proverbs are based somewhat loosely on biblical or classical texts, and these sources are acknowledged only where they are of particular interest or relevance.

A number of foreign proverbs in translation have been included in this collection. The Chinese, in particular, are renowned for their cogent and picturesque idiom (*Wise is the man who has two loaves, and sells one to buy a lily*); the origin of such proverbs is given with some measure of certainty. However, proverbs from Spain, France, and other European countries have not generally been acknowledged, as a variant of the same proverb often exists in several countries and it is usually impossible to pinpoint its origin. In the case of Latin proverbs the English version is given first, even when the Latin form is better known (*Caveat emptor*, for example, will be found under *Let the buyer beware*).

Finally, a word about the wisdom of proverbs. Proverbs have to be short, they have to be memorable, and they must not be mere platitudes. But they do not have to be true! Folk wisdom is often contradictory. *A fair face cannot have a crabbed heart* and *Fair face, foul heart* cannot both be true. If *Too many cooks spoil the broth*, in what circumstances do *Many hands make light work*?

Perhaps it is a mistake to regard proverbs as a source of accumulated wisdom. Perhaps they are better seen as a collection of tags that enable thoughts to be communicated and exchanged, without the effort of formulation. An English dictionary lists words with which to formulate ideas. This *Dictionary of Proverbs* lists a selection of preformulated ideas, ready for instant use in the appropriate situation.

ROSALIND FERGUSSON, 1983

# USING THE INDEX

The index is an important part of this dictionary. Each proverb is indexed under its first keyword and the index entry gives either the complete proverb or the opening phrase. This is followed by the category number and the number of the proverb within that category. Thus *Look before you leap* and *A stitch in time saves nine* are indexed as:

Look   L. before you leap   85:33
Stitch   A s. in time . . .   52:21

# CONTENTS

# CONTENTS

# 1 ABSENCE

*Its effect on love*

1. Absence makes the heart grow fonder.
2. Men are best loved furthest off.
3. Absence diminishes little passions and increases great ones.
4. Absence sharpens love, presence strengthens it.
5. Far from eye, far from heart.
6. Salt water and absence wash away love. [Horatio Nelson (1758–1805). "Salt water" here refers to the sea, or more precisely the separation caused by a long sea voyage]

*Its effect on friendship*

7. Friends agree best at a distance.
8. Separation secures manifest friendship. [Indian proverb]
9. Long absence changes a friend.
10. To dead men and absent there are no friends left.

*Its effect on discipline*

11. When the cat's away, the mice will play.
12. Well kens the mouse when the cat's out of the house.
13. If the dog is not at home, he barks not. [African proverb]
14. He that fears you present will hate you absent.

*Its dangers*

15. The absent are always in the wrong.
16. The absent are never without fault, nor the present without excuse.
17. The absent party is always to blame.
18. Never were the absent in the right.
19. If a person is away, his right is away. [Moorish proverb]
20. He is guilty who is not at home. [Ukrainian proverb]

*Other disadvantages*

21. Out of sight, out of mind.
22. Present to the eye, present to the mind. [Chinese proverb]
23. Unminded, unmoaned.
24. Unseen, unrued.
25. Long absent, soon forgotten.
26. Seldom seen, soon forgotten.
27. The absent get farther off every day. [Japanese proverb]
28. Absence is the mother of disillusion.
29. The absent saint gets no candle.

*Other advantages*

30. Far folk fare best.
31. They are aye good that are away.
32. Far from court, far from care.

# 2 ADVERSITY

*Its sources*

1. Misfortunes come of themselves.
2. An ill marriage is a spring of ill fortune.

*Its effects*

3. Adversity makes a man wise, not rich.
4. Trouble brings experience and experience brings wisdom.
5. The wind in one's face makes one wise. ["The wind in one's face" here implies adversity]
6. Misfortunes hasten age.
7. Adversity makes strange bedfellows. [The implication of this and the next proverb is that unlikely alliances are formed through common misfortune]
8. Woes unite foes.
9. Misfortune makes foes of friends. [For other proverbs on this theme see FRIENDS: *Their disloyalty*]
10. It is easy to bear the misfortunes of others.

*Its value*

11. Adversity is the touchstone of virtue.
12. Adversity comes with instruction in its hand.
13. Misfortunes tell us what fortune is. [This and the next proverb imply that good fortune can be better appreciated when one has experienced misfortune]
14. No man better knows what good is than he who has endured evil.
15. He that is down needs fear no fall. [John Bunyan (1628–88) *Pilgrim's Progress*]
16. Ill luck is good for something.
17. Sweet are the uses of adversity. [William Shakespeare (1564–1616) *As You Like It*]

*Its undesirability*

18. What is worse than ill luck?

19. He gains enough whom fortune loses. ["Fortune" here means "misfortune"]

### Its inevitability

20. Misfortunes find their way even on the darkest night.
21. Misfortune comes to all men and most women. [Chinese proverb]
22. There is a crook in the lot of every one. ["Crook" here means "trial, affliction"]
23. Misfortune is not that which can be avoided, but that which cannot. [Chinese proverb]

### Its method of attack

24. Misfortune arrives on horseback but departs on foot.
25. Mischief comes by the pound and goes away by the ounce.
26. Ill comes in by ells, and goes out by inches.
27. Misfortunes never come singly.
28. It never rains but it pours.
29. Of one ill come many.
30. Ill comes often on the back of worse.
31. An unhappy man's cart is eith to tumble. ["Eith to tumble" means "easy to overturn". The implication is that an unfortunate person is most susceptible to further misfortune]
32. Lightning never strikes twice in the same place.

# 3 ADVICE

### Its value

1. Good counsel has no price.
2. Good counsel never comes too late.
3. Good counsel never comes amiss.
4. Good take heed does surely speed.
5. Take heed is a fair thing.

### Its limitations

6. Advice is a stranger; if welcome he stays for the night; if not welcome he returns home the same day. [African proverb]
7. Counsel is irksome, when the matter is past remedy.
8. When a thing is done, advice comes too late.
9. We may give advice, but we cannot give conduct.
10. Counsel is no command.
11. Take counsel only of your own head.

12. Though thou hast never so many counsellors, yet do not forsake the counsel of thy own soul.
13. A good scare is worth more to a man than good advice.

### Its dangers

14. Counsel will make a man stick his own mare.
15. Ill counsel mars all.

### The importance of seeking advice

16. While the discreet advise, the fool does his business. ["Advise" here and below means "seek advice"]
17. Though old and wise, yet still advise.
18. There never came ill of good advisement.
19. He that will not be counselled, cannot be helped.

### The importance of following advice

20. Counsel must be followed, not praised.
21. In vain he craves advice that will not follow it.
22. He was slain that had warning, not he that took it.
23. Advice when most needed is least heeded.
24. The first degree of folly is to hold one's self wise, the second to profess it, the third to despise counsel.
25. Who will not be ruled by the rudder, must be ruled by the rock. [The implication is that those who will not be guided by advice and warning, must learn from disaster]
26. Write down the advice of him who loves you, though you like it not at present.
27. In wiving and thriving a man should take counsel of all the world.

### The need to be selective

28. Steer not after every mariner's direction.
29. Too much consulting confounds.
30. He that speers all opinions, comes ill speed. ["Speer" means "enquire"]
31. Like counsellor, like counsel.

### Good sources of advice

32. If you wish good advice, consult an old man.
33. Night is the mother of counsel.
34. The best advice is found on the pillow.
35. Counsel is to be given by the wise, the remedy by the rich.
36. The healthful man can give counsel to the sick.

37. An enemy may chance to give good counsel.
38. If the counsel be good, no matter who gave it.
39. A fool may give a wise man counsel.
40. The egg shows the hen the place where to hatch. [African proverb. The implication is that the advice of the young should not be despised]
41. A woman's advice is no great thing, but he who won't take it is a fool.

*Bad sources of advice*

42. Counsels in wine seldom prosper.
43. Counsel over cups is crazy.
44. Advice whispered in the ear is not worth a tare.
45. Advice whispered is worthless.
46. Take the first advice of a woman and not the second. [The implication is that the first advice, based on intuition, will be more reliable than the second, based on inferior reasoning]
47. Women's counsel is cold.

*Giving advice*

48. It is safer to hear and take counsel, than to give it.
49. It is as hard to follow good advice as to give it.
50. Give neither counsel nor salt till you are asked for it.
51. Come not to counsel uncalled.
52. Don't teach your grandmother to suck eggs.
53. Overhasty counsels are rarely prosperous.
54. Anger and haste hinder good counsel.
55. The counsel thou wouldst have another keep, first keep it thyself.
56. We have better counsel to give than to take.
57. Nothing is given so freely as advice.
58. The land is never void of counsellors.
59. He that thatches his house with turds shall have more teachers than reachers. [The implication is that people tend to offer advice rather than practical assistance to someone in an unpleasant situation]
60. Bachelors' wives and maids' children are well taught. [The implication of this and the following proverbs is that those who have no experience of a situation are only too eager to offer advice]
61. He that has no children brings them up well.
62. Every man can rule a shrew save he that has her.
63. He that has no wife, beats her oft.

# 4 AMBITION

## *Its value*

1. Ambition makes people diligent.
2. Poor by condition, rich by ambition. [Chinese proverb]
3. He who aims at the moon may hit the top of a tree; he who aims at the top of a tree is unlikely to get off the ground.
4. He that stays in the valley, shall never get over the hill.
5. Nothing crave, nothing have.
6. Nothing seek, nothing find.
7. Seek and ye shall find. [Matthew 7:7]
8. Seek mickle, and get something; seek little, and get nothing. ["Mickle" means "much"]
9. Look to a gown of gold, and you will at least get a sleeve of it.
10. Bode a robe, and wear it; bode a sack, and bear it. ["Bode" here means "expect"]
11. He begins to die that quits his desires.
12. Hitch your wagon to a star. [Ralph Waldo Emerson (1803–82) *Society and Solitude*]
13. There's always room at the top.

## *Its dangers*

14. Ambition loses many a man.
15. He who opens his heart to ambition closes it to repose.
16. Every ambitious man is a captive and every covetous one a pauper. [Arabic proverb]
17. Desire has no rest.
18. The best is the enemy of the good. [The implication is that by continually striving for the best, one may waste good opportunities]
19. Better sit still than rise and fall.
20. Hasty climbers have sudden falls.
21. High places have their precipices.
22. The higher the mountain the greater descent.
23. Hew not too high lest the chips fall in thine eye.
24. In a great river, great fish are found; but take heed lest you be drowned.
25. The ant had wings to her hurt. [A warning against aspiring to higher positions than one is equipped to cope with]

## *Against over-ambition*

26. Better be first in a village than second at Rome.
27. Better be the head of a dog than the tail of a lion. [Variants of this proverb substitute "fox", "mouse", or "lizard" for "dog". Others

substitute "ass ... horse", "pike ... sturgeon", or "yeomanry ... gentry" for "dog ... lion"]
28. Better ride on an ass that carries me than a horse that throws me.
29. Seek that which may be found.

See also GREATNESS: *Its dangers*


# 5 ANGER

### *Its undesirability*

1. He that is angry is seldom at ease.
2. An angry man never wants woe.
3. Anger makes a rich man hated, and a poor man scorned.

### *Its dangers*

4. Anger and haste hinder good counsel.
5. Anger punishes itself.
6. Wrath killeth the foolish man. [Job 5:2]
7. Wrath often consumes what goodness husbands. [Icelandic proverb]
8. Anger ends in cruelty. [Indian proverb]
9. Take heed of the wrath of a mighty man, and the tumult of the people.
10. From a choleric man withdraw a little; from him that says nothing for ever.

### *Its irrationality*

11. Anger has no eyes. [Hindi proverb]
12. When a man grows angry, his reason rides out.
13. When wrath speaks, wisdom veils her face.
14. Anger begins with folly, and ends with repentance.
15. When a man is angry, he cannot be in the right. [Chinese proverb]

### *Its causes*

16. As fire is kindled by bellows, so is anger by words.
17. A hungry man is an angry man.
18. Patience provoked turns to fury.
19. Short folk are soon angry.

### *Its duration*

20. Anger dies quickly with a good man.
21. Anger is a short madness.

22. The anger is not warrantable that has seen two suns.
23. He who slowly gets angry keeps his anger longer.

### Its remedies

24. When angry, count a hundred.
25. Delay is the antidote of anger.
26. If you be angry, you may turn the buckle of your belt behind you. [The aim of turning one's belt is apparently to provide a harmless outlet for one's anger]
27. When meat is in, anger is out.
28. A soft answer turneth away wrath. [Proverbs 15:1]

### Controlling one's anger

29. Anger restrained is wisdom gained.
30. When you enter into a house, leave the anger ever at the door.
31. He has wisdom at will, that with an angry heart can hold him still.
32. Let not the sun go down upon your wrath. [Ephesians 4:26]

### Needless anger

33. Two things a man should never be angry at; what he can help, and what he cannot help.
34. He that is angry without a cause, shall be pleased without amends.

# 6 ANTICIPATION

### Its effects

1. Expectation is better than realization.
2. Prospect is often better than possession.
3. Fear of death is worse than death itself.
4. Easter so longed for is gone in a day.
5. It is better to travel hopefully than to arrive.

### Its inadvisability

6. Don't count your chickens before they are hatched.
7. Don't sell the skin till you have caught the bear.
8. First catch your hare.
9. Never spend your money before you have it.
10. Count not four, except you have them in a wallet.
11. Don't bargain for fish which are still in the water. [Indian proverb]
12. It is ill fishing before the net.
13. Don't build the sty before the litter comes.

14. Boil not the pap before the child is born.
15. Don't spread the cloth till the pot begins to boil.
16. Gut no fish till you get them.
17. Make not your sauce, before you have caught the fish.
18. Don't eat the calf in the cow's belly.
19. It is ill prizing of green barley.
20. Do not halloo till you are out of the wood. [The implication is that one should not rejoice at extricating oneself from a difficult situation until one is sure that there are no further problems ahead]
21. Do not triumph before the victory.
22. The opera isn't over till the fat lady sings.
23. He laughs best who laughs last.
24. He who laughs last, laughs longest.
25. There's many a slip 'twixt the cup and the lip.
26. Blessed is he who expects nothing, for he shall never be disappointed. [Alexander Pope (1688–1744)]
27. He that hopes not for good, fears not evil.

### The unexpected

28. The unexpected always happens.
29. Nothing is certain but the unforeseen.

See also WORRY: *Against worrying about the future*

# 7 APPEARANCE

### Misleading appearance

1. Appearances are deceptive.
2. Things are not always what they seem.
3. All that glitters is not gold.
4. All are not maidens that wear bare hair. [A reference to the former fashion of virgins to go without hats]
5. It is not the beard that makes the philosopher.
6. If the beard were all, the goat might preach.
7. It is not the gay coat that makes the gentleman.
8. The cowl does not make the monk.
9. The face is no index to the heart.
10. He that looks in a man's face knows not what money is in his purse.
11. All are not merry that dance lightly.
12. They that are booted are not always ready.
13. All Stuarts are not sib to the king. ["Sib" means "related"]

### The need for caution

14. The bait hides the hook.
15. Bees that have honey in their mouths have stings in their tails.
16. Cats hide their claws.
17. The still sow eats up all the draff. ["Draff" means "scraps"]
18. Fair face, foul heart.
19. Fair without, false within.
20. There is many a fair thing full false.
21. Straight trees have crooked roots.
22. Vice is often clothed in virtue's habit.
23. What is sweet in the mouth is oft bitter in the stomach.
24. Poison is poison though it comes in a golden cup.
25. The fowler's pipe sounds sweet till the bird is caught.
26. Distance lends enchantment to the view. [Thomas Campbell (1777–1844) *The Pleasures of Hope*. This and the following two proverbs imply that things that appear attractive at a distance may be disappointing when viewed at close quarters]
27. Blue are the faraway hills.
28. Far fowls have fair feathers.

### Against judging by appearances

29. Never judge from appearances.
30. All clouds bring not rain.
31. None can guess the jewel by the casket.
32. You can't tell a book by its cover.
33. You cannot know the wine by the barrel.
34. Still waters run deep.
35. Truth has a good face, but bad clothes.
36. There's many a good cock come out of a tattered bag. [This proverb originated in the sport of cockfighting]
37. Crooked logs make straight fires.
38. A straight stick is crooked in the water.
39. A black plum is as sweet as a white.
40. A black hen lays a white egg.
41. In the coldest flint there is hot fire.
42. All are not thieves that dogs bark at.

### The inadequacy of disguise

43. An ape's an ape, a varlet's a varlet, though they be clad in silk or scarlet.
44. The filth under the white snow the sun discovers.
45. Fine dressing is a foul house swept before the doors.
46. A whore in a fine dress is like a clean entry to a dirty house.

47. A holy habit cleanses not a foul soul.

# 8 ASKING

### Its importance

1. He that cannot ask, cannot live.
2. A man may lose his goods for want of demanding them.
3. Bashfulness is an enemy to poverty.
4. Better to ask the way than go astray.

### Its effects

5. Ask and it shall be given you. [Matthew 7:7]
6. Speak and speed, ask and have.
7. He that demands misses not, unless his demands be foolish.

### Questions

8. Question for question is all fair.
9. Like question, like answer.
10. Ask a silly question and you'll get a silly answer.
11. Never answer a question until it is asked.
12. Ask no questions and hear no lies.
13. It is not every question that deserves an answer.
14. Every why has a wherefore.

### Refusal

15. He that asks faintly begs a denial.
16. Shameful craving must have shameful nay.
17. A civil denial is better than a rude grant.
18. Delays are not denials.
19. Don't say 'No' till you are asked.
20. If you always say 'No', you'll never be married.
21. 'No', thank you, has lost many a good butter-cake.
22. Never refuse a good offer.
23. The money you refuse will never do you good.
24. Money refused loses its brightness.

# 9 AUTHORITY

### Its advantages

1. Better to rule than be ruled by the rout.

2. It is better to be the hammer than the anvil.
3. He who has the frying-pan in his hand turns it at will.
4. He who holds the thread holds the ball.

*Its dangers*

5. Mickle power makes many enemies. ["Mickle" means "much"]
6. Out of office, out of danger.
7. It is ill putting a sword in a madman's hand.
8. Power corrupts. [This proverb is based on the words of Lord Acton (1834–1902): "Power tends to corrupt and absolute power corrupts absolutely."]

*Its effects*

9. If you wish to know a man, give him authority.
10. Authority shows the man.
11. Mastery mows the meadows down.
12. Where MacGregor sits is the head of the table. [Any other name may be substituted for MacGregor]
13. He that puts on a public gown, must put off a private person. [The implication is that those in authority must not be influenced by private interests and affairs]
14. Caesar's wife must be above suspicion. ["Caesar's wife" refers to any relative or close friend of a person in authority]

*Qualities of leadership*

15. An army of stags led by a lion would be more formidable than one of lions led by a stag. [The implication is that the strength of the leader is far more important than the strength of the army]
16. No man can be a good ruler, unless he has first been ruled.
17. One must be a servant before one can be a master.
18. Servants make the worst masters.
19. He is not fit to command others, that cannot command himself.
20. He that is master of himself, will soon be master of others.
21. Every man cannot be a master.
22. He is the best general who makes the fewest mistakes.

*The dangers of shared authority*

23. Where every man is master, the world goes to wrack. ["Wrack" means "collapse, destruction", as in "rack and ruin"]
24. One master in a house is enough.
25. There is no good accord, where every man would be a lord.
26. That voyage never has luck where each one has a vote.

27. Where grooms and householders are all alike great, very disastrous will it be for the houses and all that dwell in them.
28. Every man's man had a man, and that made the Treve fall. ["The Treve" was a Scottish castle. The warning here is of the danger of delegating authority]
29. He that has a fellow-ruler, has an over-ruler.

# 10 BADNESS

## *Its sources*

1. Covetousness is the root of all evil. [Variants of this proverb substitute "money", "riches", or "idleness" for "covetousness". See WEALTH: 29]
2. No mischief but a woman or a priest is at the bottom of it.
3. Mischief comes without calling for.
4. Weeds want no sowing.
5. He who does no good, does evil enough.
6. When the weasel and the cat make a marriage, it is a very ill presage. [The implication is that no good can come of an alliance between two bad people]

## *Its effects*

7. He that does ill, hates the light.
8. He that lives not well one year, sorrows seven after.
9. Sin is the root of sorrow. [Chinese proverb]
10. Who swims in sin shall sink in sorrow.
11. Sin plucks on sin. [This implies that one sin leads to another]
12. He that has done ill once, will do it again.
13. One might as well be hanged for a sheep as for a lamb. [A variant of this proverb substitutes "hung" for "hanged". The proverb is quoted as an excuse for indulging in further wrongdoing once one has committed a minor offence]
14. He that mischief hatches, mischief catches.
15. They that sow the wind shall reap the whirlwind. [This proverb is based on Hosea 8:7]
16. Vice is its own punishment, and sometimes its own cure.
17. A wicked man is his own hell.
18. An ill life, an ill end.
19. He that lives wickedly can hardly die honestly.
20. He that does evil, never weens good. ["Weens" means "expects"]

13

### Its value

21. The more mischief, the better sport.
22. The more wicked, the more lucky.
23. The more knave, the better luck.
24. Thieves and rogues have the best luck, if they do but scape hanging.
25. The greater the sinner, the greater the saint.

### Its dangers

26. Wickedness with beauty is the devil's hook baited.
27. Never open the door to a little vice, lest a great one enter with it.
28. The wages of sin is death. [Romans 6:23]
29. Every sin brings its punishment with it.
30. Where vice is, vengeance follows.
31. Fear nothing but sin.

### Its universality

32. It is a good world, but they are ill that are on it.
33. It is a wicked world, and we make part of it.
34. The world is full of knaves.
35. To fall into sin is human, to remain in sin is devilish.

### Characteristics of the bad

36. A bad penny always turns up.
37. Some do amend when they cannot grow worse.
38. A knave and a fool never take thought.
39. The love of the wicked is more dangerous than their hatred.
40. Show a good man his error, and he turns it to a virtue; but an ill, it doubles his fault.
41. Two false knaves need no broker.
42. Ill weeds grow apace.
43. The weeds overgrow the corn. [The implication is that the bad outnumber the good]
44. Evil doers are evil dreaders. [This implies that bad people are always the first to suspect others]

### Handling bad people

45. The best remedy against an ill man, is much ground between.
46. He who sups with the devil should have a long spoon.
47. One hates not the person, but the vice.
48. Give a thief enough rope and he'll hang himself. [A variant of this proverb substitutes "fool" for "thief". The implication is that a bad or troublesome person will eventually bring about his own downfall]

*Wrong and right*

49. The end justifies the means. [This implies that a worthy result may justify doubtful means of achieving it. The next two proverbs support the opposite view]
50. Never do evil that good may come of it.
51. Wrong has no warrant.
52. Wrong never comes right.
53. Two wrongs do not make a right.
54. Two blacks do not make a white.

See also DEEDS: *Bad deeds*; GOODNESS: *Good and evil*

# 11 BEAUTY

*Its superficiality*

1. Beauty is only skin-deep.
2. Beauty is only one layer. [Japanese proverb]
3. Beauty may have fair leaves, yet bitter fruit.
4. Fair face, foul heart.
5. The peacock has fair feathers, but foul feet.
6. There is many a fair thing full false.
7. Fair without, false within.
8. Beauty and honesty seldom agree. [The implication is that a beautiful woman is rarely honest. Variations of this proverb substitute "chastity" or "wisdom" for "honesty"]
9. Beauty and folly go often in company.
10. White silver draws black lines.

*Its influence*

11. Beauty draws more than oxen.
12. Beauty opens locked doors.
13. Beauty is eloquent even when silent.
14. A good face is a letter of recommendation.
15. A fair face is half a portion.

*Its unimportance*

16. The fair and the foul, by dark are like store.
17. All cats are grey in the dark.
18. Goodness is better than beauty.
19. Good fame is better than a good face.
20. Handsome is as handsome does.

### Its inadequacy

21. Beauty without bounty avails nought.
22. A fair woman without virtue is like palled wine.
23. Beauty won't make the pot boil.
24. No one can live on beauty, but they can die for it.
25. Prettiness makes no pottage.
26. A poor beauty finds more lovers than husbands.
27. Beauty is no inheritance.
28. Beauty is potent but money is omnipotent.

### Its ephemerality

29. Beauty fades like a flower.
30. Beauty is but a blossom.
31. The fairest flowers soonest fade.
32. The fairest rose at last is withered.
33. Grace will last, beauty will blast.
34. Prettiness dies first.

### Its subjectivity

35. Beauty is in the eye of the beholder.
36. Fair is not fair, but that which pleases.
37. A ship under sail, a man in complete armour, a woman with a great belly are three of the handsomest sights.
38. If Jack's in love, he's no judge of Jill's beauty.
39. The owl thinks her own young fairest.

### Its sources

40. Health and gaiety foster beauty.
41. Health and wealth create beauty.
42. A blithe heart makes a blooming visage.
43. The joy of the heart makes the face fair.

### Its disadvantages

44. The fairest silk is soonest stained.
45. In an ermine spots are soon discovered.
46. The fairer the paper, the fouler the blot. [The implication of this and the two preceding proverbs is that beauty shows up by contrast even the smallest fault]
47. The smaller the peas, the more to the pot; the fairer the woman, the more the giglot. ["Giglot" means "wanton"]
48. Who has a fair wife needs more than two eyes.
49. Please your eye and plague your heart.

50. A fair wife and a frontier castle breed quarrels.
51. Pretty face, poor fate. [Chinese proverb]
52. Beauty's sister is vanity, and its daughter lust.
53. A woman and a cherry are painted for their own harm.

### Its value

54. A bonny bride is soon buskit, and a short horse is soon wispit. ["Buskit" means "adorned"; "wispit" means "rubbed down"]
55. A good face needs no band, and a bad one deserves none. ["Band" here means "adornment"]
56. Who is born fair is born married.
57. A fair face cannot have a crabbed heart.
58. An enemy to beauty is a foe to nature.
59. A thing of beauty is a joy forever. [John Keats (1795–1821) *Endymion*]

# 12 BEGINNINGS

### Their importance

1. Everything must have a beginning.
2. Everything has its seed.
3. No root, no fruit.
4. Rivers need a spring.
5. First impressions are the most lasting.
6. The first blow is half the battle.

### Their difficulty

7. Every beginning is hard.
8. The first step is the hardest.
9. The greatest step is that out of doors.

### The importance of beginning well

10. If the beginning is good, the end must be perfect. [Burmese proverb]
11. A good beginning makes a good ending.
12. An ill beginning, an ill ending.
13. Such beginning, such end.
14. Well begun is half done.
15. A beard well lathered is half shaved.
16. No good building without a good foundation.

# 13 BELIEVING

*Its sources*

1. We soon believe what we desire.
2. Seeing is believing.
3. That which is easily done, is soon believed.
4. Men have greater faith in those things which they do not understand.

*Its value*

5. Believe well and have well.
6. He can who believes he can.
7. Faith will move mountains.
8. Belief is better than investigation.

*The need for caution*

9. He that believes all, misses; he that believes nothing, misses.
10. Believe nothing of what you hear, and only half of what you see.
11. Of money, wit, and virtue, believe one-fourth of what you hear.
12. Believe no tales from an enemy's tongue.
13. Thinking is very far from knowing.

*The gullible*

14. They that think none ill, are soonest beguiled.
15. No man so wise but he may be deceived.
16. A fool believes everything.
17. A fool and his money are soon parted.
18. If fools went not to market, bad wares would not be sold.

*Doubt*

19. The more one knows, the less one believes.
20. He that knows nothing, doubts nothing.
21. Doubt is the key of knowledge. [Persian proverb]
22. He that nothing questions, nothing learns.
23. The persuasion of the fortunate sways the doubtful.

# 14 BORROWING

*Against borrowing*

1. Better buy than borrow.
2. Better to pay and have little than have much and be in debt.
3. Better go to bed supperless than to rise in debt.

4. Debt is the worst poverty.
5. He who has good health is young; and he is rich who owes nothing.
6. He may well be contented who needs neither borrow nor flatter.
7. Not so good to borrow, as to be able to lend.
8. Neither a borrower nor a lender be. [William Shakespeare (1564–1616) *Hamlet*]
9. The world still he keeps at his staff's end that needs not to borrow and never will lend.

*Its disadvantages*

10. Borrowed garments never fit well.
11. He that trusts to borrowed ploughs, will have his land lie fallow.
12. He that borrows binds himself with his neighbour's rope.
13. A man in debt is caught in a net.
14. Shame fades in the morning, but debts remain from day to day [Chinese proverb]
15. Debt is an evil conscience.
16. Let him that sleeps too sound, borrow the debtor's pillow.
17. He that goes a borrowing, goes a sorrowing.
18. Woe's to them that have the cat's dish, and she aye mewing.
19. Creditors have better memories than debtors.
20. He that borrows must pay again with shame or loss.

*Debtors*

21. The borrower is servant to the lender. [Proverbs 22:7]
22. He who owes, is in all the wrong.
23. Debtors are liars.
24. Lying rides upon debt's back.

*Repayment of debts*

25. Borrowed thing will home again.
26. A borrowed loan should come laughing home.
27. A pound of care will not pay an ounce of debt.
28. An hundred pounds of sorrow pays not one ounce of debt.
29. Sorrow will pay no debt.
30. Old thanks pay not for a new debt.
31. Unpaid debts are unforgiven sins.
32. He has but a short Lent, that must pay money at Easter.
33. Pay what you owe and you'll know what you're worth.
34. Pay with the same dish you borrow.
35. Out of debt, out of danger.
36. Once paid, never craved.

37. Short reckonings make long friends. ["Short reckonings" here means "prompt repayment of debts"]
38. Death pays all debts.
39. Of ill debtors, men take oats. [The implication is that one must take what one can in repayment of a bad debt]

See also LENDING: *Usurers*

# 15 BREEDING

## *Its importance*

1. Better unborn than unbred.
2. The best bred have the best portion.
3. Birth is much, but breeding is more.
4. Nurture is above nature. [The implication is that breeding is of more importance than inherited qualities]
5. Nurture and good manners maketh man.

## *Manners*

6. Civility costs nothing. [Variants of this and the following proverb substitute "politeness" or "courtesy" for "civility"]
7. There is nothing lost by civility.
8. Courtesy is the inseparable companion of virtue.
9. Manners maketh man.
10. Manners make often fortunes.
11. Manners and money make a gentleman.
12. Meat is much, but manners is better.
13. Leave is light. [The implication is that it is easy enough to ask "leave", or permission, before doing something]
14. 'After you' is good manners.
15. It is not good manners to show your learning before ladies.
16. Speak when you are spoken to.
17. A well-bred youth neither speaks of himself, nor, being spoken to, is silent.
18. Curiosity is ill manners in another house.
19. Do on the hill as you would do in the hall.

## *The ill-bred*

20. It is an ill-bred dog that will beat a bitch.
21. The higher the ape goes, the more he shows his tail. [This implies that the higher ill-bred people are promoted, the more obvious their inadequacies become]

22. Courtesy is cumbersome to them that ken it not. [A reference to the clumsy attempts of ill-bred people to behave with good manners]
23. Dogs bark as they are bred.
24. Beware of breed. ["Breed" here refers to the ill-bred]
25. Do not cast your pearls before swine. [This proverb is based on Matthew 7:6]

### The gentry

26. Gentility is but ancient riches.
27. Gentility without ability is worse than plain beggary.
28. Gentry sent to market will not buy one bushel of corn. [The implication is that noble blood alone is of no material value]
29. Nobility, without ability, is like a pudding wanting suet.
30. Good blood makes bad puddings without groats or suet.
31. Great birth is a very poor dish at table.
32. The more noble, the more humble.
33. Kind hearts are more than coronets. [Alfred, Lord Tennyson (1809–92) *Lady Clara Vere de Vere*]
34. Better a good cow than a cow of good kind.
35. Virtue is the only true nobility.
36. He is noble that has noble conditions.
37. He is a gentleman that has gentle conditions.
38. A gentleman will do like a gentleman.
39. A gentleman without an estate is like a pudding without suet.
40. A thief passes for a gentleman when stealing has made him rich.
41. Jack would be a gentleman if he had money.
42. Jack would be a gentleman if he could speak French.
43. It is not the gay coat that makes the gentleman.
44. It takes three generations to make a gentleman.
45. The king can make a knight, but not a gentleman.
46. The Peerage is the Englishman's Bible. [A reference to *Burke's Peerage* (1826), a dictionary of peers and their genealogy]

# 16 BUILDING

### Its expense

1. Building is a thief.
2. Building is a sweet impoverishing.
3. Building and borrowing, a sack full of sorrowing.
4. Building and marrying of children are great wasters.
5. The charges of building, and making of gardens are unknown.
6. Fools build houses, and wise men buy them.
7. Who borrows to build, builds to sell. [Chinese proverb]

# 17 CHANGE

### Its value

1. A change is as good as a rest.
2. Change brings life.
3. Change your dwelling-place often, for the sweetness of life consists in variety. [Arabic proverb]
4. Variety is the spice of life.
5. Variety takes away satiety.
6. Variety is charming.
7. Changing of works is lighting of hearts.
8. Change of pasture makes fat calves.
9. New meat begets a new appetite.

### Its inadvisability

10. Better the devil you know than the devil you don't know.
11. Better rue sit than rue flit. [The implication is that it is better to stay in an unpleasant job or situation than change to another that may be worse]
12. A tree often transplanted, bears not much fruit.
13. Three removals are as bad as a fire.
14. Don't change horses in midstream. [A variant of this proverb substitutes "swap" for "change"]
15. As a tree falls, so shall it lie. [This implies that one should not attempt to change long-standing attitudes or habits in the face of death]

### Its effects

16. A rolling stone gathers no moss.
17. A new broom sweeps clean.
18. Of a new prince, new bondage.
19. New lords, new laws.

### Its inevitability

20. Times change and we with them.
21. One cannot put back the clock.
22. Paul's will not always stand. [A reference to St. Paul's Cathedral in London]
23. The world will not last alway.
24. There is nothing permanent except change.

*Conservatism*

25. Nature hates all sudden changes.
26. When a new book appears, read an old one.
27. Who leaves the old way for the new, will find himself deceived.
28. Old chains gall less than new.
29. Old shoes are easiest.
30. Old fish, old oil, and an old friend are the best.
31. Old friends and old wine and old gold are best.
32. Old wood is best to burn, old horse to ride, old books to read, and old wine to drink.
33. Old customs are best.
34. Preserve the old, but know the new. [Chinese proverb]

*Novelty*

35. Novelty always appears handsome.
36. New things are fair.
37. Everything new is fine.
38. It is a sairy brewing that is not good in the newing. ["Sairy" means "poor"; "in the newing" means "when it is new"]
39. Yule is young in Yule even, and as old in Saint Stephen. [St. Stephen's Day is December 26th. The implication of this and the preceding proverbs is that the initial attraction of new things does not last]
40. There is nothing new under the sun.
41. What is new cannot be true.
42. Newer is truer.
43. You can't put new wine into old bottles. [This proverb is based on Matthew 9:17]

# 18 CHARACTER

*Hereditary influences*

1. We may not expect a good whelp from an ill dog.
2. The tod's bairns are ill to tame. ["Tod" means "fox"]
3. Eagles do not breed doves.
4. Of an evil crow, an evil egg.
5. He that comes of a hen, must scrape.
6. How can the foal amble if the horse and mare trot?
7. The litter is like to the sire and dam.
8. The apple never falls far from the tree.
9. Of a thorn springs not a fig. [This and the following two proverbs are based on Matthew 7:16–18]

10. One cannot gather grapes of thorns or figs of thistles.
11. No good apple on a sour stock.
12. Of evil grain, no good seed can come.
13. What is bred in the bone will come out in the flesh.
14. Blood will tell.
15. A wise man commonly has foolish children. [This and the next proverb contradict the preceding ones, all of which imply that the character of the offspring must match that of its parents]
16. Many a good cow has an evil calf.

*Other influences*

17. Names and natures do often agree. [The implication is that people come to possess the character traits suggested by their name]
18. A man's studies pass into his character.
19. The cask savours of the first fill. [A reference to the influence of childhood experience on the formation of character]

*The inability to change or conceal a person's character*

20. He that is born a fool is never cured.
21. Send a fool to the market, and a fool he will return again.
22. If an ass goes a-travelling, he'll not come home a horse. [See TRAVEL: 8–12 for variants of this proverb]
23. Travellers change climates, not conditions. ["Conditions" here implies "character"]
24. It is harder to change human nature than to change rivers and mountains.
25. You can drive out nature with a pitchfork, but she keeps on coming back.
26. Cut off a dog's tail and he will be a dog still.
27. Reek comes aye down again however high it flees. ["Reek" means "smoke"]
28. Once a knave, always a knave. [Variants of this proverb substitute "bishop", "devil", "parson", "priest", "thief", or "whore" for "knave"]
29. The fox may grow grey, but never good.
30. The wolf may lose his teeth, but never his nature.
31. The leopard cannot change his spots.
32. Black will take no other hue.
33. A carrion kite will never be a good hawk.
34. You cannot make a silk purse out of a sow's ear.
35. There comes nought out of the sack but what was there.
36. Bring a cow to the hall and she'll run to the byre.
37. The frog cannot out of her bog.
38. You cannot make a crab walk straight.

39. What can you expect from a pig but a grunt?
40. A kindly aver will never make a good horse. [A "kindly aver" is a horse that is naturally suited to being a work-horse]
41. An ape's an ape, a varlet's a varlet, though they be clad in silk or scarlet.
42. Fire cannot be hidden in flax.
43. Nature and the sin of Adam can ill be concealed by fig-leaves.

# 19 CHILDREN

### Their value

1. He that has no children knows not what is love.
2. The best smell is bread, the best savour salt, the best love that of children.
3. If you live without being a father you will die without being a human being. [Russian proverb]
4. Children are poor men's riches.
5. Happy is he that is happy in his children.
6. A son is a son till he gets him a wife, but a daughter's a daughter all the days of her life.
7. A child's service is little, yet he is no little fool that despises it.

### Their disadvantages

8. He that has children, all his morsels are not his own.
9. Children suck the mother when they are young, and the father when they are old.
10. Wife and children are bills of charges.
11. Small birds must have meat.
12. The first service a child does his father is to make him foolish.
13. Children when they are little make their parents fools, when they are great they make them mad.
14. A little child weighs on your knee, a big one on your heart.
15. Children are certain cares, but uncertain comforts.

### Their shortcomings

16. Children are to be deceived with comfits and men with oaths. [The implication is that children are easily bribed and deceived]
17. Kindness is lost that's bestowed on children and old folk. [This implies that children forget former kindnesses when they grow up, and old men die before they can repay them]
18. Woe to the kingdom whose king is a child.

*Their appetite*

19. Children and chicken must be always picking.
20. A growing youth has a wolf in his belly.

*Their honesty*

21. Children and fools cannot lie.
22. The child says nothing, but what it heard by the fire.
23. What children hear at home, soon flies abroad.
24. Children pick up words as pigeons peas, and utter them again as God shall please.
25. Little pitchers have great ears. [This and the three preceding proverbs warn against discussing private affairs in front of one's children]

*Their impressionability*

26. Raw leather will stretch.
27. Soft wax will take any impression.
28. Youth and white paper take any impression.
29. As the twig is bent, so is the tree inclined.
30. Thraw the wand while it is green. ["Thraw" means "twist"]
31. Train up a child in the way he should go.

*Their behaviour*

32. Boys will be boys. [This and the following three proverbs may be used as an excuse for unruly behaviour in the young]
33. God's lambs will play.
34. Young colts will canter.
35. Youth will have its course.
36. You cannot put an old head on young shoulders.
37. Children should be seen and not heard.
38. When children stand quiet, they have done some ill.

*Care of children*

39. Let not a child sleep upon bones. [The advice here is that a child should not be allowed to sleep on a person's lap]
40. Shod in the cradle, barefoot in the stubble. [A warning against overprotectiveness]

*The child and the man*

41. The child is father of the man. [William Wordsworth (1770–1850) *My Heart Leaps Up*. This and the following four proverbs suggest that one may see in a child a model of the future adult. The remaining proverbs in this section contradict this belief]

42. Boys will be men.
43. It early pricks that will be a thorn.
44. The fine pullet shows its excellence from the egg. [Arabic proverb]
45. Timely crooks the tree, that will good cammock be. [A "cammock" is a crooked piece of wood]
46. A man at five may be a fool at fifteen.
47. Young saint, old devil.
48. Royet lads make sober men. ["Royet" means "wild"]
49. Wanton kittens make sober cats.
50. Naughty boys sometimes make good men.
51. A ragged colt may make a good horse.

*Precocity*

52. Soon ripe, soon rotten.
53. Old young, young old. [The implication is that a precocious child may compensate for his lost youth by being childish in his old age]
54. A man at sixteen will prove a child at sixty.
55. He that would be old long, must be old betimes. ["Betimes" means "early"]

*The recklessness of youth*

56. Youth never casts for peril.
57. Reckless youth makes rueful age.
58. An idle youth, a needy age.
59. If you lie upon roses when young, you'll lie upon thorns when old.
60. He sups ill who eats all at dinner. [The implication is that he who uses up all his resources in his youth will have nothing left for his old age]
61. If youth knew what age would crave, it would both get and save.
62. Spare when you're young, and spend when you're old.
63. Diligent youth makes easy age.
64. Young men's knocks old men feel.
65. Who that in youth no virtue uses, in age all honour him refuses.

See also DEATH: *Its choice of victims*; DISCIPLINE: *Disciplining children, The spoilt child*; OLD PEOPLE: *The generation gap*

# 20 CHOOSING

*Its necessity*

1. You cannot have it both ways.
2. You cannot have your cake and eat it.

3. You cannot sell the cow and sup the milk.
4. A door must either be shut or open.
5. You cannot serve God and Mammon. [Matthew 6:24. "Mammon" means "riches"; the choice here is between piety and worldliness]

### Making one's choice

6. Choose neither women nor linen by candlelight.
7. Of two evils choose the less.
8. Where bad's the best, bad must be the choice.
9. There's small choice in rotten apples. [William Shakespeare (1564–1616) *The Taming of the Shrew*]
10. No choice amongst stinking fish.
11. You pays your money and you takes your choice. [This proverb is usually used in situations where one is obliged to choose at random. The more grammatical variant, substituting "pay ... take" for "pays ... takes", is less common]
12. A maiden with many wooers often chooses the worst.

See also MARRIAGE: *Choosing a partner*

# 21 CLEANLINESS

### Its value

1. Cleanliness is next to godliness.
2. For washing his hands, none sells his lands.
3. Clean and whole makes poor clothes shine.

### Dirtiness

4. The clartier the cosier. ["Clartier" means "dirtier"]
5. Where there's muck there's brass. [A variant of this proverb substitutes "luck" for "brass", which here refers to money]
6. Muck and money go together.
7. We must eat a peck of dirt before we die. [This proverb is frequently quoted as an excuse for unwashed crockery or food. It may also be used metaphorically in a wider sense]

# 22 COMMERCE

### Its tactics

1. Ask but enough, and you may lower the price as you list.
2. Ask much to have a little.

3. When you go to buy, don't show your silver. [Chinese proverb]
4. He praises who wishes to sell.
5. He that blames would buy. [This and the following three proverbs refer to the practice of criticizing the goods one wishes to buy, in order to obtain them at a lower price]
6. Many men lack what they would fain have in their pack. ["Lack" here means "criticize"]
7. He that speaks ill of the mare would buy her.
8. Never cheapen unless you mean to buy.
9. There is a difference between 'Will you buy?' and 'Will you sell?' [The implication is that over-eagerness to sell may discourage prospective buyers, and over-eagerness to buy may encourage sellers to raise their prices]

*The need for caution*

10. Let the buyer beware. [This legal maxim is equally familiar in its Latin form, *Caveat emptor*]
11. Keep your eyes open: a sale is a sale.
12. The buyer needs a hundred eyes, the seller but one.
13. There are more foolish buyers than foolish sellers.
14. At a good bargain, think twice.

*Sound business sense*

15. The best payment is on the peck bottom. [A "peck" was a vessel used for measuring grain. The implication of this and the following proverb is that it is best to receive immediate payment for one's wares]
16. Ell and tell is good merchandise. [An "ell" was a stick used to measure length. "Tell" here refers to counting out money]
17. While the dust is on your feet, sell what you have bought. [This and the following proverb imply that rapid turnover may be more lucrative than high profits]
18. Quick returns make rich merchants.
19. A man must sell his ware after the rates of the market.
20. He that desires to make a market of his ware, must watch an opportunity to open his shop.
21. Look to the main chance.
22. Drive your business, do not let it drive you.
23. Business is business.
24. Business before pleasure.
25. Who buys dear and takes up on credit, shall ever sell to his loss.
26. Buy in the cheapest market and sell in the dearest.
27. A merchant that gains not, loses.
28. He that buys and sells is called a merchant. [The implication is that

to buy and sell without profit brings one nothing but the title of "merchant"]
29. Never open your pack, and sell no wares.
30. Buy at a fair, but sell at home.
31. He that could know what would be dear, need be a merchant but one year. [This implies that if one could predict future shortages of a particular commodity, one could buy it cheaply while it was plentiful and sell it at a high profit when it was in short supply]
32. The customer is always right.

*Honest dealings*

33. The blind man's peck should be well measured.
34. Weight and measure take away strife.
35. It is no sin to sell dear, but a sin to give ill measure.
36. Weigh justly and sell dearly.

*Bad bargains*

37. A thing you don't want is dear at any price.
38. Light cheap, lither yield. ["Lither" means "bad"]
39. Many have been ruined by buying good pennyworths.
40. A good bargain is a pick-purse.
41. Good cheap is dear. ["Good cheap" means "a bargain"]
42. Best is best cheap. [A variant of this proverb is "Best is cheapest." The implication is that good quality goods at their normal price are better value than inferior goods sold cheaply]
43. Ill ware is never cheap.

*Prices and quality*

44. To buy dear is not bounty.
45. He will never have a good thing cheap that is afraid to ask the price.
46. The dearer it is the cheaper. [The retort of one who refuses to pay a high price for goods. The implication is that doing without such goods saves money]
47. They buy good cheap that bring nothing home. [A reiteration of the sentiments of the preceding proverb, this time addressed to the buyer]
48. Good ware makes quick markets.
49. Pleasing ware is half sold.
50. Good wine needs no bush. [A reference to the bunch of ivy that formerly hung outside a wine-merchant's shop. The implication is that goods of a high quality should not need advertising]

## 23 COMPANY

*Its sources*

1. Two is company, three is none. [A variant of this proverb substitutes "a crowd" for "none"]
2. A crowd is not company.

*The value of good company*

3. Keep good men company, and you shall be of the number.
4. Choose thy company before thy drink.
5. The company makes the feast.
6. Good company upon the road is the shortest cut.
7. A merry companion is a wagon in the way. [The implication is that to have good company when travelling on foot makes the journey seem as easy as if one were riding in a wagon]

*The undesirability of bad company*

8. Better be alone than in bad company.
9. Better to be beaten than be in bad company.
10. He keeps his road well enough who gets rid of bad company.

*The influence of one's companions*

11. A man is known by the company he keeps.
12. A man is known by his friends.
13. As a man is, so is his company.
14. Sike a man as thou wald be, draw thee to sike company. ["Sike" means "such"; "wald" means "would"]
15. Tell me with whom thou goest, and I'll tell thee what thou doest.
16. Keep company with good men, and good men you'll imitate; keep company with beggars, and sleep outside some gate. [Chinese proverb]

See also CORRUPTION: *Its causes*

## 24 CONCEIT

*Its universality*

1. Men love to hear well of themselves.
2. Every bird loves to hear himself sing.
3. Every sprat now-a-days calls itself a herring.

4. There is one good wife in the country, and every man thinks he has her.
5. There is no such flatterer as a man's self.

*Its inadequacy*

6. Vainglory blossoms but never bears.
7. Brag is a good dog but dares not bite.

*Its dangers*

8. An ounce of vanity spoils a hundredweight of merit.
9. The more women look in their glass, the less they look to their house.
10. Do not triumph before the victory.
11. Never be boastful; someone may pass who knew you as a child. [Chinese proverb]

*Characteristics of the boastful*

12. A vaunter and a liar are near akin.
13. They can do least who boast loudest.
14. Great braggers, little doers.
15. Great boast, small roast.

*Modesty*

16. Modesty sets off one newly come to honour.
17. Though modesty be a virtue, yet bashfulness is a vice.
18. No man cries stinking fish. [The implication is that one should not disparage oneself or one's wares through excessive modesty]
19. Don't hide your light under a bushel. [A "bushel" is a measure or container for corn. The proverb is based on Matthew 5:15]
20. What is the good of a sundial in the shade? [A further warning against excessive modesty]

See also PRAISE: *Self-praise*

# 25 CONFORMITY

*Its necessity*

1. When in Rome, do as the Romans do.
2. If you see a town worshipping a calf, mow grass and feed him. [Egyptian proverb]
3. One must howl with the wolves.
4. It is ill sitting at Rome and striving against the Pope.

5. It is ill shaving against the wool.
6. It is ill striving against the stream.
7. Piss not against the wind. [A variant of this proverb substitutes "puff" for "piss"]
8. If you can't beat 'em, join 'em.
9. Better bend than break.
10. Better be out of the world than out of the fashion.
11. Say as men say, but think to yourself.
12. Do as most men do, then most men will speak well of you.

# 26 CONSCIENCE

*The effects of a guilty conscience*

1. A guilty conscience needs no accuser.
2. Conscience is a cut-throat.
3. Conscience is a thousand witnesses.
4. A guilty conscience feels continual fear.
5. The faulty stands on his guard.
6. He that lives ill, fear follows him.
7. Who has skirts of straw, needs fear the fire.
8. The thief doth fear each bush an officer. [William Shakespeare (1564–1616) *Henry VI*]
9. Conscience does make cowards of us all. [William Shakespeare *Hamlet*]
10. Whose conscience is cumbered and stands not clean, of another man's deeds the worse will he deem.
11. Who is in fault suspects everybody.
12. He that commits a fault, thinks everyone speaks of it.
13. The truest jests sound worst in guilty ears.

*The value of a clear conscience*

14. A clear conscience fears not false accusations.
15. Men whose consciences are clear, of a knock at midnight have no fear. [Chinese proverb]
16. Do right and fear no man.
17. Preserve a clear conscience, and sleep without fear in the desert. [Arabic proverb]
18. A quiet conscience sleeps in thunder.
19. A good conscience makes an easy couch.
20. A good conscience is a soft pillow.
21. A good conscience is the best divinity.
22. A good conscience is a continual feast.
23. A clear conscience is like a coat of mail.

*Innocence*

24. No protection is as sure as innocence.
25. Innocent actions carry their warrant with them.
26. Every one is held to be innocent until he is proved guilty.
27. Innocence is no protection.

# 27 CONTEMPT

*Its sources*

1. Familiarity breeds contempt.
2. A maid oft seen, and a gown oft worn, are disesteemed and held in scorn.
3. Scorn comes commonly with scathe. ["Scathe" means "harm, injury"]
4. Where the demand is a jest, the fittest answer is a scoff.
5. To be too busy, gets contempt.

*Its effects*

6. Contempt will sooner kill an injury than revenge.
7. Contempt is the sharpest reproof.
8. Some evils are cured by contempt.
9. Scorn at first makes after-love the more.
10. Contempt pierces even through the shell of the tortoise.
11. Many can bear adversity, but few contempt.
12. Never was a scornful person well received.

*The value of respect*

13. If the laird slight the lady, so will all the kitchen boys.
14. He that respects not is not respected.
15. Respect a man, he will do the more.
16. He is a silly man that can neither do good nor ill. ["Silly" here means "sorry, poor". The implication of this and the following proverb is that it may be in one's interest to treat even the meanest with respect]
17. Better to have a dog fawn on you than bite you.

# 28 CONTENTMENT

*Its value*

1. Content is all.
2. He has nothing, that is not contented.

3. Content is more than a kingdom.
4. Content is happiness.
5. Content is the philosopher's stone, that turns all it touches into gold.
6. He who is content in his poverty, is wonderfully rich.
7. He is not rich that possesses much, but he that is content with what he has.
8. A contented mind is a continual feast.
9. Who is contented, enjoys.

*Its sources*

10. Content lodges oftener in cottages than palaces.
11. He may well be contented who needs neither borrow nor flatter.
12. A little with quiet is the only diet.

*Having enough*

13. He is at ease who has enough.
14. Enough is as good as a feast.
15. More than enough is too much.
16. Of enough, men leave. [The implication of this and the following proverb is that only when something is left over, can we be sure that there was enough to start with]
17. There was never enough where nothing was left.
18. That which suffices, is not little.
19. Women, priests, and poultry, have never enough.

*Humble desires*

20. He that desires but little has no need of much.
21. He has enough who is contented with little.
22. Humble hearts have humble desires.
23. Little things please little minds.
24. Little things are great to little men.
25. A little bird is content with a little nest.
26. A little wood will heat a little oven.
27. The greatest wealth is contentment with a little.
28. Nature is content with a little.
29. A wise man cares not for what he cannot have.

*Discontent*

30. Discontent is the first step in progress.
31. A man's discontent is his worst evil.
32. A discontented man knows not where to sit easy.
33. He that has nothing, is not contented.
34. He that studies his content, wants it.

35. No man is content with his lot.
36. None says his garner is full.
37. Though stone were changed to gold, the heart of man would not be satisfied. [Chinese proverb]
38. Vast chasms can be filled, but the heart of man never. [Chinese proverb]
39. Man's heart is never satisfied, the snake would swallow the elephant. [Chinese proverb]
40. The grass is always greener on the other side of the fence.
41. The apples on the other side of the wall are the sweetest.
42. Our neighbour's ground yields better corn than ours.
43. Acorns were good till bread was found.

*Accepting one's lot*

44. Worse things happen at sea.
45. Let every man be content with his own kevel. ["Kevel" means "lot"]
46. Gnaw the bone which is fallen to thy lot.
47. When you are an anvil, hold you still; when you are a hammer, strike your fill.
48. If thou hast not a capon, feed on an onion.
49. He that may not do as he would, must do as he may.
50. The goat must browse where she is tied.
51. We must not look for a golden life in an iron age.
52. A man must plough with such oxen as he has.

# 29 CORRUPTION

*Its causes*

1. Evil communications corrupt good manners. [1 Corinthians 15:33]
2. The unrighteous penny corrupts the righteous pound.
3. The rotten apple injures its neighbours.
4. One ill weed mars a whole pot of pottage.
5. One drop of poison infects the whole tun of wine.
6. One scabbed sheep will mar a whole flock.
7. Near vermilion one gets stained pink. [Chinese proverb]
8. He who squeezes in between the onion and the peel, picks up its stink. [Arabic proverb]
9. A hog that's bemired endeavours to bemire others.
10. He that deals in dirt has aye foul fingers.
11. He that touches pitch shall be defiled.
12. He that has to do with what is foul, never comes away clean.
13. Keep not ill men company, lest you increase the number.
14. Who keeps company with the wolf, will learn to howl.

15. He that dwells next door to a cripple, will learn to halt. ["Halt" here means "limp"]
16. If you lie down with dogs, you will get up with fleas.
17. He who lives with cats will get a taste for mice.
18. He who goes into a mill comes out powdered.
19. Power corrupts. [This proverb is based on the words of Lord Acton (1834–1902): "Power tends to corrupt and absolute power corrupts absolutely."]
20. Fish begins to stink at the head. [The implication is that corruption begins in the highest ranks of an organization]
21. No man ever became thoroughly bad all at once.

*Its effects*

22. The corruption of one thing is the generation of another. [Learned illustrations of this proverb include "the corruption of a poet is the generation of a critic" (John Dryden 1631–1700) and "the corruption of pipes is the generation of stoppers" (Jonathan Swift 1667–1745)]
23. Corruption of the best becomes the worst.
24. Who trusts to rotten boughs, may fall.
25. One is not smelt where all stink.

*Bribery*

26. Neither bribe, nor lose thy right.
27. A bribe will enter without knocking.
28. Gifts enter everywhere without a wimble. [A "wimble" is a gimlet]
29. Gold goes in at any gate except heaven's.
30. What cannot gold do?
31. No lock will hold against the power of gold.
32. Every man has his price.
33. There is no wool so white but a dyer can make it black.
34. Gifts blind the eyes.
35. Who greases his way travels easily.

*Religious corruption*

36. The devil gets up to the belfry by the vicar's skirts.
37. No penny, no pardon.
38. No penny, no paternoster. [The implication of this and the preceding proverb is that without payment, the priest will not perform the duties and services expected of him]

*Corruption at law*

39. Law is a flag, and gold is the wind that makes it wave. [Russian proverb]
40. A pocketful of right needs a pocketful of gold.
41. A golden handshake is better than ten witnesses.
42. The devil makes his Christmas-pies of lawyer's tongues and clerk's fingers.
43. Home is home, as the devil said when he found himself in the Court of Session. [The Court of Session is the supreme civil court in Scotland]
44. A basket-justice will do justice right or wrong. [A "basket-justice" was a judge who could be bribed with a basket of game]
45. He whose father is judge, goes safe to his trial.
46. Show me the man, and I'll show you the law. [A reference to biased judges]
47. Little thieves are hanged, but great ones escape.

# 30 COUNTRY LORE

*Agriculture*

1. A field requires three things; fair weather, sound seed, and a good husbandman.
2. Lime makes a rich father and a poor son. [The implication is that liming the soil will provide improved crops in the short term, but in the long term will damage the soil]
3. He who marls sand, may buy the land. ["Marl" is a mixture of clay and lime, a valuable fertilizer for sandy soil]
4. It is time to cock your hay and corn, when the old donkey blows his horn. [The implication is that the braying of the donkey presages heavy rain]
5. Corn and horn go together. [A reference to the market prices of corn and cattle, which generally rise and fall together]
6. When the corn is in the shock, the fish are on the rock. [This refers to the coincidence of the harvest and the fishing season]
7. If you cut oats green, you get both king and queen. [The advice here is to cut oats before they are fully ripe, so as not to lose the largest grains at the top of the heads]
8. Oats will mow themselves.
9. A famine in England begins at the horse-manger. [The implication is that a shortage of oats is generally accompanied by a shortage of other crops]
10. Hops make or break. [A reference to the unreliability of this expensive crop]

11. Plenty of ladybirds, plenty of hops.
12. Sow wheat in dirt, and rye in dust.
13. Sow in the slop, 'twill be heavy at top. [The advice here is to sow wheat in wet ground for maximum yield]
14. This rule in gardening never forget, to sow dry and to set wet.
15. Sow beans in the mud, and they'll grow like a wood.
16. One for the mouse, one for the crow, one to rot and one to grow. [This proverb refers to the mishaps that commonly befall a crop of beans, and suggests that only a 25% yield may be expected]
17. Sow peas and beans in the wane of the moon; who soweth them sooner, he soweth too soon.
18. A crooked man should sow beans, and a wud man peas. ["Crooked" here means "lame"; "wud" means "mad". The implication is that beans may be thickly sown, whereas peas should be sown more thinly]
19. Turnips like a dry bed but a wet head.

*Dairy produce*

20. Butter is once a year in the cow's horn. [A reference to the time of year when a cow gives no milk]
21. Butter is mad twice a year. [This refers to the summer, when butter is too soft to spread, and to the winter, when it is too hard]
22. If you will have a good cheese and hav'n old, you must turn'n seven times before he is cold.
23. Cheese and money should always sleep together one night. [A former saying of farmers, who insisted that payment for cheese should be received before the cheese was dispatched]
24. A red cow gives good milk.

*Animals*

25. A leap year is never a good sheep year.
26. He that has sheep, swine, and bees, sleep he, wake he, he may thrive.
27. Pigs see the wind. [An allusion to the restlessness of pigs when a wind is approaching]
28. Look to the cow, and the sow, and the wheat mow, and all will be well enow.
29. Roast meat does cattle. ["Does" means "fattens". The implication is that the burnt grass of a dry season is more fattening than the grass of a wet season]
30. The ox is never woe, till he to the harrow go. [A reference to the comparative discomfort of pulling a harrow rather than a plough]
31. Quey calves are dear veal. ["Quey" means "heifer"]
32. You may beat a horse till he be sad, and a cow till she be mad.

*Birds*

33. He who will have a full flock, must have an old stag and a young cock. ["Stag" here means "gander"]
34. He that will have his farm full, must keep an old cock and a young bull.
35. When the cuckoo comes to the bare thorn, sell your cow and buy you corn: but when she comes to the full bit, sell your corn and buy you sheep.
36. When the pigeons go a benting, then the farmers lie lamenting. ["Benting" is feeding on the seeds of grasses]
37. The pigeon never knows woe, but when she does a-benting go.
38. If the partridge had the woodcock's thigh, it would be the best bird that ever did fly.

*Trees and plants*

39. He that plants a tree plants for posterity.
40. Set trees poor and they will grow rich, set them rich and they will grow poor. [The advice is to move trees out of a barren soil into a fertile soil, rather than vice versa]
41. Red wood makes gude spindles. ["Red wood" here refers to the wood found at the heart of trees]
42. Every elm has its man. [A reference to the potential danger of the elm, which is frequently uprooted or sheds its branches in a storm]
43. The willow will buy a horse before the oak will pay for a saddle. [This refers to the speed at which a willow grows]
44. A cherry year, a merry year; a plum year, a dumb year; a pear year, a dear year.
45. Plant pears for your heirs.
46. He who plants a walnut-tree, expects not to eat of the fruit.
47. If you would fruit have, you must bring the leaf to the grave. [The advice here is to transplant trees as the leaves are falling, so that they have time to take root before the frosts of winter. To move them earlier would disturb the motion of the sap]
48. Short boughs, long vintage.
49. Make the vine poor, and it will make you rich. [This and the preceding proverb refer to the advantages of pruning vines]
50. When elder's white, brew and bake a peck; when elder's black, brew and bake a sack.
51. When the sloe tree is as white as a sheet, sow your barley whether it be dry or wet.
52. When the gorse is out of bloom, kissing's out of fashion. [An excuse for kissing or being kissed at any time of the year, based on the fact that gorse is never out of bloom]
53. When the fern is as high as a spoon, you may sleep an hour at noon.

54. Parsley seed goes nine times to the devil. [A reference to the slow germination of parsley seed]

See also MONTHS; SEASONS; WEATHER

# 31 COURAGE

### Its value

1. Courage and resolution are the spirit and soul of virtue.
2. Courage and perseverance conquer all before them.
3. Valour is the nobleness of the mind.
4. Fear can keep a man out of danger, but courage can support him in it.
5. Great things are done more through courage than through wisdom.
6. Fortune favours the bold.
7. A bold heart is half the battle.

### Its necessity

8. Faint heart never won fair lady.
9. None but the brave deserves the fair. [John Dryden (1631–1700) *Alexander's Feast*]
10. Put a stout heart to a stey brae. [The advice here is to face difficulties with courage. "Stey brae" means "steep slope"]

### Its sources

11. Valour is born with us, not acquired.
12. Despair gives courage to a coward.
13. Necessity and opportunity may make a coward valiant.

### Characteristics of the brave

14. A valiant man's look is more than a coward's sword.
15. The weapon of the brave is in his heart.
16. A man of courage never wants weapons.
17. A brave arm makes a short sword long.
18. A brave man's wounds are seldom on his back.
19. A brave man may fall, but he cannot yield.
20. Bold men have generous hearts.
21. To the real hero life is a mere straw. [Indian proverb]
22. Valour delights in the test.
23. Calamity is the touchstone of a brave mind. [This implies that bravery can only be assessed in time of danger]
24. To a brave and faithful man nothing is difficult.

*False courage*

25. Hares may pull dead lions by the beard.
26. Who takes a lion when he is absent, fears a mouse present.
27. Every cock will crow upon his own dung-hill.
28. Every dog is valiant at his own door.
29. Every dog is a lion at home.

*Foolhardiness*

30. It is a bold mouse that breeds in the cat's ear.
31. Nothing so bold as a blind mare.
32. Discretion is the better part of valour. [The implication of this and the following proverb is that what appears to be cowardice may be wise caution, and what appears to be valour may be foolish rashness]
33. Valour would fight, but discretion would run away.

# 32 COWARDICE

*Its effects*

1. Cowards run the greatest danger of any man in a battle. [A reference to the danger of turning one's back on one's enemy]
2. Cowards die often. [The implication of this and the following two proverbs is that to the coward, the mere prospect of danger is as bad as death]
3. Cowards die many times before their deaths. [William Shakespeare (1564–1616) *Julius Caesar*]
4. To fazarts, hard hazards are death ere they come there. ["Fazarts" means "cowards"]
5. He that forecasts all perils, will never sail the sea.
6. The mother of the coward does not worry about him. [Arabic proverb]
7. Faint heart never won fair lady.

*Its shame*

8. Cowardice is afraid to be known or seen.
9. Better die with honour than live with shame.
10. Of cowards no history is written.
11. He that forecasts all perils, will win no worship.

*Its value*

12. It is better to be a coward for a minute than dead for the rest of your life.

13. It is good sleeping in a whole skin.
14. One pair of heels is often worth two pairs of hands.
15. He that fights and runs away, may live to fight another day.

*Characteristics of the cowardly*

16. Cowards are cruel.
17. A bully is always a coward.
18. Many would be cowards, if they had courage enough. [This and the following proverb imply that in some situations it may be more difficult to run away than to stay and fight]
19. Some have been thought brave because they were afraid to run away.
20. Put a coward to his mettle, and he'll fight the devil. [The implication of this and the following two proverbs is that in desperate situations even the cowardly can be brave]
21. Despair gives courage to a coward.
22. Necessity and opportunity may make a coward valiant.
23. The virtue of a coward is suspicion.
24. Who has not a heart, let him have legs. ["Heart" is used here in the sense of "courage"]

# 33 CRIME

*Its causes*

1. Poverty is the mother of crime.
2. He that brings up his son to nothing, breeds a thief.
3. It is a hard task to be poor and leal. ["Leal" means "honest"]
4. It is hard for a greedy eye to have a leal heart.
5. The postern door makes thief and whore. [The implication is that the back door of a house provides the necessary concealment for dishonest servants and unfaithful wives]
6. The back door robs the house.
7. Two daughters and a back door are three arrant thieves. ["Two daughters" refers to the expense of bringing up daughters]
8. A careless hussy makes many thieves. ["Hussy" here means "housewife"]
9. He that is suffered to do more than is fitting, will do more than is lawful.
10. The more laws, the more offenders.

*Its effects*

11. He that does what he should not, shall feel what he would not.
12. Crimes are made secure by greater crimes.

13. The law grows of sin, and chastises it.
14. Stolen waters are sweet. [Proverbs 9:17. Variants of this proverb substitute "pleasures" or "fruit" for "waters"]

### Its dangers

15. Frost and fraud both end in foul.
16. He that steals honey should beware of the sting.
17. He that eats the king's goose shall be choked with the feathers.
18. Murder will out.
19. If you steal for others, you shall be hanged yourself.

### Its unprofitability

20. Crime does not pay.
21. Ill-gotten goods never prosper.
22. Stolen goods never thrive.
23. The devil's meal is all bran.
24. Ill gotten, ill spent.
25. Come with the wind, go with the water. [This proverb reiterates the sentiments of the preceding one]

### Criminals

26. He that will steal a pin, will steal a better thing.
27. He that will steal an egg, will steal an ox.
28. Hang a thief when he's young, and he'll no steal when he's old.
29. Set a thief to catch a thief.
30. An old poacher makes the best gamekeeper.
31. The wolf knows what the ill beast thinks.
32. A true man and a thief think not the same.
33. Show me a liar, and I will show thee a thief.
34. A tale-bearer is worse than a thief.
35. The receiver is as bad as the thief.
36. If there were no receivers, there would be no thieves.
37. One thief robs another.
38. A thief knows a thief as a wolf knows a wolf.
39. The thief is sorry he is to be hanged, but not that he is a thief. [The implication is that the thief does not repent his misdeeds, he merely regrets their consequences]
40. Thieves' handsel ever unlucky. ["Handsel" means "gift"]
41. A cut-purse is a sure trade, for he has ready money when his work is done.

See also TEMPTATION: *Its sources*

# 34 CRITICISM

*Its effects*

1. Hard words break no bones.
2. Lacking breeds laziness, praise breeds pith. ["Lacking" here means "censure"; "pith" means "effort"]
3. Judge not, that ye be not judged. [Matthew 7:1]

*Against criticizing others*

4. Live and let live.
5. Those who live in glass houses should not throw stones. [The implication of this and the following proverbs is that people should not be too eager to criticize in others faults they possess themselves]
6. Every man's censure is first moulded in his own nature.
7. The pot calls the kettle black.
8. The kettle calls the pot burnt-arse.
9. Ill may the kiln call the oven burnt-tail.
10. The frying-pan said to the kettle, 'Avaunt, black brows!'
11. The snite need not the woodcock betwite. ["Snite" means "snipe"; "betwite" means "criticize". The proverb refers to the long bills of these birds]
12. He should have a hale pow, that calls his neighbour nitty know. ["Pow" means "head"; "know" means "hillock". To call a person "nitty know" would imply that he was stupid]
13. The camel never sees its own hump, but that of its brother is always before its eyes. [Arabic proverb]
14. The hunchback does not see his own hump, but sees his companion's.
15. The eye that sees all things else sees not itself. [This and the following proverbs imply that those who criticize others are often blind to their own faults]
16. We see not what is in the wallet behind. [A reference to Aesop's idea that everyone carries two packs, one hanging in front of him and one behind. Into the first, which is always before his eyes, he puts the faults of others, but he hides his own faults in the one behind his back]
17. You can see a mote in another's eye but cannot see a beam in your own. [A "mote" is a particle of dust. The metaphor originated in Matthew 7:3]
18. Point not at others' spots with a foul finger.
19. Physician, heal thyself. [Luke 4:23]
20. Every one's faults are not written in their foreheads. [A retort made to those who criticize, implying that their faults, though less obvious, are as bad]

21. If every man would sweep before his own door, the city would soon be clean.

### The critical

22. He may find fault that cannot mend. [This and the following proverb imply that correcting faults is of more value than finding them]
23. One mend-fault is worth twenty spy-faults.
24. The most high God, sees, and bears: my neighbour knows nothing, and yet is always finding fault.

### Handling criticism

25. When all men say you are an ass, it is time to bray.
26. If one, two, or three tell you you are an ass, put on a bridle.
27. Fling at the brod was ne'er a good ox. ["Brod" means "goad"; "fling" here means "kick". The implication is that those who spurn criticism will never improve themselves]
28. If the cap fits, wear it.

# 35 CRUELTY

### Its evil

1. A man of cruelty is God's enemy.
2. Cruelty deserves no mercy.
3. Cruelty is the first attribute of the devil.
4. Cruelty is the strength of the wicked.

### Its value

5. Sometimes severity is better than gentleness.
6. Sometimes clemency is cruelty, and cruelty clemency.
7. Knock a carle, and ding a carle, and that's the way to win a carle. ["Ding" means "beat"; "carle" means "fellow". The proverb implies that some people respond best to rough or harsh treatment]

### Its effects

8. He that hurts another hurts himself.
9. Malice hurts itself most.
10. He threatens many that hurts any.
11. Tramp on a snail, and she'll shoot out her horns. [The implication is that not even the most lowly will tolerate cruelty without retaliation]

*Cruelty and fear*

12. Cruelty is a tyrant that's always attended with fear.
13. Cowards are cruel. [This and the following proverb imply that the cruellest people are generally the least brave]
14. A bully is always a coward.

See also TALKING: *The tongue as a weapon*

# 36 CUNNING

*Its value*

1. Cunning surpasses strength.
2. Wiles help weak folk.
3. If the lion's skin cannot, the fox's shall. [The implication is that what cannot be gained by strength must be gained by cunning]

*Its limitations*

4. Too much cunning undoes.
5. At length the fox is brought to the furrier.
6. Though the fox run, the chicken has wings.

*Characteristics of the cunning*

7. A crafty knave needs no broker.
8. Full of courtesy, full of craft. [This and the following two proverbs refer to the hypocrisy of the cunning]
9. When the fox preaches, then beware your geese.
10. It is an ill sign to see a fox lick a lamb.
11. The fox preys farthest from his home.

*Handling the cunning*

12. The fox knows much, but more he that catcheth him.
13. To a crafty man, a crafty and a half. [The implication is that a crafty person will only be caught by one more crafty than he]
14. An old fox is not easily snared.
15. If you deal with a fox, think of his tricks.
16. He that will deceive the fox must rise betimes.

# 37 DANGER

*Its sources*

1. Far from home, near thy harm.
2. A man far from his good is near his harm.
3. When we have gold, we are in fear; when we have none we are in danger.
4. Love and pease-pottage are two dangerous things. [The implication is that one attacks the heart and the other the stomach]
5. No safe wading in an unknown water.
6. What is not wisdom, is danger.
7. He that is not in the wars, is not out of danger.
8. There is a scorpion under every stone.
9. The post of honour is the post of danger.
10. He lives unsafely that looks too near on things.
11. A running horse is an open grave.
12. When you ride a young colt, see your saddle be well girt.

*Its effects*

13. Any port in a storm. [This implies that in time of danger, any refuge is better than none]
14. While the thunder lasted, two bad men were friends. [The implication of this and the following three proverbs is that danger may have good effects, which unfortunately do not last once the danger is past]
15. When it thunders, the thief becomes honest.
16. Danger makes men devout.
17. Vows made in storms are forgotten in calms.
18. Calamity is the touchstone of a brave mind. [This and the following proverb imply that bravery can only be assessed in time of danger]
19. In a calm sea, every man is a pilot.
20. He that dallies with his enemy, dies by his own hand.
21. He that brings himself into needless dangers, dies the devil's martyr.
22. They that bourd wi' cats, maun count on scarts. ["Bourd" means "jest"; "maun" means "must"; "scarts" means "scratches"]
23. The fly that plays too long in the candle, singes his wings at last.
24. You may play with a bull till you get his horn in your eye.
25. He that steals honey, should beware of the sting.
26. Dear bought is the honey that is licked from the thorn.
27. He that handles thorns shall prick his fingers.
28. Who remove stones, bruise their fingers.

*Its importance*

29. The more danger, the more honour.

30. Danger is next neighbour to security. [This implies that one cannot be truly secure unless one has experienced danger]
31. Danger itself is the best remedy for danger.
32. Without danger we cannot get beyond danger.

### The dangers of the sea

33. He that would sail without danger, must never come on the main sea.
34. He who travels not by sea, knows not what the fear of God is.
35. He that will learn to pray, let him go to sea.

### Taking a risk

36. Nothing ventured, nothing gained. [Variants of this proverb substitute "venture" for "ventured" and "gain", "have", or "win" for "gained"]
37. Nothing stake, nothing draw.
38. Nought lay down, nought take up.
39. Adventures are to the adventurous.
40. He that is afraid to shake the dice will never throw a six. [Chinese proverb]
41. Take your venture, as many a good ship has done.
42. If you do not enter a tiger's den, you cannot get his cubs. [Chinese proverb]

### Against taking risks

43. Don't go near the water until you learn how to swim.
44. Children and fools must not play with edged tools.
45. It is ill jesting with edged tools.
46. It is ill contending with the master of thirty legions.
47. Be not too bold with your biggers or betters.
48. If you play with fire you get burnt.
49. Bourd not with Bawty, lest he bite you. ["Bourd" means "jest"; "Bawty" is a watch-dog]
50. Though the mastiff be gentle, yet bite him not by the lip.
51. Three things are not to be trusted: a cow's horn, a dog's tooth, and a horse's hoof.

# 38 DAYS

### Popular rhymes

1. Monday for wealth, Tuesday for health, Wednesday the best day of all; Thursday for crosses, Friday for losses, Saturday no luck at all.

[A reference to the good or ill fortune associated with the day of one's wedding]

2. Monday's child is fair of face, Tuesday's child is full of grace; Wednesday's child is full of woe, Thursday's child has far to go; Friday's child is loving and giving, Saturday's child works hard for its living; and the child that's born on the Sabbath day, is fair and wise and good and gay.
3. Monday is Sunday's brother, Tuesday is such another; Wednesday you must go to church and pray, Thursday is half-holiday; on Friday it is too late to begin to spin, then Saturday is half-holiday agen. [An excuse for being idle all week]

*Particular days*

4. Thursday come, and the week is gone.
5. Friday and the week is seldom alike.
6. Friday night's dream on the Saturday told, is sure to come true be it never so old.
7. Friday's hair, and Saturday's horn, goes to the devil on Monday morn. [The implication is that it is unlucky to cut one's hair on Friday and to cut one's nails on Saturday]
8. Friday's moon, come when it will, comes too soon.
9. There is never a Saturday without some sunshine.
10. Saturday's servants never stay, Sunday servants run away.
11. A Saturday's moon, if it comes once in seven years, it comes too soon.
12. Saturday's new, and Sunday's full, was never fine and never wool. ["Wool" means "will be". The proverb refers to the moon]

See also RELIGION: *Sunday*

# 39 DEATH

*Its inevitability*

1. All men are mortal.
2. Grass and hay, we are all mortal.
3. All men must die.
4. Charon waits for all. [In Greek mythology, Charon was the ferryman who conveyed the souls of the dead across the river Styx to Hades]
5. Death is sure to all.
6. Nothing is certain but death and taxes.
7. Nothing so certain as death.
8. Death is the black camel that kneels before every door.
9. Every door may be shut but death's door.

10. Arthur himself had but his time. [A reference to the mortality of great men such as King Arthur]
11. Dying is as natural as living.
12. It is as natural to die as to be born. [Francis Bacon (1561–1626) *Essay on Death*]
13. As soon as man is born he begins to die.
14. The first breath is the beginning of death.
15. He that is once born, once must die.
16. No man has a lease of his life.
17. When thou dost hear a toll or knell, then think upon thy passing bell.
18. Death defies the doctor.
19. Death is deaf to our wailings.
20. Death does not recognize strength. [African proverb]

*Its unpredictability*

21. Death keeps no calendar.
22. At every hour death is near.
23. Death surprises us in the midst of our hopes.
24. Men know where they were born, not where they shall die.
25. No man knows when he shall die, although he knows he must die.
26. Today a man, tomorrow none.

*Its finality*

27. Death is the end of all.
28. Stone-dead has no fellow.
29. A dead bee makes no honey.
30. There is a remedy for all things but death.
31. There is hope from the mouth of the sea, but none from the mouth of the grave.
32. The evening crowns the day. [The implication of this and the following four proverbs is that only at the end of his life can a man be truly judged]
33. Praise a fair day at night.
34. Praise no man till he is dead.
35. Call no man happy till he dies.
36. Death's day is doom's day.

*Its consolations*

37. A dead mouse feels no cold.
38. Death is a remedy for all ills.
39. A ground sweat cures all disorders.
40. Death is the poor man's best physician.

41. Death rather frees us from ills, than robs us of our goods.
42. Death pays all debts.
43. A man can die but once.
44. Our birth made us mortal, our death will make us immortal.
45. Death is a dying man's friend.
46. Look upon death as a going home. [Chinese proverb]
47. Earth is the best shelter.

### Its advantages

48. Dead dogs bark not.
49. Dead men don't bite.
50. Dead men tell no tales.
51. The death of a young wolf never comes too soon. [Such a death is advantageous from the shepherd's or farmer's point of view]
52. The death of the wolves is the safety of the sheep.

### Its causes

53. There is but one way to enter this life, but the gates of death are without number.
54. One funeral makes many. [This superstition may be based on the unhealthy practice of mourners standing around a grave in a cold churchyard]
55. Old men, when they marry young women, make much of death. [The implication is that when an old man embraces his young wife he embraces death, for she will bring him to an early grave]
56. A green Yule makes a fat churchyard. [This and the following proverb comment on the unhealthy effects of mild weather at certain times of the year]
57. A hot May makes a fat churchyard.
58. A young physician fattens the churchyard.
59. War is death's feast.

### Its effects

60. Dying men speak true.
61. When death is on the tongue, repentance is not difficult.

### Its choice of victims

62. The best go first.
63. Whom the gods love dies young.
64. The good die young.
65. Death is the only master who takes his servants without a character.
66. In Golgotha are skulls of all sizes. [The implication of this and subsequent proverbs is that none are too young to die]

67. Graves are of all sizes.
68. Death devours lambs as well as sheep.
69. As soon goes the young sheep to the pot as the old.
70. As soon goes the young lamb's skin to the market as the old ewe's.

### Equality in death

71. Death is the great leveller.
72. A piece of churchyard fits everybody.
73. We shall lie all alike in our graves.
74. All our pomp the earth covers.
75. Six feet of earth make all men equal.
76. On the turf all men are equal – and under it.
77. The end makes all equal.
78. Death makes us equal in the grave and unequal in eternity.
79. Death combs us all with the same comb.
80. Death carries a fat tsar on his shoulders as easily as a lean beggar. [Russian proverb]

### Fear of death

81. Fear of death is worse than death itself.
82. He that fears death lives not.
83. Men fear death as children fear to go in the dark. [Francis Bacon *Essay on Death*]
84. Death hath not so ghastly a face at a distance, as it hath at hand.

### The manner of death

85. A good life makes a good death.
86. They die well that live well.
87. An ill life, an ill end.
88. He dies like a beast who has done no good while he lived.
89. Such a life, such a death.
90. Let all live as they would die.
91. A fair death honours the whole life.

### Our attitude to the dead

92. Never speak ill of the dead.
93. Speak only what is true of the living and what is honourable of the dead.
94. Dead men are of no family, and are akin to none.
95. To dead men and absent there are no friends left.
96. Dead men have no friends.
97. The dead are always wrong.
98. Let the dead bury their dead. [Matthew 8:22. The implication is that

the living have more important things to do than to attend to the needs of the dead]
99. We must live by the living, not by the dead.
100. To lament the dead avails not and revenge vents hatred.

See also OLD PEOPLE: *Old age and death*

# 40 DECEIT

*Its sources*

1. Believe no tales from an enemy's tongue.
2. A false tongue will hardly speak truth.
3. There is falsehood in fellowship.
4. Trust is the mother of deceit.
5. Debtors are liars.
6. Lying rides upon debt's back.
7. Half the truth is often a whole lie.
8. Where there is whispering there is lying.
9. In many words a lie or two may escape.

*Its dangers*

10. A liar can go round the world but cannot come back. [The implication is that the liar dare not return to those people he has previously deceived]
11. The liar is sooner caught than the cripple.
12. A blister will rise upon one's tongue that tells a lie.
13. One lie makes many.
14. Oh, what a tangled web we weave, when first we practise to deceive! [Walter Scott (1771–1832) *Marmion*]
15. A liar is not believed when he speaks the truth.
16. He that once deceives, is ever suspected.
17. Liars begin by imposing upon others, but end by deceiving themselves.
18. Falsehood never made a fair hinder end.
19. Women and wine, game and deceit, make the wealth small, and the wants great.
20. Cheats never prosper.

*Its sinfulness*

21. Deceiving those that trust us, is more than a sin.
22. A lie is the curse of God.
23. The liar and the murderer are children of the same village.

24. A liar is worse than a thief.

*Its permissibility*

25. To deceive a deceiver is no deceit.
26. No law for lying. [This implies that lying is not against the law]
27. Old men and travellers may lie by authority.
28. Painters and poets have leave to lie.
29. Better a lie that heals than a truth that wounds.

*Concealing lies*

30. Though a lie be well drest, it is ever overcome.
31. Almost and well nigh saves many a lie. [The implication is that saying a task is almost completed, when it is scarcely begun, may be considered less deceitful than to say that the task is done]

*Self-deception*

32. Who thinks to deceive God has already deceived himself.
33. To deceive oneself is very easy.

*Characteristics of the deceitful*

34. A liar should have a good memory.
35. He that will lie, will steal.
36. He that will swear, will lie.
37. He that will cheat at play, will cheat you anyway.
38. False with one can be false with two.
39. Deceivers have full mouths and empty hands.
40. You can't kid a kidder.

# 41 DEEDS

*Their value*

1. 'Tis action makes the hero.
2. Our own actions are our security, not others' judgments.
3. Well is, that well does.
4. By his deeds we know a man. [African proverb]
5. Action is the proper fruit of knowledge.

*Words and deeds*

6. Actions speak louder than words.
7. The effect speaks, the tongue needs not.
8. Deeds are fruits, words are but leaves.

9. Words are mere bubbles of water, but deeds are drops of gold. [Chinese proverb]
10. A man of words and not of deeds, is like a garden full of weeds.
11. Deeds will show themselves, and words will pass away.
12. Doing is better than saying.
13. It is better to do well than to say well.
14. A little help is worth a deal of pity.
15. Say well, and do well, end with one letter; say well is good, but do well is better.
16. Good words without deeds are rushes and reeds.
17. The shortest answer is doing.
18. The greatest talkers are the least doers.
19. There is great difference between word and deed.
20. Saying and doing are two things.
21. Saying is one thing, and doing another.
22. From word to deed is a great space.
23. Easier said than done.
24. Fair words and foul deeds cheat wise men as well as fools.
25. Fair words and foul play cheat both young and old.
26. Good words and ill deeds deceive wise men and fools.

### Action and intention

27. The good intention excuses the bad action.
28. Every deed is to be judged by the doer's intention.
29. Take the will for the deed. [The implication is that where something has been left undone, the intention or will to do it is all that matters]
30. Man punishes the action, but God the intention.

### Good deeds

31. One good deed atones for a thousand bad ones. [Chinese proverb]
32. A good deed is never lost.
33. To see a man do a good deed is to forget all his faults. [Chinese proverb]
34. Do good: thou doest it for thyself.
35. Do well and have well.
36. He that does well, wearies not himself.
37. One never loses by doing a good turn.
38. One good turn deserves another.
39. Never be weary of well doing.

### Bad deeds

40. An ill deed cannot bring honour.
41. Better suffer ill than do ill.

42. An evil deed remains with the evil-doer. [Japanese proverb]
43. An ill turn is soon done.
44. Who would do ill, ne'er wants occasion.
45. If you do no ill, do no ill like. [This implies that to refrain from doing evil is of no avail if one still condones the bad deeds of others]
46. Whoso will no evil do, shall do nothing that belongs thereto.
47. Evil deeds are like perfume, difficult to hide. [African proverb]
48. Do wrong once and you'll never hear the end of it.
49. Ten good turns lie dead and one ill deed report abroad does spread. [The implication of this and the following four proverbs is that while good deeds are soon forgotten, the memory of bad deeds and past injuries can never be effaced]
50. Old sins cast long shadows.
51. Injuries are written in brass.
52. Injuries don't use to be written on ice.
53. The evil that men do lives after them, the good is oft interred with their bones. [William Shakespeare (1564–1616) *Julius Caesar*]

See also PROMISES: *Promise and performance*; TALKING: *Its inadequacy*

# 42 DEFAMATION

## Its effects

1. Throw dirt enough, and some will stick.
2. If the ball does not stick to the wall, it will at least leave a mark.
3. Slander leaves a score behind it. ["Score" here means "mark"]
4. Slander is a shipwreck by a dry tempest.
5. Slander cannot make a good man bad; when the water recedes the stone is still there. [Chinese proverb]
6. He that falls into the dirt, the longer he stays there the fouler he is. [The advice here is to clear oneself of defamatory accusations as soon as possible]
7. Give a dog a bad name and hang him.
8. He that has an ill name is half hanged.
9. An ill wound is cured, not an ill name.
10. The fox fares best when he is cursed.
11. He that flings dirt at another, dirtieth himself most.
12. Slander flings stones at itself.
13. The slanderer kills a thousand times, the assassin but once. [Chinese proverb]
14. The devil is not so black as he is painted.

*Handling insults*

15. The more you tramp on a turd, the broader it grows. [The implication is that to make a great fuss about an undeserved insult serves only to draw further attention to it]
16. The wise forget insults, as the ungrateful a kindness. [Chinese proverb]
17. Neglect will kill an injury sooner than revenge.
18. No reply is best.
19. The remedy for injuries, is not to remember them.
20. There were no ill language, if it were not ill taken.
21. It was never ill said that was not ill taken.
22. Patience under old injuries invites new ones.

See also GOSSIP; TALKING: *Speaking ill*

# 43 DELAY

*Its dangers*

1. Delays are dangerous.
2. While the grass grows, the horse starves.
3. While men go after a leech, the body is buried.
4. 'Time enough' lost the ducks. [A reference to the danger of delaying such precautionary measures as locking up the ducks to protect them from the fox]
5. Time lost cannot be recalled.

*Its advantages*

6. That delay is good which makes the way the safer.
7. Desires are nourished by delays.
8. If today will not, tomorrow may.
9. Put off the evil hour as long as you can.
10. Delay is the antidote of anger.

*Its effects*

11. Cruelty is more cruel, if we defer the pain.
12. Hope deferred maketh the heart sick. [Proverbs 13:12]
13. Long tarrying takes all the thanks away.
14. He loses his thanks who promises and delays.
15. Tarry-long brings little home.
16. After a delay comes a let. ["Let" here means "hindrance"]
17. What is deferred is not abandoned.
18. The thing that's fristed is not forgiven. ["Fristed" means "delayed".

This and the previous proverb warn that delay neither releases one from an obligation nor spares one from punishment]

*Against procrastination*

19. Procrastination is the thief of time. [Edward Young (1683–1765) *Night Thoughts*]
20. Never put off till tomorrow what you can do today.
21. One hour today is worth two tomorrow.
22. One today is worth two tomorrows.
23. Tomorrow never comes.
24. One of these days is none of these days.
25. Sooner begun, sooner done.
26. No time like the present.

See also OPPORTUNITY

# 44 DESERVING

*Rightful reward*

1. A good dog deserves a good bone.
2. One good turn deserves another.
3. He that blows best, bears away the horn.
4. He that serves well, needs not ask his wages.
5. Desert and reward seldom keep company.
6. The labourer is worthy of his hire. [Luke 10:7. The implication of this and the following two proverbs is that everybody deserves to be paid for work done or services rendered]
7. Good hand, good hire. ["Hire" here and in the preceding proverb means "payment, reward"]
8. It is an ill dog that deserves not a crust.

*Just deserts*

9. He that sows thistles shall reap prickles.
10. The deed comes back upon the doer.
11. The biter is sometimes bit.
12. An arrow shot upright falls on the shooter's head.
13. Who spits against the wind, it falls in his face.
14. Curses, like chickens, come home to roost.
15. After your fling, watch for the sting.
16. Sweet meat will have sour sauce.
17. Like fault, like punishment.
18. Such answer as man gives, such will he get.

19. One ill word asks another.
20. If you give a jest, you must take a jest.
21. Punishment is lame, but it comes.

### The undeserving

22. He deserves not the sweet that will not taste the sour.
23. He that cannot abide a bad market, deserves not a good one.
24. He is worth no weal that can bide no woe.
25. Into the mouth of a bad dog, often falls a good bone.
26. The worst hog often gets the best pear.

See also GOD: *Divine retribution*

# 45 DESTINY

### Its inescapability

1. Destiny has four feet, eight hands, and sixteen eyes; how then shall the ill-doer with only two of each hope to escape? [Chinese proverb]
2. No flying from fate.
3. Flee never so fast you cannot flee your fortune.
4. Do what you ought, and come what can.
5. What must be, must be. [Variants of this proverb substitute "will" or "shall" for "must". The proverb is also familiar in its Italian form, *Che sarà, sarà*]
6. Fate leads the willing, but drives the stubborn.
7. He that is born to be hanged, shall never be drowned.
8. Every bullet has its billet.
9. There's a divinity that shapes our ends, rough-hew them how we will. [William Shakespeare (1564–1616) *Hamlet*]

### Its mystery

10. A man's destiny is always dark. [The implication is that nobody knows what fate has in store for him]
11. She is an old wife that wats her weird. ["Wats" means "knows"; "weird" means "fortune"]

# 46 DEVIL

### His trickery

1. The devil is subtle, yet weaves a coarse web.

2. The devil can cite Scripture for his purpose. [William Shakespeare (1564–1616) *The Merchant of Venice*]
3. When the devil prays, he has a booty in his eye.
4. The devil sometimes speaks the truth.

*His evil*

5. The devil always leaves a stink behind him.
6. It is an ill battle where the devil carries the colours.
7. When rogues go in procession, the devil holds the cross.

*His power*

8. He that the devil drives, feels no lead at his heels.
9. The devil knows many things because he is old.
10. There is no redemption from hell.

*His persistence*

11. Where the devil cannot come, he will send.
12. The devil will play small game before he will sit out. [The implication is that when the devil cannot take full possession of a person, he will still attempt to take a small part of his soul]

*His omnipresence*

13. The devil is a busy bishop in his own diocese. [This implies that the devil is never out of his own diocese, for it has no boundaries]
14. The devil is at home. [A reminder that not even at home can one escape the temptations of the devil]
15. The devil lurks behind the cross.

*Handling the devil*

16. The devil loves no holy water.
17. They that deal wi' the devil, get a dear pennyworth.
18. He is fond of barter that niffers with Old Nick. ["Niffers" means "bargains"]
19. He must rise betimes that will cozen the devil. ["Betimes" means "early"; "cozen" means "cheat"]

See also GOD: *God and the devil*

# 47 DIFFERENCES

### Their existence

1. It takes all sorts to make a world.
2. There's nowt so queer as folk. ["Nowt" means "nothing"]
3. All feet tread not in one shoe.
4. Every shoe fits not every foot.
5. All things fit not all persons.
6. There may be blue and better blue.
7. Every couple is not a pair.
8. Every man after his fashion.
9. Every man buckles his belt his ain gate. ["His ain gate" means "his own way"]
10. So many men, so many opinions.

### Different tastes

11. There is no accounting for tastes.
12. There is no disputing about tastes.
13. Every one to his taste.
14. One man's meat is another man's poison.
15. All meat pleases not all mouths.
16. No dish pleases all palates alike.
17. All meats to be eaten, and all maids to be wed. [The implication of this and the following proverb is that what is rejected by one person will be taken up by another]
18. If one will not, another will.
19. If minds were alike goods would age in the shops. [Arabic proverb]
20. Every man as he loves, quoth the good man when he kissed his cow.

### Different needs

21. You can't please everyone.
22. He that would please all and himself too, undertakes what he cannot do.
23. He had need rise betimes that would please everybody. ["Betimes" means "early"]
24. He that all men will please shall never find ease.
25. Not God above gets all men's love. [The implication is that not even God can satisfy the needs of everybody simultaneously]

### Different methods

26. There are more ways to the wood than one.
27. There is more than one way to skin a cat.
28. There are more ways to kill a cat than choking it with cream. [A

variant of this proverb substitutes "dog ... butter" for "cat ...
cream"]
29. There are more ways to kill a dog than hanging it.
30. All roads lead to Rome.

# 48 DILIGENCE

*Its value*

1. If a job's worth doing, it's worth doing well. [A variant of this
   proverb substitutes "thing" for "job"]
2. Diligence is the mother of good fortune.
3. Care and diligence bring luck.
4. Diligence makes an expert workman.
5. Diligence is a great teacher. [Arabic proverb]
6. Lice do not bite busy men.
7. Better wear out shoes than sheets.
8. Without business, debauchery. [In this and the next proverb, "business" means "being busy"]
9. Business is the salt of life.
10. Labour overcomes all things.
11. A diligent scholar, and the master's paid.
12. Better to wear out than to rust out.
13. Elbow grease gives the best polish.
14. The gear that is gifted is never so sweet as the gear that is won. [The
    implication is that goods that have been earned by honest hard work
    are worth far more than gifts]
15. A little labour, much health.
16. Where bees are, there is honey. [This and the following proverbs
    refer to the material gains of hard work]
17. No bees, no honey; no work, no money.
18. Keep your shop and your shop will keep you.
19. The mill gets by going.
20. A going foot is aye getting.
21. He that labours and thrives, spins gold.
22. Industry is fortune's right hand, and frugality her left.
23. Plough deep, while sluggards sleep; and you shall have corn to sell
    and to keep.
24. The diligent spinner has a large shift.
25. Win gold and wear gold. [A variant of this proverb substitutes
    "purple" for "gold"]
26. That which is well done is twice done. [The implication is that a
    thing done well is done for ever, whereas a thing done badly must be
    done again]

*Its necessity*

27. It is good to work wisely lest a man be prevented.
28. Labour as long lived, pray as ever dying.
29. God gives the milk, but not the pail. [The implication is that hard work is needed to make the most of nature's benefits]
30. Footprints on the sands of time are not made by sitting down.
31. No sweet without sweat.
32. Ninety per cent of inspiration is perspiration.
33. Genius is an infinite capacity for taking pains.
34. Without diligence, no prize.
35. No pains, no gains.
36. You don't get something for nothing.
37. He that will eat the kernel, must crack the nut.
38. He that would have the fruit, must climb the tree.
39. If you put nothing into your purse, you can take nothing out.
40. It is not with saying 'Honey, honey,' that sweetness will come into the mouth.
41. If you won't work you shan't eat.
42. He that will not endure labour in this world, let him not be born.
43. The race is got by running.
44. Think of ease, but work on.

*Its effects*

45. Busiest men find the most leisure time.
46. Those that make the best use of their time, have none to spare.
47. Work expands to fill the time available. [This facetious notion was formulated by C. Northcote Parkinson (1909–   ), and is known as Parkinson's Law]

*The dangers of working too hard*

48. To be too busy, gets contempt.
49. Ever busy, ever bare. [The implication is that the busiest people do not have the most wealth and possessions]
50. All work and no play makes Jack a dull boy.
51. Mix work with leisure and you will never go mad. [Russian proverb]
52. There are only twenty-four hours in the day.
53. Many irons in the fire, some must cool.
54. He who begins many things, finishes but few.
55. If you run after two hares, you will catch neither.
56. He that does most at once, does least.
57. One thing at a time, and that done well, is a very good thing, as many can tell.

*Diligent people*

58. For the diligent the week has seven todays, for the slothful seven tomorrows.
59. Not a long day, but a good heart rids work.
60. The workman is known by his work.

*Making an effort*

61. You never know what you can do till you try.
62. If the mountain will not come to Mahomet, Mahomet must go to the mountain.

# 49 DISCIPLINE

*Its importance*

1. Reward and punishment are the walls of a city.
2. Corn is cleansed with wind, and the soul with chastenings.
3. He that corrects not small faults, will not control great ones.
4. The best horse needs breaking, and the aptest child needs teaching.
5. It is the bridle and spur that makes a good horse.
6. A boisterous horse must have a rough bridle.
7. The plough goes not well if the ploughman hold it not.
8. He that chastens one, chastens twenty.
9. He that chastises one, amends many.

*Disciplining children*

10. Better children weep than old men. [The implication is that it is better to punish children, however cruel it may seem, than to let them develop faults which will cause more sorrow in later life]
11. Rule youth well, and age will rule itself.
12. Give me a child for the first seven years, and you may do what you like with him afterwards.
13. The kick of the dam hurts not the colt.
14. Time is the rider that breaks youth.
15. She spins well that breeds her children.

*The spoilt child*

16. A child may have too much of his mother's blessing.
17. He that cockers his child, provides for his enemy. ["Cockers" means "spoils"]
18. Give a child while he craves, and a dog while his tail doth wave, and you'll have a fair dog, but a foul knave.

19. A pitiful mother makes a scabby daughter. ["Scabby" here means "nasty"]
20. Dawted daughters make daidling wives. ["Dawted" means "spoilt"; "daidling" means "lazy"]
21. A blate cat makes a proud mouse. ["Blate" means "bashful". The implication is that a lenient parent or master makes impertinent children or servants]

*Corporal punishment*

22. Spare the rod and spoil the child.
23. A whip for a fool, and a rod for a school, is always in good season.
24. The rod breaks no bones.
25. Birchen twigs break no ribs.
26. A woman, a dog, and a walnut-tree, the more you beat them the better they be.
27. Spaniels that fawn when beaten, will never forsake their masters.
28. He that is sick of a fever lurden, must be cured by the hazel gelding. ["Fever lurden" means "laziness"]
29. You may ding the devil into a wife, but you'll never ding him out of her. ["Ding" means "beat"]
30. Never take the tawse when a word will do the turn. [The "tawse" is a leather strap with split end, used in Scotland for corporal punishment]

*Self-discipline*

31. Happy is he that chastens himself.
32. He that is master of himself, will soon be master of others.
33. He is not fit to command others, that cannot command himself.
34. He gets a double victory, who conquers himself.

*The watchful master*

35. The eye of the master will do more work than both his hands. [The implication of this and the following proverbs is that discipline in a household can only be maintained when the master is present to supervise and inspect]
36. One eye of the master sees more than ten of the servants.
37. The master's eye makes the horse fat. [A reference to the need for supervision of stable-hands]
38. The master's footsteps fatten the soil, and his foot the ground.
39. A sleepy master makes his servant a lout.

See also ABSENCE: *Its effect on discipline*

## 50 DRESS

*Its effects*

1. Clothes make people, priests make brides.
2. God makes and apparel shapes.
3. Apparel makes the man.
4. The tailor makes the man.
5. Good clothes open all doors.
6. Fine feathers make fine birds.
7. Dress up a stick and it does not appear to be a stick.
8. Fine dressing is a foul house swept before the doors.
9. Ugly women, finely dressed, are the uglier for it.
10. Clothes do not make the man.

*Fashion*

11. The present fashion is always handsome.
12. Fools may invent fashions that wise men will wear.
13. What has been the fashion will come into fashion again. [Japanese proverb]
14. Better be out of the world than out of the fashion.

*Sunday best*

15. Alike every day makes a clout on Sunday. ["Clout" means "rag". This and the following proverb are addressed to those who wear their Sunday best all week]
16. Every day braw makes Sunday a daw. ["Braw" means "fine"; "daw" means "drab"]

## 51 DRINKING

*Drunkenness*

1. When the wine is in, the wit is out.
2. Ale will make a cat speak.
3. Drunkards and fools cannot lie.
4. There is truth in wine. [This proverb is equally familiar in its Latin form, *In vino veritas*]
5. What soberness conceals, drunkenness reveals.
6. Drunkenness does not produce faults, it discovers them. [Chinese proverb]
7. Wine wears no breeches. [The implication is that drink reveals a man's failings]
8. Wine is the glass of the mind.

9. When wine sinks, words swim.
10. Wine does not intoxicate men: men intoxicate themselves. [Chinese proverb]
11. Drunken days have all their tomorrows.
12. Let but the drunkard alone, and he will fall of himself.
13. A drunkard's purse is a bottle.
14. You cannot make people sober by Act of Parliament. [A reference to laws restricting the sale of alcoholic liquor]
15. The best cure for drunkenness is while sober to see a drunken man. [Chinese proverb]

### Its advantages

16. Drunken folks seldom take harm.
17. There are more old drunkards than old doctors.
18. Wine is the best broom for troubles. [Japanese proverb]
19. A cask of wine works more miracles than a church full of saints. [Italian proverb]
20. A good drink makes the old young.
21. Wine makes old wives wenches.
22. Wine and youth increase love.
23. A spur in the head is worth two in the heel. [The implication is that a drunken man rides faster]
24. Wine is a whetstone to wit.

### Its dangers

25. Bacchus has drowned more men that Neptune. [Bacchus is the god of wine, Neptune the god of the sea]
26. There is a devil in every berry of the grape.
27. He that kills a man when he is drunk shall be hanged when he is sober.
28. Wine and wealth change wise men's manners.
29. The first glass for thirst, the second for nourishment, the third for pleasure, and the fourth for madness.
30. Dicing, drabbing and drinking bring men to destruction. [A "drab" is a prostitute]
31. Gaming, women, and wine, while they laugh, they make men pine.
32. Play, women, and wine undo men laughing.
33. Wine and wenches empty men's purses.
34. Women and wine, game and deceit, make the wealth small, and the wants great.

### Beer

35. Good ale is meat, drink, and cloth.

36. He that buys land buys many stones; he that buys flesh buys many bones; he that buys eggs buys many shells; but he that buys good ale buys nothing else.
37. Heresy and beer came into England both in a year.
38. Every one has a penny to spend at a new ale-house.
39. He goes not out of his way that goes to a good inn.

### Wine

40. The vine brings forth three grapes: the first of pleasure, the second of drunkenness, the third of sorrow.
41. Wine is a turncoat. [The implication is that although wine is pleasant to drink, it has unpleasant after-effects]
42. Wine is old men's milk.
43. Wine makes all sorts of creatures at table.
44. It is a good wind that blows a man to the wine.
45. The wine is the master's, the goodness is the butler's. [This implies that the credit for a good wine should go to the butler, who selects and serves it, rather than to the master, who merely pays for it]
46. Of wine the middle, of oil the top, and of honey the bottom, is the best.
47. Fish must swim thrice. [The implication is that fish should first swim in the water, then in the sauce in which it is cooked, and finally in the wine with which it is drunk]
48. The peach will have wine and the fig water.
49. After melon, wine is a felon.
50. Drink wine in winter for cold, and in summer for heat.

### Water

51. Water is the king of food. [African proverb]
52. Adam's ale is the best brew. ["Adam's ale" is water]
53. Drinking water neither makes a man sick, nor in debt, nor his wife a widow.
54. Those who drink but water will have no liquor to buy.
55. Drink only with the duck. [The advice is to drink only water]
56. Water drinkers bring forth nothing good.

### Healthy drinking habits

57. Drink less, and go home by daylight.
58. Eat at pleasure, drink by measure.
59. Clothe thee warm, eat little, drink enough, and thou shalt live.
60. Of all victuals, drink digests the quickest. [An excuse for drinking after a meal]
61. Never mix your liquor. [This may be taken to mean either that one

should not mix different types of liquor or, facetiously, that one should not mix liquor with water to dilute it]
62. Our fathers which were wondrous wise, did wash their throats before their eyes.
63. Do not drink between meals.
64. Drink as much after an egg as after an ox. [The implication is that one should drink as much with a small meal as with a large]
65. Good wine engenders good blood.
66. If you would live ever, you must wash milk from your liver. [This and the following proverb refer to the belief that wine should be drunk after milk]
67. Milk says to wine, Welcome friend.

*Unhealthy drinking habits*

68. He who drinks a little too much drinks much too much.
69. If you drink in your pottage, you'll cough in your grave. [The implication is that it is unwise to drink with soup]
70. Drink wine, and have the gout; drink no wine, and have the gout too. [An excuse for drinking wine]
71. He that drinks not wine after salad is in danger of being sick.

*Thirst*

72. He who is master of his thirst is master of his health.
73. He is not thirsty who doesn't drink water.
74. Many words would have much drink.
75. Salt beef draws down drink apace.
76. A drunken man is always dry.
77. Ever drunk, ever dry.
78. He that goes to bed thirsty, rises healthy.

# 52 EARLINESS

*Its advantages*

1. The early bird catches the worm.
2. The sleepy fox has seldom feathered breakfasts.
3. The cow that's first up, gets the first of the dew.
4. He that comes first to the hill, may sit where he will.
5. First come, first served.
6. He that rises first, is first dressed.
7. Early to bed and early to rise, makes a man healthy, wealthy and wise.

8. He that will thrive, must rise at five; he that has thriven, may lie till seven; but he that will never thrive may lie till eleven.
9. Go to bed with the lamb, and rise with the lark.
10. Some work in the morning may trimly be done, that all the day after may hardly be won.
11. An hour in the morning is worth two in the evening.
12. He who works before dawn will soon be his own master.
13. The early man never borrows from the late man.
14. Early sow, early mow.
15. Sooner begun, sooner done.

*Its necessity*

16. He that will deceive the fox must rise betimes. ["Betimes" means "early"]
17. He must rise betimes that will cozen the devil. ["Cozen" means "cheat"]
18. He had need rise betimes that would please everybody.
19. A green wound is soon healed. [The implication of this and the next proverb is that a wound is best healed if treated early]
20. It is ill healing of an old sore.
21. A stitch in time saves nine. [This and the following three proverbs illustrate the value of prompt action in avoiding future trouble]
22. Who repairs not his gutter, repairs his whole house.
23. He that repairs not a part, builds all.
24. Destroy the lion while he is yet but a whelp.

*Its inadequacy*

25. God's help is better than early rising.
26. Though you rise early, yet the day comes at his time, and not till then.
27. In vain they rise early that used to rise late.

*The importance of punctuality*

28. Punctuality is the politeness of princes.
29. Punctuality is the soul of business.

# 53 EATING

*Its importance*

1. Bread is the staff of life.
2. An army marches on its stomach.
3. The belly carries the legs.

4. Stuffing holds out storm. [The advice here is that one should eat a good meal before setting off on a journey in bad weather]
5. The guts uphold the heart, and not the heart the guts.
6. The way to an Englishman's heart is through his stomach. [A variant of this proverb substitutes "man" for "Englishman"]
7. Without Ceres and Bacchus, Venus grows cold. [Ceres is the goddess of agriculture, Bacchus the god of wine, and Venus the goddess of love. The implication of this and the next proverb is that without food and wine a man loses his desire to make love]
8. If it wasn't for meat and good drink, the women might gnaw the sheets.
9. When meat is in, anger is out.
10. Spread the table, and contention will cease.
11. All griefs with bread are less.
12. Meat and mass never hindered any man.
13. The mouth is the executioner and the doctor of the body. [The implication is that a bad or good diet may either kill or cure]
14. He was an ingenious man that first found out eating and drinking. [Jonathan Swift (1667–1745) *Dialogues*]

## Its unimportance

15. Man cannot live by bread alone. [This proverb is based on Deuteronomy 8:3]
16. Meat is much, but manners is more.
17. It is better to want meat than guests or company.

## Appetite

18. All things require skill but an appetite.
19. The eye is bigger than the belly.
20. Better fill a man's belly than his eye.
21. One shoulder of mutton draws down another. [This proverb, contrary to the next, suggests that appetite increases with eating]
22. Eating and drinking takes away one's stomach.
23. The first dish is aye best eaten.
24. The first dish pleases all. [The implication of this and the preceding proverb is that the first course of a meal will always be the best appreciated because it takes the edge off one's appetite]
25. A growing youth has a wolf in his belly.

## Desirable foods

26. The best food is that which fills the belly. [Arabic proverb]
27. The best smell is bread, the best savour salt, the best love that of children.

28. Salt seasons all things.
29. Good kail is half a meal. ["Kail" means "broth"]
30. Kail spares bread.
31. Of soup and love, the first is the best.
32. Milk is white, and lies not in the dyke, but all men know it good meat.
33. Tripe's good meat if it be well wiped.
34. A meal without flesh is like feeding on grass. [Indian proverb]
35. He that has breams in his pond is able to bid his friend welcome. [This proverb originated in France, where bream were highly valued as food]
36. The wholesomest meat is at another man's cost.
37. It is good beef that costs nothing.

### Undesirable foods

38. He was a bold man that first ate an oyster.
39. Oysters are ungodly, because they are eaten without grace; uncharitable because we leave nought but shells; and unprofitable because they must swim in wine.
40. Garlic makes a man wink, drink, and stink.
41. There is no such thing as good small beer, good brown bread, or a good old woman.
42. Hare is melancholy meat.
43. Parsley fried will bring a man to his saddle, and a woman to her grave.
44. Every pease has its veaze, and a bean fifteen. ["Veaze" literally means "a sudden rush", here referring to flatulence. The implication is that although peas are flatulent, beans are fifteen times more so]
45. Raw pulleyn, veal, and fish, make the churchyards fat. ["Pulleyn" means "poultry"]
46. Sweet things are bad for the teeth.
47. In a shoulder of veal, there are twenty and two good bits. [The implication is not that there are twenty-two good bits in a shoulder of veal, but rather that there are twenty indifferent bits and just two good ones]

### Cheese

48. After cheese comes nothing. [Cheese is traditionally the last course of a meal]
49. Cheese digests everything but itself.
50. An apple-pie without some cheese is like a kiss without a squeeze.

*Healthy eating habits*

51. After dinner sit awhile, after supper walk a mile.
52. When the belly is full, the bones would be at rest.
53. Clothe thee warm, eat little, drink enough, and thou shalt live.
54. Feed by measure and defy the physician.
55. He that eats least eats most. [This implies that eating sparingly enables one to live longer, and thus eat more]
56. Eat to live and not live to eat.
57. Eat at pleasure, drink by measure.
58. Eat an apple going to bed, make the doctor beg his bread.
59. An apple a day keeps the doctor away.
60. Eat leeks in Lide and ramsins in May, and all the year after physicians may play. ["Lide" is a dialect word for "March"; "ramsins" means "garlic"]
61. He that would live for aye, must eat sage in May.
62. If they would drink nettles in March, and eat mugwort in May, so many fine maidens wouldn't go to the clay. [Nettle juice and mugwort are herbal remedies]
63. Oysters are only in season in the R months. [The R months are those that have the letter R in their name. The implication is that oysters should not be eaten in the summer months, namely May, June, July, and August]

*Unhealthy eating habits*

64. Whatsoever was the father of a disease, an ill diet was the mother.
65. Many dishes make many diseases.
66. Much meat, much malady.
67. Often and little eating makes a man fat.

*Table manners and superstitions*

68. Fingers were made before forks, and hands before knives. [An apology for picking food up in one's fingers]
69. None but fools and fiddlers sing at their meat.
70. He loved mutton well that licked where the ewe lay. [This and the following two proverbs are addressed to those who scrape or lick their dish after a good meal]
71. He loves bacon well that licks the swinesty door.
72. He loves roast meat well that licks the spit.
73. Never be ashamed to eat your meat.
74. Speak not of a dead man at the table.
75. To speak of a usurer at the table mars the wine.
76. Help you to salt, help you to sorrow.

*Cooks*

77. If you want your dinner, don't offend·the cook. [Chinese proverb]
78. God sends meat and the devil sends cooks.

See also GLUTTONY; HUNGER

# 54 EDUCATION

*Its importance*

1. Education polishes good natures, and correcteth bad ones.
2. Learn not and know not.
3. The best horse needs breaking, and the aptest child needs teaching.
4. Better unborn than untaught.

*The process of learning*

5. Knowledge has bitter roots but sweet fruits. [This and the following two proverbs refer to the suffering involved in learning, and its final reward]
6. The rain of tears is necessary to the harvest of learning. [Indian proverb]
7. Learn weeping, and you shall gain laughing.
8. There is no royal road to learning. [This proverb is based on the reply given by Euclid (c. 300 BC) to Ptolemy I, when he asked if there was an easy way to master the science of geometry]
9. Soon learnt, soon forgotten.

*The ideal time*

10. Learn young, learn fair.
11. Whoso learns young, forgets not when he is old.
12. Learning in one's youth is engraving in stone.
13. What's learnt in the cradle lasts till the tomb.
14. What youth is used to, age remembers.
15. What we first learn, we best can.
16. Never too late to learn.
17. A man may learn wit every day.

*Teachers and pupils*

18. Teaching of others, teacheth the teacher.
19. In every art, it is good to have a master.
20. He teaches ill, who teaches all. [The implication is that a good

teacher always leaves something for his pupils to work out for themselves]
21. Better untaught than ill taught.
22. Those who can, do; those who can't, teach. [This modern proverb is a variant of one of George Bernard Shaw's *Maxims for Revolutionists* (1903), "He who can, does. He who cannot, teaches."]
23. He that teaches himself, has a fool for his master.
24. Every good scholar is not a good schoolmaster.
25. He can ill be master that never was scholar.
26. A good master, a good scholar.
27. An ill master, an ill scholar.
28. The scholar may waur the master. ["Waur" means "be better than"]
29. Silly child is soon ylered. ["Silly" here means "good"; "ylered" means "taught"]

See also EXPERIENCE: *Learning by experience*

# 55 ENDINGS

*Their importance*

1. The end crowns the work.
2. Think on the end before you begin.
3. Look to the end.
4. At the game's end, we shall see who gains.
5. All's well that ends well.

*Their inevitability*

6. Everything has an end.
7. All good things must come to an end.
8. The best of friends must part.

*The end result*

9. Garbage in, garbage out. [This proverb originated in computer science; the acronym GIGO is also used]
10. If better were within, better would come out.
11. Such beef, such broth.
12. Whether you boil snow or pound it, you can have but water of it.

See also BEGINNINGS: *The importance of beginning well*; OPTIMISM: *Nothing is permanent*

# 56 ENDURANCE

*Its value*

1. He conquers who endures.
2. He that endures is not overcome.

*Its necessity*

3. What can't be cured, must be endured.
4. Bear and forbear.
5. He that will not endure to itch, must endure to smart.

*Its limitations*

6. Even a worm will turn. [The implication is that even the most lowly will tolerate only a limited amount of abuse]
7. The orange that is too hard squeezed yields a bitter juice.
8. An ass endures his burden, but not more than his burden.
9. A man may bear till his back break.
10. It is not the burden, but the over-burden that kills the beast.
11. Too long burden makes weary bones.
12. Bind the sack before it be full.
13. Double charge will rive a cannon. [This implies that an excess of anything, whether it be food, drink, or work, may have disastrous results]
14. Too-too will in two.
15. A bow long bent at last waxes weak.
16. The pitcher goes so often to the well that it is broken at last.
17. Put not the bucket too often in the well.
18. Strings high stretched either soon crack or quickly grow out of tune.
19. When the well is full, it will run over.
20. The last drop makes the cup run over.
21. The last straw breaks the camel's back.
22. The cord breaks at last by the weakest pull.

*Its dangers*

23. All lay load on the willing horse.
24. If thou suffer a calf to be laid on thee, within a little they'll clap on the cow.
25. The submitting to one wrong brings on another.
26. He that makes himself a sheep, shall be eaten by the wolf. [The implication is that those who meekly endure insults and injuries will only receive more]

# 57 ENEMIES

## *Their value*

1. An enemy may chance to give good counsel.
2. If you have no enemies, it's a sign fortune has forgot you.

## *Their danger*

3. There is no little enemy.
4. One enemy can do more hurt than ten friends can do good.
5. One enemy is too many; and a hundred friends too few.
6. An enemy's mouth seldom speaks well.
7. No friend to a bosom friend; no enemy to a bosom enemy. [The implication is that while there is no better friend than a bosom friend, there is no worse enemy than a bosom enemy]
8. Nothing worse than a familiar enemy. ["Familiar" here means "of one's own household"]
9. Better a thousand enemies outside the house than one inside. [Arabic proverb]
10. A secret foe gives a sudden blow.
11. Better go by your enemy's grave than by his gate.

## *Handling one's enemies*

12. Make your enemy your friend.
13. For a flying enemy make a golden bridge. [The advice here is to facilitate the retreat of one's enemy, thereby discouraging him from fighting on]
14. Speak well of your friend, of your enemy say nothing.

## *Words of caution*

15. Believe no tales from an enemy's tongue.
16. Though thy enemy seem a mouse, yet watch him like a lion.
17. If we are bound to forgive an enemy, we are not bound to trust him.
18. Fear the Greeks bearing gifts. ["The Greeks" here refers to any enemy]
19. He that gives honour to his enemy, is like to an ass.
20. The only good Indian is a dead Indian. [Many variants of this proverb exist, the word "Indian" (which here refers to the North American Indians) being replaced by the nationality of the enemy concerned]
21. Take heed of reconciled enemies.
22. Take heed of wind that comes in at a hole, and a reconciled enemy.
23. Trust not a new friend nor an old enemy.

# 58 ENGLAND

*Attitudes to England*

1. England is a good land, and a bad people.
2. England is the paradise of women, the hell of horses, and the purgatory of servants.
3. England is the ringing island. [A reference to the large number of bells in the country]
4. With all the world have war, but with England do not jar.
5. England is a little garden full of very sour weeds.
6. Shoulder of mutton and English beer, make the Flemings tarry here.
7. There is more good victuals in England, than in seven other kingdoms.
8. The English are a nation of shop-keepers. [This saying is generally attributed to Napoleon Bonaparte (1769–1821), although he was not the first to use it]

*Characteristics of the English*

9. Gluttony is the sin of England.
10. The way to an Englishman's heart is through his stomach.
11. The English have one hundred religions, but only one sauce. [This French proverb refers to the lack of variety in English cooking. Compare PEOPLE AND PLACES: 5]
12. An Englishman's word is his bond.
13. The English are the swearing nation.
14. Every English archer beareth under his girdle twenty-four Scots.
15. One Englishman can beat three Frenchmen.
16. The English never know when they are beaten.
17. A right Englishman knows not when a thing is well.
18. An Englishman loves a lord.
19. It is an Englishman's privilege to grumble.
20. An Englishman's home is his castle. [A reference to the Englishman's love of privacy. A variant of this proverb substitutes "house" for "home"]
21. Long beards heartless; painted hoods witless; gay coats graceless; makes England thriftless. [A contemptuous Scottish proverb]

*Regions and counties*

22. Blessed is the eye, that is betwixt Severn and Wye. [This refers to the pleasant countryside of Hereford and Worcester]
23. What Lancashire thinks today, all England will think tomorrow. [This proverb was coined in the days of the Anti-Corn Law League,

a political movement which originated in Lancashire in 1839. See also proverb 55 below]

24. He that would take a Lancashire man at any time or tide, must bait his hook with a good egg-pie, or an apple with a red side.
25. When all the world shall be aloft, then Hallamshire shall be God's croft. ["Hallamshire" was the area around Sheffield]
26. When Sheffield Park is ploughed and sown, then little England hold thine own.
27. Yorkshire born and Yorkshire bred, strong in the arm and weak in the head. [Variants of his proverb substitute other northern counties or towns for Yorkshire]
28. Give a Yorkshireman a halter, and he'll find a horse. [This and the following proverb refer to the Yorkshireman's love of riding]
29. Shake a bridle over a Yorkshire tike's grave, and he'll rise again.
30. Shake a Leicestershire man by the collar, and you shall hear the beans rattle in his belly.
31. Suffolk is the land of churches.
32. Essex stiles, Kentish miles, Norfolk wiles, many a man beguiles.
33. Some places of Kent have health and no wealth, some wealth and no health, some health and wealth, some have neither health nor wealth.
34. Sussex won't be druv. ["Druv" means "driven". The proverb implies that the people of Sussex cannot be forced to do anything against their will]
35. Hampshire ground requires every day in the week a shower of rain and on Sunday twain.
36. The Isle of Wight has no monks, lawyers, or foxes. [A former boast, probably without foundation, of the inhabitants of the Isle of Wight. Monks, lawyers, and foxes were all considered undesirable characters]
37. All Cornish gentlemen are cousins. [The implication is that the Cornish upper classes generally intermarry]
38. The devil will not come into Cornwall, for fear of being put into a pie. [A reference to the Cornish tendency to make pies of anything edible]
39. Cornwall will bear a shower every day, and two on Sunday.
40. There are more saints in Cornwall than in heaven.
41. The north of England for an ox, the south for a sheep, and the middle part for a man.
42. The north for greatness, the east for health; the south for neatness, the west for wealth.
43. Out of the north, all ill comes forth.
44. Three ills come from the north, a cold wind, a shrinking cloth, and a dissembling man.
45. Cold weather and knaves come out of the north.

*Rivers and mountains*

46. Hengsten Down well wrought is worth London town dear bought. [Hengsten (or Hingston) Down in Cornwall was once a valuable source of tin]
47. Ingleborough, Pendle, and Penyghent, are the highest hills between Scotland and Trent. [Pendle Hill is in Lancashire, Ingleborough and Pen-y-Ghent are in Yorkshire. The proverb is inaccurate, as there are higher peaks than these in the northern part of the Pennines]
48. Kent and Keer have parted many a good man and his mare. [A reference to the dangers of fording the rivers Kent and Keer, which flow into Morecambe Bay]
49. River of Dart! O river of Dart! every year thou claimest a heart. [This refers to the river Dart in Devon, which was said to claim the life of at least one person every year]
50. Witham pike: England has none like. [The river Witham is in Lincolnshire]
51. Salisbury Plain is seldom without a thief or twain.

*Towns and villages*

52. Oxford is the home of lost causes.
53. When Oxford draws knife, England's soon at strife.
54. Oxford for learning, London for wit, Hull for women, and York for a tit. ["Tit" here means "horse"]
55. What Manchester says today, the rest of England says tomorrow. [A modern variant of proverb 23 above]
56. From hell, Hull, and Halifax, good Lord deliver us. [This proverb is also known as "the thieves' litany". Until 1650, thieves were beheaded at the Halifax Gibbet for stealing cloth (Halifax was the centre of the cloth trade for that area)]
57. Said the devil when flying o'er Harrogate Wells, I think I am getting near home by the smells. [A reference to the sulphur springs at Harrogate]
58. Northampton stands on other men's legs. [Northampton was a centre of the shoemaking trade]
59. The Mayor of Northampton opens oysters with his dagger. [A reference to the distance of Northampton from the sea. Oysters and other seafood would be rather stale by the time they reached the town]
60. If Poole was a fish-pool, and the men of Poole fish, there'd be a pool for the devil and fish for his dish.
61. When Plymouth was a vuzzy down, Plympton was a borough town. ["Vuzzy" means "covered in gorse". The proverb gives evidence of local rivalry between the smaller but more ancient town of Plympton and the larger town of Plymouth. Variants of this proverb substitute

Dartmouth and Kingswear, or Exon (Exeter) and Kirton (Crediton, for Plymouth and Plympton. All are places in Devon]

62. Salisbury Cathedral was built upon wool-packs. [The implication is that the funds for building the cathedral were obtained from the revenue from the wool trade]

63. A Royston horse and a Cambridge master of arts will give way to nobody. [Royston is in Cambridgeshire]

64. Sutton for mutton, Carshalton for beeves; Epsom for whores, and Ewell for thieves. [This and the following proverb refer to towns in Surrey]

65. Sutton for good mutton, Cheam for juicy beef, Croydon for a pretty girl, and Mitcham for a thief.

66. Tring, Wing, and Ivinghoe, three dirty villages all in a row, and never without a rogue or two. Would you know the reason why? Leighton Buzzard is hard by. [Tring is in Hertfordshire, Wing and Ivinghoe in Buckinghamshire, and Leighton Buzzard in Bedfordshire]

67. The Mayor of Altrincham, lies in bed while his breeches are mending. [Altrincham, in Cheshire, was reputed to be so poor that the mayor could only afford one pair of breeches]

68. Through the pass of Alton, poverty might pass without peril of robbing. [The pass of Alton, in Hampshire, was heavily wooded and therefore an ideal place for outlaws to ambush travellers]

69. It is written upon a wall in Rome, Ribchester was as rich as any town in Christendom. [Ribchester, a Roman town, is in Lancashire]

70. Rising was, Lynn is, and Downham shall be, the greatest seaport of the three. [A reference to Castle Rising, King's Lynn, and Downham Market, in Norfolk]

71. Rising was a seaport town, and Lynn it was a wash, but now Lynn is a seaport town, and Rising fares the worst.

72. Gimmingham, Trimmingham, Knapton and Trunch, North Repps and South Repps are all of a bunch. [This refers to six Norfolk villages which lie close together]

73. The stoutest beggar that goes by the way, can't beg through Long on an midsummer's day. [A reference to the straggling village of Longdon in Staffordshire]

74. All the maids in Wanswell may dance in an eggshell. [Wanswell is in Gloucestershire]

### London

75. When a man is tired of London, he is tired of life. [Samuel Johnson (1709–84)]

76. Who goes to Westminster for a wife, to Paul's for a man, and to Smithfield for a horse, may meet with a whore, a knave, and a jade.

77. The streets of London are paved with gold. [The implication is that it

is easy to make one's fortune in London. The inaccuracy of the proverb has been found out by many to their cost]
78. London Bridge was made for wise men to go over, and fools to go under. [This implies that it was considered safer to go across the bridge than under it]

*English names*

79. In 'ford', in 'ham', in 'ley', and 'ton', the most of English surnames run.
80. By Tre, Pol, and Pen, you shall know the Cornish men. [A reference to three common prefixes of Cornish surnames]
81. In Cheshire there are Lees as plenty as fleas, and as many Davenports as dogs' tails.
82. The people of Clent are all Hills, Waldrons, or devils. [Clent is near Birmingham. "Hill" and "Waldron" were common surnames in the area]

# 59 ENVY

*Its dangers*

1. Envy eats nothing but its own heart.
2. Envy shoots at others, and wounds herself.
3. Envy never dies.
4. Envy and covetousness are never satisfied.
5. The envious man shall never want woe.
6. An envious man waxes lean with the fatness of his neighbour.

*Its effects*

7. Envy and idleness married together begot curiosity.
8. Nothing sharpens sight like envy.
9. Envy envies itself.
10. He who envies admits his inferiority.
11. Envy never enriched any man.

*Its universality*

12. If envy were a fever, all mankind would be ill.
13. One potter envies another. [This implies that every man envies potential rivals within his own field]

# 60 EQUALITY

### Its effects

1. When Greek meets Greek, then comes the tug of war. [A reference to any contest between two sides of equal strength. The proverb is based on a line from *The Rival Queens* by Nathaniel Lee (1655–92)]
2. At a round table, there's no dispute of place.
3. If all were equal, if all were rich, and if all were at table, who would lay the cloth?
4. You a lady, I a lady, who will milk the cow? [Variants of this proverb exist in many languages throughout the world]

### Basic equality

5. We are all Adam's children.
6. Homo is a common name to all men.
7. Before God and the bus-conductor we are all equal.
8. In church, in an inn, and in a coffin, all men are equal.
9. Human blood is all of a colour.
10. All blood is alike ancient.
11. There is no difference of bloods in a basin.
12. The sun shines upon all alike.
13. The rain falls on every roof. [African proverb]

### Equality of the great and the lowly

14. A cat may look at a king.
15. Every ass thinks himself worthy to stand with the king's horses.
16. As good horses draw in carts, as coaches.
17. The lower millstone grinds as well as the upper.
18. Every groom is a king at home.
19. It is as hard to please a knave as a knight.
20. When Adam delved and Eve span, who was then a gentleman?
21. Every beggar is descended from some king, and every king is descended from some beggar.
22. Jack is as good as his master.
23. At the end of the game the king and pawn go into the same bag.
24. Put the poor man's penny and the rich man's penny in ae purse, and they'll come out alike. ["Ae" means "one"]
25. Joan is as good as my lady in the dark.
26. The balance distinguishes not between gold and lead.

See also AUTHORITY: *The dangers of shared authority*; DEATH: *Equality in death*

# 61 EXAMPLE

*Example and precept*

1. Practise what you preach.
2. Example is better than precept.
3. Precepts may lead but examples draw.
4. Precept begins, example accomplishes.
5. A good example is the best sermon.
6. He preaches well that lives well.
7. Do as I say, not as I do.
8. Do as the friar says, not as he does.
9. We live by laws not by examples.

*Setting an example*

10. Do as you would be done by.
11. Do unto others as you would they should do unto you. [This proverb is based on Luke 6:31]
12. Law makers should not be law breakers.
13. Where the dam leaps over, the kid follows.
14. One sheep follows another.
15. If one sheep leap o'er the dyke, all the rest will follow.
16. No marvel if the imps follow when the devil goes before.

# 62 EXPERIENCE

*Its value*

1. Experience is the mother of wisdom.
2. Trouble brings experience and experience brings wisdom.
3. Experience is good, if not bought too dear.
4. Experience without learning is better than learning without experience.
5. Knowledge without practice makes but half an artist.
6. Experience is a precious gift, only given a man when his hair is gone. [Turkish proverb]
7. The tongue of experience has most truth. [Arabic proverb]
8. An ounce of practice is worth a pound of precept.
9. Practice makes perfect.
10. Custom makes all things easy.
11. Use makes mastery.
12. Use is all.

*Learning by experience*

13. Experience is the best teacher.
14. Live and learn.
15. In doing we learn.
16. By writing you learn to write.
17. Failure teaches success.
18. Experience must be bought.
19. Experience is the mistress of fools.
20. Experience keeps a dear school, but fools learn in no other.
21. Once bitten, twice shy.
22. The burnt child dreads the fire.
23. Wherever an ass falls, there will he never fall again.
24. Though the wound be healed, yet a scar remains.
25. Birds once snared fear all bushes.
26. He that has been bitten by a serpent, is afraid of a rope.
27. Whom a serpent has bitten, a lizard alarms.
28. A scalded cat fears hot water.
29. The escaped mouse ever feels the taste of the bait.
30. He complains wrongfully on the sea that twice suffers shipwreck.
31. He that deceives me once, shame fall him; if he deceives me twice, shame fall me.
32. It is a silly fish that is caught twice with the same bait.
33. He that stumbles twice over one stone, deserves to break his shins.
34. In war, it is not permitted twice to err.
35. Better learn by your neighbour's skaith than by your own. ["Skaith" means "harm"]
36. Wise men learn by other men's harms, fools, by their own.
37. It is good to beware by other men's harms.
38. It is good to learn at other men's cost.
39. Let another's shipwreck be your sea-mark.

See also OLD PEOPLE: *Their wisdom*

# 63 EYES

*The eye and the mind*

1. The eyes are the window of the soul. [Variants of this proverb substitute "heart" or "mind" for "soul"]
2. In the forehead and the eye, the lecture of the mind doth lie.
3. The heart's letter is read in the eyes.

*The importance of seeing*

4. Seeing is believing.
5. One eyewitness is better than two hear-so's.

*The need for watchfulness*

6. Keep your weather-eye open.
7. Keep your mouth shut and your eyes open.
8. Let the cat wink, and let the mouse run.

See also DISCIPLINE: *The watchful master*

# 64 FAME

*Its sources*

1. He that sows virtue, reaps fame.
2. Fame is the perfume of heroic deeds.
3. There are many ways to fame.
4. Reputation is often got without merit, and lost without crime.

*Its effects*

5. Fame is a magnifying glass.
6. He who leaves the fame of good works after him does not die.
7. From fame to infamy is a beaten road.
8. All fame is dangerous: good, bringeth envy; bad, shame.
9. Any publicity is good publicity.

*Attitudes to fame*

10. Fame is but the breath of the people.
11. Fame is a thin shadow of eternity.
12. Fame, like a river, is narrowest at its source and broadest afar off.
13. Brave men lived before Agamemnon. [Agamemnon was a Greek hero. The implication is that the famous may be neither the first nor the most outstanding in their field]

*The value of a good reputation*

14. Good fame is better than a good face.
15. A good name is better than riches.
16. A good name is a rich heritage.
17. A good name keeps its lustre in the dark.
18. Win a good reputation, and sleep at your ease.
19. Reputation serves to virtue, as light does to a picture.

20. The name of an honest woman is mickle worth. ["Mickle" means "much"]
21. He that has lost his credit, is dead to the world.
22. Credit lost is like a Venice-glass broken.
23. A wounded reputation is seldom cured.
24. A good name is sooner lost than won.

# 65 FAMILIARITY

*Its effects*

1. Familiarity breeds contempt.
2. Respect is greater from a distance.
3. Those near the temple deride the gods. [Chinese proverb]
4. Intimacy lessens fame.
5. No man is a hero to his valet.
6. A prophet is not without honour, save in his own country. [Matthew 13:57]
7. The reed-player of your own street does not charm. [Egyptian proverb]
8. No man fears what he has seen grow. [African proverb]
9. A maid oft seen, and a gown oft worn, are disesteemed and held in scorn.
10. Goods that are much on show lose their colour. [Brazilian proverb]
11. Custom takes the taste from the most savoury dishes.

*Against over-familiarity*

12. You should know a man seven years before you stir his fire.

# 66 FEAR

*Its sources*

1. When we have gold, we are in fear; when we have none, we are in danger.
2. Riches bring care and fears.
3. Love is full of fear.

*Its effects*

4. Fear gives wings.
5. Fear has a quick ear.
6. Fear has magnifying eyes.
7. Fear is a great inventor.

8. 'Twas fear that first put on arms.
9. Who fears to suffer, suffers from fear.

*Its undesirability*

10. All fear is bondage.
11. Fear is the prison of the heart.
12. Better pass a danger once, than be always in fear.
13. Better a fearful end than fear without end.

*Its value*

14. Fear is one part of prudence.
15. Wise fear begets care.

*Its power*

16. Fear is stronger than love.
17. All the weapons of war will not arm fear.
18. There is no medicine for fear.
19. There is no remedy for fear but cut off the head.

*Trivial fears*

20. He that is afraid of the wagging of feathers, must keep from among wild fowl.
21. He that is afraid of wounds, must not come nigh a battle.
22. He that fears every bush must never go a-birding.
23. He that fears every grass must not piss in a meadow.
24. He that fears leaves, let him not go into the wood.

See also CRUELTY: *Cruelty and fear*; DEATH: *Fear of death*

# 67 FINE ARTS

*Painting*

1. Art improves Nature.
2. Pictures are the books of the unlearned.
3. On painting and fighting look aloof. [The implication is that a picture may lose some of its effect when viewed at close quarters, and it is dangerous to be close to the scene of fighting]
4. A good painter can draw a devil as well as an angel.
5. Painters and poets have leave to lie.

*Poetry*

6. There are pictures in poems and poems in pictures. [Chinese proverb]
7. The poet, of all sorts of artificers, is the fondest of his works.
8. A poet is born not made.
9. He's a blockhead that can't make two verses, and he's a fool that makes four.

*Music*

10. Music is the food of love.
11. Music has charms to soothe a savage breast. [William Congreve (1670–1729) *The Mourning Bride*. This is frequently misquoted, "beast" being substituted for "breast"]
12. Music is the eye of the ear.
13. Music helps not the toothache.
14. Women and music should never be dated.

# 68 FLATTERY

*Its value*

1. Flattery sits in the parlour, when plain-dealing is kicked out of doors.
2. Better fleech the devil than fight him. ["Fleech" means "flatter"]
3. Whoso will dwell in court must needs curry favour.

*Its sources and effects*

4. Imitation is the sincerest form of flattery.
5. Praise the child, and you make love to the mother.
6. Tell a woman she is fair, and she will soon turn fool.
7. Make yourself all honey, and the flies will devour you. [The warning here is that excessive flattery and obsequious behaviour may arouse contempt]

*Its insincerity*

8. Dogs wag their tails not so much in love to you as to your bread.
9. Every man bows to the bush he gets bield of. ["Bield" means "shelter"]
10. Call the bear 'uncle' till you are safe across the bridge. [Turkish proverb]

*Mutual flattery*

11. One complimentary letter asks another.

12. Scratch my back and I'll scratch yours.
13. Scratch my breech and I'll claw your elbow.
14. Claw me, and I'll claw thee.

*Flatterers*

15. The most deadly of wild beasts is a backbiter, of tame ones a flatterer.
16. Beware of one who flatters unduly; he will also censure unjustly. [Arabic proverb]
17. As a wolf is like a dog, so is a flatterer like a friend.
18. No foe to a flatterer.
19. A flatterer's throat is an open sepulchre.
20. When the flatterer pipes, then the devil dances.
21. When a lackey comes to hell's door, the devils lock the gates. [A "lackey" is an obsequious or servile person]

# 69 FOOLISHNESS

*Its advantages*

1. Children and fools have merry lives.
2. The folly of one man is the fortune of another.
3. Fortune favours fools.
4. God sends fortune to fools.
5. Better be a fool than a knave.

*Its dangers*

6. Fools and madmen ought not to be left in their own company.
7. Children and fools must not play with edged tools.
8. Fools should not have chopping sticks.
9. Take heed of mad fools in a narrow place.

*Its causes*

10. The first service a child does his father is to make him foolish.
11. No folly to being in love.
12. Too much money makes one mad.
13. Much learning makes men mad.
14. When the moon's in the full, then wit's in the wane.

*Its incurability*

15. He that is born a fool is never cured.
16. Send a fool to the market and a fool he will return again.

17. Fools will be fools still.
18. Once wood, never wise. ["Wood" here means "mad"]
19. Whom Heaven at his birth has endowed as a fool, 'tis a waste of instruction to teach. [Chinese proverb]
20. Fools grow without watering.

### Its universality

21. The world is full of fools.
22. Folly is the product of all countries and ages.
23. We have all been fools once in our lives.
24. Every man a little beyond himself is a fool.
25. If folly were grief, every house would weep.
26. Every man is a fool sometimes, and none at all times.
27. If all fools wore feathers we should seem a flock of geese.
28. If all fools had baubles, we should want fuel. [The implication is that if all fools carried the jester's "bauble" or stick, firewood would be in short supply]
29. Who has neither fools nor beggars nor whores among his kindred, was born of a stroke of thunder.

### Foolish acts

30. The fool asks much, but he is more fool that grants it.
31. He has great need of a fool, that plays the fool himself.
32. Make not a fool of thyself, to make others merry.
33. He is a fool that forgets himself.
34. He is a fool that kisses the maid when he may kiss the mistress.
35. He is a fool that makes a hammer of his fist.
36. He is not the fool that the fool is, but he that with the fool deals.
37. He is a fool that thinks not that another thinks.
38. He is a fool who makes his physician his heir.
39. It is a foolish sheep that makes the wolf his confessor.
40. It is a blind goose that comes to the fox's sermon.
41. A barber learns to shave by shaving fools. [The implication is that only a fool allows himself to be practised on by a learner]
42. One cannot do a foolish thing once in one's life, but one must hear of it a hundred times.
43. Wise men make proverbs and fools repeat them.
44. He is an ass that brays against another ass.
45. A white wall is a fool's paper. [The implication is that it is foolish to scribble on walls]
46. Fools live poor to die rich.
47. He that talks to himself, speaks to a fool.

*Characteristics of fools*

48. The first degree of folly is to hold one's self wise, the second to profess it, the third to despise counsel.
49. What the fool does in the end, the wise man does at the beginning.
50. Little things please little minds.
51. Riches serve a wise man but command a fool.
52. A wise man changes his mind, a fool never.
53. Children and fools cannot lie.
54. Experience is the mistress of fools. [The implication of this and the following two proverbs is that fools only learn by making mistakes]
55. Experience keeps a dear school, but fools learn in no other.
56. Wise men learn by other men's harms; fools, by their own.
57. A fool's bolt is soon shot.
58. Fat paunches have lean pates.
59. Mickle head, little wit. ["Mickle" here means "large"]
60. Seldom is a long man wise, or a low man lowly. ["Long" here means "tall"]

*The recklessness of fools*

61. Fools rush in where angels fear to tread. [Alexander Pope (1688–1744) *An Essay on Criticism*]
62. While the discreet advise, the fool does his business. ["Advise" here means "seek advice"]
63. Wise men propose, and fools determine.
64. A fool always rushes to the fore.
65. A knave and a fool never take thought.
66. From a foolish judge, a quick sentence.
67. Haste and wisdom are things far odd.

*The gullibility of fools*

68. A fool and his money are soon parted.
69. A fool believes everything.
70. An easy fool is a knave's tool.
71. Fair words make fools fain. [The implication is that fools easily succumb to flattery and false promises. "Fain" means "willing"]
72. Fools rejoice at promises.
73. If fools went not to market, bad wares would not be sold.
74. A nod from a lord is a breakfast for a fool.

*The talkativeness of fools*

75. Empty vessels make the greatest sound.
76. Toom bags rattle. ["Toom" means "empty"]
77. Shallow streams make the most din.

78. A fool's bell is soon rung.
79. A fool's tongue is long enough to cut his own throat.
80. Foolish tongues talk by the dozen.
81. Every ass likes to hear himself bray.
82. The wise hand does not all that the foolish mouth speaks.
83. Wise men silent, fools talk.
84. Wise men have their mouth in their heart, fools their heart in their mouth.
85. If the fool knew how to be silent he could sit amongst the wise.
86. Fools are wise as long as silent.
87. For mad words deaf ears.
88. Change of weather is the discourse of fools.

*The wisdom of fools*

89. A fool may give a wise man counsel.
90. A fool may sometimes speak to the purpose.
91. A fool's bolt may sometimes hit the mark.
92. A fool knows more in his own house than a wise man in another's.
93. A fool may ask more questions in an hour than a wise man can answer in seven years.
94. A fool may throw a stone into a well, which a hundred wise men cannot pull out.
95. Fools set stools for wise folks to stumble at.
96. None is so wise, but the fool overtakes him.
97. Folly and learning often dwell together.
98. Fools are wise men in the affairs of women.

*Old fools*

99. There's no fool like an old fool.
100. A fool at forty is a fool indeed.


# 70 FORESIGHT

*Its value*

1. One good forewit, is worth two afterwits.
2. He is wise who looks ahead.
3. He that looks not before, finds himself behind.
4. A word before is worth two behind.
5. Prevention is better than cure.

*The importance of being prepared*

6. Providing is preventing.

7. Force without forecast is of little avail. [The implication of this and the following three proverbs is that foreseeing problems and being prepared for them is of more use than great strength or skill]
8. Forewarned is forearmed.
9. Forecast is better than work-hard.
10. He is wise that is ware in time.
11. Forethought is easy, repentance hard. [Chinese proverb]
12. Provide for the worst; the best will save itself.
13. In fair weather prepare for foul.
14. Thatch your roof before the rain begins.
15. Have not thy cloak to make when it begins to rain.
16. Although it rain, throw not away your watering-pot.
17. Although the sun shine, leave not your cloak at home.
18. Never rued the man that laid in his fuel before St. John. [St. John's Day is December 27th]
19. If you go into a labyrinth, take a clew with you. [A "clew" is a ball of thread, such as that used by the Greek hero Theseus to find his way out of the labyrinth of King Minos in Crete]

### Providing for the future

20. First thrive and then wive.
21. Before you marry, be sure of a house wherein to tarry.
22. Honour a physician before thou hast need of him.
23. It is good to work wisely lest a man be prevented.
24. This world is unstable, so saith sage: therefore gather in time, ere thou fall into age.

# 71 FORGIVENESS

### Its value

1. Pardons and pleasantness are great revenges of slanders.
2. The noblest vengeance is to forgive.
3. Pardon is the choicest flower of victory. [Arabic proverb]
4. He that forgives gains the victory. [African proverb]
5. There is no austerity like forgiveness. [Indian proverb]
6. Mercy surpasses justice.
7. To err is human; to forgive, divine. [Alexander Pope (1688–1744) *An Essay on Criticism*]
8. He who forgives others, God forgives him. [Arabic proverb]
9. Forgiveness from the heart is better than a box of gold. [Moorish proverb]

*Its dangers*

10. Pardon one offence and you encourage many.
11. Pardon makes offenders.
12. Pardoning the bad is injuring the good.
13. Mercy to the criminal may be cruelty to the people.

*Its conditions*

14. The lion spares the suppliant.
15. Forgiving the unrepentant is like making pictures on water. [Japanese proverb]
16. Past shame, past grace.

*The need to forgive*

17. Let bygones be bygones.
18. Forgive and forget.
19. Forgiveness is perfect when the sin is not remembered. [Arabic proverb]
20. Forgive all but thyself.
21. Wink at small faults.

*The unforgiving*

22. He that does you an ill turn will never forgive you.
23. The offender never pardons.

*The forgiving*

24. He that sharply chides, is the most ready to pardon.
25. God gives his wrath by weight, and without weight his mercy.
26. The first faults are theirs that commit them, the second theirs that permit them. [The implication is that those who forgive a person a second time for committing the same fault are themselves in the wrong]

# 72 FRIENDS

*Their value*

1. Better lose a jest than a friend.
2. A friend in court is better than a penny in purse.
3. A friend in the market is better than money in the chest.
4. It is good to have some friends both in heaven and hell.
5. He quits his place well that leaves his friend there.
6. Life without a friend, is death without a witness.

7. It's merry when friends meet.
8. When friends meet, hearts warm.
9. One enemy is too many; and a hundred friends too few.
10. One God, no more, but friends good store.
11. Friends tie their purse with a cobweb thread. [The implication is that friends are not miserly]
12. If friends have faith in each other, life and death are of no consequence. [Chinese proverb]

*Their danger*

13. Hatred with friends is succour to foes.
14. Better an open enemy than a false friend.
15. It is better to be stung by a nettle than pricked by a rose. [The implication is that it is better to be wronged by an enemy than by a friend]
16. God defend me from my friends; from my enemies I can defend myself.
17. Friends are thieves of time.
18. A reconciled friend is a double enemy.

*Their disloyalty*

19. Dead men have no friends.
20. Remember man and keep in mind, a faithful friend is hard to find.
21. When good cheer is lacking, our friends will be packing.
22. Misfortune makes foes of friends.
23. Penny in purse will bid me drink, when all the friends I have will not.
24. Poor folks' friends soon misken them. ["Misken" means "desert, disown"]
25. Fresh fish and poor friends become soon ill savoured.
26. Poverty parts fellowship.
27. In time of prosperity, friends will be plenty; in time of adversity, not one amongst twenty.
28. He that ceases to be a friend, never was a good one.
29. Tell nothing to thy friend that thine enemy may not know.
30. Love your friend, but look to yourself. [This and the following proverb advise caution in putting one's complete trust in a friend]
31. Whensoever you see your friend, trust to yourself.

*Their falseness*

32. A false friend and a shadow attend only while the sun shines.
33. There is falsehood in fellowship.
34. All are not friends that speak us fair.

97

35. He that has a full purse never wanted a friend.
36. Rich folk have many friends.
37. The rich knows not who is his friend.
38. When two friends have a common purse, one sings and the other weeps.

### True friendship

39. A friend in need is a friend indeed.
40. A friend is never known till a man have need.
41. Prosperity makes friends, adversity tries them.
42. Friends are made in wine and proved in tears.
43. At marriages and funerals, friends are discerned from kinsfolk.
44. Real friendship does not freeze in winter.
45. A friend is another self.
46. A good friend is my nearest relation.
47. Among friends all things are common.
48. Perfect friendship cannot be without equality.
49. A good friend never offends.
50. A true friend is the best possession.
51. They are rich who have true friends.
52. No physician like a true friend.
53. He is a good friend that speaks well of us behind our backs.
54. Greater love hath no man than this, that a man lay down his life for his friends. [John 15:13]

### Worthless friends

55. His own enemy is no one's friend.
56. A friend to everybody is a friend to nobody.
57. Trencher friends are seldom good neighbours. [A "trencher" was a platter for serving food. The implication is that such friends will disappear when one can no longer provide them with food and drink]

### Old friends

58. The best mirror is an old friend.
59. Friendship, the older it grows, the stronger it is.
60. Old fish, old oil, and an old friend are the best.
61. Old friends and old wine and old gold are best.
62. Old acquaintance will soon be remembered.

### Choosing friends

63. Have but few friends, though many acquaintances.
64. Books and friends should be few but good.

65. Select your friend with a silk-gloved hand and hold him with an iron gauntlet.
66. Before you make a friend eat a bushel of salt with him. [As only a small amount of salt is eaten at each meal, the implication is that one should spend a long time with a person before becoming his friend]
67. Sudden friendship, sure repentance.
68. Trust not a new friend nor an old enemy.
69. Prove your friend ere you have need.
70. Try your friend before you trust.
71. Go down the ladder when you marry a wife; go up when you choose a friend.

*Maintaining friendship*

72. Make not thy friend thy foe.
73. Have patience with a friend rather than lose him forever.
74. Love your friend with his fault.
75. Friendship cannot stand always on one side. [The implication is that friendship is based on mutual help and kindness]
76. Friendship increases in visiting friends, but in visiting them seldom.
77. A hedge between keeps friendship green.
78. Little intermeddling makes good friends.
79. When a friend asks, there is no tomorrow. [The implication is that one should not put off a friend's requests with vain promises]
80. Speak well of your friend, of your enemy say nothing.
81. Treat a friend as if he might become a foe.
82. Friendship is a plant which must be often watered.

*Losing friends*

83. A broken friendship may be soldered, but will never be sound.
84. One may mend a torn friendship but it soon falls in tatters.
85. Fall not out with a friend for a trifle.
86. A friend is not so soon gotten as lost.
87. Lend your money and lose your friend.
88. When love puts in, friendship is gone.

See also ABSENCE: *Its effect on friendship*

# 73 GAIN

*Its value*

1. Great gain makes work easy.
2. Great pain and little gain will make a man soon weary.

3. No gaining, cold gaming.
4. The gains will quit the pains.
5. Pain is forgotten where gain follows.
6. A blow that is profitable does not hurt the neck. [Arabic proverb]
7. Profit gives no headache.
8. Praise without profit puts little in the pot.

*Its sources*

9. Gain savours sweetly from anything. [The implication is that the pleasure of gain is not affected by its source, however unsavoury]
10. No pains, no gains.
11. Honour and profit lie not in one sack.
12. The greatest burdens are not the gainfullest.

*Loss and gain*

13. There's no great loss without some gain.
14. Where profit is, loss is hidden nearby. [Japanese proverb]
15. He that loses anything and gets wisdom by it is a gainer by the loss.
16. Sometimes the best gain is to lose.
17. A man may lose more in an hour than he can get in seven.
18. What you lose on the swings you gain on the roundabouts.
19. What is lost in the hundred will be found in the shire. [A "hundred" is a former division of a county or "shire"]
20. One man's loss is another man's gain.

*Losing*

21. Loss embraces shame.
22. He loses indeed that loses at last.
23. He that is not sensible of his loss has lost nothing.
24. You cannot lose what you never had.
25. It signifies nothing to play well if you lose.
26. Win at first and lose at last.
27. Losers are always in the wrong.
28. Give losers leave to speak. [This implies that losers should be given the chance to express their feelings]

# 74 GAMBLING

*Its dangers*

1. The devil goes shares in gaming.
2. Keep flax from fire and youth from gaming.
3. Gaming, women, and wine, while they laugh, they make men pine.

4. Play, women, and wine undo men laughing.
5. Women and wine, game and deceit, make the wealth small, and the wants great.
6. He that plays his money ought not to value it.

*Cards*

7. Cards are the devil's books.
8. Lucky at cards, unlucky in love.

*Dice*

9. The devil is in the dice.
10. Dicing, drabbing and drinking bring men to destruction.
11. The best throw of the dice, is to throw them away.

*Betting*

12. A wager is a fool's argument.
13. In a bet there is a fool and a thief.
14. On the turf all men are equal – and under it.

*Gamblers*

15. The better gamester, the worser man.
16. Gamesters and race-horses never last long.
17. If the gambler can change, then there is medicine for leprosy. [Chinese proverb]

# 75 GIVING

*Its value*

1. Riches are like muck, which stink in a heap, but spread abroad make the earth fruitful.
2. Better an apple given than eaten.
3. It is more blessed to give than to receive. [Acts 20:35. A variant of this proverb substitutes "better" for "more blessed"]
4. Better give a shilling than lend and lose half a crown.
5. They are welcome that bring.
6. Give and spend, and God will send. [The implication of this and the following proverbs is that one loses nothing by being generous]
7. The charitable give out at the door and God puts in at the window.
8. He who gives discreetly gains directly.
9. The hand that gives, gathers.
10. Giving much to the poor, doth enrich a man's store.

11. Alms never make poor.
12. Great almsgiving lessens no man's living.
13. What we spent we had; what we gave we have; what we left we lost.

*The need for caution*

14. He who gives to the unworthy loses doubly.
15. Be just before you are generous.
16. He that has a good memory, gives few alms. [The implication is that shrewd people remember persistent beggars]
17. He that gives his goods before he be dead, take up a mallet and knock him on the head. [A reference to the ingratitude of children, who will neglect an ageing parent once he has given up all his wealth and possessions]
18. He learned timely to beg that could not say 'Nay'.

*The need for promptness*

19. He gives twice who gives quickly.
20. To refuse and to give tardily is all the same.
21. He that is long a giving knows not how to give.
22. A gift much expected is paid, not given.
23. Long tarrying takes all the thanks away.

*Generous people*

24. Friends tie their purse with a cobweb thread.
25. It is a good goose that's ay dropping.
26. The higher the hill, the lower the grass. [The implication is that the richest people are not the most generous]
27. He is more noble that deserves, than he that confers benefits.

*False generosity*

28. He is free of fruit that wants an orchard. [This and the following two proverbs imply that some people are always ready to give away what they do not have, or what belongs to another]
29. He is free of horse that never had one.
30. Hens are free of horse corn.
31. Give a thing and take a thing, to wear the devil's gold ring. [A children's rhyme used when a person takes back a gift]

*Small gifts*

32. Small gifts make friends, great ones make enemies.
33. He that gives me small gifts, would have me live.
34. He that gives thee a bone, would not have thee die.

35. A little given seasonably, excuses a great gift.

*Receiving gifts*

36. Who receives a gift, sells his liberty.
37. Benefits make a man a slave. [Arabic proverb]
38. Benefits bind.
39. Nothing costs so much as what is given us.
40. Nothing freer than a gift. [This would appear to be a direct contradiction of the preceding proverb]
41. She that takes gifts, herself she sells, and she that gives, does not else.
42. Fear the Greeks bearing gifts. ["The Greeks" here refers to any enemy]

# 76 GLUTTONY

*Its disadvantages*

1. A belly full of gluttony will never study willingly.
2. Fat paunches have lean pates.
3. A fat belly does not breed a subtle mind.
4. A full belly neither fights nor flies well.
5. If it were not for the belly, the back might wear gold. [A reference to those who spend more money on food and drink than on clothes]
6. The nearer the bone, the sweeter the flesh. [This implies that slim people are more attractive than fat people. See also proverb 18 below]

*Its dangers*

7. He that eats till he is sick, must fast till he is well.
8. Many dishes make many diseases.
9. Much meat, much malady.
10. A swine over fat, is the cause of his own bane.
11. Greedy eaters dig their graves with their teeth.
12. Gluttony kills more than the sword.
13. By suppers, more have been killed than Galen ever cured. [Galen (130–201) was a Greek physician]

*Characteristics of gluttons*

14. Gluttony is the sin of England.
15. A glutton is never generous.
16. He that has a wide therm had never a long arm. ["Therm" means "belly". This proverb reiterates the sentiments of the previous one]

*Excuses for gluttony*

17. Better belly burst than good meat lost.
18. The flesh is aye fairest that is farthest from the bone. [A direct contradiction of proverb 6 above]

*Needless eating*

19. There's little difference between a feast and a bellyful. [The implication is that once hunger has been satisfied, there is nothing to be gained from eating more]
20. Hunger makes dinners, pastime suppers. [The implication is that eating supper is a pleasure rather than a necessity]

# 77 GOD

*His omnipotence*

1. God is above all.
2. All must be as God will.
3. That God will have see, shall not wink.
4. Where God will help, nothing does harm.
5. What God will, no frost can kill.
6. When God will, no wind but brings rain.
7. The tree that God plants, no wind hurts it.
8. All things are possible with God.
9. When it pleases not God, the saint can do little.
10. He sits above that deals acres.

*His wisdom*

11. Do the likeliest, and God will do the best.
12. God complains not, but does what is fitting.
13. God is no botcher.
14. God knows well which are the best pilgrims.
15. They are well guided that God guides.
16. To whom God gives the task, he gives the wit.
17. If God does not give us what we want he gives us what we need.

*His goodness*

18. That never ends ill which begins in God's name.
19. God, and parents, and our master, can never be requited.
20. God is a good man.
21. He who serves God, serves a good master.

*His compassion*

22. God tempers the wind to the shorn lamb.
23. God makes the back for the burden.
24. God sends cold after clothes.
25. Since God has not bent the top of the palm-tree, he has given a long neck to the giraffe. [Arabic proverb]
26. God strikes not with both hands, for to the sea he made havens, and to rivers fords.
27. Heaven takes care of children, sailors, and drunken men.
28. God strikes with his finger, and not with all his arm.

*His reliability*

29. God comes at last when we think he is farthest off.
30. God provides for him that trusts.
31. He that sows, trusts in God.
32. God never sends mouth but he sends meat. [The implication is that when a new child is born God will always provide sufficient food for it]
33. The constancy of the benefit of the year in their seasons argues a Deity.

*His help*

34. God helps them that help themselves.
35. God reaches us good things by our own hands.
36. We must not lie down and cry, 'God help us.'
37. God is a good worker, but he loves to be helped.
38. God gives the grain, but we must make the furrow. [Bohemian proverb]
39. For a web begun God sends the thread.
40. God gives, but he does not lock the gate of the fold. [Bulgarian proverb]
41. Get thy spindle and thy distaff ready and God will send thee flax.
42. God himself is the help of the helpless. [Indian proverb]
43. Man's extremity is God's opportunity. [The implication is that God is best able to help when man most needs him]
44. God's help is better than early rising.
45. God's help is nearer than the fair even.

*His grace*

46. Divine grace was never slow.
47. God's grace and Pilling Moss are boundless. ["Pilling Moss" is a large stretch of land near Fleetwood]
48. Well thrives he whom God loves.

49. Who has God for his friend has the saints in his pocket.
50. Whom God loves, his bitch brings forth pigs.
51. When God loathes aught, men presently loathe it too. [A reference to the dangers of losing God's grace]
52. The grace of God is enough.
53. The grace of God is worth a fair.

### His mysterious ways

54. God moves in a mysterious way. [William Cowper (1731–1800) *Olney Hymns* No. 35]
55. Afflictions are sent to us by God for our good.
56. God heals, and the physician has the thanks.

### His forgiveness

57. God gives his wrath by weight, and without weight his mercy.
58. The most high God, sees, and bears: my neighbour knows nothing, and yet is always finding fault.
59. God forgives sins, otherwise heaven would be empty.
60. He who forgives others, God forgives him. [Arabic proverb]
61. Who errs and mends, to God himself commends. [The implication is that God forgives the repentant]

### Divine retribution

62. God comes with leaden feet, but strikes with iron hands. [The implication is that God is not quick to punish, allowing time for repentance, but when he strikes it is with force]
63. The feet of the avenging deities are shod with wool. [A warning of the silent approach of divine retribution]
64. God stays long, but strikes at last.
65. The mills of God grind slowly, yet they grind exceeding small. [Friedrich von Logau (1604–55) *Retribution*, translated by H. W. Longfellow]
66. God is a sure paymaster.

### God and the devil

67. The devil is God's ape. [The implication is that the devil strives to counterfeit or parody the works of God]
68. Where God has his church, the devil will have his chapel.
69. Where God dwells, the devil also has his nest.
70. God sends corn and the devil mars the sack.
71. That which God will give, the devil cannot reave. ["Reave" means "take away"]

*God and man*

72. God makes and man shapes.
73. God made the country, and man made the town.
74. Man does what he can, and God what he will.
75. Man proposes, God disposes.

# 78 GOODNESS

*Its value*

1. Virtue joins man to God.
2. Virtue and happiness are mother and daughter.
3. Riches adorn the dwelling; virtue adorns the person. [Chinese proverb]
4. Virtue is a jewel of great price.
5. Virtue is the beauty of the mind.
6. Goodness is better than beauty.
7. There is no poverty where there is virtue, no riches where virtue is not. [Chinese proverb]
8. Virtue and a trade are the best portion for children.
9. A good heart conquers ill fortune.
10. A good life makes a good death.
11. He dies like a beast who has done no good while he lived.
12. They die well that live well.
13. Virtue has all things in itself.
14. Virtue is its own reward.
15. Virtue is more important than blood.
16. Virtue is the only true nobility.
17. Virtue never grows old.
18. He that sows virtue, reaps fame.
19. Honour is the reward of virtue.
20. Praise is the reflection of virtue.
21. A handful of good life, is better than a bushel of learning.
22. He that lives well is learned enough.
23. It is not how long, but how well we live.
24. It is good to be good in your time, for you know not how long it will last.
25. A house is a fine house when good folks are within.

*Its limitations*

26. There is no virtue that poverty destroys not.
27. None so good that it's good to all.
28. That which is good for the back, is bad for the head.

29. That which is good for the head, is evil for the neck and the shoulders.
30. Good for the liver may be bad for the spleen.

## Its disadvantages

31. Good things are hard.
32. The good is the enemy of the best. [The implication is that being content with good prevents one from striving for better]
33. Good is good, but better carries it.

## Its scarcity

34. Good folks are scarce.
35. There are two good men: one dead, the other unborn. [Chinese proverb]
36. Virtue is praised by all, but practised by few.

## Characteristics of the good

37. A good heart cannot lie.
38. A good man can no more harm than a sheep.
39. He lives long that lives well.
40. Good men must die, but death cannot kill them quite.
41. The sun is never the worse for shining on a dunghill. [The implication is that those who are pure and virtuous are not easily corrupted]
42. Good men suffer much. [Chinese proverb]
43. Good people walk on, whatever befall. [Japanese proverb]
44. Show a good man his error, and he turns it to a virtue; but an ill, it doubles his fault.

## Good and evil

45. Good and evil are chiefly in the imagination.
46. There is not the thickness of a sixpence between good and evil.
47. Set good against evil.
48. Good is to be sought out and evil attended.
49. Better good afar off than evil at hand.
50. It costs more to do ill than to do well.
51. Vice makes virtue shine.
52. Virtue and vice divide the world, but vice has got the greater share.
53. Vice is often clothed in virtue's habit.

See also DEEDS: *Good deeds*

# 79 GOSSIP

## Its accuracy or inaccuracy

1. Common fame is seldom to blame. [The implication of this and the following three proverbs is that gossip generally has an element of truth in it]
2. There's no smoke without fire.
3. Where there are reeds, there is water.
4. There was aye some water where the stirk drowned. [A "stirk" is a young bullock]
5. One learns to know oneself best behind one's back.
6. Gossiping and lying go together.
7. Where there is whispering there is lying.
8. Common fame is a liar.
9. 'They say so' is half a lie.
10. The tale runs as it pleases the teller.
11. A tale never loses in the telling. [A reference to the embellishments added to an item of gossip as it passes from person to person]

## Its dangers

12. The gossip of two women will destroy two houses. [Arabic proverb]
13. An ill tongue may do much.
14. He who speaks much of others burns his tongue.
15. He that speaks the thing he should not, hears the thing he would not.
16. He that speaks lavishly shall hear as knavishly.

## Its dissemination

17. Go abroad and you'll hear news of home.
18. What is told in the ear of a man is often heard a hundred miles away. [Chinese proverb]
19. Whispered words are heard afar. [Chinese proverb]
20. The noise of the kettledrum goes far. [Arabic proverb]
21. Confide in an aunt and the world will know.
22. If the Nile knows your secret it will soon be known in the desert. [African proverb]
23. Fields have eyes, and woods have ears.
24. Walls have ears.
25. Give a lie twenty-four hours' start, and you can never overtake it.

## Gossips and talebearers

26. A gossip speaks ill of all, and all of her.
27. Gossips are frogs, they drink and talk.
28. 'Tis merry when gossips meet.

29. A rouk-town's seldom a good housewife at home. [A "rouk-town" is a gossip]
30. Put no faith in tale-bearers.
31. A tale-bearer is worse than a thief.
32. He that is a blab is a scab.
33. Don't tell tales out of school.
34. No names, no pack-drill. ["Pack-drill" is a form of military punishment]
35. Avoid a questioner, for he is also a tattler.
36. Who chatters *to* you, will chatter *of* you.
37. The dog that fetches, will carry. [A reiteration of the sentiments of the preceding proverb]
38. Were there no hearers, there would be no backbiters. [The implication of this and the following proverb is that those who listen to gossip are as much at fault as those who speak it]
39. There is nothing to choose between bad tongues and wicked ears.

*Telling secrets*

40. Thy secret is thy prisoner; if thou let it go, thou art a prisoner to it.
41. He that tells a secret, is another's servant.
42. Three may keep a secret, if two of them are dead.

# 80 GRATITUDE

*Its value*

1. Gratitude preserves old friendships, and procures new.
2. To a grateful man, give money when he asks. [This implies that the requests of the grateful are more likely to be granted than those of the ungrateful]

*Its necessity*

3. Do not forget little kindnesses and do not remember small faults. [Chinese proverb]
4. When you drink from the stream, remember the spring. [Chinese proverb]
5. Never look a gift horse in the mouth.
6. Throw no gift again at the giver's head.
7. Beggars can't be choosers.
8. Half a loaf is better than no bread. [The implication of this and the following proverbs is that one must be thankful for what one has, however little]
9. A crust is better than no bread.

10. Better a louse in the pot than no flesh at all.
11. Better are small fish than an empty dish.
12. Better some of a pudding than none of a pie.
13. A churl's feast is better than none at all.
14. Half an egg is better than an empty shell.
15. They that have no other meat, bread and butter are glad to eat.
16. It is better to sup with a cutty than want a spoon. [A "cutty" is a pipe]
17. Better a lean jade than an empty halter. [A "jade" is an old horse]
18. A bad bush is better than the open field.
19. A bad excuse is better than none at all.
20. Better a bare foot than none.
21. One foot is better than two crutches.
22. Better eye sore than all blind.
23. Better to have one eye than be blind altogether.
24. A man were better to be half blind than have both his eyes out.
25. Better my hog dirty home than no hog at all.
26. Something is better than nothing.

### Ingratitude

27. Gratitude is the least of virtues, but ingratitude is the worst of vices.
28. Who gives not thanks to men, gives not thanks to God. [Arabic proverb]
29. He is an ill guest that never drinks to his host.
30. The hog never looks up to him that threshes down the acorns.
31. Many a man serves a thankless master.
32. He that keeps another man's dog, shall have nothing left him but the line.
33. All is lost that is put into a riven dish. [The implication is that generosity is wasted on the ungrateful]

# 81 GREATNESS

### Its dangers

1. A great tree attracts the wind.
2. Great winds blow upon high hills.
3. The bigger they are, the harder they fall.
4. The highest branch is not the safest roost.
5. The highest tree has the greatest fall.
6. He sits not sure that sits too high.
7. Oaks may fall when reeds stand the storm.
8. High cedars fall when low shrubs remain.
9. Little fishes slip through nets, but great fishes are taken.

111

10. The bigger the man, the better the mark. ["Mark" here means "target"]
11. He who stands high is seen from afar.
12. It is height makes Grantham steeple stand awry. [A reference to the steeple of St. Wulfram's church, Grantham, which is 280 feet high. The implication of this proverb is that envy prompts people to find fault with the great, however honest they may be]

### Its sources

13. Goodness is not tied to greatness, but greatness to goodness. [This implies that while a man's goodness may make him great, his greatness does not necessarily make him good.]
14. Some are born great, some achieve greatness, and some have greatness thrust upon them. [William Shakespeare (1564–1616) *Twelfth Night*]
15. In the country of the blind, the one-eyed man is king. [The implication is that even the mediocre may appear great when surrounded by those more incompetent or foolish than themselves]

### Its limitations

16. Great trees are good for nothing but shade.
17. The greatest vessel has but its measure.

### Characteristics of the great

18. An oak is not felled at one stroke.
19. A truly great man never puts away the simplicity of a child. [Chinese proverb]
20. The boughs that bear most, hang lowest. [A reference to the humility of the great]
21. All things that great men do are well done.
22. Great persons seldom see their face in a true glass.
23. Great men have great faults.
24. The greater the man, the greater the crime.
25. Great men's sons seldom do well.
26. A great man and a great river are often ill neighbours.
27. Great men's favours are uncertain.
28. Hall benches are slippery. [This and the next proverb reiterate the warning contained in the preceding proverb]
29. There is a sliddery stone before the hall door. ["Sliddery" means "slippery"]
30. Serve a great man, and you will know what sorrow is.
31. Eagles don't catch flies. [The implication is that the great do not concern themselves with trivial matters]

*The great and the small*

32. The great and the little have need one of another.
33. If great men would have care of little ones, both would last long.
34. There would be no great ones if there were no little ones.
35. Great oaks from little acorns grow.
36. Every oak has been an acorn.
37. Small is the seed of every greatness.
38. From small beginnings come great things.
39. The little cannot be great unless he devour many.
40. Great businesses turn on a little pin.
41. Great engines turn on small pivots.
42. Great weights hang on small wires.
43. Big fish eat little fish.
44. The great put the little on the hook.
45. Great trees keep down the little ones.

# 82 GREED

*Its sources*

1. Riches have made more covetous men, than covetousness hath made rich men.
2. Need makes greed.

*Its effects*

3. Appetite comes with eating.
4. Covetousness is always filling a bottomless vessel.
5. The greedy mouth of covetousness is not filled except by the earth of the grave. [Arabic proverb]
6. The more you get, the more you want.
7. Much would have more.
8. Covetousness is the father of unsatisfied desires. [African proverb]
9. The pleasure of what we enjoy, is lost by coveting more.
10. Covetousness often starves other vices.
11. Many a one for land takes a fool by the hand. [A reference to those who marry for money]

*Its dangers*

12. Covetousness is the root of all evil.
13. Covetousness breaks the sack.
14. Over covetous was never good.
15. Catch not at the shadow and lose the substance. [A reference to one of Aesop's fables, in which a dog carrying a bone in his mouth

catches sight of his reflection in a pond and snaps greedily at the bone reflected there. In doing so, the real bone slips out of his mouth and is lost. The following four proverbs reiterate the moral of this story]

16. Grasp all, lose all.
17. All covet, all lose.
18. Kill not the goose that lays the golden egg. [This refers to another fable, concerning a goose that laid a golden egg every day. The greedy owner of the bird killed it, in the vain hope of finding a store of gold inside it, and thus lost his regular source of income]
19. Covetousness brings nothing home.

*Characteristics of the greedy*

20. It is hard for a greedy eye to have a leal heart. ["Leal" means "honest"]
21. The greedy man and the gileynour are soon agreed. [A "gileynour" is a cheat]
22. Greedy folks have long arms. [A reference to the ability of the greedy to obtain what they desire, by fair means or foul]
23. Where the carcase is, there shall be the eagles gathered together. [This proverb is based on Matthew 24:28]
24. The covetous spends more than the liberal.
25. Lechery and covetousness go together.
26. There is little for the rake after the besom. [The implication is that there is little left after the greedy have had their fill]
27. Three things are insatiable, priests, monks, and the sea.
28. Beggars' bags are bottomless.
29. He is not poor that has little, but he that desires much.

See also MISERLINESS

# 83 HABIT

*Its power*

1. Habit is a second nature.
2. Men do more things through habit than through reason.
3. Old habits die hard.
4. It is hard to break a hog of an ill custom.
5. It is hard to make an old mare leave flinging. ["Flinging" here means "kicking"]
6. Custom reconciles us to everything.

*Its development*

7. Habits are at first cobwebs, at last cables.
8. Pursuits become habits.
9. Once a use and ever a custom.

# 84 HAPPINESS

*Its sources*

1. Content is happiness.
2. Children and fools have merry lives.
3. Laughter is the hiccup of a fool.
4. It is comparison that makes men happy or miserable.
5. Let him that would be happy for a day, go to the barber; for a week, marry a wife; for a month, buy him a new horse; for a year, build him a new house; for all his life time, be an honest man.
6. Happy is he that chastens himself.
7. Happy is he that is happy in his children.
8. Happy is he whose friends were born before him. [This and the following proverb are ironic references to those who inherit rich estates]
9. Happy is that child whose father goes to the devil. [There is also a reference here to the ill-gotten gains inherited by the son of a criminal]
10. Happy is she who marries the son of a dead mother.
11. Happy is the country which has no history.
12. Peace in a thatched hut – that is happiness. [Chinese proverb]
13. Sadness and gladness succeed each other.
14. Seill comes not till sorrow be gone. ["Seill" means "happiness"]
15. True happiness consists in making happy. [Hindi proverb]
16. All happiness is in the mind.
17. He is happy, that knoweth not himself to be otherwise.
18. He who leaves his house in search of happiness pursues a shadow. [Chinese proverb. The implication is that happiness is to be found at home]
19. Who will in time present pleasure refrain, shall in time to come the more pleasure obtain.
20. Who can sing so merry a note, as he that cannot change a groat?

*Its effects*

21. Pleasant hours fly past.
22. A blithe heart makes a blooming visage.
23. The joy of the heart makes the face fair.

24. A man of gladness seldom falls into madness.
25. Laughter makes good blood.
26. Laugh and grow fat.
27. As long lives a merry man as a sad.
28. With happiness comes intelligence to the heart. [Chinese proverb]
29. When a man is happy he does not hear the clock strike.
30. Merry meet, merry part.

### Its value

31. Laugh, and the world laughs with you; weep, and you weep alone.
    [Ella Wheeler Wilcox (1850–1919) *Solitude*]
32. Better be happy than wise.
33. To weep for joy is a kind of manna.
34. One joy scatters a hundred griefs. [Chinese proverb]
35. Laughter is the best medicine.
36. One day of pleasure is worth two of sorrow.
37. An ounce of mirth is worth a pound of sorrow.
38. Aye be as merry as be can, for love ne'er delights in a sorrowful man.
39. When good cheer is lacking, our friends will be packing.
40. A merry heart goes all the way.
41. Mirth is the sugar of life.
42. Mustard is a good sauce, but mirth is better.

### Its disadvantages

43. Pleasure has a sting in its tail.
44. No joy without annoy.
45. No pleasure without pain.
46. Short pleasure, long pain.
47. Pleasure is not pleasant unless it cost dear.
48. Take a pain for a pleasure all wise men can.
49. Great happiness, great danger.
50. Sudden joy kills sooner than excessive grief.
51. It is misery enough to have once been happy.
52. Merry is the feast-making till we come to the reckoning.
53. Sorrow is at parting if at meeting there be laughter.

### Its ephemerality

54. The mirth of the world dureth but a while.
55. Over jolly dow not. ["Dow not" means "does not last"]
56. Joy and sorrow are next door neighbours.
57. God send you joy, for sorrow will come fast enough.
58. Laugh at leisure, you may greet ere night. ["Greet" means "weep"]
59. Laugh before breakfast, you'll cry before supper.

60. If you sing before breakfast, you'll cry before night.
61. He that sings on Friday, will weep on Sunday.

*Handling happiness*

62. Happiness is not a horse, you cannot harness it. [Chinese proverb]
63. Possessed of happiness, don't exhaust it.
64. We should publish our joys, and conceal our griefs.
65. Mirth without measure is madness. [This and the following two proverbs recommend moderation in one's joy]
66. It is good to be merry and wise.
67. He laughs ill that laughs himself to death.
68. Of thy sorrow be not too sad, of thy joy be not too glad.
69. He that talks much of his happiness, summons grief.

*Jollity*

70. There is no jollity but has a smack of folly.
71. It is a poor heart that never rejoices.
72. It is good to be merry at meat.
73. It is merry in hall when beards wag all.
74. It's merry when maltmen meet. [Variants of this proverb substitute "friends", "gossips", or "knaves" for "maltmen"]
75. The more the merrier; the fewer the better fare.
76. A cheerful look makes a dish a feast.

# 85 HASTE

*Its dangers*

1. Haste is from the devil.
2. It is the pace that kills.
3. Untimeous spurring spills the steed. ["Untimeous" means "untimely"; "spills" here means "spoils". The implication is that an attempt to speed up the natural course of events may be more destructive than constructive]
4. Haste is the sister of repentance. [African proverb]
5. Oft rape rueth. ["Rape" here means "haste"]
6. He that soon deemeth, soon repenteth. [This and the next proverb imply that hasty decisions are often regretted]
7. He that passes judgment as he runs, overtakes repentance.
8. Marry in haste, and repent at leisure.
9. A hasty man never wants woe.
10. Hurry bequeaths disappointment. [African proverb]
11. Anger and haste hinder good counsel.

12. He begins to build too soon that has not money to finish it.
13. He that rides ere he be ready, wants some of his gear.
14. The hasty bitch brings forth blind whelps.
15. Haste comes not alone. [The implication is that haste always causes trouble of one kind or another]
16. Haste makes waste.
17. The hasty leaps over his opportunities.
18. Haste trips up its own heels.
19. That tongue does lie that speaks in haste.
20. In haste is error.
21. Haste is the mother of imperfection. [Brazilian proverb]
22. Hasty work, double work.
23. Good and quickly seldom meet. [This implies that what is done in a hurry is seldom done well]

*Its inadvisability*

24. Make haste slowly.
25. There is luck in leisure.
26. Nothing should be done in haste but gripping a flea.
27. Soon enough, if well enough.
28. Be not too hasty to outbid another.
29. Hate not at the first harm.
30. Love not at the first look.
31. Affairs, like salt fish, ought to be a good while a-soaking.

*Against recklessness*

32. First think, and then speak.
33. Look before you leap.
34. Think on the end before you begin.
35. Score twice before you cut once. [A reference to the need for careful preparation before taking an irreversible action. "Score" refers to the marking of leather by shoemakers]
36. Don't stitch your seam before you've tacked it.
37. He thinks not well, that thinks not again.
38. Second thoughts are best.
39. Don't throw out your dirty water until you get in fresh.
40. Don't cut the bough you are standing on.
41. Don't throw the baby out with the bathwater.

*Haste and speed*

42. More haste, less speed.
43. Fool's haste is no speed.
44. A hasty man drinks his tea with a fork. [Chinese proverb]

45. The nearest way is commonly the foulest. [The implication of this and the following two proverbs is that short cuts do not always save time]
46. The longest way round is the shortest way home.
47. Better to go about than to fall into the ditch.
48. Slow but sure wins the race.
49. Soft pace goes far.
50. Fair and softly goes far.
51. Ride softly, that we may come sooner home.
52. He that goes softly goes safely.

See also CHILDREN: *The recklessness of youth*; FOOLISHNESS: *The recklessness of fools*

# 86 HATRED

*Its dangers*

1. Hatred is worse than murder.
2. Hatred blasts the crop on the land; envy the fish in the sea.
3. Hatred with friends is succour to foes.

*Its relationship to love*

4. Love and hate are blood relations.
5. He that cannot hate cannot love.
6. They that too deeply loved too deeply hate.
7. The greatest hate springs from the greatest love.
8. Hatred is blind, as well as love.
9. Better a dinner of herbs where love is than a stalled ox where hate is. [This proverb is based on Proverbs 15:17. The words "where love is" are frequently omitted]

*Its persistence*

10. Old hate never wearies.
11. Rancour sticks long by the ribs.

# 87 HEALTH

*Its value*

1. Health and gaiety foster beauty.
2. Health and wealth create beauty.
3. Health and money go far.

4. Health is great riches.
5. Health is better than wealth.
6. A good wife and health is a man's best wealth.
7. He who has good health, is young; and he is rich who owes nothing.
8. He that wants health wants all.
9. Health is not valued till sickness comes.

*Its sources*

10. There's nothing so good for the inside of a man as the outside of a horse. [A reference to the value of horse-riding as a healthy pastime]
11. A cool mouth, and warm feet, live long.
12. Dry feet, warm head, bring safe to bed.
13. The head and feet keep warm, the rest will take no harm.
14. Wash your hands often, your feet seldom, and your head never.
15. Early to bed and early to rise, makes a man healthy, wealthy, and wise.
16. A little labour, much health.
17. Poverty is the mother of health.
18. Temperance is the best physic.
19. Where the sun enters, the doctor does not.
20. An apple a day keeps the doctor away.

*Sources of ill health*

21. Diseases are the price of ill pleasures.
22. Ill air slays sooner than the sword.
23. The air of a window is as the stroke of a cross-bow. [This and the following three proverbs refer to the dangers of sitting in a draught]
24. If cold wind reach you through a hole, say your prayers, and mind your soul.
25. Back to the draught is face to the grave. [Chinese proverb]
26. Take heed of wind that comes in at a hole, and a reconciled enemy.

*Effects of ill health*

27. The sickness of the body may prove the health of the soul.
28. Sickness shows us what we are.
29. Sickness soaks the purse.
30. The chamber of sickness is the chapel of devotion.
31. A creaking gate hangs longest. [A variant of this proverb substitutes "door" for "gate". The implication is that the chronically sick often outlive the healthy]
32. A dry cough is the trumpeter of death.
33. A priest sees people at their best, a lawyer at their worst, but a doctor sees them as they really are.

*Remedies*

34. A disease known is half cured.
35. The best doctors are Dr. Diet, Dr. Quiet, and Dr. Merryman. [The implication is that sensible eating, quiet, and a cheerful spirit are the surest remedies for ill health]
36. Kitchen physic is the best physic. [A further reference to the value of good food as a substitute for drugs and medicaments]
37. Feed a cold and starve a fever. [A variant of this proverb substitutes "stuff" for "feed". Now generally interpreted as an encouragement to eat well when suffering from a cold, the proverb was originally a warning that feeding a cold will bring on a fever]
38. When the sun rises, the disease will abate. [This superstition is based on a story concerning the Old Testament figure, Abraham, who wore a precious stone with healing properties around his neck. It is said that God placed this stone in the sun after Abraham's death]
39. Who pays the physician does the cure.
40. Ready money is a ready medicine.
41. No pain, no cure. [The implication is that painful remedies, such as iodine applied to a wound, are the most effective]

*The limitations of medicine*

42. When a disease returns, no medicine can cure it. [Chinese proverb]
43. Death defies the doctor.
44. A deadly disease neither physician nor physic can ease.
45. If physic do not work, prepare for the kirk.
46. St. Luke was a saint and a physician, and yet he died.
47. To the gout, all physicians are blind. [A reference to the incurability of gout]
48. Medicines are not meat to live by. [This and the following proverb warn against relying too heavily on drugs and medicines]
49. Make not thy stomach an apothecary's shop.

*Doctors*

50. If the doctor cures, the sun sees it; but if he kills, the earth hides it.
51. One doctor makes work for another.
52. The doctor is often more to be feared than the disease.
53. Physicians kill more than they cure.
54. Leeches kill with licence. ["Leech" is a former slang term for a doctor]
55. A young physician fattens the churchyard. [The implication is that an inexperienced doctor may make fatal mistakes]
56. If you have a physician for your friend, tip your hat and send him to your enemy.

57. Few lawyers die well, few physicians live well.
58. God heals, and the physician has the thanks.
59. A physician is an angel when employed, but a devil when one must pay him.
60. Hide nothing from thy minister, physician, and lawyer.
61. Every man is a fool or a physician. [The implication is that any man who does not know enough about health to be his own doctor, must be a fool]
62. A good surgeon must have an eagle's eye, a lion's heart, and a lady's hand.
63. Surgeons cut, that they may cure.

See also DRINKING: *Healthy drinking habits, Unhealthy drinking habits*; EATING: *Undesirable foods, Healthy eating habits, Unhealthy eating habits*

# 88 HELPING

### Its sources

1. One can't help many, but many can help one.
2. All is not at hand that helps. [The implication is that help may come from unexpected sources]
3. He that is fallen cannot help him that is down.

### Its value

4. Many hands make light work.
5. Three helping one another, bear the burthen of six.
6. Two heads are better than one.
7. Four eyes see more than two.
8. He must needs swim, that is held up by the chin. [This implies that those who receive assistance and support cannot fail to thrive]

### Its dangers

9. Too many cooks spoil the broth.
10. Two boys are half a boy, and three boys are no boy at all. [A reiteration of the sentiments of the preceding proverb]
11. He that helps the evil hurts the good.
12. Never catch at a falling knife or a falling friend.
13. Save a stranger from the sea, and he'll turn your enemy.
14. Save a thief from the gallows and he'll cut your throat.
15. A beggar pays a benefit with a louse.

*Its timing*

16. When need is highest, help is nighest.
17. When the child is christened, you may have godfathers enough. [The implication is that people are always most ready to offer assistance after the job is done]
18. Slow help is no help.

*Mutual help*

19. One good turn deserves another.
20. One hand washes the other.
21. One kindness is the price of another.
22. Kindness lies not aye in one side of the house.
23. He that pities another remembers himself.
24. Scratch my back and I'll scratch yours.
25. Scratch my breech and I'll claw your elbow.
26. Claw me, and I'll claw thee.
27. Give me fire and I'll give you a light. [Arabic proverb]
28. Help, for help in harvest. [The implication is that the person one helps now will return the favour in time of need]

See also GOD: *His help*

# 89 HONESTY

*Its value*

1. Honesty is the best policy.
2. Honesty may be dear bought, but can never be an ill pennyworth.
3. No honest man ever repented of his honesty.
4. Knavery may serve for a turn, but honesty is best at the long run.
5. Plain dealing is a jewel.
6. Plain dealing is best.
7. Open confession is good for the soul.
8. A man never surfeits of too much honesty.
9. Better beg than steal.
10. An honest look covers many faults.

*Its disadvantages*

11. Honesty is ill to thrive by.
12. Honesty is praised and starves.
13. Plain dealing is a jewel, but they that use it die beggars.
14. Confess and be hanged.

### Its rarity

15. Plain dealing is praised more than practised.
16. Honesty is a fine jewel; but much out of fashion.
17. Plain dealing is dead, and died without issue.
18. He that resolves to deal with none but honest men, must leave off dealing.

### Characteristics of the honest

19. An honest man's word is as good as his bond.
20. Leal heart lied never. ["Leal" means "honest"]
21. Leal folks never wanted gear. ["Gear" means "possessions"]
22. A thread will tie an honest man better than a rope will do a rogue.
23. A true man and a thief think not the same.
24. Honesty keeps the crown of the causeway. [The implication is that the honest have nothing to be ashamed or afraid of]
25. Honest men marry soon, wise men not at all.
26. He is wise that is honest.

# 90 HONOUR

### Its effects

1. Honours change manners.
2. Honour shows the man.

### Its inadequacy

3. Honour buys no beef in the market.
4. Honour without profit is a ring on the finger.
5. Honour and profit lie not in one sack.

### Its drawbacks

6. Honour and ease are seldom bedfellows.
7. Where there is no honour, there is no grief.
8. Great honours are great burdens.
9. The post of honour is the post of danger.

### Being worthy of honour

10. He that desires honour, is not worthy of honour.
11. It is a worthier thing to deserve honour than to possess it.
12. Honour is the reward of virtue.
13. Who that in youth, no virtue uses, in age all honour him refuses.

# 91 HOPE

*Its value*

1. Hope is the poor man's bread.
2. If it were not for hope, the heart would break.
3. Hope keeps man alive.
4. Never was cat or dog drowned, that could but see the shore.
5. Hope is grief's best music.
6. A good hope is better than a bad possession.
7. Great hopes make great men.
8. There is more delight in hope than in enjoyment. [Japanese proverb]
9. Tine heart, tine all. ["Tine" means "lose"]
10. If fortune torments me, hope contents me.
11. In the land of hope there is never any winter.

*Its constancy*

12. Hope springs eternal in the human breast. [Alexander Pope (1688–1744) *An Essay on Man*]
13. Hope is the last thing to abandon the unhappy.
14. A drowning man will clutch at a straw.
15. Death alone can kill hope.

*Its disadvantages*

16. Too much hope deceives.
17. Hope often deludes the foolish man.
18. Hope is but the dream of those that wake.
19. Hope is a good breakfast but a bad supper.
20. Who lives by hope will die by hunger.
21. He that lives in hope dances to an ill tune.
22. Hopers go to hell.
23. Hope deferred maketh the heart sick. [Proverbs 13:12]

*Hopeful attitudes*

24. Hope for the best. [A variant of this proverb adds " . . . and prepare for the worst"]
25. Hope well and have well.
26. While there's life there's hope.
27. Bear with evil and expect good.
28. Tomorrow is another day.
29. He has not lost all who has one cast left. ["Cast" here refers to a throw of the dice]

See also OPTIMISM

# 92 HOSPITALITY

*Its value*

1. If a man receives no guests at home, when abroad he'll have no hosts. [Chinese proverb]
2. The guest of the hospitable learns hospitality. [Arabic proverb]
3. Good will and welcome is your best cheer.
4. He that is welcome fares well.
5. Welcome is the best dish.
6. Such welcome, such farewell.
7. It is a sin against hospitality, to open your doors and shut up your countenance.

*The guest's behaviour*

8. To the man submit at whose board you sit. [Chinese proverb]
9. He is an ill guest that never drinks to his host.

*Outstaying one's welcome*

10. Do not wear out your welcome.
11. A constant guest is never welcome.
12. Long visits bring short compliments. [Chinese proverb]
13. Fish and guests smell in three days.
14. The first day a guest, the second day a guest, the third day a calamity. [Indian proverb]
15. The guest who outstays his fellow-guests loses his overcoat. [Chinese proverb]

*The uninvited guest*

16. An unbidden guest knows not where to sit.
17. An unbidden guest must bring his stool with him.
18. Who comes uncalled, sits unserved.

# 93 HUNGER

*Its causes*

1. After a famine in the stall, comes a famine in the hall. [The implication is that a bad harvest leads to a lack of animal feed, and both contribute to the hunger of the people]
2. Where coin is not common, commons must be scant. ["Commons" means "provisions"]
3. They must hunger in frost that will not work in heat.

*Its effects*

4. Who goes to bed supperless, all night tumbles and tosses.
5. An empty belly bears no body.
6. A sharp stomach makes short devotion.
7. The belly wants ears. [A reference to the futility of reasoning with a hungry person who is intent on eating]

*Its advantages*

8. Hunger finds no fault with the cookery.
9. Hunger is good kitchen meat. ["Kitchen meat" is anything served as a relish with bread]
10. Hunger is the best sauce.
11. Hunger makes hard beans sweet.
12. A hungry horse makes a clean manger.
13. All's good in a famine.
14. Hunger increases the understanding. [Lithuanian proverb]

*Its dangers*

15. Hunger and cold deliver a man up to his enemy.
16. A hungry man is an angry man.

*Its intensity*

17. Hunger is sharper than the sword.
18. Hunger is stronger than love.
19. A hungry man smells meat afar off.

*The desperation of the hungry*

20. Hunger breaks stone walls.
21. Hunger drives the wolf out of the wood.
22. Hungry dogs will eat dirty puddings.
23. A hungry man is glad to get boiled wheat. [Chinese proverb]

*Fasting*

24. Who fasts and does no other good, spares his bread and goes to hell.
25. He fasts enough that has had a bad meal.
26. He fasts enough whose wife scolds all dinner-time.
27. Two hungry meals make the third a glutton. [The implication is that fasting improves the appetite]
28. He whose belly is full believes not him who is fasting.

See also EATING: *Appetite*

# 94 HYPOCRISY

*Its value*

1. Who knows not how to dissemble, knows not how to live.
2. Speak fair and think what you will.
3. Lip-honour costs little, yet may bring in much.

*Hypocritical acts*

4. The cat and dog may kiss, yet are none the better friends.
5. Many kiss the hand they wish cut off.
6. Many kiss the child for the nurse's sake.
7. He that gives to be seen, will relieve none in the dark.
8. Carrion crows bewail the dead sheep, and then eat them.
9. The cat shuts its eyes while it steals cream.

*Hypocritical words*

10. Fine words dress ill deeds.
11. Many a one says well that thinks ill.
12. A honey tongue, a heart of gall.
13. He that speaks me fair and loves me not, I'll speak him fair and trust him not.
14. All are not friends that speak us fair.

*Religious hypocrisy*

15. Pretended holiness is double iniquity.
16. All are not saints that go to church.
17. Bells call others, but themselves enter not into the church.
18. When the fox preaches, then beware your geese.
19. The friar preached against stealing, and had a goose in his sleeve.
20. Some make a conscience of spitting in the church, yet rob the altar.
21. No rogue like to the godly rogue.
22. If you want to see black-hearted people, look among those who never miss their prayers. [Chinese proverb]

*Against hypocrisy*

23. Be what you would seem to be.
24. Kythe in your own colours, that folk may ken you. ["Kythe" means "appear"]

# 95 IDLENESS

## *Its causes*

1. A light-heeled mother makes a heavy-heeled daughter. ["Light-heeled" means "nimble"; "heavy-heeled" means "lazy"]
2. Work for nought makes folks dead sweir. ["Sweir" means "lazy"]
3. Lacking breeds laziness, praise breeds pith. ["Lacking" here means "criticism"; "pith" means "effort"]

## *Its effects*

4. Idleness is the shipwreck of chastity.
5. Love is the fruit of idleness.
6. Pride and laziness would have mickle upholding. ["Mickle" means "much". A reference to the expense of providing ornaments for the vain and servants for the lazy]
7. Sweet in the bed, and sweir up in the morning, was never a good housewife. ["Sweir" here means "late"]
8. Standing pools gather filth.
9. A sluggard takes an hundred steps because he would not take one in due time.
10. Idle folks have the least leisure.
11. Who is more busy, than he that has least to do? [The implication of this and the preceding proverb is either that lazy people avoid work by claiming to have no spare time, or that they use up all their spare time in the effort to avoid work]
12. It is more pain to do nothing than something.
13. The dog that is idle barks at his fleas, but he that is hunting feels them not.

## *Its dangers*

14. The devil finds work for idle hands to do.
15. If the devil find a man idle, he'll set him to work.
16. An idle brain is the devil's workshop.
17. An idle person is the devil's cushion.
18. The devil tempts all, but the idle man tempts the devil.
19. He that is busy, is tempted by but one devil; he that is idle, by a legion.
20. By doing nothing we learn to do ill.
21. Of idleness comes no goodness.
22. Idleness is the root of all evil.
23. Idleness turns the edge of wit.
24. Sloth, like rust, consumes faster than labour wears.
25. Sloth breeds a scab.

26. They must hunger in frost that will not work in heat.
27. An idle youth, a needy age.
28. Idleness is the key of beggary.
29. Laziness goes so slowly that poverty overtakes it.
30. Idleness must thank itself if it goes barefoot.
31. He that lies long abed, his estate feels it.
32. He who sleeps all the morning, may go a begging all the day after.
33. The slothful man is the beggar's brother.
34. The sluggard must be clad in rags.
35. He that gapes until he be fed, well may he gape until he be dead.

*Dealing with idleness*

36. A lazy ox is little better for the goad.
37. He that is sick of a fever lurden, must be cured by the hazel gelding. ["Fever lurden" means "laziness"]
38. A horse that will not carry a saddle must have no oats.
39. A lean fee is a fit reward for a lazy clerk.

*Lazy people*

40. He that does nothing, does ever amiss.
41. Every day is holiday with sluggards.
42. The sluggard's convenient season never comes.
43. For the diligent the week has seven todays, for the slothful seven tomorrows.
44. Idle folks lack no excuses.
45. The slothful is the servant of the counters. ["Counters" here means "prisons"]
46. Sluggards are never great scholars.
47. A lazy sheep thinks its wool heavy.
48. As good be an addled egg as an idle bird.

# 96 IGNORANCE

*Its advantages*

1. Ignorance is the peace of life.
2. Ignorance and incuriosity are two very soft pillows.
3. Wonder is the daughter of ignorance.
4. He that knows nothing, doubts nothing.
5. Where ignorance is bliss, 'tis folly to be wise. [Thomas Gray (1716–71) *Ode on a Distant Prospect of Eton College*]
6. What the eye doesn't see, the heart doesn't grieve over.
7. What you don't know can't hurt you.

8. He that never ate flesh, thinks a pudding a dainty.
9. Acorns were good till bread was found. [The implication of this and the preceding proverb is that ignorance of the finer things of life is better than the discontented knowledge that one cannot have them]

### Its disadvantages

10. Ignorance is the night of the mind. [Chinese proverb]
11. There is no blindness like ignorance.
12. The devil never assails a man except he find him either void of knowledge, or of the fear of God.
13. Science has no enemy but the ignorant.
14. Art has no enemy but ignorance.
15. If the blind lead the blind, both shall fall into the ditch. [Matthew 15:14]

### Its effects

16. Ignorance is the mother of impudence.
17. Ignorance is the mother of devotion. ["Devotion" is used here in the religious sense]
18. He that knows little, often repeats it.
19. It is profound ignorance that inspires the dogmatic tone.

# 97 IMPERFECTION

### Nobody is perfect

1. Every man has his faults.
2. He is lifeless that is faultless.
3. No man is infallible.
4. To err is human. [See also FORGIVENESS: 7]
5. If you don't make mistakes you don't make anything.
6. The best may amend.
7. Every man has his weak side.
8. He is good that failed never.
9. It is a sound head that has not a soft piece in it.
10. Every man is mad on some point.
11. No living man all things can.
12. He who makes no mistakes, makes nothing.
13. He rides sure that never fell.
14. He stands not surely that never slips.
15. Accidents will happen in the best regulated families.
16. Homer sometimes nods. [A reference to the Greek poet Homer. The

implication of this and the following three proverbs is that even the great have their limitations]

17. Bernard did not see everything. [A reference to the theologian St. Bernard of Clairvaux (1091–1153)]
18. Arthur could not tame woman's tongue. [A reference to King Arthur]

*Nothing is perfect*

19. The best things may be abused.
20. Nothing so good but it might have been better.
21. The best-laid schemes of mice and men gang aft agley. [Robert Burns (1759–96) *To a Mouse*. "Gang aft agley" means "often go awry"]
22. There are spots even in the sun.
23. The best cloth may have a moth in it.
24. The best cart may overthrow.
25. No garden without its weeds.
26. No land without stones, or meat without bones.
27. No silver without its dross.
28. There is no pack of cards without a knave.
29. No rose without a thorn.
30. Every light has its shadow.
31. No sun without a shadow.
32. No day so clear but has dark clouds.
33. No summer, but has its winter.
34. There was never a good town but had a mire at one end of it.
35. Wherever a man dwell, he shall be sure to have a thorn-bush near his door.
36. No larder but has its mice.
37. Every bean has its black.
38. Every path has a puddle.
39. It is a good tree that has neither knap nor gaw. [A "knap" is a knob; a "gaw" is a blemish]
40. He is a gentle horse that never cast his rider.
41. It is a good horse that never stumbles.
42. He who wants a mule without fault, must walk on foot.
43. He that seeks a horse or a wife without fault, has neither steed in his stable nor angel in his bed.

See also WISDOM: *The fallibility of the wise*

# 98 INCONVENIENCE

*Its necessity*

1. No convenience without its inconvenience.

2. Every commodity has its discommodity.
3. Suffer the ill and look for the good.
4. The cat would eat fish and would not wet her feet.
5. He that would have eggs must endure the cackling of hens.
6. Better a mischief than an inconvenience. [The implication is that it is better to have a small inconvenience now than to have to endure greater inconvenience at a later date]
7. A stumble may prevent a fall.
8. It is better to kiss a knave than to be troubled with him.

# 99 INQUISITIVENESS

*Its dangers*

1. Curiosity killed the cat.
2. Curiosity is endless, restless, and useless.
3. Listeners never hear good of themselves.
4. He who peeps through a hole, may see what will vex him.
5. He that gazes upon the sun, shall at last be blind.
6. He that pries into every cloud, may be stricken with a thunderbolt.
7. That fish will soon be caught that nibbles at every bait.
8. Spur a jade a question, and she'll kick you an answer. [The implication is that the over-inquisitive may not be pleased with what they hear]
9. Ask no questions and hear no lies.

*Against meddling*

10. Mind your own business.
11. Meddle not with another man's matter.
12. Skeer your own fire. ["Skeer" means "rake out"]
13. The stone that lies not in your gate breaks not your toes.
14. Enquire not what boils in another's pot.
15. Put not thy hand between the bark and the tree. [A warning against meddling in family quarrels]
16. Little intermeddling makes good friends.
17. Little meddling makes much rest.
18. Come not to counsel uncalled.
19. Every man knows his own business best.

# 100 JUSTICE

## *Its value*

1. In justice is all virtue found in sum.
2. Justice will not condemn even the devil himself wrongfully.
3. Though the sword of justice is sharp, it will not slay the innocent. [Chinese proverb]
4. Right wrongs no man.
5. A just war is better than an unjust peace.

## *Injustice*

6. Extreme justice is extreme injustice. [The implication is that to apply a law to the letter, without taking any extenuating circumstances into account, is a form of injustice]
7. Much law, but little justice.
8. There's one law for the rich, and another for the poor.
9. One man may steal a horse, while another may not look over a hedge. [This implies that through personal favour or prejudice, the misdeeds of one person may be overlooked whilst a trivial action by another is condemned]

## *Fair judgment*

10. Hear all parties.
11. There are two sides to every question.
12. Every medal has its reverse.
13. Give the devil his due.
14. Give credit where credit is due.
15. Comparisons are odious. [The implication is that one should not pass judgment on one person by comparing him with another]
16. Circumstances alter cases.

## *Fair play*

17. Fair play's a jewel.
18. Fair exchange is no robbery.
19. What's sauce for the goose is sauce for the gander.
20. One dog, one bull. [A reference to the former sport of bull-baiting]
21. Two to one is odds. [This and the following proverb refer to the unfairness of an uneven match]
22. Many dogs may easily worry one hare.

## *Sharing fairly*

23. Share and share alike.

24. It is no play where one greets and another laughs. ["Greets" here means "cries"]
25. Turn about is fair play.

## 101 KINDNESS

*Its value*

1. A kind heart loseth nought at last.
2. It is cheap enough to say, 'God help you.'
3. Pity is akin to love.
4. Charity construes all doubtful things in good part.
5. Charity covers a multitude of sins.
6. Kindness is the noblest weapon to conquer with.
7. An iron anvil should have a hammer of feathers. [The implication is that a kind, gentle approach may be the best way to win over a stubborn person]
8. The rough net is not the best catcher of birds.
9. To fright a bird is not the way to catch her.
10. Honey catches more flies than vinegar.
11. Where men are well used, they'll frequent there.

*Its dangers*

12. Tender-handed stroke a nettle, and it stings you for your pains; grasp it like a man of mettle, and it soft as silk remains. [Aaron Hill (1685–1750) *Verses Written on a Window*]
13. Kind hearts are soonest wronged.
14. Let an ill man lie in thy straw, and he looks to be thy heir. [This and the following two proverbs warn that unscrupulous people may take advantage of one's kindness]
15. Give a clown your finger, and he will take your hand.
16. Give him an inch and he'll take a yard. [A variant of this proverb substitutes "ell" for "yard"]
17. Sometimes clemency is cruelty, and cruelty clemency.

*Its sources*

18. Kindness cannot be bought for gear.
19. Kindness comes of will.
20. We can poind for debt but not for kindness. ["Poind" means "distrain". The implication of this and the two preceding proverbs is that kindness cannot be obtained by force]

135

*Kind words*

21. Fair words break no bones.
22. Fair words hurt not the mouth.
23. Good words are good cheap.
24. A good word costs no more than a bad one.
25. Good words cost nought.
26. There is great force hidden in a sweet command. [The implication is that gentle words may be more effective than massive threats]

# 102 KNOWLEDGE

*Its sources*

1. Doubt is the key of knowledge. [Persian proverb]
2. He that nothing questions, nothing learns.
3. He that travels far, knows much.
4. Knowledge is a wild thing and must be hunted before it can be tamed. [Persian proverb]

*Its effects*

5. Learning makes a good man better and an ill man worse.
6. A man's studies pass into his character.
7. Pursuits become habits.

*Its value*

8. Knowledge is the mother of all virtue; all vice proceeds from ignorance.
9. Knowledge is power.
10. Knowledge is no burthen.
11. Learning is a treasure which accompanies its owner everywhere. [Chinese proverb]
12. Learning makes a man fit company for himself.
13. Learning is the eye of the mind.
14. Wit without learning is like a tree without fruit.
15. A man of great memory without learning, has a rock and a spindle, and no stuff to spin. ["Rock" here means "distaff"]
16. When house and land are gone and spent, then learning is most excellent. [The implication is that learning enables one to survive without material wealth]
17. No knave to the learned knave.
18. With Latin, a horse, and money, you may travel the world. ["Latin" here symbolizes learning]

19. A dwarf on a giant's shoulders sees further of the two. [A reference to the value of knowledge acquired from one's predecessors]

*Its inadequacy*

20. Knowledge makes one laugh, but wealth makes one dance.
21. Knowledge without practice makes but half an artist.
22. Learning without wisdom is a load of books on an ass's back. [Japanese proverb]
23. Experience without learning is better than learning without experience.
24. The greatest scholars are not the best preachers.
25. The greatest clerks are not the wisest men.

*Its unimportance*

26. He that lives well is learned enough.
27. A handful of good life is better than a bushel of learning.

*Its dangers*

28. Knowledge is folly, except grace guide it.
29. Learning in the breast of a bad man is as a sword in the hand of a madman.
30. Much learning makes men mad.
31. Much science, much sorrow.
32. A little learning is a dangerous thing. [Alexander Pope (1688–1744) *An Essay on Criticism*]

*Characteristics of scholars*

33. The love of money and the love of learning rarely meet.
34. Poverty is the common fate of scholars. [Chinese proverb]
35. He that robs a scholar, robs twenty men. [The implication is that many of the things stolen from a scholar will have been previously borrowed from other people]

# 103 LATENESS

*Its disadvantages*

1. Who comes late, lodges ill.
2. He that comes last to the pot, is soonest wroth. ["Wroth" means "angry"]
3. Far behind must follow the faster.
4. Late-comers are shent. ["Shent" means "ruined"]

5. He that rises not early, never does a good day's work.
6. He that rises late, must trot all day.
7. The gods send nuts to those who have no teeth. [A reference to opportunities that come too late to be of any use]

### Its compensations

8. Better late than never.
9. Better late ripe and bear, than early blossom and blast.
10. Late was often lucky.
11. They are far behind that may not follow.
12. Never too late to learn. [Variants of this proverb substitute "mend", "repent", or "do well" for "learn"]
13. The last suitor wins the maid.

See also REGRET: *Its futility, The futility of hindsight*

# 104 LAW

### Its sources

1. Good laws often proceed from bad manners.
2. The law grows of sin, and chastises it.
3. Many lords, many laws.
4. New lords, new laws.
5. Law governs man, reason the law.

### Its inconsistency

6. There's one law for the rich, and another for the poor.
7. The law is not the same at morning and at night.
8. The law is an ass. [This proverb was familiarized by Charles Dickens (1812–70) in *Oliver Twist*]
9. Laws catch flies but let hornets go free.

### Its inadequacy

10. You cannot make people honest by Act of Parliament.
11. A coach and four may be driven through any Act of Parliament.
12. Every law has a loophole.
13. Where drums beat, laws are silent. [The implication is that the law has little weight in a state of war]
14. Much law, but little justice.
15. A penny-weight of love is worth a pound of law.
16. In a thousand pounds of law, there's not an ounce of love.

17. We can poind for debt but not for kindness. ["Poind" means "distrain"]
18. Law cannot persuade, where it cannot punish.
19. Many things lawful are not expedient.

### Its dangers

20. Law is a bottomless pit.
21. The more laws, the more offenders.
22. One suit of law breeds twenty.
23. Wrong laws make short governance.

### Its expense

24. Agree, for the law is costly.
25. A lean agreement is better than a fat judgment.
26. Law is a lickpenny.
27. Lawsuits consume time, and money, and rest, and friends.
28. Win your lawsuit and lose your money. [Chinese proverb]
29. Go to law for a sheep and lose your cow.
30. A lawyer's opinion is worth nothing unless paid for.
31. Lawyers' gowns are lined with the wilfulness of their clients.

### Keeping the law

32. Abundance of law breaks no law. [The implication is that it is better to do more than is required by law than to break the law]
33. Law makers should not be law breakers.
34. We live by laws not by examples.

### Lawyers

35. A good lawyer, an evil neighbour.
36. The better lawyer is the worse Christian.
37. A client twixt his attorney and counsellor is like a goose twixt two foxes.
38. A good lawyer must be a great liar.
39. Few lawyers die well, few physicians live well.
40. A lawyer never goes to law himself.
41. He that is his own lawyer has a fool for a client.
42. Hide nothing from thy minister, physician, and lawyer.
43. Kick an attorney downstairs and he'll stick to you for life.
44. Two attorneys can live in a town, when one cannot. [The implication is that one attorney makes work for the other]

### Judges

45. A good judge conceives quickly, judges slowly.
46. From a foolish judge, a quick sentence.
47. A judge knows nothing unless it has been explained to him three times.

### Legal maxims

48. No wrong without a remedy.
49. The law does not concern itself about trifles.
50. Ignorance of the law excuses no man.
51. No man is bound to criminate himself.
52. Every one is held to be innocent until he is proved guilty.
53. Possession is nine points of the law.
54. The act of God does wrong to none.
55. Every dog is allowed one bite. [A reference to the leniency of the law with regard to a person's first offence]
56. Once a way and aye a way. [The implication is that nobody has the authority to close or divert a public right of way]
57. The father to the bough, the son to the plough. [This refers to the law that allowed the offspring of a hanged criminal to inherit his lands]

### Customs

58. With customs we live well, but laws undo us.
59. The command of custom is great.
60. Custom rules the law.
61. Custom has the force of law.
62. Custom is the plague of wise men, and the idol of fools.
63. Custom without reason is but ancient error.
64. A bad custom is like a good cake, better broken than kept.
65. So many countries, so many customs.
66. Every land has its own law.

See also CORRUPTION: *Corruption at law*

# 105 LENDING

### Against lending

1. Better give a shilling than lend and lose half a crown.
2. Lend only that which you can afford to lose.
3. Lend never that thing thou needest most.
4. He who has but one coat cannot lend it.
5. Lend sitting and you will run to collect.

6. Neither a borrower nor a lender be. [William Shakespeare (1564–1616) *Hamlet*]
7. The world still he keeps at his staff's end, that needs not to borrow and never will lend.
8. A horse, a wife, and a sword may be shewed, but not lent.

### Its dangers

9. If you would make an enemy, lend a man money, and ask it of him again.
10. Lend your money and lose your friend. [The implication is not that you will lose your friend through lending him money, but rather for demanding repayment of the loan]
11. Lending nurses enmity. [Arabic proverb]
12. When I lent, I was a friend; and when I asked, I was unkind.
13. Lend, and lose the loan, or gain an enemy.
14. Give a loan and buy a quarrel. [Indian proverb]
15. Lend money to a bad debtor and he will hate you. [Chinese proverb]
16. He that lends, gives.
17. Lending is like throwing away; being paid is like finding something. [Chinese proverb]
18. The leeful man is the beggar's brother. ["Leeful" means "ready to lend"]
19. Lend and lose; so play fools.
20. He that lends his pot may seethe his kail in his loof. ["Kail" is broth; "loof" means "palm of the hand"]
21. Lend your horse for a long journey, you may have him return with his skin.

### Usurers

22. God keep me from four houses, a usurer's, a tavern, a spital, and a prison.
23. Usury is murder. [Hebrew proverb]
24. Usurers are always good husbands.
25. Usurers live by the fall of heirs, as swine by the dropping of acorns.
26. To speak of a usurer at the table mars the wine.

# 106 LIBERTY

### Its value

1. Liberty is more worth than gold.
2. Liberty is a jewel.
3. Freedom is a fair thing.

4. Lean liberty is better than fat slavery.
5. A bean in liberty is better than a comfit in prison.
6. Better hand loose than in an ill tethering. [This and the following proverb are often used as a warning against marriage]
7. An ox, when he is loose, licks himself at pleasure.
8. No love is foul, nor prison fair.

*Its effects*

9. Too much liberty spoils all.
10. Liberty is not licence. [A warning of the possible abuse of liberty]

*Losing one's liberty*

11. Who loses his liberty loses all.
12. Who receives a gift, sells his liberty.
13. He that marries for wealth, sells his liberty.

## 107 LIFE

*Its brevity*

1. Life is but a span.
2. Life is half spent before we know what it is.
3. Man's life is like a candle in the wind, or hoar-frost on the tiles. [Chinese proverb]
4. Art is long, life is short.[This proverb is also used in its Latin form, *Ars longa, vita brevis*. Its original meaning was that life is too short to acquire skills or learning in any depth. However it is now frequently used to imply that painting, sculpture, etc., last for longer than the brief span of human life]
5. Life is short and time is swift.

*Its unpleasant aspects*

6. Long life has long misery.
7. Life is not all beer and skittles.
8. Life would be too smooth, if it had no rubs in it.

*Attitudes to life*

9. Life is sweet.
10. The life of man is a winter's day and a winter's way.
11. Our whole life is but a greater and longer childhood.
12. Life begins at forty.
13. Life means strife.

14. Life is a pilgrimage.
15. Life is a shadow.
16. Every day of thy life is a leaf in thy history.
17. Life is just a bowl of cherries.

### The value of long life

18. They who live longest, will see most.
19. The longer we live, the more farlies we see. ["Farlies" means "wonders"]

See also DEATH: *The manner of death*

# 108 LIKELIHOOD

### Probability

1. A thousand probabilities do not make one truth.
2. Likely lies in the mire, and unlikely gets over. [The implication is that the probable often gives way to the improbable]

### Possibility

3. Possibilities are infinite.
4. All things are possible with God.
5. Whatever man has done, man may do.
6. Every may be has a may not be.
7. May-bee was ne'er a gude honey bee.
8. If ifs and ans were pots and pans, there'd be no trade for tinkers.
9. 'If' and 'An' spoils many a good charter.
10. Like to die fills not the churchyard.

### Improbability

11. Pigs might fly, if they had wings. [A variant of this proverb is "Pigs may fly, but they are very unlikely birds"]
12. If the sky falls we shall catch larks.
13. If my aunt had been a man, she'd have been my uncle.
14. The age of miracles is past.

### Impossibility

15. Nothing is impossible to a willing heart.
16. Nought's impossible, as t'auld woman said when they told her calf had swallowed grindlestone. ["Grindlestone" means "grindstone"]
17. The difficult is done at once; the impossible takes a little longer.

18. No one is bound to do impossibilities.
19. No man can do two things at once.
20. No man can sup and blow together.
21. A man cannot be in two places at once.
22. No man can flay a stone.
23. It is hard to sail over the sea in an egg-shell.
24. Solomon was a wise man, and Sampson was a strong man, yet neither of them could pay money before they had it.
25. You can't get blood out of a stone. [This proverb is often applied to those who have no money with which to pay their debts]
26. You can't get a quart into a pint pot.
27. You can't make bricks without straw.
28. Nothing comes of nothing.

## 109 LOVE

### Its blindness

1. Love is blind.
2. If Jack's in love, he's no judge of Jill's beauty.
3. Love sees no faults.
4. In the eyes of the lover, pock-marks are dimples.
5. No love is foul, nor prison fair.

### Its irrationality

6. Love is without reason.
7. Love is lawless.
8. Affection blinds reason.
9. No folly to being in love.
10. One cannot love and be wise.
11. Lovers are madmen.

### Its value

12. To be beloved is above all bargains.
13. A penny-weight of love is worth a pound of law.
14. Love covers many infirmities.
15. Where love fails, we espy all faults.
16. Faults are thick where love is thin.
17. Labour is light where love doth pay.
18. Love makes one fit for any work.
19. He that has love in his breast, has spurs in his sides.
20. Love is free.
21. In love is no lack.

22. Love locks no cupboards.
23. True love kythes in time of need. ["Kythes" means "shows itself"]
24. All the world loves a lover.
25. Love is the touchstone of virtue.
26. 'Tis better to have loved and lost than never to have loved at all. [Alfred, Lord Tennyson (1809–92) *In Memoriam*. The basic sentiment of this now proverbial quotation was first expressed many centuries earlier]

*Its power*

27. Love conquers all.
28. Love rules his kingdom without a sword.
29. Love makes the world go round.
30. Love makes all men equal.
31. Love and business teach eloquence.
32. Love makes a wit of the fool.
33. Love makes all hard hearts gentle.
34. Love laughs at locksmiths.
35. Love will find a way.
36. Love will go through stone walls.
37. Love cannot be compelled.
38. A man has choice to begin love, but not to end it.
39. Perfect love casteth out fear. [1 John 4:18]
40. Love is as strong as death. [Song of Solomon 8:6]
41. Love and a cough cannot be hid. [Variations of this proverb substitute or add "light", "fire", "smoke", "gout", and "an itch" as things that can no more be concealed than love]

*Its universality*

42. He that does not love a woman, sucked a sow.
43. Love and leprosy few escape. [Chinese proverb]

*Its steadfastness*

44. Old love will not be forgotten.
45. Old love does not rust.
46. Sound love is not soon forgotten.
47. True love never grows old.
48. Love will creep where it may not go. [The implication is that love will always do what little it can to help]
49. Love without end has no end. [This implies that true love will last forever, whereas false love, which has a particular aim in view, will fade as soon as its goal is attained]

145

*Its ups and downs*

50. The course of true love never did run smooth. [William Shakespeare (1564–1616) *Midsummer Night's Dream*]
51. Never rely on love or the weather.
52. Of honey and gall in love there is store.
53. Love is sweet in the beginning but sour in the ending.
54. Love is a sweet torment.
55. War, hunting, and love are as full of trouble as pleasure.

*Its disadvantages*

56. Love is full of fear.
57. When love puts in, friendship is gone.

*Its dangers*

58. Love and pease-pottage are two dangerous things. [The implication is that one attacks the heart and the other the stomach]
59. The love of the wicked is more dangerous than their hatred.
60. They love too much that die for love.

*Its inadequacy*

61. Fear is stronger than love.
62. Of soup and love, the first is the best.
63. 'Sweet-heart' and 'Honey-bird' keeps no house.

*Its silence*

64. Love speaks, even when the lips are closed.
65. When love is greatest, words are fewest.
66. Whom we love best, to them we can say least.
67. Next to love, quietness.

*Its sources*

68. Congruity is the mother of love.
69. Likeness causes liking.
70. Looks breed love.
71. Love begets love.
72. Love is the loadstone of love.
73. Love is the true reward of love.
74. Love needs no teaching.
75. Love is not found in the market.
76. Love is the fruit of idleness.

*Its remedies*

77. Cold pudding will settle your love.
78. Time, not the mind, puts an end to love.
79. In love's wars, he who flies is conqueror. [The implication is that the only remedy for love is to run away]
80. No herb will cure love.

*Its rules and conditions*

81. All is fair in love and war.
82. Love is a game in which both players always cheat.
83. Love me, love my dog. [The implication is that in loving a person one must also love those who are close to him]

*Its tactics*

84. Love delights in praise.
85. Scorn at first makes after-love the more.
86. He that would the daughter win, must with the mother first begin.
87. Follow love and it will flee thee: flee love and it will follow thee.
88. The last suitor wins the maid.
89. He that woos a maid, must seldom come in her sight; but he that woos a widow must woo her day and night.
90. Puddings and paramours should be hotly handled. [The implication is that neither puddings nor love should be allowed to grow cold]

*Courtship*

91. To woo is a pleasure in a young man, a fault in an old.
92. A man may woo where he will, but he will wed where his hap is.
93. Happy is the wooing that is not long a-doing.
94. Sunday's wooing draws to ruin.
95. When petticoats woo, breeks may come speed. [A reference to women courting men]

*Lover's quarrels*

96. Lovers' quarrels are soon mended.
97. The quarrel of lovers is the renewal of love.
98. Jove laughs at lovers' perjuries.
99. Biting and scratching is Scots folk's wooing.

*Young love*

100. Calf love, half love; old love, cold love.
101. Love of lads and fire of chats is soon in and soon out. ["Chats" are wood-chips]

102. Lad's love's a busk of broom, hot awhile and soon done.
103. No love like the first love.

### New love

104. The new love drives out the old love.
105. One love expels another.
106. It is best to be off with the old love before you are on with the new.
107. As good love comes as goes.
108. Many a heart is caught in the rebound.

### Unrequited love

109. Love without return is like a question without an answer.
110. There is more pleasure in loving than in being beloved.

### Parental love

111. It is a dear collop that is cut out of thine own flesh. [A "collop" is a slice, here referring to one's offspring]
112. A mother's love never ages.
113. A mother's love is best of all.
114. No love to a father's.
115. Love the babe for her that bare it. [The implication of this and the next two proverbs is that if a man loves a woman he must also love her children]
116. If you love the boll, you cannot hate the branches.
117. He that loves the tree, loves the branch.

### Love and faith

118. Love asks faith, and faith asks firmness.
119. Where love is, there is faith.
120. Where there is no trust there is no love.

### Love and jealousy

121. Love being jealous, makes a good eye look asquint.
122. Love is never without jealousy.
123. Love and lordship like no fellowship. [This proverb may be interpreted in two ways: that neither love nor lordship will tolerate a rival, or that love and lordship are not compatible. The first interpretation applies here]

### Love and money

124. Love does much, money does everything.
125. Love lasts as long as money endures.

126. Money is the sinews of love as well as of war.
127. When poverty comes in at the door, love flies out of the window.
128. Love lives in cottages as well as in courts.

See also ABSENCE: *Its effect on love*; HATRED: *Its relationship to love*;
MARRIAGE: *Marriage and love*

# 110 LOYALTY

*Its value*

1. Loyalty is worth more than money.
2. Faithfulness is a sister of love.
3. The subject's love is the king's lifeguard.

*Loyalty between companions*

4. There is honour among thieves.
5. One thief will not rob another.
6. Dog does not eat dog.
7. Hawks will not pick out hawks' eyes.
8. One mule scrubs another.
9. One barber shaves another gratis.
10. Tarry breeks pays no fraught. ["Tarry breeks" refers to seamen; "fraught" means "freight"]

*Divided loyalties*

11. No man can serve two masters. [Matthew 6:24]
12. You cannot run with the hare and hunt with the hounds.
13. If you can't ride two horses at once, you shouldn't be in the circus. [A contradiction of the preceding proverb]

*Disloyalty*

14. Rats desert a sinking ship.
15. No tie can oblige the perfidious.

# 111 LUCK

*Its unpredictability*

1. God sends good luck and God sends bad.
2. A blind man may sometimes hit the mark.
3. It chances in an hour, that happens not in seven years.

149

4. Fortune is blind.
5. Fortune is fickle.
6. Fortune to one is mother, to another is stepmother.
7. You never know your luck.

### Its uncertainty

8. The footsteps of fortune are slippery.
9. The highest spoke in fortune's wheel, may soon turn lowest.
10. Fortune is weary to carry one and the same man always.
11. Fortune is made of glass.
12. When a fool finds a horseshoe, he thinks aye the like to do. [The implication is that it is foolish to rely on perpetual good fortune after just one lucky occurrence]
13. He that quits certainty and leans to chance, when fools pipe he may dance.

### Its value

14. It is better to be born lucky than rich.
15. Good luck reaches further than long arms.
16. An ounce of luck is worth a pound of wisdom.
17. Better be born lucky than wise.
18. Hap and halfpenny goods enough. ["Hap" means "luck". The implication is that as long as one has luck, great wealth is unnecessary]

### Its drawbacks

19. Great fortune brings with it great misfortune.
20. When the wagon of fortune goes well, spite and envy hang on to the wheels. [Chinese proverb]
21. Every flow has its ebb.

### Ill luck

22. If anything can go wrong, it will. [This modern proverb is known as Murphy's (or Sod's) Law]
23. The bread never falls but on its buttered side.
24. There's no fence against ill fortune.
25. Bad luck often brings good luck.
26. The worse luck now, the better another time.

### The power of fortune

27. Fortune is the mistress of the field.
28. Fortune, not prudence, rules the life of men.

29. No man can make his own hap.
30. Fortune can take from us nothing but what she gave us.

*The lucky*

31. Lucky men need no counsel.
32. He dances well to whom fortune pipes.
33. A cat has nine lives. [A reference to the cat's apparent ability to escape death, either through agility or sheer good luck]
34. Fortune favours those who use their judgment.
35. Fortune favours fools.
36. A little wit will serve a fortunate man.
37. The more knave, the better luck.
38. The more wicked, the more lucky.
39. Thieves and rogues have the best luck, if they do but scape hanging.
40. Fortune knocks once at least at every man's gate.
41. Every dog has his day.
42. Some have the hap, some stick in the gap.
43. The devil looks after his own. [This and the following proverb are quoted when other people have a stroke of good fortune]
44. The devil's children have the devil's luck.

See also SUPERSTITIONS

# 112 LUST

*Its causes*

1. When the belly is full, the mind is among the maids.
2. Without Ceres and Bacchus, Venus grows cold. [Ceres is the goddess of agriculture, Bacchus the god of wine, and Venus the goddess of love. The implication of this and the next proverb is that without food and wine a man loses his desire to make love]
3. If it wasn't for meat and good drink, the women might gnaw the sheets.
4. Wine and youth increase love.
5. Beauty's sister is vanity, and its daughter lust.
6. The postern door makes thief and whore. [The implication is that the back door of a house provides the necessary concealment for dishonest servants and unfaithful wives]

*Its effects*

7. When the heart is full of lust, the mouth's full of leasings. [A

reference to the lies told by a lustful person in order to win over the object of his desires]

8. Lechery and covetousness go together.
9. A lewd bachelor makes a jealous husband.
10. Grass grows not upon the highway. [A reference to the supposed barrenness of prostitutes]

### Its dangers

11. A libertine life is not a life of liberty.
12. Of the myriad vices lust is the worst. [Chinese proverb]
13. Hunting, hawking, and paramours, for one joy a hundred displeasures.
14. Dicing, drabbing and drinking bring men to destruction. [A "drab" is a prostitute]
15. Gaming, women, and wine, while they laugh, they make men pine.
16. Play, women, and wine undo men laughing.
17. Thieves and whores meet at the gallows.

### Its expense

18. Three things cost dear: the caresses of a dog, the love of a whore, and the invitation of a host.
19. Whores affect not you but your money.
20. Wine and wenches empty men's purses.
21. Whoring and bawdry do often end in beggary.
22. Women and wine, game and deceit, make the wealth small, and the wants great.
23. What is got over the devil's back is spent under his belly. [The implication is that ill-gotten gains are often squandered in dissolute living]

### Its universality

24. A man is known to be mortal by two things, sleep and lust.
25. Who has neither fools nor beggars nor whores among his kindred, was born of a stroke of thunder.
26. It is a poor kin that has neither whore nor thief in it.

### Whores

27. Once a whore and ever a whore.
28. A whore repents as often as water turns to sour milk. [Arabic proverb]
29. Never was strumpet fair.
30. A whore in a fine dress is like a clean entry to a dirty house.
31. Whoredom and grace dwelt ne'er in one place.

152

32. Whores and rogues always speak of their honour.

# 113 MARRIAGE

### Its advantages

1. He that is needy when he is married, shall be rich when he is buried.
2. Age and wedlock tames man and beast.
3. Single long, shame at length.
4. He who marries might be sorry; he who does not will be sorry.
5. The married man has many cares, the unmarried one many more.
6. A man without a wife is but half a man.
7. A good wife and health is a man's best wealth.
8. A cheerful wife is the joy of life.
9. A good wife's a goodly prize, saith Solomon the wise.
10. Two things do prolong thy life: a quiet heart and a loving wife.
11. As your wedding ring wears, your cares will wear away.

### Its disadvantages

12. Wedlock is a padlock.
13. A married man turns his staff into a stake. [The implication is that the staff carried by the unmarried man becomes, on marriage, a stake to which he is tethered]
14. A married woman has nothing of her own but her wedding-ring and her hair-lace.
15. Maids want nothing but husbands, and when they have them they want everything.
16. Wife and children are bills of charges.
17. Mills and wives are ever wanting.
18. It is hard to wive and thrive both in a year.
19. A young man married is a man that's marr'd. [William Shakespeare (1564–1616) *All's Well that Ends Well*]
20. He that has a wife, has strife.
21. Matrimony is a school in which one learns too late.

### Its undesirability

22. Advise none to marry or go to war.
23. Better hand loose than in an ill tethering. [The implication is that the freedom of celibacy is preferable to a bad marriage]
24. An ox, when he is loose, licks himself at pleasure. [A further reference to the freedom of celibacy]
25. Why buy a cow when milk is so cheap?
26. Honest men marry soon, wise men not at all.

27. Next to no wife, a good wife is best.
28. An ill marriage is a spring of ill fortune.
29. Better be half hanged, than ill wed.
30. Needles and pins, needles and pins: when a man marries his trouble begins.
31. Many a man sings that wife home brings; wist he what he brought, weep he might.
32. We bachelors laugh and show our teeth, but you married men laugh till your hearts ache.

*Its risks*

33. Marriage is a lottery.
34. Marriage makes or mars a man.
35. Marriage halves our griefs, doubles our joys, and quadruples our expenses.

*Its inevitability*

36. Marriages are made in heaven.
37. Marriage is destiny.
38. Hanging and wiving go by destiny.
39. A man may woo where he will, but he will wed where his hap is. [The implication is that a man has no freedom of choice when it comes to marriage]
40. Wives must be had, be they good or bad.

*The need for caution*

41. Marry in haste, and repent at leisure. [Modern corruptions of this proverb include "Marry in haste, and repent in the suburbs" and "Marry in haste, and repent at Reno" (Reno is an American city in which divorces may be easily obtained)]
42. Marriage rides upon the saddle and repentance upon the crupper.
43. In wiving and thriving a man should take counsel of all the world.
44. Keep your eyes wide open before marriage, and half shut afterwards.

*The importance of material well-being*

45. First thrive and then wive.
46. Before you marry, be sure of a house wherein to tarry.
47. More belongs to marriage, than four bare legs in a bed.
48. Bare walls make giddy housewives.
49. A house well-furnished makes a woman wise.
50. Toom pokes will strive. ["Toom" means "empty"; a "poke" is a bag or sack. The implication is that lack of food and money causes quarrels in a household]

51. Haste makes waste, and waste makes want, and want makes strife between the goodman and his wife.

*The dowry*

52. Better a portion in a wife than with a wife. ["Portion" means "dowry"]
53. A great dowry is a bed full of brambles.
54. He that marries for wealth, sells his liberty.
55. Never marry for money, ye'll borrow it cheaper.
56. Marry not an old crony, or a fool, for money.
57. Many a one for land takes a fool by the hand.
58. Money makes marriage.
59. A tocherless dame sits long at home. ["Tocherless" means "without a dowry"]
60. A poor beauty finds more lovers than husbands.
61. A poor man gets a poor marriage.

*Choosing a partner*

62. The good or ill hap of a good or ill life, is the good or ill choice of a good or ill wife.
63. In choosing a wife, and buying a sword, we ought not to trust another.
64. Refuse a wife with one fault, and take one with two. [The advice here is not to be too particular when choosing a wife]
65. A maid marries to please her parents; a widow to please herself.
66. He has fault of a wife, that marries mam's pet.
67. Take a vine of a good soil, and the daughter of a good mother.
68. It is good grafting on a good stock.
69. It is better to marry a shrew than a sheep.
70. One sheaf of a stook is enough. [The advice here is against marrying twice into the same family]
71. Better be an old man's darling than a young man's slave.
72. A young maid married to an old man is like a new house thatched with old straw.
73. Old men, when they marry young women, make much of death. [The implication is that when an old man embraces his young wife he embraces death, for she will bring him to an early grave]
74. An old man who weds a buxom young maiden, bids fair to become a freeman of Buckingham. ["Freeman of Buckingham" here means "cuckold"]
75. Better wed over the mixen than over the moor. [This implies that it is better to marry someone from one's own neighbourhood. The "mixen" or "midden" was a compost heap in the back yard]
76. Like blood, like good, and like age, make the happiest marriage.

77. Marry your like.
78. Better one house spoiled than two. [The implication is that two ill-tempered people should marry each other, so that only one household is marred by their presence]
79. Go down the ladder when you marry a wife; go up when you choose a friend.
80. A wife is sought for her virtue, a concubine for her beauty. [Chinese proverb]
81. Choose not a wife by the eye only.
82. Choose a wife by your ear rather than by your eye.
83. Choose a wife on a Saturday rather than a Sunday. [The implication is that on a Sunday women are dressed in their best clothes and are therefore not seen in their true light]
84. An ugly wife and a lean piece of ground protect the house. [Chinese proverb]
85. A fair wife and a frontier castle breed quarrels.
86. Who has a fair wife needs more than two eyes.
87. He that has a white horse and a fair wife, never wants trouble.

### The ideal time

88. He that marries ere he be wise, will die ere he thrive.
89. A young man should not marry yet, an old man not at all.
90. Early wed, early dead.
91. It is good to marry late or never.
92. He that marries late, marries ill.
93. It is time to set in, when the oven comes to the dough. [The implication of this and the next proverb is that the right time to marry is when the woman courts the man]
94. It is time to yoke, when the cart comes to the caples. ["Caples" means "horses"]
95. He is a fool that marries his wife at Yule, for when the corn's to shear the bairn's to bear.

### The husband's importance

96. A good husband makes a good wife.
97. When the goodman is from home, the good wife's table is soon spread. [The implication is that money for food will be short when the husband is away]
98. He is an ill husband who is not missed.
99. If the husband be not at home, there is nobody.

### The wife's importance

100. A good wife makes a good husband.

101. He that will thrive must ask leave of his wife. [A reference to the wife's responsibility for the household finances]
102. The wife is the key of the house.
103. The grey mare is the better horse. [The "grey mare" here signifies the wife]
104. The foot on the cradle and hand on the distaff is the sign of a good housewife.

## The dominant wife

105. He that has a wife has a master.
106. The most master wears no breech. [The implication is that the wife, who does not wear breeches or trousers, is the more dominant member of a household]
107. Where the mistress is the master, the parsley grows the faster.
108. An obedient wife commands her husband.
109. It is a sorry flock where the ewe bears the bell. [This implies that it is a sorry household where the wife is in command]
110. As the goodman says, so say we; but as the good wife says, so must it be.

## The scolding wife

111. Scolds and infants never lin bawling. ["Lin" means "cease"]
112. A groaning horse and a groaning wife never fail their master.
113. If a hen does not prate, she will not lay. [The implication is that a scolding wife is a good housewife]
114. A deaf husband and a blind wife are always a happy couple.
115. Husbands are in heaven whose wives scold not.
116. Wae's the wife that wants the tongue, but weel's the man that gets her. ["Wae's" means "woe is"]
117. It is a good horse that never stumbles, and a good wife that never grumbles.
118. It is a sad house where the hen crows louder than the cock.
119. Three things drive a man out of his house – smoke, rain, and a scolding wife.
120. Who has a scold, has sorrow to his sops.

## Handling one's wife

121. You may ding the devil into a wife, but you'll never ding him out of her. ["Ding" means "beat"]
122. If you make your wife an ass, she will make you an ox.
123. He that lets his horse drink at every lake, and his wife go to every wake, shall never be without a whore and a jade.

124. He that tells his wife news, is but newly married. [The implication is that it is unwise to confide in one's wife]
125. If you sell your purse to your wife, give your breeks into the bargain. [The warning here is that a wife who has control over her husband's money has total control in the household]

### Losing one's wife

126. He that loses his wife and sixpence, has lost a tester. ["Tester" is a former slang word for sixpence]
127. 'Tis a sweet sorrow to bury an outrageous wife.
128. A dead wife's the best goods in a man's house.

### The in-laws

129. Happy is she who marries the son of a dead mother.
130. She is well married, who has neither mother-in-law nor sister-in-law by her husband.
131. Mother-in-law and daughter-in-law are a tempest and hail storm.
132. The mother-in-law remembers not that she was a daughter-in-law.

### Marriage and love

133. Marriage is the tomb of love.
134. Love is a fair garden and marriage a field of nettles.
135. It is unlucky to marry for love.
136. Who marries for love without money, has good nights and sorry days.
137. Love is a flower which turns into fruit at marriage.
138. Marry first, and love will follow.
139. Where there's marriage without love, there will be love without marriage.

### Superstitions concerning marriage

140. A growing moon and a flowing tide are lucky times to marry in.
141. Marry in Lent, and you'll live to repent.
142. Marry in May, rue for aye.
143. They that marry in green, their sorrow is soon seen.
144. Happy is the bride the sun shines on, and the corpse the rain rains on.
145. Change your name but not the letter, change for worse, and not for better. [The implication is that it is unlucky for the initial letter of one's married name to be the same as that of one's maiden name]
146. If you carry a nutmeg in your pocket, you'll be married to an old man.
147. Two bachelors drinking to you at once; you'll soon be married.

148. One wedding brings another.

*Remarriage*

149. The first wife is matrimony, the second company, the third heresy.
150. Frequent remarriage gives room for scandal.
151. The woman who marries many is disliked by many.

*Marrying widows*

152. He that marries a widow and two children marries three thieves.
153. He that marries a widow, will often have a dead man's head thrown in his dish. [This and the next proverb refer to the unfavourable comparisons a widow may make between her old and new husbands]
154. Never marry a widow unless her first husband was hanged.
155. Marry a widow before she leaves mourning.
156. Take heed of a person marked and a widow thrice married.

*Marrying off one's children*

157. Building and marrying of children are great wasters. [A reference to the expense of wedding festivities]
158. Marry your daughter and eat fresh fish betimes. [The implication is that the marriage of one's daughter, like the eating of fresh fish, should be done as soon as possible]
159. Marry your daughters betimes, lest they marry themselves.
160. Marry your son when you will, your daughter when you can.

# 114 MIND

*Its importance*

1. The mind is the man.
2. What is a man but his mind?
3. A man is well or woe as he thinks himself so.
4. There is nothing either good or bad but thinking makes it so. [William Shakespeare (1564–1616) *Hamlet*]
5. A mind enlightened is like heaven; a mind in darkness is like hell. [Chinese proverb]
6. It is the riches of the mind only that make a man rich and happy.
7. If the brain sows not corn, it plants thistles.

*Changing one's mind*

8. A man will never change his mind if he has no mind to change.
9. A wise man changes his mind, a fool never.

10. A woman's mind and winter wind change oft.

*Freedom of thought*

11. Thought is free.
12. One may think that dares not speak.
13. The rope has never been made that binds thoughts.

*Misunderstanding*

14. Misunderstanding brings lies to town.
15. Who understands ill, answers ill.
16. Who wrong hears, wrong answer gives.
17. Ill hearing makes ill rehearsing.

*The power of reason*

18. Reason rules all things.
19. Reason binds the man.
20. Reason governs the wise man and cudgels the fool.
21. Hearken to reason, or she will be heard.
22. A man without reason is a beast in season.

See also EYES: *The eye and the mind*

# 115 MISERLINESS

*Its effects*

1. Avarice hoards itself poor; charity gives itself rich.
2. Little good comes of gathering.
3. If a man is a miser, he will certainly have a prodigal son.
4. Narrow gathered, widely spent.
5. He that measures oil shall anoint his fingers.
6. Sow thin and mow thin.
7. Nothing enters into a close hand.
8. Covetous men's chests are rich, not they.
9. Gold does not belong to the miser, but the miser to gold. [Arabic proverb]
10. Don't spoil the ship for a ha'porth of tar. [The warning here and in the following proverb is that refusing to make a small expense may result in great loss. The proverb originally referred to sheep (pronounced "ship" in certain parts of the country), and the use of tar to treat their wounds]
11. Many tine half-mark whinger for the halfpenny thong. ["Tine" means "lose"; a "whinger" is a small dagger]

### Characteristics of the miserly

12. Poverty wants many things, and avarice all.
13. A poor man wants some things, a covetous man all things.
14. Fools live poor to die rich.
15. Covetous men live drudges, to die wretches.
16. He that hoards up money, takes pains for other men.
17. A rich miser is poorer than a poor man. [Arabic proverb]
18. The covetous man is good to none and worst to himself.
19. The ass loaded with gold still eats thistles. [A reference to the refusal of the miser to spend money on personal luxuries]
20. The brother had rather see the sister rich than make her so.
21. The devil's mouth is a miser's purse.

### Avarice and age

22. Avarice is the only passion that never ages.
23. When all sins grow old, covetousness is young.
24. The older the bird the more unwillingly it parts with its feathers.

# 116 MODERATION

### Its value

1. Moderation in all things.
2. Measure is treasure.
3. Measure is medicine.
4. The half is better than the whole.
5. Measure is a merry mean.
6. The mean is the best.
7. Virtue is found in the middle.
8. Safety lies in the middle course.
9. It is good to be neither too high nor too low. [Chinese proverb]
10. Reason lies between the spur and the bridle.
11. Too much spoils, too little does not satisfy.
12. Soft fire makes sweet malt.
13. Love me little, love me long.

### Against excess

14. Better go away longing than loathing.
15. Leave off with an appetite.
16. Make not your sail too big for the ballast.
17. Sow with the hand, and not with the whole sack.
18. Take no more on than you're able to bear.

19. Do not all you can; spend not all you have; believe not all you hear; and tell not all you know.
20. Never take a stone to break an egg, when you can do it with the back of your knife.
21. Never draw your dirk when a dunt will do. ["Dunt" means "blow"]
22. Take not a musket to kill a butterfly.
23. Burn not your house to fright the mouse away.
24. There is measure in all things.
25. You can have too much of a good thing.

*The dangers of excess*

26. Too much of ought is good for nought.
27. Too much pudding will choke a dog.
28. Too much honey cloys the stomach.
29. If in excess even nectar is poison.
30. Mirth without measure is madness.
31. A little wind kindles, much puts out the fire.
32. He that forsakes measure, measure forsakes him.
33. He that measures not himself is measured.

*Extremes*

34. Every extremity is a fault.
35. Extreme law is extreme wrong. [The implication is that to apply a law to the letter, without taking any extenuating circumstances into account, is a form of injustice]
36. No extreme will hold long.
37. Extremes meet. [This and the following proverb imply that any virtue, belief, emotion, etc., indulged in to excess, may approach the opposite extreme. Thus a person may verge on extreme arrogance by being excessively humble]
38. Too far east is west.
39. From the sublime to the ridiculous is only a step.
40. Extremes are dangerous.

See also CONTENTMENT: *Having enough*

# 117 MONTHS

*January*

1. Who in Janiveer sows oats, gets gold and groats; who sows in May, gets little that way. ["Janiveer" is January]
2. If grass look green in Janiveer, 'twill look the worser all the year.

3. If one knew how good it were to eat a hen in Janivere; had he twenty in the flock, he'd leave but one to go with the cock.
4. At Twelfth Day the days are lengthened a cock-stride. [Twelfth Day is January 6th]
5. On St. Distaff's Day neither work nor play. [St. Distaff's Day (January 7th) is so called because it is the day when work is resumed after the Christmas festivities]
6. Yule is come and Yule is gone, and we have feasted well; so Jack must to his flail again, and Jenny to her wheel.

*February*

7. Februeer doth cut and shear.
8. On Candlemas Day, you must have half your straw and half your hay. [Candlemas Day is February 2nd]
9. On Candlemas Day, throw candle and candlestick away. [A reference to a religious custom. Candles were not used at vespers and litanies between Candlemas Day and All Saints' Day (November 1st)]
10. Sow or set beans in Candlemas waddle. ["Waddle" means "wane of the moon"]
11. On St. Valentine, all the birds of the air in couples do join. [St. Valentine's Day is February 14th]
12. St. Valentine, set thy hopper by mine. [A "hopper" is a seed-basket]
13. On St. Valentine's Day cast beans in clay, but on St. Chad sow good or bad. [St. Chad's Day is March 2nd]
14. On Valentine's Day, will a good goose lay; if she be a good goose, her dame well to pay, she will lay two eggs before Valentine's Day.
15. St. Matthee shut up the bee. [A reference to St. Matthias's Day (February 24th)]
16. St. Matthi lay candlesticks by.
17. St. Matthie sends sap into the tree.
18. St. Mattho, take thy hopper, and sow.

*March*

19. March borrowed from April three days, and they were ill. [A reference to bad weather in March]
20. March comes in like a lion and goes out like a lamb.
21. March comes in with adder heads and goes out with peacock tails.
22. In March, kill crow, pie, and cadow, rook, buzzard, and raven; or else go desire them to seek a new haven. ["Pie" means "magpie"; "cadow" means "jackdaw"]
23. In March, the birds begin to search; in April the corn begins to fill; in May, the birds begin to lay.
24. If you kill one flea in March, you kill a hundred.
25. On the first of March, the crows begin to search.

26. St. David's Day, put oats and barley in the clay. [St. David's Day is March 1st]
27. David and Chad: sow peas good or bad. [St. Chad's Day is March 2nd]
28. Before St. Chad every goose lays, both good and bad.
29. First comes David, next comes Chad, and then comes Winneral as though he were mad. ["Winneral" refers to St. Winwaloe's Day (March 3rd)]
30. St. Benedick, sow thy pease, or keep them in thy rick. [St. Benedict's Day is March 21st]
31. Salmon and sermon have their season in Lent.
32. Marry in Lent, and you'll live to repent.
33. On Mothering Sunday, above all other, every child should dine with its mother.
34. At Easter, let your clothes be new, or else be sure you will it rue.
35. When Easter Day lies in our Lady's lap, then, O England, beware of a clap. ["Lady" refers to the Feast of the Annunciation, or Lady Day (March 25th). It is apparently a bad omen for Easter Day to fall on this date]

### April

36. On the first of April, you may send a fool whither you will.
37. On the first of April, hunt the gowk another mile. ["Gowk" means "fool"]
38. The cuckoo comes in April, and stays the month of May; sings a song at midsummer, and then goes away.
39. On the third of April comes in the cuckoo and nightingale.
40. The cuckoo goes to Beaulieu Fair to buy him a greatcoat. [Beaulieu Fair was held on April 15th, the day when the cuckoo was supposed to arrive, contrary to the implications of the preceding proverb]
41. Mackerel's in season when Balaam's ass speaks in church. [A reference to the lesson for the second Sunday after Easter (Numbers 22), which concerns Balaam and his ass]
42. If they blow in April, you'll have your fill; but if in May, they'll all go away. [A reference to the blossoming of fruit trees]

### May

43. A swarm in May is worth a load of hay; a swarm in June is worth a silver spoon; but a swarm in July is not worth a fly.
44. May makes or mars the wheat.
45. Set sage in May, and it will grow alway.
46. Shear your sheep in May, and shear them all away.
47. He that is in a town in May, loses his spring.

48. May-day, pay-day, pack rags and go away. [A reference to the hiring of workers on May 1st]
49. A May cold is a thirty-day cold. [The implication is that colds caught in May are hard to shake off]
50. He that is hanged in May, will eat no flannes in midsummer. ["Flannes" are custards or pancakes]
51. Marry in May, rue for aye.
52. May birds come cheeping. [The implication is that children born in May are sickly and unhealthy]
53. May never goes out without a wheat-ear.
54. Be it weal or be it woe, beans blow before May does go.
55. Ne'er cast a clout till May be out. [The advice here is not to discard winter clothing until the end of May or, following an erroneous alternative interpretation, until the may (hawthorn) blossom appears]

*June*

56. If you look at your corn in May, you'll come weeping away; if you look at the same in June, you'll come home in another tune.
57. He who bathes in May, will soon be laid in clay; he who bathes in June, will sing a merry tune.
58. Barnaby bright, Barnaby bright, the longest day and the shortest night. [Before the calendar reform of 1752, St. Barnabas's Day (June 11th) was the longest day of the year]

*July*

59. Till St. James's Day be come and gone, you may have hops or you may have none. [St. James's Day is July 25th]

*August*

60. After Lammas corn ripens as much by night as by day. [Lammas is August 1st]
61. St. Bartholomew brings the cold dew. [St. Bartholomew's Day is August 24th]

*September*

62. September blow soft, till the fruit's in the loft.
63. On Holyrood Day the devil goes a-nutting. [Holyrood Day is September 14th]
64. St. Matthew get candlesticks new. [St. Matthew's Day is September 21st]
65. Michaelmas chickens and parsons' daughters never come to good. [Michaelmas is September 29th]
66. The Michaelmas moon rises aye alike soon.

67. Michaelmas rot comes never in the pot. [A reference to sheep afflicted with the liver disease known as "rot"]
68. The devil sets his foot on the blackberries on Michaelmas Day.

*October*

69. On St. Luke's Day the oxen have leave to play. [St. Luke's Day is October 18th. The ox was once the symbol of St. Luke]
70. Simon and Jude all the ships on the sea home they do crowd. [The feast day of SS. Simon and Jude is October 28th]

*November*

71. November take flail; let ship no more sail. [The advice is that in November the thresher should take up his flail, and sailors should not venture out to sea]
72. On the first of November, if the weather holds clear, an end of wheat-sowing do make for this year.
73. Set trees at Allhallontide and command them to prosper; set them after Candlemas and entreat them to grow. [Allhallontide (All Hallows) is the first week in November]
74. St. Andrew the King, three weeks and three days before Christmas comes in. [St. Andrew's Day is November 30th]

*December*

75. On Lady Day the latter, the cold comes on the water. [A reference to the Festival of the Conception (December 8th)]
76. St. Thomas gray! St. Thomas gray! the longest night and the shortest day. [St. Thomas's Day is December 21st]
77. On St. Thomas the Divine kill all turkeys, geese, and swine.
78. Blessed be St. Stephen, there is no fast upon his even. [St. Stephen's Day is December 26th]
79. If you bleed your nag on St. Stephen's Day, he'll work your work for ever and aye.

See also WEATHER

# 118 NAMES

*Their importance*

1. A man lives a generation; a name to the end of all generations. [Japanese proverb]
2. Names and natures do often agree.

3. Names are debts. [The implication is that a person is obliged to live according to the meaning of his name]

*Their unimportance*

4. What's in a name? [This and the following proverb are quotations from William Shakespeare's *Romeo and Juliet*]
5. A rose by any other name would smell as sweet.
6. Man dies and leave a name; the tiger dies and leaves a skin. [Chinese proverb]

See also ENGLAND: *English names*; FAME: *The value of a good reputation*

# 119 NATURE

*Her power*

1. Nature draws more than ten teams.
2. Nature will have her course.
3. Fix thy pale in Severn, Severn will be as before. [A reference to the river Severn, implying the futility of any attempt to alter the course of Nature]
4. Let Uther-Pendragon do what he can, the river Eden will run as it ran. [Uther-Pendragon was a legendary Welsh prince, who is said to have attempted to change the course of the river Eden in order to fortify his castle]

*Her wisdom*

5. Nature is the true law.
6. Nature does nothing in vain.
7. Nature is no botcher.
8. Nature, time, and patience are the three great physicians.
9. He that follows Nature, is never out of his way.

*Other characteristics*

10. Nature abhors a vacuum.
11. Nature hates all sudden changes.
12. Nature is content with a little.
13. Nature is conquered by obeying her.

*Nature and art*

14. Art improves Nature.

15. Nature passes art. ["Passes" here means "surpasses"]
16. That which Nature paints never fades.

# 120 NECESSITY

*Its power*

1. Necessity knows no law.
2. Necessity is a powerful weapon.
3. There is no such conquering weapon as the necessity of conquering.
4. Necessity breaks iron.
5. Necessity has no holiday.
6. Needs must when the devil drives.

*Its effects*

7. Necessity is the mother of invention.
8. Necessity and opportunity may make a coward valiant.

# 121 NEIGHBOURS

*Their importance*

1. No one is rich enough to do without his neighbour.
2. We can live without our friends, but not without our neighbours.
3. Choose your neighbour before your house and your companion before the road. [Arabic proverb]
4. You must ask your neighbour if you shall live in peace.
5. A good neighbour, a good morrow.
6. To have a good neighbour is to find something precious. [Chinese proverb]
7. A near neighbour is better than a far-dwelling kinsman.
8. All is well with him who is beloved of his neighbours.
9. It is not as thy mother says, but as thy neighbours say.
10. He who wants to know himself should offend two or three of his neighbours.

*Bad neighbours*

11. An ill neighbour is an ill thing.
12. A great man and a great river are often ill neighbours.
13. A good lawyer, an evil neighbour.
14. He's an ill neighbour that is not missed.

*Privacy*

15. Love your neighbour, yet pull not down your hedge.
16. A hedge between keeps friendship green.
17. Good fences make good neighbours.
18. An Englishman's home is his castle. [Variants of this proverb substitute "man" for "Englishman" or "house" for "home"]

# 122 NEWS

*Good news*

1. No news is good news.
2. He that brings good news, knocks hard.

*Bad news*

3. Bad news travels fast.
4. Ill news comes apace.
5. Ill news comes unsent for.
6. Ill news never comes too late.
7. Ill news comes often on the back of worse.
8. Ill news is too often true.

*Hearing news*

9. If you will learn news, you must go to the oven or the mill.
10. Go abroad and you'll hear news of home.
11. Stay a little, and news will find you.

*Telling news*

12. Good news may be told at any time, but ill in the morning.
13. He that tells his wife news, is but newly married.

# 123 OBEDIENCE

*Its value*

1. Obedience is the mother of success.
2. He that cannot obey, cannot command.
3. Do as you're bidden and you'll never bear blame.

*Its effects*

4. An obedient wife commands her husband.

169

5. Obedience is much more seen in little things than in great.
6. Nature is conquered by obeying her.

*Its necessity*

7. Obedience is the first duty of a soldier.
8. They that are bound must obey.
9. Do as I say, not as I do.
10. Do as the friar says, not as he does.

*Disobedience*

11. Forbid a thing, and that women will do.
12. Forbidden fruit is sweet.
13. That which one most foreheets, soonest comes to pass. ["Foreheets" means "forbids"]

# 124 OCCUPATIONS

*The value of a trade*

1. Who hath a good trade, through all waters may wade.
2. Who has a trade, has a share everywhere.
3. He who has an art, has everywhere a part.
4. They that can cobble and clout, shall have work when others go without.
5. Trade is the mother of money.
6. A handful of trade is a handful of gold.
7. A useful trade is a mine of gold.
8. An occupation is as good as land.
9. He that learns a trade, has a purchase made.
10. Virtue and a trade are the best portion for children.
11. He that has no good trade, it is to his loss.
12. A trade is better than service.
13. A man of many trades, begs his bread on Sunday. [This and the following two proverbs imply that to specialize in one trade is far more profitable than to dabble in many]
14. A dozen trades, thirteen miseries.
15. Jack of all trades, master of none.

*The need for tradesmen*

16. If things did not break, or wear out, how would tradesmen live?
17. Let all trades live. [A remark made when something is accidentally broken, referring to the sentiments of the preceding proverb]
18. Tradesmen live upon lack.

*Rivalry between trades*

19. Two of a trade never agree.
20. One potter envies another.
21. A vinegar seller does not like another vinegar seller. [Arabic proverb]

*Sticking to one's trade*

22. Let the cobbler stick to his last.
23. The gunner to his linstock, and the steersman to the helm.
24. Every man to his trade.

*Millers and bakers*

25. Millers are the last to die of famine. [The implication is that the miller always steals a little from the grain brought to him to be ground. The following proverbs all refer to the alleged dishonesty of millers and bakers]
26. Millers and bakers do not steal: people bring it to them.
27. Three dear years will raise a baker's daughter to a portion.
28. The miller is honest who has hair on his teeth.
29. What is bolder than a miller's neck-cloth, which takes a thief by the neck every morning?
30. Put a miller, a weaver, and a tailor in a bag, and shake them; the first that comes out will be a thief.

*Tailors*

31. Tailors and writers must mind the fashion.
32. The tailor must cut three sleeves to every woman's gown. [This and the following proverbs refer to the alleged dishonesty of tailors]
33. A hundred tailors, a hundred millers, and a hundred weavers are three hundred thieves.
34. Never trust a tailor that does not sing at his work.
35. There is knavery in all trades, but most in tailors.

*Nurses*

36. Nurses put one bit in the child's mouth and two in their own.
37. One year a nurse, and seven years the worse.
38. The nurse is valued till the child has done sucking.
39. The nurse's tongue is privileged to talk.

*Sailors*

40. Sailors' fingers must all be fish-hooks.
41. Sailors have a port in every storm.
42. Sailors go round the world without going into it.

43. Sailors get money like horses, and spend it like asses.
44. Seamen are the nearest to death, the furthest from God.
45. A seaman, if he carries a millstone, will have a quart out of it. [A reference to the drinking habits of sailors]

*Soldiers*

46. Nails are not made from good iron, nor soldiers from good men. [Chinese proverb]
47. To take from a soldier ambition, is to take off his spurs.
48. Old soldiers never die, they simply fade away.
49. Soldiers in peace are like chimneys in summer.
50. The blood of the soldier makes the glory of the general.
51. Soldiers fight, and kings are heroes. [Hebrew proverb]
52. It is better to have no son than one who is a soldier. [Chinese proverb]

See also HEALTH: *Doctors*; LAW: *Lawyers, Judges*; SERVANTS

# 125 OLD PEOPLE

*Their wisdom*

1. An old man's sayings are seldom untrue.
2. If you wish good advice, consult an old man.
3. If the old dog bark, he gives counsel.
4. An old dog barks not in vain.
5. The devil knows many things because he is old.
6. Years know more than books.
7. It is good to follow the old fox.
8. The ox when weariest treads surest.
9. Let aye the belled wether break the snow. [A "belled wether" is a ram with a bell tied round its neck. The implication of this and the two preceding proverbs is that it is best to follow the lead of the old and experienced]
10. Old foxes want no tutors.
11. An old fox is not easily snared.
12. You cannot catch old birds with chaff.
13. No playing with a straw before an old cat.
14. An old knave is no babe.
15. No knave to the old knave.
16. Put an old cat to an old rat. [This implies that only the experience of the old can match the wiliness of their contemporaries]

*Their value*

17. There is beild aneath an auld man's beard. ["Beild" means "shelter"]
18. An old wise man's shadow is better than a young buzzard's sword.
19. It is good sheltering under an old hedge.
20. The best wine comes out of an old vessel.
21. There's many a good tune played on an old fiddle.
22. Good broth may be made in an old pot.
23. An old cart well used may outlast a new one abused.
24. An old man in a house is a good sign.
25. An old ox makes a straight furrow. [A reference to the value of an old person's experience]

*Their uselessness*

26. When bees are old, they yield no honey.
27. Old cattle breed not.
28. An old man is a bed full of bones.
29. Old vessels must leak.

*Their folly*

30. There's no fool like an old fool.
31. The brains don't lie in the beard.
32. Old age doesn't protect from folly.
33. Both folly and wisdom come upon us with years.
34. Though old and wise, yet still advise. ["Advise" here means "seek advice"]
35. Never too old to learn.
36. Old men are twice children.

*Their infirmities*

37. Old age is sickness of itself.
38. Old age is a hospital that takes in all diseases.
39. A hundred disorders has old age.
40. Old age is a malady of which one dies.
41. Old churches have dim windows. [A reference to the failing eyesight of the old]

*Their influence*

42. As the old cock crows, so crows the young.
43. The young pig grunts like the old sow.
44. Where old age is evil, youth can learn no good.

*Their tales*

45. When the teeth fall out, the tongue wags loose. [Chinese proverb]
46. An old man never wants a tale to tell.
47. Old men and travellers may lie by authority.
48. Old wives were aye good maidens. [A reference to old people's boasts of past virtue]

*Handling the old*

49. An old ox will find a shelter for himself.
50. He wrongs not an old man that steals his supper from him. [The implication is that the old should not be overfed]
51. Remove an old tree and it will wither to death. [A warning against forcing old people to move house]
52. You can't teach an old dog new tricks. [This implies that old people, who are set in their ways, cannot cope with new ideas]
53. An old dog bites sore. [The advice here is not to provoke an old person]

*The generation gap*

54. Youth and age will never agree.
55. Young men think old men fools, and old men know young men to be so.
56. The old cow thinks she was never a calf.

*The inevitability of old age*

57. Old age comes stealing on.
58. You cannot have two forenoons in the same day.
59. Old be, or young die.
60. If you would not live to be old, you must be hanged when you are young.

*Old age and death*

61. They that live longest, must die at last.
62. The cure for old age is the grave.
63. The more thy years, the nearer thy grave.
64. An old man's staff is the rapper of death's door.
65. Death sends his challenge in a grey hair. [Arabic proverb]
66. Grey hairs are death's blossoms.
67. Of young men die many, of old men scape not any.
68. Young men may die, but old must die.
69. Old men go to death, death comes to young men.

70. The old man has his death before his eyes; the young man behind his back.
71. When age is jocund, it makes sport for death.
72. None so old that he hopes not for a year of life.
73. When an old man will not drink, go to see him in another world. [The implication is that death is at hand when an old person refuses a drink]

See also CHILDREN: *The recklessness of youth*


# 126 OPPORTUNITY

*Making the most of opportunities*

1. Opportunity seldom knocks twice.
2. Christmas comes but once a year.
3. Make hay while the sun shines.
4. Strike while the iron is hot.
5. Hoist your sail when the wind is fair.
6. Gather ye rosebuds while ye may. [Robert Herrick (1591–1674) *Hesperides*]
7. Put out your tubs when it is raining.
8. If heaven drops a date, open your mouth. [Chinese proverb]
9. Take the goods the gods provide.
10. When the shoulder of mutton is going, 'tis good to take a slice.
11. Make not a balk of good ground. [A "balk" is a ridge of land left unploughed]
12. The tide must be taken when it comes.
13. Time and tide wait for no man.
14. Take time by the forelock.
15. Take time when time comes.
16. Life is short and time is swift.
17. An occasion lost cannot be redeemed.
18. The mill cannot grind with the water that is past.
19. He that will not when he may, when he will he shall have nay.
20. When fortune smiles, embrace her.


# 127 OPTIMISM

*Optimistic attitudes*

1. Look on the bright side.
2. When one door shuts, another opens.
3. There are as good fish in the sea as ever came out of it.

4. When the sun sets, the moon rises; when the moon sets, the sun rises. [Chinese proverb]
5. Bode good, and get it. ["Bode" means "expect"]
6. Nothing so bad but it might have been worse.
7. Nothing is to be presumed on, or despaired of.
8. God's in his heaven; all's right with the world.
9. All is for the best in the best of all possible worlds. [The sentiments of this proverb were expressed in Voltaire's *Candide* (1759), satirizing the optimistic doctrine of Leibnitz]

*Things will improve*

10. He that falls today may rise tomorrow.
11. It will all come right in the wash.
12. When things are at the worst they begin to mend.
13. There is a good time coming.
14. All is not lost that is in danger.
15. The darkest hour is that before the dawn.
16. A foul morning may turn to a fair day.
17. Cloudy mornings turn to clear afternoons.
18. After black clouds, clear weather.
19. After a storm comes a calm.

*Nothing is all bad*

20. Every cloud has a silver lining.
21. It's an ill wind that blows nobody any good.
22. It's a hard-fought field, where no man escapes unkilled.
23. It is an ill bargain where no man wins.
24. There is good land where there is foul way.
25. Ill for the rider, good for the abider. [The implication of this and the preceding proverb is that the most fertile land is usually muddy and thus inconvenient for the rider]
26. Of evil manners, spring good laws.
27. After a typhoon there are pears to gather up.
28. No great loss but some small profit. ["But" here means "without"]
29. Ill luck is good for something.
30. Nothing but is good for something.
31. Nothing so bad in which there is not something of good.
32. The bee sucks honey out of the bitterest flowers.

*Nothing is permanent*

33. All wrong will end.
34. Nothing that is violent is permanent.
35. All that is sharp is short.

36. The sharper the storm, the sooner it's over.
37. Be the day never so long, at length comes evensong.
38. The longest day has an end.
39. The longest night will have an end.
40. Even the weariest river winds somewhere safe to sea.
41. It is a long lane that has no turning.
42. The tide never goes out so far but it always comes in again.

See also HOPE

## 128 PARENTS

*Their importance*

1. God, and parents, and our master, can never be requited.
2. A father's goodness is higher than the mountains; a mother's goodness is deeper than the sea. [Japanese proverb]
3. One father is enough to govern one hundred sons, but not a hundred sons one father.
4. One father is more than a hundred schoolmasters.
5. An ounce of mother is worth a ton of priest.
6. A man's mother is his other God. [African proverb]

*Their influence*

7. Parents are patterns.
8. Like father, like son.
9. Like mother, like daughter.
10. The birth follows the belly. [The implication of this and the next proverb is that the mother is likely to have a greater influence than the father over the child]
11. The mother's side is the surest.
12. The hand that rocks the cradle rules the world.

*Their subjectivity*

13. He whose father is judge, goes safe to his trial.
14. The owl thinks her own young fairest.
15. There's only one pretty child in the world, and every mother has it.
16. It is not as thy mother says, but as thy neighbours say.

*The mother's kindness*

17. The good mother says not, 'Will you?' but gives.
18. The mother's breath is aye sweet.

*Old parents*

19. The old pearl-oyster produces a pearl. [Chinese proverb]
20. Late children, early orphans.
21. The offspring of those that are very old, or very young, lasts not.

*Step-parents*

22. With the arrival of the stepmother the father becomes a stepfather. [Afghan proverb]
23. Take heed of a stepmother: the very name of her suffices.
24. Put another man's child in your bosom, and he'll creep out at your elbow. [The implication is that a child will never have any natural affection for an adoptive or step-parent]

See also CHARACTER: *Hereditary influences*; LOVE: *Parental love*

# 129 PASSION

*Its sources*

1. There is no heat of affection, but is joined with some idleness of brain.
2. A man is a lion in his own cause.

*Its effects*

3. Glowing coals sparkle oft.
4. When the heart is a fire, some sparks will fly out of the mouth.
5. He that burns most, shines most.
6. Hot love, hasty vengeance.
7. The end of passion is the beginning of repentance.
8. Hot love is soon cold.
9. Soon hot, soon cold.
10. Nothing that is violent is permanent.
11. After a storm comes a calm.
12. No man can guess in cold blood what he may do in a passion.
13. To a boiling pot, flies come not.
14. The stream stopped swells the higher. [This and the following proverb refer to the effect of suppressing passion]
15. Fire that's closest kept burns most of all.

*Its value*

16. He freezes who does not burn.
17. Never do things by halves.

*Its dangers*

18. Zeal without knowledge is a runaway horse.
19. Zeal is fit only for wise men, but is found mostly in fools.
20. Zeal without prudence is frenzy.
21. Mettle is dangerous in a blind horse.
22. Zeal, when it is a virtue, is a dangerous one.
23. Serving one's own passions is the greatest slavery.

# 130 PATIENCE

*Its importance*

1. Patience is a virtue.
2. Let patience grow in your garden alway. ["Patience" was a popular name for a species of dock, *Rumex patientia*. Hence the reference to the garden in this and the next proverb]
3. Patience is a flower that grows not in every one's garden.
4. Patience is the best buckler against affronts.
5. Patience surpasses learning.
6. Patience is the knot which secures the seam of victory. [Chinese proverb]
7. Patience is the key of joy, but haste is the key of sorrow. [Arabic proverb]
8. Though God take the sun out of heaven, yet we must have patience.
9. He that will be served, must be patient.
10. They also serve who only stand and wait. [John Milton (1608–74) *On His Blindness*]

*Its rewards*

11. Patient men win the day.
12. The world is for him who has patience.
13. Everything comes to him who waits.
14. Long looked for comes at last.
15. Be still, and have thy will.
16. He that can stay, obtains.
17. Patience, time, and money accommodate all things.
18. He that has patience, has fat thrushes for a farthing.
19. Who has no haste in his business, mountains to him seem valleys.
20. The hindmost dog may catch the hare.
21. With patience the mulberry leaf becomes a silk gown. [Chinese proverb]
22. With the trowel of patience we dig out the roots of truth.
23. It is in the garden of patience that strength grows best.

*Its dangers*

24. Patience provoked turns to fury.
25. The string of a man's sack of patience is generally tied with a slip knot.
26. Patience under old injuries invites new ones. [This implies that to tolerate injuries or insults with patience may provoke further attack]

*Patience as a remedy*

27. Patience is the remedy of the world.
28. Patience is a remedy for every grief.
29. Patience is a plaster for all sores.
30. No remedy but patience.
31. Patience with poverty is all a poor man's remedy.
32. Nature, time, and patience are the three great physicians.

*Against impatience*

33. A little impatience will spoil great plans. [Chinese proverb]
34. A watched pot never boils. [The implication is that time appears to pass more slowly when one is impatiently waiting for something to happen]
35. Rome was not built in a day. [This and the following proverbs are aimed at those who are impatient to see the results of their labours]
36. A strong town is not won in an hour.
37. An oak is not felled at one stroke.
38. No man is his craft's master the first day.
39. All things are difficult before they are easy.
40. Children learn to creep ere they can go.
41. First creep, and then go.
42. We must learn to walk before we can run.
43. Learn to say before you sing.
44. First things first.
45. He who would climb the ladder must begin at the bottom.

# 131 PAYING

*Its necessity*

1. Mills will not grind if you give them not water.
2. As good play for nought as work for nought.
3. Work for nought makes folks dead sweir. ["Sweir" means "lazy"]
4. Service without reward is punishment.

## Its effects

5. Corn him well, he'll work the better. [This proverb originally referred to horses, but it can also be applied in a wider sense to any person whose industriousness is directly related to the size of his fee]
6. The purse of the patient protracts the disease. [Contrary to the sentiments of the preceding proverb, this implies that those who are being well paid for their work may draw it out longer than is necessary]
7. Wage will get a page.
8. Merry is the feast-making till we come to the reckoning.
9. Sweet appears sour when we pay.
10. The reckoning spoils the relish.

## The dangers of not paying

11. He that cannot pay, let him pray.
12. He must pay with his body that cannot pay with money.
13. He that cannot pay in purse must pay in person.
14. If you pay not a servant his wages, he will pay himself.

## Methods of payment

15. Pay beforehand was never well served.
16. Pay beforehand and your work will be behindhand.
17. Payment in advance is evil payment.
18. He who wants the work badly done has only to pay in advance.
19. He that pays last never pays twice.
20. The best payment is on the peck bottom. [A "peck" was a vessel used for measuring grain. The implication is that it is best to receive immediate payment for one's wares]
21. It is best to take half in hand and the rest by and by.

## Good and bad payers

22. A good payer is master of another's purse.
23. A good paymaster needs no surety.
24. A good paymaster never wants workmen.
25. A good paymaster may build Paul's. [A reference to St. Paul's Cathedral in London]
26. If you pay peanuts, you get monkeys.
27. An ill paymaster never wants excuse.
28. Sore cravers are aye ill payers. [The implication is that those who are most earnest to obtain something are least prompt in paying for it]
29. Trust is dead, ill payment killed it.

*Privileges of the one who pays*

30. He who pays the piper calls the tune.
31. Let him that pays the lawing choose the lodging. ["Lawing" means "reckoning"]

*The mercenary*

32. He that serves God for money, will serve the devil for better wages.
33. Virtue flies from the heart of a mercenary man.

See also BORROWING: *Repayment of debts*


# 132 PEACE

*Its value*

1. Where there is peace, God is.
2. To live peaceably with all breeds good blood.
3. Peace makes plenty.
4. By wisdom peace, by peace plenty.
5. The secret wall of a town is peace.

*War and peace*

6. He that will not have peace, God gives him war.
7. If you want peace, you must prepare for war.
8. Clothe thee in war: arm thee in peace.
9. A just war is better than an unjust peace.
10. He that makes a good war, makes a good peace.
11. Better a lean peace than a fat victory.
12. Better an egg in peace than an ox in war.
13. War makes thieves, and peace hangs them.
14. Of all wars, peace is the end.
15. It is a great victory that comes without blood.

*Making peace*

16. The stick is the surest peacemaker. [The implication of this and the following proverbs is that peace can best be achieved by violence or by the threat of violence]
17. 'Tis safest making peace with sword in hand.
18. Weapons breed peace.
19. One sword keeps another in the sheath.

# 133 PEOPLE AND PLACES

## Africa

1. Africa always brings something new.
2. The African race is an indiarubber ball; the harder you dash it to the ground, the higher it will rise. [African proverb]
3. The riches of Egypt are for the foreigners therein. [Arabic proverb. A reference to the fact that most of Egypt's rulers were foreigners]
4. Truly at weaving wiles the Egyptians are clever.

## Asia

5. In China we have only three religions, but we have a hundred dishes we can make from rice. [Chinese proverb. Compare ENGLAND: 11]
6. In China are more tutors than scholars, and more physicians than patients. [Chinese proverb]
7. A Chinaman is ill only once in his life, and that is when he is dying. [Russian proverb]
8. If a Bengali is a man, what is a devil? [Indian proverb]
9. The more you plunder a Turk the richer he is.
10. Where the Turk's horse once treads, the grass never grows. [A reference to the destructive power of the former Turkish empire]
11. The tyranny of the Turk is better than the justice of the Arab. [Arabic proverb]
12. The understanding of an Arab is in his eyes. [Arabic proverb]

## Europe

13. The emperor of Germany is the king of kings; the king of Spain, king of men; the king of France, king of asses; the king of England, the king of devils.
14. The Italians are wise before the deed, the Germans in the deed, the French after the deed.
15. In settling an island, the first building erected by a Spaniard will be a church; by a Frenchman, a fort; by a Dutchman, a warehouse; and by an Englishman, an alehouse.
16. Learn in Italy; clothe yourself in Germany; flirt in France; banquet in Poland.
17. In Spain, the lawyer; in Italy, the doctor; in France, the flirt; in Germany, the artisan; in England, the merchant; in the Balkans, the thief; in Turkey, the soldier; in Poland, a Treasury official; in Moscow, the liar – can all make a living.
18. Malta would be a delightful place if every priest were a tree.
19. Every Czech is a musician.

20. Finland is the devil's country. [A reference to the physical geography of the country, rather than to its inhabitants]

### France

21. France is a meadow that cuts thrice a year.
22. He that will France win, must with Scotland first begin.
23. The day of France's ruin, is the eve of the ruin of England.
24. Every French soldier carries a marshal's baton in his knapsack. [This saying has been attributed both to Louis XVIII (1755–1824) and to Napoleon Bonaparte (1769–1821)]
25. The French would be the best cooks in Europe if they had got any butcher's meat.
26. Have the Frenchman for thy friend, not for thy neighbour.
27. The Frenchman is a scoundrel.
28. The English love; the French make love.
29. When the Ethiopian is white, the French will love the English.
30. The friendship of the French is like their wine, exquisite but of short duration.
31. Only a dog and a Frenchman walks after he has eaten.
32. Good Americans, when they die, go to Paris.
33. The Bourbons learn nothing and forget nothing. [The Bourbons were a ruling family of France and Spain]

### Italy

34. The Englishman Italianate is a devil incarnate.
35. All things are to be bought at Rome.
36. Genoa has mountains without wood, sea without fish, women without shame, and men without conscience.
37. See Naples and die. [A reference to the beauty of Naples and its environs]
38. The Neapolitan is wide-mouthed and narrow-handed. ["Narrow-handed" here means "tight-fisted, mean"]
39. A man would live in Italy, but he would choose to die in Spain. [The implication is that while Italy is the more pleasant place to live, the Catholic religion is more strictly practised in Spain]

### Spain and Portugal

40. Nothing ill in Spain but that which speaks.
41. The Spaniard is a bad servant, but a worse master.
42. The Basque is faithful.
43. He who has not seen Seville, has not seen a wonder.
44. A bad Spaniard makes a good Portuguese. [This implies that the best of the Portuguese are no better than the worst Spaniards]

45. A blue eye in a Portuguese woman is a mistake of nature.

### Germany

46. When a snake gets warm on ice, then a German will wish well to a Czech.
47. The German's wit is in his fingers. [The implication is that a German's practical skills are superior to his intellectual ability]

### Holland

48. The Netherlands are the cockpit of Christendom. ["Cockpit" here refers to an area of civil strife and war. "The Netherlands" is used in the historical sense of "the Low Countries", namely Holland, Belgium, and Luxembourg]
49. God made the earth but the Dutch made Holland.

### Hungary

50. Outside Hungary there is no life; if there is any it is not the same.
51. Where there is a Hungarian there is anger; where there is a Slovak there is a song.
52. Do not trust a Hungarian unless he has a third eye on his forehead.

### Poland

53. Poland is the peasant's hell, the Jew's paradise, the citizen's purgatory, the noble's heaven, and the grave of the stranger's gold.
54. What an Englishman cares to invent, a Frenchman to design, or a German to patch together, the stupid Pole will buy.
55. When God made the world He sent to the Poles some reason and the feet of a gnat, but even this little was taken away by a woman.
56. God save us from a Polish bridge!

### Russia

57. In Russia as one must; in Poland as one wishes. [This Polish proverb was coined in the days of Russian serfdom]
58. Russian friendship does not get sour.
59. The cold is Russia's cholera.
60. Scratch a Russian and you'll find a Tartar.
61. If you can deal with an Armenian, you can deal with the devil. [Persian proverb]
62. Trust a snake before a Jew, a Jew before a Greek, but never trust an Armenian.

*Greece*

63. After shaking hands with a Greek, count your fingers.
64. The Greeks only tell the truth once a year.

*Britain*

65. All countries stand in need of Britain, and Britain of none.
66. An Englishman is never happy but when he is miserable, a Scotchman never at home but when he is abroad, and an Irishman never at peace but when he is fighting.
67. The Englishman weeps, the Irishman sleeps, but the Scottishman gangs while he gets it. ["Gangs while" means "goes until". The proverb is supposed to refer to the behaviour of the English, Irish, and Scottish when they need food]
68. The Irishman for a hand, The Welshman for a leg, the Englishman for a face, and the Dutchman for a beard. [The implication is that the Irish have the best hands, the Welsh the best legs, and so on]

*Scotland*

69. A Scot, a rat, and a Newcastle grindstone travel all the world over.
70. The Scot will not fight till he sees his own blood.
71. Biting and scratching is Scots folk's wooing.
72. A Scotsman is always wise behind the hand.
73. Forth bridles the wild Highlandman. [A reference to the river Forth as a protection against Highland raids]
74. A Scottish mist will wet an Englishman to the skin.
75. Had Judas betrayed Christ in Scotland he might have repented before he could have found a tree to hang himself on. [This proverb was evidently coined at a time when Scotland had few trees]

*Ireland*

76. An Irishman before answering a question always asks another. [The other question referred to is, "Why do you ask?"]
77. Put an Irishman on the spit, and you can always get another Irishman to baste him. [A reference to the civil strife within Ireland]
78. Will any, but an Irishman, hang a wooden kettle over the fire?
79. The citizens of Cork are all akin. [The implication is that the people of Cork mistrust outsiders, and therefore only marry amongst themselves]
80. Limerick was, Dublin is, and Cork shall be, the finest city of the three.

*Wales*

81. Anglesey is the mother of Wales. [A reference to the fertility of the farming land on the island of Anglesey]
82. Powys is the paradise of Wales.
83. Snowdon will yield sufficient pasture for all the cattle of Wales put together.
84. The older the Welshman, the more madman.
85. The Welshman keeps nothing until he has lost it. [This implies that the Welsh work hard to protect their lands only after they have been lost and regained]

See also ENGLAND

# 134 PERSEVERANCE

*Its value*

1. Perseverance kills the game.
2. It's dogged as does it.
3. Have at it, and have it.
4. Slow but sure wins the race. [The implication of this and the following two proverbs is that one may achieve more by steady perseverance than by rash haste]
5. The tortoise wins the race while the hare is sleeping. [A reference to one of Aesop's fables]
6. The race is not to the swift, nor the battle to the strong. [Ecclesiastes 9:11]
7. The snail slides up the tower at last, though the swallow mounteth it sooner.
8. Better never to begin than never to make an end.
9. Good to begin well, better to end well. [This implies that a good beginning is of no value unless one perseveres to the end]
10. Things that are hard to come by are much set by.
11. The best fish swim near the bottom.
12. The best things are hard to come by. [This and the two preceding proverbs are an encouragement to persevere even in the face of difficulties]

*Its effects*

13. Feather by feather, the goose is plucked.
14. Grain by grain, and the hen fills her belly.
15. Step after step the ladder is ascended.
16. By one and one the spindles are made.

17. Spit on a stone, and it will be wet at the last.
18. Constant dripping wears away the stone.
19. Little strokes fell great oaks.
20. A mouse in time may bite in two a cable.

*Against giving up*

21. Never say die.
22. Seek till you find, and you'll not lose your labour.
23. If at first you don't succeed, try, try, try again.
24. He that shoots oft at last shall hit the mark.
25. Oft ettle, whiles hit. ["Ettle" means "aim"; "whiles" means "sometimes"]
26. Forsaken by the wind, you must use your oars.
27. That which will not be butter, must be made into cheese. [The implication of this and the preceding proverb is that after an initial failure, one should try a different approach rather than abandon the enterprise]

*Seeing things through*

28. In for a penny, in for a pound. [This and the following proverb imply that once one has embarked on an enterprise, however difficult, costly, or dangerous it may be, one must see it through to the end]
29. He who rides a tiger is afraid to dismount.

# 135 POSSESSION

*Its value*

1. A bird in the hand is worth two in the bush. [A few of the numerous variants of this proverb are listed below]
2. Better a sparrow in the hand than a pigeon on the roof.
3. A thousand cranes in the air are not worth one sparrow in the fist. [Arabic proverb]
4. A pullet in the pen is worth a hundred in the fen.
5. A bird in the soup is better than an eagle's nest in the desert. [Chinese proverb]
6. A feather in hand is better than a bird in the air.
7. Better an egg today than a hen tomorrow.
8. Better to have than wish.
9. Better is one *Accipe*, than twice to say *Dabo tibi*. [*Accipe* is Latin for "take it"; *dabo tibi* is Latin for "I shall give it to you"]
10. Have is have.

11. Own is own.

*Having and keeping*

12. Better keep now than seek anon.
13. Better say 'here it is', than 'here it was'.
14. He who gets does much, but he who keeps does more.
15. What you have, hold.

*Laws of possession*

16. Possession is nine points of the law.
17. Finders keepers, losers seekers. [A variant of this proverb substitutes "weepers" for "seekers"]
18. Finding's keeping.
19. *Meum, tuum, suum,* set all the world together by the ears. [*Meum, tuum, suum* is Latin for "mine, yours, his". The proverb refers to disputes over ownership]
20. Every man should take his own.
21. What's yours is mine and what's mine is my own.

*True possession*

22. The gown is his that wears it, and the world his that enjoys it.
23. Goods are theirs that enjoy them.
24. A man has no more goods than he gets good of.

# 136 POVERTY

*Its causes*

1. Who dainties love, shall beggars prove.
2. There are God's poor and the devil's poor. ["God's poor" are those whose poverty results from misfortune; "the devil's poor" are those who have brought poverty upon themselves by greed or extravagance]
3. Who spends before he thrives, will beg before he thinks.
4. He that has it and will not keep it; he that wants it and will not seek it; he that drinks and is not dry, shall want money as well as I.
5. Nothing is to be got without pains except poverty.
6. An idle youth, a needy age.
7. Idleness is the key of beggary.
8. Idleness must thank itself if it go barefoot.
9. Plenty makes poor.
10. He who of plenty will take no heed, shall find default in time of need.

### Its effects

11. Poverty is an enemy to good manners.
12. A moneyless man goes fast through the market.
13. Need makes the naked man run.
14. Need makes the old wife trot.
15. The worth of a thing is best known by the want of it.
16. Wealth is best known by want.
17. When poverty comes in at the door, love flies out of the window.

### Its advantages

18. A beggar can never be bankrupt.
19. It is a good thing to eat your brown bread first. [The implication is that poverty in early life is good preparation for future wealth]
20. Poor folk are fain of little. [This and the following two proverbs imply that poor people are easily pleased]
21. Where nothing is, a little does ease.
22. Poor folks are glad of porridge.
23. A horn spoon holds no poison. [The implication is that those who can afford nothing better than a horn spoon are not worth poisoning, therefore they need have no fear of murderers or thieves. This sentiment is echoed in several of the following proverbs]
24. He that has nothing need fear to lose nothing.
25. He that has no money needs no purse.
26. No naked man is sought after to be rifled.
27. The beggar may sing before the thief.
28. If we have not the world's wealth, we have the world's ease.
29. Who can sing so merry a note, as he that cannot change a groat?
30. Little gear, less care. ["Gear" means "goods, possessions"]
31. Little wealth, little care.
32. Lowly sit, richly warm.
33. Small riches hath most rest.
34. The poor sit on the front benches in Paradise.
35. He that has little is the less dirty.
36. Nothing have, nothing crave.
37. Poor folk fare the best.
38. Poverty is the mother of all arts.
39. Poverty is the mother of health.

### Its disadvantages

40. A poor man's table is soon spread.
41. Where coin is not common, commons must be scant. ["Commons" means "provisions"]
42. Want of money, want of comfort.

43. An empty purse causes a full heart.
44. A light purse makes a heavy heart.
45. An empty purse fills the face with wrinkles.
46. It is easier to commend poverty than to endure it.
47. Poverty is no disgrace, but it is a great inconvenience.
48. Health without money is half an ague.
49. He that has little shall have less.
50. He that has nought shall have nought.
51. He that has nothing is not contented.
52. A man without money is no man at all.
53. The poor man pays for all.
54. The poor suffer all the wrong.
55. The poor man's shilling is but a penny. [The implication is that the poor man has no bargaining power and must therefore pay the top price for everything]
56. He that is in poverty, is still in suspicion.
57. No woe to want.
58. Poor men have no souls. [This and the following proverb refer to the former religious custom of saying funeral masses only for those rich enough to pay]
59. Penniless souls must pine in purgatory.

*Its dangers*

60. Poverty is the mother of crime.
61. He that brings up his son to nothing, breeds a thief.
62. The devil dances in an empty pocket.
63. The poorer one is, the more devils one meets. [Chinese proverb]
64. An empty sack cannot stand upright. [A reference either to the moral or to the physical weakness of the poor]
65. It is a hard task to be poor and leal. ["Leal" means "honest"]
66. There is no virtue that poverty destroys not.
67. Poverty obstructs the road to virtue.
68. Poverty is the worst guard for chastity.
69. Need makes greed.
70. Poverty breeds strife.
71. When we have gold, we are in fear; when we have none we are in danger.

*Its relative unimportance*

72. He who is content in his poverty, is wonderfully rich.
73. He is not poor that has little, but he that desires much.
74. Poverty does not hurt him who has not been rich before.
75. Poor men go to heaven as soon as rich.

76. Put the poor man's penny and the rich man's penny in ae purse, and they'll come out alike. ["Ae" means "one"]
77. He is poor that God hates. [The implication is that to lack God's grace is far more serious than to lack money]
78. Poverty is not a shame; but the being ashamed of it is.
79. Poverty is not a crime.
80. Want of wit is worse than want of gear.
81. It is better to be a beggar than a fool.
82. Better beg than steal.

### Poverty and wealth

83. Poverty and wealth are twin sisters.
84. From clogs to clogs is only three generations. [Clogs were shoes worn by workers in the north of England. The implication is that if a poor man works hard to ensure a comfortable life for his children, they will squander all his accumulated wealth and their own children will once again be obliged to work for their living. A modern variant of this proverb substitutes "shirtsleeves" for "clogs"]
85. Bear wealth, poverty will bear itself.
86. Better go to heaven in rags than to hell in embroidery.
87. Better a wee fire to warm us than a mickle fire to burn us. [This implies that it is better to have the comforts of a small amount of money than the dangers of a large fortune]
88. Content lodges oftener in cottages than palaces.
89. Better be envied than pitied.
90. Better leave than lack. [The implication is that it is better to have too much than not enough]
91. The dainties of the great are the tears of the poor.
92. The pleasures of the mighty are the tears of the poor.
93. The pride of the rich makes the labour of the poor.
94. The rich man spends his money, the poor man his strength. [Chinese proverb]
95. A poor man's cow dies, a rich man's child.
96. The rich man has his ice in the summer and the poor man gets his in the winter.
97. The sorrows of the rich are not real sorrows; the comforts of the poor are not real comforts. [Chinese proverb]
98. Poor men seek meat for their stomach; rich men stomach for their meat.
99. The rich man may dine when he will, the poor man when he may.
100. The rich man thinks of the future, the poor man thinks of today. [Chinese proverb]
101. Rich men are stewards for the poor. [The implication is that the rich

are caretakers rather than owners of their wealth, and as such should
always be ready to give to the poor]
102. Beggars breed, and rich men feed.

### Contempt for the poor

103. The devil wipes his tail with the poor man's pride.
104. God help the rich, the poor can beg.
105. There's one law for the rich, and another for the poor.
106. Little Jock gets the little dish, and it holds him aye long little. [The
implication is that poverty is prolonged by bad treatment of the
poor]
107. The poor man is aye put to the worst.
108. A poor man's tale cannot be heard.
109. The reasons of the poor weigh not.
110. Wood in a wilderness, moss in a mountain, and wit in a poor man's
breast, are little thought of.
111. The skilfullest wanting money is scorned.

### Qualities of the poor

112. Under a ragged coat lies wisdom.
113. Poor and liberal, rich and covetous.
114. Patience with poverty is all a poor man's remedy.
115. Be patient in poverty and you may become rich. [Chinese proverb]
116. Poverty and anger do not agree. [Arabic proverb]
117. Bashfulness is an enemy to poverty.
118. He that has no honey in his pot, let him have it in his mouth. [The
implication of this and the next proverb is that the poor man must
be a glib speaker]
119. He that has not silver in his purse, should have silk on his tongue.

See also MARRIAGE: *The importance of material well-being*; PRIDE:
*Pride and poverty*

# 137 PRAISE

### Its value

1. True praise roots and spreads.
2. Praise is always pleasant.
3. Praise is the reflection of virtue.
4. They that value not praise, will never do any thing worthy of praise.
5. Praise youth and it will prosper.

6. Lacking breeds laziness, praise breeds pith. ["Lacking" here means "censure"; "pith" means "effort"]

*Its dangers*

7. Too much praise is a burden.
8. Praise none too much, for all are fickle.
9. Praise by evil men is dispraise.

*Its effects*

10. Praise is a spur to the good, a thorn to the evil.
11. Praise makes good men better, and bad men worse.
12. Praise the child, and you make love to the mother.
13. Who praises St. Peter does not blame St. Paul.
14. Good words anoint us, and ill do unjoint us.

*Its inadequacy*

15. Praise is not pudding.
16. Praises fill not the belly.
17. Praise without profit puts little in the pot.

*Self-praise*

18. Self-praise is no recommendation.
19. A man's praise in his own mouth stinks.
20. He that praises himself, spatters himself.
21. He has ill neighbours, that is fain to praise himself.
22. Neither praise nor dispraise thyself; thy actions serve the turn.

## 138 PRIDE

*Its dangers*

1. Pride goes before a fall. [A misquotation from Proverbs 16:18. The full quotation is, "Pride goeth before destruction, and an haughty spirit before a fall."]
2. Pride goes before, and shame follows after.
3. When pride rides, shame lacqueys. [To "lacquey" is to follow or attend]
4. Pride is the sworn enemy to content.
5. Pride is a flower that grows in the devil's garden.
6. Pride increases our enemies, but puts our friends to flight.
7. Pride, joined with many virtues, chokes them all.

*Its sources*

8. Heresy is the school of pride.
9. Plenty breeds pride.

*Its effects*

10. Pride and grace dwelt never in one place.
11. Pride and laziness would have mickle upholding. ["Mickle" means "much". A reference to the expense of providing ornaments for the vain and servants for the lazy]
12. I proud and thou proud, who shall bear the ashes out?

*Pride and poverty*

13. Pride and poverty are ill met, yet often seen together.
14. Charity and pride do both feed the poor.
15. Pride may lurk under a threadbare coat.
16. A proud mind and a beggar's purse agree not together.

*Characteristics of the proud*

17. It is good beating proud folks, for they'll not complain.
18. Bastard brood is always proud.
19. Pride had rather go out of the way than go behind. [The implication is that proud people will not accept advice or guidance]
20. Likeness begets love, yet proud men hate one another.
21. Pride with pride will not abide.
22. Pride will spit in pride's face.
23. Pride often wears the cloak of humility. [This and the following two proverbs imply that to proclaim one's humility is in itself a form of pride]
24. There are those who despise pride with a greater pride.
25. It is not a sign of humility to declaim against pride.

*The need for humility*

26. No man so good, but another may be as good as he.
27. No man is indispensable.
28. The best of men are but men at best.
29. Remember you are but a man.
30. He that will not stoop for a pin, shall never be worth a pound.
31. It is a proud horse that will not bear his own provender.
32. He is a proud tod that will not scrape his own hole. ["Tod" means "fox"]

# 139 PROMISES

### Their unreliability

1. Promises are like pie-crust, made to be broken.
2. Eggs and oaths are easily broken.
3. Promises are either broken or kept.
4. A man apt to promise, is apt to forget.
5. The day obliterates the promise of the night. [Arabic proverb]
6. Vows made in storms are forgotten in calms.
7. Men may promise more in a day than they will fulfil in a year.
8. Many fair promises in marriage making, but few in tocher paying. ["Tocher" means "dowry"]
9. Words and feathers the wind carries away.
10. Words are but wind.

### Their obligation

11. Promise is debt.
12. An ox is taken by the horns, and a man by his word.

### Breaking one's word

13. A man that breaks his word, bids others be false to him.
14. To him that breaks his trust, let trust be broken.
15. He loses his thanks who promises and delays.

### Promising too much

16. He that promises too much, means nothing. [The implication of this and the following proverbs is that those who make lavish promises are unlikely to be able to keep them]
17. To offer much, is a kind of denial.
18. Who gives to all, denies all.

### Promise and performance

19. Promises may make friends, but 'tis performances keep them.
20. One acre of performance, is worth twenty of the land of promise.
21. Between promising and performing, a man may marry his daughter.
22. A long tongue is a sign of a short hand. [The implication is that those who are most eager to make promises are the least likely to keep them]

# 140 PROVERBS

*Their value*

1. A good maxim is never out of season.
2. The genius, wit, and spirit of a nation are discovered in its proverbs. [Francis Bacon (1561–1626)]
3. Great consolation may grow out of the smallest saying.
4. A proverb is an ornament to language.
5. The proverb cannot be bettered.
6. Hold fast to the words of your ancestors.

*Their truth*

7. Common proverb seldom lies.
8. Old saws speak truth.
9. There is no disputing a proverb, a fool, and the truth.
10. Proverbs cannot be contradicted.
11. Though the proverb is abandoned, it is not falsified.

*Their sources*

12. Proverbs are the children of experience.
13. Maxims are the condensed good sense of nations.
14. Proverbs are the wisdom of the streets.
15. Wise men make proverbs and fools repeat them.
16. A proverb is the wit of one and the wisdom of many.
17. A proverb comes not from nothing.

*Their brevity*

18. Death and proverbs love brevity.
19. A proverb is shorter than a bird's beak.

*Their permanence*

20. Time passes away, but sayings remain.
21. Proverbs are like butterflies, some are caught, others fly away.

# 141 QUARRELLING

*Its sources*

1. Contention's roots are three: women, land, and gold. [Indian proverb]
2. Women and dogs set men together by the ears.
3. Poverty breeds strife.

4. It takes two to make a quarrel.
5. The second word makes the quarrel. [Japanese proverb]
6. Two cats and a mouse, two wives in one house, two dogs and a bone, never agree in one.
7. Two sparrows on one ear of corn make an ill agreement.
8. Two suns cannot shine in one sphere.
9. Youth and age will never agree.
10. The mother of mischief is no bigger than a midge's wing. [A reference to the trivial causes of many quarrels]

*Its effects*

11. Quarrelling dogs come halting home.
12. Quarrelsome dogs get dirty coats.
13. Brabbling curs never want sore ears. ["Brabbling" means "brawling"]
14. Brawling booteth not. ["Booteth" means "profits"]
15. Two dogs strive for a bone, and a third runs away with it.
16. Yelping curs will raise mastiffs. [The implication is that a trivial quarrel may lead to more serious disputes]
17. By scratching and biting, cats and dogs come together.
18. In too much dispute truth is lost.
19. Strife never begets a gentle child. [African proverb]
20. Broken bones well set become stronger. [This implies that a quarrel between two parties, once settled, may help to strengthen their relationship]
21. Woe to the house where there is no chiding.
22. When thieves fall out, honest men come by their own.
23. It is good fishing in troubled waters. [This and the following proverb imply that situations of unrest or dispute may be successfully exploited by a third party]
24. Divide and rule.

*The need to agree*

25. Fools bite one another, but wise men agree together.
26. Agree, for the law is costly.
27. One bad general is better than two good ones. [The implication is that two generals may not agree as to the best course of action]
28. United we stand, divided we fall.
29. A house divided against itself cannot stand. [This proverb is based on Mark 3:25]
30. Kingdoms divided soon fall.
31. Birds in their little nests agree. [Isaac Watts (1674–1748) *Love Between Brothers and Sisters*]

### The quarrelsome

32. Of two disputants, the warmer is generally in the wrong.
33. Wranglers never want words.
34. Cavil will enter at any hole, and if it find none it will make one. [This implies that those who are determined to quarrel will always find some excuse to do so]

### Settling a quarrel

35. Spread the table, and contention will cease.
36. The difference is wide that the sheets will not decide. [The implication is that most quarrels between a couple may be settled in bed]
37. Dogs will redd swine. ["Redd" means "settle, put in order". The proverb refers to the use of a third party to settle disputes]
38. He that can make a fire well, can end a quarrel.

## 142 REGRET

### Its futility

1. What's done cannot be undone. [A variant of this proverb is "What's done is done"]
2. It is too late to call back yesterday.
3. Things past cannot be recalled.
4. It is too late to grieve when the chance is past.
5. It is no use crying over spilt milk.
6. Never grieve for what you cannot help.
7. Past cure, past care.
8. A word spoken is past recalling.
9. For a lost thing, care not.
10. A hundred pounds of sorrow pays not one ounce of debt.
11. Sorrow will pay no debt.
12. Win or lose, never regret. [Chinese proverb]
13. Repentance comes too late.
14. Repentance is the virtue of fools.

### Its undesirability

15. Fly that pleasure which pains afterward.
16. Repentance is a bitter physic.
17. Repentance is a pill unwillingly swallowed.

### Its sources

18. Remorse is lust's dessert.

19. No pleasure without repentance.
20. Short pleasure, long repentance.
21. The end of passion is the beginning of repentance.
22. Short acquaintance brings repentance.
23. Sudden friendship, sure repentance.
24. From hearing, comes wisdom; from speaking, repentance.

*The futility of hindsight*

25. It is easy to be wise after the event.
26. If things were to be done twice, all would be wise.
27. Beware of 'Had I wist'.
28. After wit comes ower late. ["Ower" means "ever"]
29. After wit is dear bought.
30. A word before is worth two behind.
31. It's too late to shut the stable door after the horse has bolted.
32. When the daughter is stolen, shut Pepper Gate. [A reference to a former gate of the city of Chester, through which the mayor's daughter was once stolen. The mayor is alleged to have had the gate shut up after the incident]
33. It is no time to stoop when the head is off.
34. We never know the worth of water till the well is dry.

*The value of repentance*

35. Repentance is the loveliest of the virtues. [Chinese proverb]
36. Repentance is not to be measured by inches and hours.
37. Repentance is good, but innocence is better.
38. Who errs and mends, to God himself commends.
39. A fault confessed is half redressed.
40. Never too late to repent.

# 143 RELATIONS

*Their value*

1. Blood is thicker than water.
2. Kinsman helps kinsman, but woe to him that has nothing.
3. It is good to be near of kin to land.

*Their unreliability*

4. Many kinsfolk, few friends.
5. At marriages and funerals, friends are discerned from kinsfolk.
6. A near neighbour is better than a far-dwelling kinsman.
7. Wheresoever you see your kindred, make much of your friends.

8. Do no business with a kinsman. [Indian proverb]

*Undesirable relations*

9. There's a black sheep in every flock.
10. Every family has a skeleton in the cupboard.
11. Even the Son of Heaven has his poor relations. [Chinese proverb]
12. It is a poor kin that has neither whore nor thief in it.
13. It is a sairy wood that has never a withered bough in it. ["Sairy" means "poor"]
14. In good pedigrees there are governors and chandlers.
15. Who has neither fools nor beggars nor whores among his kindred, was born of a stroke of thunder.
16. Every family cooking-pot has one black spot. [Chinese proverb]
17. Shame in a kindred cannot be avoided.
18. A man cannot bear all his kin on his back. [The implication is that nobody can be held responsible for the faults of his relations]

*Looking after one's relations*

19. Charity begins at home.
20. A man should keep from the blind and give to his kin.
21. Keep your ain fish-guts to your ain sea-maws. ["Ain" means "own"; "sea-maws" are gulls]

*Family affairs*

22. It is an ill bird that fouls its own nest. [The implication is that one should not publicly criticize or denigrate one's own family]
23. Don't wash your dirty linen in public. [This implies that one should not discuss family scandals or quarrels in public]

# 144 RELIGION

*Its value*

1. Religion is the rule of life.
2. A man without religion is like a horse without a bridle.
3. One may live without father or mother, but one cannot live without God.
4. The devil never assails a man except he find him either void of knowledge, or of the fear of God.
5. Have God and have all.
6. He loses nothing who keeps God for his friend.
7. The best way to travel is towards heaven.
8. Meat and mass never hindered any man.

9. When God is made the master of a family, he orders the disorderly.

### Its limitations

10. Put your trust in God, but keep your powder dry. [Advice allegedly given by Oliver Cromwell (1599–1658) to his troops while crossing a river. This and the following proverb imply that one should not allow one's faith in God to prevent one from being practical]
11. Praise the Lord and pass the ammunition. [First said by a U.S. chaplain at Pearl Harbour (1941)]
12. The man of God is better for having his bows and arrows about him.
13. It matters not what religion an ill man is of. [The implication is that religion can do little to improve an evil person]
14. St. Luke was a saint and a physician, and yet he died.

### The need for respect

15. Religion, credit, and the eye are not to be touched.
16. Jest not with the eye, or with religion.
17. King Harry robbed the church, and died a beggar. [A reference to Henry VIII and the Reformation]
18. Never dog barked against the crucifix but he ran mad.

### Heaven and hell

19. Better go to heaven in rags than to hell in embroidery.
20. Hell is wherever heaven is not.
21. Heaven and hell are within the heart. [Chinese proverb]
22. All of heaven and hell is not known till hereafter.
23. This world is nothing, except it tend to another.

### The way to heaven

24. No coming to heaven with dry eyes.
25. Crosses are ladders that lead to heaven. ["Crosses" here means "suffering"]
26. In rain and sunshine cuckolds go to heaven.
27. He that will enter into Paradise must have a good key.
28. A man must go old to the court, and young to a cloister, that would go from thence to heaven.
29. There is no going to heaven in a sedan.
30. Gold goes in at any gate except heaven's.
31. Poor men go to heaven as soon as rich.
32. The way to heaven is alike in every place.
33. The way to heaven is as ready by water as by land.

## The way to hell

34. The descent to hell is easy.
35. The road to hell is paved with good intentions.
36. Who fasts and does no other good, spares his bread and goes to hell.
37. Hell is always open.
38. Hopers go to hell.
39. Long in court, deep in hell.

## False devotion

40. The devil was sick, the devil a saint would be; the devil was well, the devil a saint was he. [The implication of this and the following proverbs is that people tend to turn to religion in time of need, only to discard it again when things take a turn for the better]
41. Danger makes men devout.
42. Some are atheists only in fair weather.
43. The porter calls upon God only when he is under the load. [Arabic proverb]

## Heresy

44. Heresy is the school of pride.
45. Heresy may be easier kept out than shook off.
46. Turkey, heresy, hops, and beer came into England all in one year.
47. For the same man to be a heretic and a good subject, is impossible.
48. With the gospel, one becomes a heretic.

## Religious differences

49. An atheist is one point beyond the devil.
50. A complete Christian must have the works of a Papist, the words of a Puritan, and the faith of a Protestant.
51. The Jews spend at Easter, the Moors at marriages, the Christians in suits. ["Suits" here refers to lawsuits]
52. Henry the Eighth pulled down monks and their cells, Henry the Ninth should pull down bishops and their bells. [A reference to the Reformation]
53. 'Pater noster' built churches, and 'Our Father' pulls them down. [A further reference to the dispute between the Catholic Church (here represented by the Latin form Pater noster) and the Church of England]
54. There is no rain – the Christians are the cause. [A popular proverb in ancient Rome]
55. He that is of all religions is of no religion.

### Religious martyrs

56. No religion but can boast of its martyrs.
57. The blood of the martyrs is the seed of the church.
58. It is not the suffering, but the cause which makes a martyr.
59. It is better to be a martyr than a confessor.

### The church

60. The church is an anvil which has worn out many hammers.
61. The nearer the church, the farther from God.
62. The kirk is aye greedy.
63. What the church takes not, the exchequer carries away.

### Sunday

64. The better the day, the better the deed. [An excuse for doing something that should not be done on the Sabbath day]
65. A man had better ne'er been born as have his nails on a Sunday shorn.
66. He that hangs himself on Sunday, shall hang still uncut down on Monday.
67. If you go nutting on Sundays, the devil will come to help and hold the bough for you.
68. Sunday's wooing draws to ruin.
69. When Sunday comes it will be holy day.
70. If you have done no ill the six days, you may play the seventh.

### Men of the church

71. A house-going parson makes a church-going people.
72. Like people, like priest. [Hosea 4:9]
73. Such priest, such offering.
74. Clergymen's sons always turn out badly.
75. Once a parson always a parson. [Variants of this proverb substitute "bishop" or "priest" for "parson"]
76. Parsons are souls' waggoners.
77. He that preaches, gives alms.
78. Saturday is the working day and Monday the holiday of preachers.
79. The greatest scholars are not the best preachers.
80. A pope by voice, a king by birth, an emperor by force.
81. If you would be pope, you must think of nothing else.
82. A monk out of his cloister is like a fish out of water.
83. He that cannot do better, must be a monk.
84. Take heed of an ox before, of a horse behind, of a monk on all sides.
85. The devil and the dean begin with a letter; when the devil gets the dean, the kirk will be the better.

86. Weel's him and wae's him that has a bishop in his kin. [The implication is that there are both advantages and disadvantages of having relatives in the church]
87. Pigeons and priests make foul houses.
88. No mischief but a woman or a priest is at the bottom of it.
89. Women, priests, and poultry, have never enough.
90. Three things are insatiable, priests, monks, and the sea.

### Prayer

91. A short prayer penetrates heaven.
92. The fewer the words, the better the prayer.
93. If your heart is in your prayer, God will know it.
94. Even the prayers of an ant reach to heaven. [Japanese proverb]
95. Labour as long lived, pray as ever dying.
96. Prayer should be the key of the day and the lock of the night.
97. Prayers and provender hinder no man's journey.
98. The prayers of the wicked won't prevail.
99. The family that prays together stays together.

### The Bible

100. The Bible is the religion of Protestants.
101. There is nothing patent in the New Testament that is not latent in the Old.
102. Prosperity is the blessing of the Old Testament, adversity the blessing of the New.

See also CORRUPTION: *Religious corruption*; DEVIL; GOD; HYPOCRISY: *Religious hypocrisy*

# 145 REMEDIES

### Their reliability

1. No wrong without a remedy.
2. There is a salve for every sore.
3. There is a remedy for all things but death.
4. There is a remedy for everything, could men find it.
5. For every evil under the sun, there is a remedy or there is none: if there be one, try and find it; if there be none, never mind it.

### The nature of the remedy

6. Adapt the remedy to the disease. [Chinese proverb]
7. Seek your salve where you get your sore.

8. The hand that gave the wound must give the cure.
9. Take a hair of the dog that bit you. [The advice here is that the unpleasant after-effects of drunkenness may be relieved by consuming more alcohol]
10. One poison drives out another. [Variants of this proverb substitute "nail", "love", "fire", or "heat" for "poison"]
11. The smell of garlic takes away the smell of onions.
12. Desperate cuts must have desperate cures.
13. Take away the cause, and the effect must cease.
14. Destroy the nests and the birds will fly away.
15. If you don't like the heat, get out of the kitchen.
16. The remedy may be worse than the disease. [This implies that measures taken to solve a problem may themselves cause a worse problem]

See also ANGER: *Its remedies*; DEATH: *Its consolations*; HEALTH: *Remedies*; LOVE: *Its remedies*; PATIENCE: *Patience as a remedy*; SORROW: *Remedies for sorrow*

# 146 RESOLUTION

*Its value*

1. Bold resolution is the favourite of providence.
2. Every task is easy to a resolute man. [Chinese proverb]
3. The resolved mind has no cares.
4. In things that must be, it is good to be resolute.
5. A cat in gloves catches no mice. [A warning against over-cautiousness]

*Indecision*

6. He who hesitates is lost.
7. The woman that deliberates is lost.
8. The longer you look at it the less you will like it.
9. Between two stools one falls to the ground.
10. When in doubt, do nowt. ["Nowt" means "nothing"]

# 147 RESPONSIBILITY

*Personal responsibility*

1. Every man is the architect of his own fortune.
2. Every man is the son of his own works.

3. Let every sheep hang by his own shank.
4. Every herring must hang by its own gill.
5. Every tub must stand on its own bottom.
6. Let every pedlar carry his own burden.
7. A burthen of one's own choice is not felt.
8. That sick man is not to be pitied who has his cure in his sleeve.
9. The evils we bring on ourselves are the hardest to bear.
10. As you make your bed, so you must lie on it. [This and the following proverbs imply that one must be held responsible for the consequences of one's own actions, however unpleasant they may be]
11. As you sow, so you reap. [This proverb is based on Galatians 6:7]
12. As you bake so shall you eat. [A variant of this proverb substitutes "brew ... drink" for "bake ... eat"]
13. He that takes the devil into his boat, must carry him over the sound.
14. He that has shipped the devil, must make the best of him.
15. He that has his hand in the lion's mouth, must take it out as well as he can.
16. If you leap into a well, Providence is not bound to fetch you out.
17. Wite yourself if your wife be with bairn. ["Wite" means "blame"]
18. That which a man causes to be done, he does himself.
19. They that dance must pay the fiddler.

*Joint responsibility*

20. It takes two to tango.
21. Everybody's business is nobody's business. [The implication of this and the following proverb is that where responsibility is shared, it is likely to be neglected]
22. A pot that belongs to many is ill stirred and worse boiled.
23. Corporations have neither bodies to be punished nor souls to be damned.

*Shifting the blame*

24. A bad workman always blames his tools.
25. A bad shearer never had a good sickle.
26. The absent party is always to blame.
27. Deaf men go away with the blame.
28. Many a one blames his wife for his own unthrift.
29. Every one puts his fault on the times.
30. One does the scathe, and another has the scorn. ["Scathe" means "harm"]
31. When one falls, it is not one's foot that is to blame. [Chinese proverb]
32. He that cannot beat the ass, beats the saddle.
33. How can the cat help it, if the maid be a fool? [The implication is

that if the cat steals food or causes some other damage, it is the
maid's fault for not putting things out of the animal's reach]
34. The dog bites the stone, not him that throws it.
35. Put the saddle on the right horse.

### Making excuses

36. He who excuses himself, accuses himself.
37. Bad excuses are worse than none.
38. A bad excuse is better than none at all.
39. It is good to have a cloak for the rain. ["A cloak for the rain" here
refers to an excuse]
40. A good shift may serve long, but it will not serve for ever. ["Shift"
here means "excuse"]
41. He that would hang his dog, gives out first that he is mad. [A
reference to excuses made for illegal or unworthy actions]
42. It is easy to find a stick to beat a dog.
43. Idle folks lack no excuses.
44. An ill paymaster never wants excuse. ["Wants" here means "lacks"]
45. A woman need but look on her apron-string to find an excuse.
46. Find a woman without an excuse, and find a hare without a meuse.
[A "meuse" is a gap in a hedge]

## 148 REVENGE

### Its inevitability

1. Blood will have blood.
2. Where blood has been spilt the tree of forgetfulness cannot flourish.
[Brazilian proverb]
3. Where vice is, vengeance follows.

### Its sources

4. The noblest vengeance is to forgive.
5. Pardons and pleasantness are great revenges of slanders.
6. Neglect will kill an injury sooner than revenge.
7. The remedy for injuries is not to remember them.
8. Living well is the best revenge.

### Its effects

9. To lament the dead avails not and revenge vents hatred.
10. Revenge never repairs an injury.
11. To take revenge is often to sacrifice oneself. [African proverb]
12. Don't cut off your nose to spite your face.

*Attitudes to revenge*

13. Revenge is sweet.
14. Revenge is a morsel for God.
15. He who cannot revenge himself is weak, he who will not is vile.
16. An eye for an eye, and a tooth for a tooth. [This concept of revenge is expressed on a number of occasions in the Old Testament. It is condemned in Matthew 5:38 by Christ, on whose teachings the following proverb is based]
17. Turn the other cheek.

*Delayed revenge*

18. Revenge, the longer it is delayed, the crueller it grows.
19. Revenge is a dish that can be eaten cold.
20. Revenge of a hundred years still has its sucking teeth.

# 149 ROYALTY

*Its power*

1. The king can do no wrong.
2. Kings have long arms.
3. Kings have many ears and many eyes.
4. What the king wills, that the law wills.
5. He whom a prince hates, is as good as dead.
6. The king never dies. [The implication of this and the following proverb is that although individual monarchs may die, the monarchy continues]
7. The king is dead; long live the king!

*Its drawbacks*

8. Crowns have cares.
9. Uneasy lies the head that wears a crown. [William Shakespeare (1564–1616) *Henry IV, Part 2*]
10. Content lodges oftener in cottages than palaces.
11. Many eyes are upon the king.
12. It is the lot of a king to do well but to be ill spoken of.

*Its inadequacy*

13. A crown is no cure for the headache.
14. Content is more than a kingdom.

### Characteristics of the monarch

15. The king's word is worth more than another man's oath.
16. A king's face should give grace.
17. Princes are venison in heaven. [The implication is that princes go t<sup></sup> heaven as rarely as venison is eaten in England]
18. Kings are out of play. [A reference to the immunity of monarchs and their affairs]

### The monarch and his subjects

19. Like king, like people.
20. He that is hated of his subjects, cannot be counted a king.
21. The subject's love is the king's lifeguard.
22. When the prince fiddles, the subject must dance.
23. When the king makes a mistake, all the people suffer. [Chinese proverb]
24. When the head aches, all the body is the worse. [The "head" here refers to the king, and the "body" to his people]

### Serving the monarch

25. No service to the king's.
26. King's chaff is worth other men's corn. [This implies that although the monarch's service may not carry the best wages, it has other advantages and benefits]

### Courtiers

27. At court, every one for himself.
28. Whoso will dwell in court must needs curry favour.
29. The king's cheese goes half away in parings. [A reference to the dishonesty of courtiers]

### The insecurity of court life

30. A king's favour is no inheritance.
31. Favour will as surely perish as life.
32. Courtiers are shod with watermelon rind.
33. He that lives in court dies upon straw.

### The dangers of court life

34. Nearest the king, nearest the widdie. ["Widdie" means "gallows"]
35. Far from Jupiter, far from thunder.
36. Far from court, far from care.
37. Long in court, deep in hell.

# 150 SACRIFICE

*Its necessity*

1. You can't make an omelette without breaking eggs.
2. You must lose a fly to catch a trout.
3. He who does not kill hogs, will not get black puddings.

*Its value*

4. A hook's well lost to catch a salmon.
5. Venture a small fish to catch a great one.
6. Throw out a sprat to catch a mackerel.
7. Better a little loss than a long sorrow.
8. Better cut the shoe than pinch the foot.
9. If thine eye offend thee, pluck it out. [Matthew 18:9]
10. Better eye out than always ache.
11. Lose a leg rather than a life.

# 151 SAFETY

*Its sources*

1. There is safety in numbers.
2. It is safe riding in a good haven.
3. The death of the wolves is the safety of the sheep.
4. Out of debt, out of danger.
5. Out of office, out of danger.
6. Nought is never in danger. ["Nought" here refers to a worthless person or thing]
7. He that never climbed never fell. [A variant of this proverb substitutes "rode" for "climbed"]
8. A hole in the ice is dangerous only to those who go skating. [Chinese proverb]
9. The way to be safe is never to be secure. [The implication of this and the following proverb is that a sense of security may make one careless and unaware of potential danger]
10. He that is secure is not safe.
11. Safety lies in solitude. [Persian proverb]
12. Safe bind, safe find.

*The value of security*

13. Better be safe than sorry. [A variant of this proverb substitutes "sure" for "safe"]
14. It is best to be on the safe side.

211

15. It is good walking with a horse in one's hand. [This and the following proverbs refer to the importance of having contingency plans]
16. Good riding at two anchors, men have told, for if one break the other may hold.
17. Venture not all in one bottom. ["Bottom" here means "vessel"]
18. Don't put all your eggs in one basket.
19. The mouse that has but one hole is quickly taken.

# 152 SEASONS

## Spring

1. When you can tread on nine daisies at once, spring has come.
2. A late spring is a great blessing.
3. The spring is not always green.
4. Plan the whole year in the spring. [Chinese proverb]
5. In the spring a young man's fancy lightly turns to thoughts of love. [Alfred, Lord Tennyson (1809–1892) *Locksley Hall*]
6. When the cuckoo comes, he eats up all the dirt. [The implication is that the arrival of the cuckoo announces the end of the unpleasant weather of winter and heralds the beginning of spring]

## Summer

7. Summer is a seemly time.
8. Look for summer on the top of an oak tree. [A reference to the sprouting of the oak tree, which is supposed to herald the beginning of summer]
9. An English summer, two fine days and a thunderstorm.

## Autumn

10. Of fair things the autumn is fair.
11. When fern grows red, then milk is good with bread. [This proverb was based on the belief that milk is thicker in the autumn than in the summer]
12. A grassy autumn presages a spring of many deaths.

## Winter

13. A good winter brings a good summer.
14. Winter eats what summer lays up.
15. Winter is summer's heir.
16. He that passes a winter's day, escapes an enemy.

17. Every mile is two in winter. [A reference to the difficulty of travelling in the winter]
18. If Candlemas Day be fair and bright, winter will have another flight; if on Candlemas Day it be shower and rain, winter is gone, and will not come again. [Candlemas Day is February 2nd]

See also WEATHER

# 153 SELF

*Protecting one's own interests*

1. When everyone takes care of himself, care is taken of all.
2. Look after number one. ["Number one" refers to oneself]
3. Number one is the first house in the row.
4. Yourself first, others afterward. [Chinese proverb]
5. Every man for himself, and the devil take the hindmost.
6. Every man for himself, and God for us all.
7. He that is ill to himself will be good to nobody.
8. He helps little that helps not himself.
9. God helps them that help themselves.
10. Mind other men, but most yourself.
11. Near is my coat, but nearer is my shirt. [This and the following two proverbs may also refer to the interests of one's close relations]
12. Near is my shirt, but nearer is my skin.
13. The shoemaker's son always goes barefoot. [A reference to those who tend to neglect their own interests]
14. Self-preservation is the first law of nature.
15. Everything would fain live.
16. Look to thyself when thy neighbour's house is on fire.
17. No man fouls his hands in his own business.
18. If tha does owt for nowt, do it for thysen. ["Owt" means "anything"; "nowt" means "nothing"]

*Selfishness*

19. He is a slave of the greatest slave, who serves nothing but himself.
20. We are not born for ourselves.
21. Sel, sel, has half-filled hell. ["Sel" means "self"]
22. He is unworthy to live who lives only for himself.
23. Who eats his cock alone, must saddle his horse alone.
24. Every man will have his own turn served.
25. Every man is nearest himself.
26. The parson always christens his own child first.

27. The tod never sped better than when he went his own errand. ["Tod" means "fox"]
28. He that is warm thinks all so.

### Against relying on others

29. If you would be well served, serve yourself.
30. If thou thyself canst do it, attend no other's help or hand.
31. If you want a thing well done, do it yourself.
32. If you want a thing done, go; if not, send.
33. Command your man, and do it yourself.
34. He that by the plough would thrive, himself must either hold or drive.
35. Self do, self have.
36. He who depends on another dines ill and sups worse.

### The dangers of oneself

37. Every man is his own worst enemy.
38. No man has a worse friend than he brings from home.
39. Beware of no man more than thyself.

### Subjectivity

40. Every man likes his own thing best.
41. Our own opinion is never wrong.
42. Men are blind in their own cause.
43. No one ought to be judge in his own cause.
44. A fox should not be of the jury at a goose's trial.
45. Lookers-on see most of the game. [A reference to the objectivity of the neutral observer]
46. Each priest praises his own relics.
47. Ask mine host whether he have good wine.

### Self-knowledge

48. Know thyself.
49. Every man is best known to himself.
50. Who knows himself knows others. [Chinese proverb]
51. No man is the worse for knowing the worst of himself.
52. No man has ever yet thoroughly mastered the knowledge of himself.

### Self-pity

53. Every horse thinks its own pack heaviest.
54. Every one thinks his sack heaviest.

55. He that bewails himself has the cure in his hands.

See also DISCIPLINE: *Self-discipline*; PRAISE: *Self-praise*; RESPONSI-
BILITY: *Personal responsibility*

## 154 SERVANTS

### Hiring servants

1. Choose none for thy servant who has served thy betters.
2. If you would have a good servant, take neither a kinsman nor a
   friend.
3. Choose a horse made, and a man to make. [The implication is that
   while an unschooled horse is difficult to handle, the best servants are
   those who may be moulded to one's own needs]
4. He that is manned with boys, and horsed with colts, shall have his
   meat eaten, and his work undone. [A warning against hiring servants
   who are too young]
5. Who wishes to be ill-served, let him keep plenty of servants. [The
   advice here is not to have too many servants]
6. He that would be well served, must know when to change his
   servants.
7. A servant and a cock must be kept but a year.

### The good servant

8. A good servant should never be in the way and never out of the way.
9. A good servant should have the back of an ass, the tongue of a
   sheep, and the snout of a swine.
10. A servant is known by his master's absence.
11. A good servant must come when you call him, go when you bid him,
    and shut the door after him.
12. A servant that is diligent, honest, and good, must sing at his work
    like a bird in the wood.
13. He that serves well needs not ask his wages.

### Handling one's servants

14. A good servant must have good wages.
15. If you would wish the dog to follow you, feed him.
16. If you pay not a servant his wages, he will pay himself.
17. Servants will not be diligent, where the master's negligent.
18. Master easy, servant slack. [Chinese proverb]
19. Like master, like man.

*Making use of one's servants*

20. Why keep a dog and bark yourself?

*Their potential danger*

21. So many servants, so many enemies.
22. Give a slave a rod, and he'll beat his master.
23. Hounds and horses devour their masters.
24. A mastiff grows the fiercer for being tied up.

*Servants as masters*

25. Servants make the worst masters.
26. Neither beg of him who has been a beggar, nor serve him who has been a servant.
27. An ill servant will never be a good master.
28. One must be a servant before one can be a master.

*Good and bad masters*

29. He that serves a good master shall have good wages.
30. Serve a noble disposition, though poor, the time comes that he will repay thee.
31. Serve a great man, and you will know what sorrow is.
32. Many a man serves a thankless master.

*The undesirability of servitude*

33. He who serves is not free.
34. Lean liberty is better than fat slavery.
35. No man loves his fetters, be they made of gold.
36. Service is no inheritance. [This and the following proverb refer to the financial insecurity of working as a servant]
37. A young serving-man, an old beggar.

*The need for subservience*

38. If the master say the crow is white, the servant must not say 'tis black.
39. Servants should put on patience, when they put on a livery.
40. As long as you serve the tod, you must bear up his tail. ["Tod" means "fox". The implication is that the servant should not consider any task too menial]
41. An ass pricked must needs trot.
42. An ass must be tied where the master will have him.
43. They that are bound must obey.

# 155 SHAME

*Its sources*

1. Loss embraces shame.
2. Poverty is not a shame; but the being ashamed of it is.
3. Single long, shame at length.
4. Long a widow weds with shame.

*Its effects*

5. Better die with honour than live with shame.
6. So long as there is shame, there is hope for virtue.

*The shameless*

7. Past shame, past grace.
8. He that has no shame, has no conscience.
9. He who has no shame before the world, has no fear before God.
10. He who is without shame, all the world is his.

*Hiding one's shame*

11. When an ass kicks you, never tell it.
12. Who is a cuckold and conceals it, carries coals in his bosom.
13. He that has horns in his bosom, let him not put them on his head.
    [This and the following proverb refer to the symbolic horns of the cuckold]
14. Wise men wear their horns on their breasts, fools on their foreheads.

# 156 SILENCE

*Its value*

1. Silence is golden.
2. Silence is of the gods. [Chinese proverb]
3. Silence is the sweet medicine of the heart. [Chinese proverb]
4. A good bestill is worth a groat. ["Bestill" is a command to be silent]
5. A close mouth catches no flies.
6. It is good to have a hatch before the door. [The implication of this and the following proverb is that one should be able to keep silent when necessary]
7. Good that the teeth guard the tongue.
8. A still tongue makes a wise head.
9. No wisdom to silence.
10. A wise head makes a close mouth.

11. Silence never makes mistakes. [Hindi proverb]
12. If you keep your tongue prisoner, your body may go free.
13. He knows enough that knows nothing if he knows how to hold his peace.
14. Neglect will kill an injury sooner than revenge. [This and the next proverb imply that it is more effective to remain silent than to retaliate when insulted]
15. No reply is best.
16. Silence is a woman's best garment.
17. Quietness is a great treasure.
18. Silence catches a mouse.
19. Sorrow makes silence her best orator.

### Its effects

20. Silence means consent. [A variant of this proverb substitutes "gives" for "means"]
21. Silence and thinking can no man offend.
22. Silence does seldom harm.

### Silence and speech

23. Speech is silver, silence is golden.
24. Talking comes by nature, silence by understanding.
25. Wise men silent, fools talk.
26. He that speaks sows, and he that holds his peace gathers.
27. There is a time to speak and a time to be silent.
28. More have repented speech than silence.
29. Better say nothing, than not to the purpose.
30. Speak fitly, or be silent wisely.

### Characteristics of the silent

31. He that is silent, gathers stones.
32. Still waters run deep.
33. Beware of a silent man and still water.
34. From a choleric man withdraw a little; from him that says nothing for ever.
35. Dumb dogs are dangerous.

See also TALKING: *Hearing and speaking, Saying little*

# 157 SIMILARITY

*Its sources*

1. Like breeds like.
2. Like father, like son. [The variants of this proverb are too numerous to list]

*Its effects*

3. Like cures like.
4. Like blood, like good, and like age, make the happiest marriage.
5. Likeness causes liking.
6. No like is the same. [The implication is that similar things are not identical]
7. Great minds think alike.
8. Like will to like.
9. Birds of a feather flock together.
10. Jackdaw always perches by jackdaw.
11. Scabby donkeys scent each other over nine hills.
12. Hedgehogs lodge among thorns, because themselves are prickly

# 158 SKILL

*Its value*

1. Skill and confidence are an unconquered army.
2. Skill will accomplish what is denied to force.
3. 'Tis skill, not strength, that governs a ship.
4. Sticking goes not by strength, but by guiding of the gully. ["Sticking" means "stabbing"; "gully" means "knife"]
5. Great strokes make not sweet music. [The implication is that skilful handling of an instrument will produce better results than force]
6. Skill is no burden.

*Its necessity*

7. Well to work and make a fire, it does care and skill require.
8. There is an art even in roasting apples.
9. Will is no skill.
10. If thy hand be bad, mend it with good play.

*Its inadequacy*

11. The skilfullest wanting money is scorned.
12. Often a full dexterous smith forges a very weak knife.

13. Nature passes art. ["Art" here means "skill, craft"]

*Its evidence*

14. A good archer is not known by his arrows, but his aim.
15. The best carpenter makes the fewest chips.

# 159 SLEEP

*Its value*

1. Sleep is better than medicine.
2. The beginning of health is sleep.
3. Sleep is a priceless treasure; the more one has of it the better it is. [Chinese proverb]
4. Sleep is the poor man's treasure.
5. In sleep all passes away.

*Its effects*

6. In sleep, what difference is there between Solomon and a fool?
7. One slumber invites another.
8. A man is known to be mortal by two things, sleep and lust.
9. Sleep is the greatest thief, for it steals half one's life.

*The right amount*

10. One hour's sleep before midnight, is worth two after.
11. Five hours sleeps a traveller, seven a scholar, eight a merchant, and eleven every knave.
12. Nature requires five, custom takes seven, idleness takes nine, and wickedness eleven.
13. Six hours' sleep for a man, seven for a woman, and eight for a fool.
14. Seven hours' sleep will make a clown forget his design.

*Against sleeping too long*

15. There will be sleeping enough in the grave.
16. He who sleeps all the morning, may go a begging all the day after.
17. The sleepy fox has seldom feathered breakfasts.

*Sleep and death*

18. Sleep is the brother of death.
19. Sleep is the image of death.

*Dreams*

20. Dream of a funeral and you hear of a marriage.
21. After a dream of a wedding comes a corpse.
22. Friday night's dream on the Saturday told, is sure to come true be it never so old.
23. Morning dreams come true.
24. Dreams go by contraries.
25. Dreams are lies.
26. To believe in one's dreams is to spend all one's life asleep. [Chinese proverb]
27. Golden dreams make men awake hungry.
28. A dream grants what one covets when awake.
29. In dreams and in love nothing is impossible.
30. God creates dreams. [African proverb]
31. When troubles are few, dreams are few. [Chinese proverb]

# 160 SMALL THINGS

*Their value*

1. The best things come in small packages. [Variants of this proverb substitute "good" for "the best" or "parcels" for "packages"]
2. A little body often harbours a great soul.
3. Small is beautiful.
4. Little fish are sweet.
5. Little sticks kindle the fire; great ones put it out.
6. A little wind kindles, much puts out the fire.
7. Every little helps.
8. Everything helps, quoth the wren, when she pissed into the sea.
9. One grain fills not a sack, but helps his fellow.
10. Many a little makes a mickle. ["A mickle" means "a lot"]
11. Many a mickle makes a muckle. [A nonsensical variant of the preceding proverb; "mickle" and "muckle" are synonymous]
12. Many small make a great.
13. Many drops make a shower.
14. Many sands will sink a ship.
15. Penny and penny laid up will be many.
16. Little and often fills the purse.
17. Small rain lays great dust.
18. Small rain allays great winds.
19. One may see day at a little hole.
20. The little wimble will let in the great anger. [A "wimble" is a gimlet]
21. No hair so small but has his shadow.
22. For want of a nail the shoe was lost; for want of a shoe the horse

was lost; for want of a horse the rider was lost. [This proverb illustrates the importance of such small details as the nail in a horse's shoe]
23. Straws show which way the wind blows. [The implication is that trivial incidents may indicate or herald momentous events]

### Their potential danger

24. A little fire burns up a great deal of corn.
25. Of a small spark, a great fire.
26. A small leak will sink a great ship.
27. A little stone in the way overturns a great wain.
28. There is no man, though never so little, but sometimes he can hurt
29. No viper so little, but has its venom.
30. The fly has her spleen, and the ant her gall.
31. Hair and hair makes the carl's head bare. ["Carl" means "man". The implication is that many small expenditures may eventually cause financial ruin]

### The unimportance of size

32. God oft has a great share in a little house.
33. A short prayer penetrates heaven.
34. The greatest calf, is not the sweetest veal.
35. The greatest crabs be not all the best meat.
36. An inch is as good as an ell. [An "ell" is a former measure of length (45 inches)]
37. They think a calf a muckle beast that never saw a cow. ["Muckle" means "large". The implication is that the perception of size is relative]
38. A little and good fills the trencher. [This implies that it is the quality rather than the quantity of food that is important]

### Small people

39. Men are not to be measured by inches.
40. Seldom is a long man wise, or a low man lowly. [The implication is that tall people are rarely wise, and small people are rarely meek and humble]
41. Short folk are soon angry.
42. Short folk's heart is soon at their mouth.
43. A little pot is soon hot.
44. As sore fight wrens as cranes. [This implies that a small person, when provoked, will fight as ardently as anyone else]

See also GREATNESS: *The great and the small*

# 161 SOLITUDE

*Its effects*

1. Solitude dulls the thought, too much company dissipates it.
2. Solitude is the nest of thought.
3. A wise man is never less alone than when he is alone.
4. A soul alone neither sings nor weeps.

*Its advantages*

5. Solitude is often the best society.
6. Better be alone than in bad company.
7. Safety lies in solitude. [Persian proverb]
8. A man is safe when alone. [Arabic proverb]
9. He travels fastest who travels alone.

*Its disadvantages*

10. It is better to want meat than guests or company.
11. Better strife than solitude.
12. No joy emanates from a lonely person.
13. Misery loves company.
14. Woe to him that is alone. [This proverb is part of a quotation from Ecclesiastes 4:10]
15. The lone sheep is in danger of the wolf.

*Characteristics of the solitary*

16. Man if he lives alone is either a god or a devil.
17. A solitary man is either a beast or an angel.

*Loneliness in a crowd*

18. A great city, a great solitude.
19. A crowd is not company.


# 162 SORROW

*Its sources*

1. It is comparison that makes men happy or miserable.
2. It is misery enough to have once been happy.
3. Much science, much sorrow.
4. It is a sad burden to carry a dead man's child.
5. Sadness and gladness succeed each other.
6. Sorrow is born of excessive joy. [Chinese proverb]

7. When it thunders in March, it brings sorrow.
8. Sorrow is at parting if at meeting there be laughter.
9. He that talks much of his happiness, summons grief.
10. Will is the cause of woe.
11. Will will have will, though will woe win. [The implication is that although wilfulness invariably causes sorrow, the wilful person still insists on having his own way]

*Its effects*

12. When good cheer is lacking, our friends will be packing.
13. Grief pent up will break the heart.
14. The wound that bleeds inwardly is most dangerous.
15. The greater grief drives out the less.
16. New grief awakens the old.
17. Sorrow kills not, but it blights.
18. Aye be as merry as be can, for love ne'er delights in a sorrowful man.
19. Sorrow and an evil life makes soon an old wife.
20. Small sorrows speak; great ones are silent. [The implication is that true grief cannot be put into words]
21. Sorrow makes silence her best orator.
22. Sorrow makes websters spin.

*Its compensations*

23. The remembrance of past sorrows is joyful.
24. No weal without woe.
25. No coming to heaven with dry eyes.
26. Nothing dries sooner than tears.
27. A bellowing cow soon forgets her calf. [The implication of this and the preceding proverb is that sorrow, once expressed, is short-lived]

*Its inevitability*

28. You cannot prevent the birds of sadness from flying over your head, but you can prevent them from nesting in your hair. [Chinese proverb]
29. Life and misery began together.
30. We weeping come into the world, and weeping hence we go.
31. No day passes without some grief.
32. He is a fool that is not melancholy once a day.
33. Long life has long misery.
34. Sorrow comes unsent for.

*Its undesirability*

35. Better a little loss than a long sorrow.

36. Better two skaiths than one sorrow. ["Skaith" means "harm". The implication of this and the preceding proverb is that losses can be made up, whereas sorrow has a lasting effect on the soul]

*Handling sorrow*

37. Hang sorrow, cast away care.
38. Never lay sorrow to your heart when others lay it to their heels. [This implies that one should not allow oneself to be upset by the desertion or ingratitude of others]
39. He bears misery best, that hides it most.
40. He is worth no weal that can bide no woe.
41. When sorrow is asleep, wake it not.
42. Make not two sorrows of one. [The advice here is that while lamenting a loss, one should not increase one's sadness by lamenting one's sorrow at the loss]
43. Of thy sorrow be not too sad, of thy joy be not too glad.
44. It is ill to put a blithe face on a black heart. [This refers to the difficulty of disguising one's sorrow]

*Remedies for sorrow*

45. A cure for all sorrows is conversation.
46. Misery loves company.
47. He grieves sore who grieves alone.
48. Two in distress make sorrow less.
49. Grief is lessened when imparted to others.
50. Time tames the strongest grief.
51. Patience is a remedy for every grief.
52. A sorrow is an itching place which is made worse by scratching. [Japanese proverb]
53. There's no cure for sorrow but to put it underfoot.
54. All griefs with bread are less. [The implication is that eating is a remedy for sorrow]

See also HAPPINESS: *Its ephemerality*


# 163 SPENDING

*Its dangers*

1. Who spends before he thrives, will beg before he thinks.
2. Young prodigal in a coach, will be an old beggar barefoot.
3. Who spends more than he should, shall not have to spend when he would.

4. Who will not keep a penny, never shall have many.
5. Who more than he is worth does spend, he makes a rope his life to end.
6. Always taking out of the meal-tub, and never putting in, soon comes to the bottom.
7. A small leak will sink a great ship. [The implication is that constant expenditure, however small, will eventually bring ruin]
8. He who flings gold away with his hands seeks it with his feet.

### Its causes

9. Easy come, easy go. [This implies that money gained with little effort is spent as easily. Variants of the proverb substitute "lightly" or "quickly" for "easy"]
10. Soon gotten, soon spent.
11. So got, so gone.
12. Early master, long knave. [The implication is that a person will squander his inheritance if he receives it too soon]
13. Narrow gathered, widely spent.

### Its effects

14. Fat housekeepers make lean executors. [This implies that those who spend all their money in their lifetime have little to leave in their will]
15. Silks and satins put out the fire in the chimney. [A reference to the hardship caused by spending money on luxuries]
16. Who dainties love, shall beggars prove.
17. Lavishness is not generosity.
18. The prodigal robs his heir; the miser himself.

### Living within one's income

19. Cut your coat according to your cloth.
20. Let your purse be your master.
21. Spend as you get.
22. Stretch your arm no further than your sleeve will reach.
23. Everyone stretches his legs according to the length of his coverlet.
24. Lay your wame to your winning. ["Wame" means "spending"]

### Wise spending

25. If you can spend much, put the more to the fire.
26. Spend not where you may save; spare not where you must spend.
27. To a good spender, God is the treasurer.
28. Spend and be free, but make no waste.

226

29. Know when to spend and when to spare, and you need not be busy; you'll ne'er be bare.
30. That penny is well spent that saves a groat.
31. Sow with the hand, and not with the whole sack.
32. Scatter with one hand, gather with two.

### Characteristics of the prodigal

33. Great spenders are bad lenders.
34. He that has but four and spends five, has no need of a purse.
35. Sailors get money like horses, and spend it like asses.

See also THRIFT: *Its drawbacks*

# 164 STRENGTH

### Its sources

1. Strength grows stronger by being tried.
2. He may bear a bull that has borne a calf. [A reference to a Greek parable in which a wrestler built up his strength by carrying a calf around on his shoulders]
3. Union is strength.
4. Weak things united become strong.
5. Men, not walls make a city safe. [The implication of this and the following proverb is that the courage and loyalty of its inhabitants may prove a stronger means of defence for a city or castle than walls of stone]
6. Better a castle of bones than of stones.

### Its power

7. Might is right.
8. The strong man and the waterfall channel their own path.
9. God is always on the side of the big battalions. [A variant of this proverb substitutes "Providence" for "God". The proverb implies that although both sides in a battle may claim to have God's support, it is the stronger side that wins]

### Its limitations

10. Not even Hercules could contend against two.
11. A man can do no more than he can.
12. You may break a horse's back, be he never so strong.
13. The race is not to the swift, nor the battle to the strong. [Ecclesiastes 9:11]

14. Sticking goes not by strength, but by guiding of the gully. ["Sticking" here means "stabbing"; "gully" means "knife"]
15. If the lion's skin cannot, the fox's shall. [The implication is that what cannot be gained by strength must be gained by cunning]
16. Wisdom is better than strength.
17. Policy goes beyond strength.
18. Subtlety is better than force.
19. A chain is no stronger than its weakest link.

## 165 SUCCESS

*Its value*

1. Nothing succeeds like success.
2. He plays best that wins.
3. In all games, it is good to leave off a winner.

*Its effects*

4. Success makes a fool seem wise.
5. He seems wise with whom all things thrive.
6. On the day of victory no fatigue is felt. [Arabic proverb]
7. Success has many friends.

*Failure*

8. You can't win them all.
9. You win some, you lose some.
10. Failure teaches success.
11. Man learns little from success, but much from failure. [Arabic proverb]
12. The vulgar will keep no account of your hits, but of your misses.
13. A miss is as good as a mile. [The implication is that when an objective is missed, the margin of failure is irrelevant]

## 166 SUFFERING

*Its sources*

1. Afflictions are sent to us by God for our good.
2. Who knows much will suffer much.
3. To have a stomach and lack meat; to have meat and lack a stomach; to lie in bed and cannot rest; are great miseries.

*Its effects*

4. Who suffers much is silent.
5. Suffering does not manifest itself.
6. Small pain is eloquent. [The implication is that true suffering cannot be put into words, and people only complain about minor ills]

*Its compensations*

7. Crosses are ladders that lead to heaven.
8. No cross, no crown. ["Cross" in this and the preceding proverb refer to the cross of Christ, a symbol of suffering]
9. Pain is forgotten where gain follows.
10. Pain is gain.
11. No pleasure without pain.
12. Take a pain for a pleasure all wise men can.
13. Of sufferance, comes ease.
14. Suffering is better than care.
15. Suffering is bitter, but its fruits are sweet.
16. Bitter pills may have blessed effects.

*Its inevitability*

17. We must suffer much or die young.
18. He that lives long suffers much.
19. Mickle must a good heart thole. ["Mickle" means "much"; "thole" means "suffer"]
20. Each cross has its inscription. [The implication is that suffering does not come by chance, specific afflictions being destined for particular people]
21. Pain is the price that God puts upon all things.

*Physical pain*

22. There is no pain like the gout and toothache.
23. Pride feels no pain.
24. Pride must be pinched. [This and the preceding proverb refer to the suffering inflicted by tight shoes, low-cut dresses, etc., worn for the sake of vanity]

## 167 SUPERSTITIONS

*Good luck*

1. He that would have good luck in horses, must kiss the parson's wife.
2. There is luck in odd numbers.

3. Third time lucky.
4. The third is a charm.
5. The third time pays for all.
6. All things thrive at thrice.
7. Shitten luck is good luck.
8. Turn the money in your pocket when you hear the cuckoo. [This action is supposed to ensure that one will not be short of money throughout the following year]
9. The robin and the wren are God's cock and hen; the martin and the swallow are God's mate and marrow. [This refers to the belief that it is lucky to have swallows and martins nesting around one's house, and that it is unlucky to kill a robin or wren]

### Bad luck

10. Lucky at cards, unlucky in love.
11. Lucky at life, unlucky in love.
12. A whistling woman and a crowing hen are neither fit for God nor men.
13. A whistling girl does rouse the devil.

### Averting misfortune

14. He who would wish to thrive, must let spiders run alive.
15. Touch wood; it's sure to come good.
16. Rowan tree and red thread make witches tine their speed. ["Tine" means "lose". A reference to the former belief that a rowan cross tied to the door with a red thread would keep witches away]

### Omens of death

17. The croaking raven bodes death.
18. Soon tod, soon with God. ["Tod" here means "having teeth". The implication is that babies who cut their teeth early will die young]
19. No moon no man. [This refers to the belief that children born between the old and new moons will not survive to adulthood]

### Physical characteristics

20. Cold hands, warm heart.
21. A moist hand argues an amorous nature.
22. A dimple in the chin, your living comes in; a dimple in the cheek, your living to seek.
23. A dimple in the chin, a devil within.
24. Blue eyes, true eyes.
25. To a red man read thy rede; with a brown man break thy bread; at a pale man draw thy knife; from a black man keep thy wife. [A

reference to the colour of a man's hair as an indicator of his personality. To "read one's rede" means to discuss one's plans]

*Miscellaneous omens and charms*

26. When a picture leaves the wall, someone then receives a call.
27. If you rock the cradle empty then you shall have babies plenty.
28. Meet on the stairs and you won't meet in heaven.
29. See a pin and pick it up, all the day you'll have good luck; see a pin and let it lie, you'll want a pin before you die.
30. Yellow's forsaken, and green's forsworn, but blue and red ought to be worn.
31. One for sorrow, two for mirth; three for a wedding, four for a birth; five for silver, six for gold; seven for a secret, not to be told; eight for heaven, nine for hell; and ten for the devil's own sel. ["Sel" means "self". The proverb may refer to magpies or crows, and there are numerous variants]

*The superstitious*

32. Nothing but what is ominous, to the superstitious.
33. He that follows freits, freits will follow him. ["Freits" means "omens"]

See also DAYS; EATING: *Table manners and superstitions*; MARRIAGE: *Superstitions concerning marriage*; SLEEP: *Dreams*

# 168 TALKING

*Its dangers*

1. Birds are entangled by their feet, and men by their tongues.
2. He that strikes with his tongue, must ward with his head.
3. The tongue talks at the head's cost.
4. The ass that brays most eats least.
5. A bleating sheep loses her bit.
6. Many words, many buffets.
7. Much babbling is not without offence.
8. He who says what he likes shall hear what he does not like.
9. A man may say too much, even upon the best subjects.
10. When all men speak, no man hears.
11. Let not thy tongue run away with thy brains.
12. Let not your tongue run at rover. ["At rover" means "unrestrained"]
13. Little can a long tongue lein. ["Lein" means "conceal"]
14. Talk much, and err much.

15. Better the foot slip than the tongue.
16. Words have wings, and cannot be recalled.
17. A word and a stone let go cannot be called back.
18. While the word is in your mouth, it is your own; when 'tis once spoken 'tis another's.
19. Words bind men.

### Its value

20. The lame tongue gets nothing.
21. Dumb men get no lands.
22. Spare to speak and spare to speed. [The implication is that those who are reluctant to speak out will not make much progress in life]
23. Speak and speed, ask and have.
24. The squeaking wheel gets the grease.
25. He that speaks well, fights well.
26. The tongue is the rudder of our ship.
27. The voice is the best music.
28. Good words cool more than cold water.
29. The bird is known by his note, the man by his words.

### Its inadequacy

30. Fine words butter no parsnips. [A variant of this proverb substitutes "fair" for "fine"]
31. Fair words fill not the belly.
32. Fair words will not make the pot play. ["Play" here means "boil"]
33. He who gives fair words, feeds you with an empty spoon.
34. Good words fill not a sack.

### Its futility

35. Talk is but talk; but 'tis money buys land.
36. Talking pays no toll.
37. Save your breath to cool your porridge.

### Idle threats

38. Barking dogs seldom bite.
39. Great barkers are no biters.
40. Dogs that bark at a distance bite not at hand.
41. Threatened folk live long. [The implication of this and the following three proverbs is that threats need not be feared as they are rarely carried out]
42. There are more men threatened than stricken.
43. Warned folks may live.
44. Long mint, little dint. ["Mint" means "warn"; "dint" means "blow"]

45. If you cannot bite, never show your teeth.

*The tongue as a weapon*

46. A good tongue is a good weapon.
47. Under the tongue men are crushed to death.
48. The tongue breaks bone, and herself has none.
49. The tongue stings.
50. The tongue is more venomous than a serpent's sting.
51. There is no venom to that of the tongue.
52. The tongue is not steel yet it cuts.
53. Words cut more than swords.
54. Words are but wind, but blows unkind.
55. Words may pass, but blows fall heavy.
56. Sticks and stones may break my bones, but words will never hurt me.

*Speaking ill*

57. Never speak ill of the dead.
58. It is a good tongue that says no ill, and a better heart that thinks none.
59. To speak ill of others is the fifth element. [The elements referred to are earth, air, fire, and water, the four basic elements of Nature according to medieval philosophy. A fifth element is therefore something that is contrary to Nature]
60. Say well or be still.
61. Of him that speaks ill, consider the life more than the word.
62. Ill will never said well.
63. Ill words are bellows to a slackening fire.
64. Good words anoint us, and ill do unjoint us.

*The truth of the spoken word*

65. What the heart thinks, the tongue speaks.
66. Speech is the picture of the mind.
67. In many words, a lie or two may escape.
68. In many words, the truth goes by.

*Hearing and speaking*

69. From hearing, comes wisdom; from speaking, repentance.
70. Hear much, speak little.
71. Hear and see and say nothing.
72. He that hears much and speaks not at all, shall be welcome both in bower and hall.
73. Keep your mouth shut and your ears open.

74. Nature has given us two ears, two eyes, and but one tongue; to the end we should hear and see more than we speak.
75. It is better to play with the ears than the tongue.
76. Hear twice before you speak once.

### Saying little

77. Brevity is the soul of wit.
78. Few words are best.
79. Deliver your words not by number but by weight.
80. Least said soonest mended.
81. Who knows most, speaks least.
82. Tell not all you know, all you have, or all you can do.
83. Whom we love best, to them we can say least.
84. Half a word is enough for a wise man. [This and the following three proverbs imply that a small hint or indirect suggestion is sufficient for those who understand quickly]
85. A word to the wise is enough. [This proverb is also known as *Verb. sap.*, an abbreviation of its Latin form *Verbum sapienti sat est*]
86. Send a wise man on an errand and say nothing to him.
87. A nod is as good as a wink to a blind horse.

### The need for tact

88. All truths are not to be told.
89. Ale sellers should not be tale-tellers.
90. Masters should be sometimes blind, and sometimes deaf.
91. Discreet women have neither eyes nor ears.
92. Name not a rope, in his house that hanged himself.
93. Although there exist many thousand subjects for elegant conversation, there are persons who cannot meet a cripple without talking about feet. [Chinese proverb]

### Language

94. That is not good language which all understand not.
95. Think with the wise, but talk with the vulgar. [The implication is that one's thoughts should be those of the wise, but one's language should be that of the common people]

### Conversation

96. Conversation makes one what he is.
97. Conversation teaches more than meditation.
98. Education begins a gentleman, conversation completes him.
99. He that converses not, knows nothing.
100. Sweet discourse makes short days and nights.

101. Talk of the devil, and he is bound to appear. [A remark made when a person mentioned in conversation unexpectedly arrives on the scene]

*Characteristics of the talkative*

102. Many speak much who cannot speak well.
103. He cannot speak well, that cannot hold his tongue.
104. Flow of words is not always flow of wisdom.
105. Empty vessels make the most sound.
106. Great talkers fire too fast to take aim.
107. The mill that is always going grinds coarse and fine. [This implies that those who talk constantly will often say what is better left unsaid]
108. Great talkers are like leaky pitchers, everything runs out of them.
109. He must have leave to speak who cannot hold his tongue. [A reference to the often impolite insistence of the talkative to voice their opinions]
110. The eternal talker neither hears nor learns.
111. The tongue of idle persons is never still.

See also DEEDS: *Words and deeds*; FOOLISHNESS: *The talkativeness of fools*; SILENCE: *Silence and speech*; WOMEN: *Their tongue*

# 169 TEMPTATION

*Its sources*

1. All temptations are found either in hope or fear.
2. The righteous man sins before an open chest.
3. An open door may tempt a saint.
4. At open doors dogs come in.
5. The hole calls the thief.
6. Opportunity makes the thief.
7. A bad padlock invites a picklock.
8. He that shows his purse, longs to be rid of it.
9. He that is busy, is tempted by but one devil; he that is idle, by a legion.
10. The devil tempts all, but the idle man tempts the devil.
11. How can a crow sleep soundly when the figs are ripe? [Indian proverb]

*Handling temptation*

12. Everything tempts the man who fears temptation.

13. Greater is he who is above temptation than he who, being tempted, overcomes.
14. Better keep the devil at the door than turn him out of the house. [The implication is that it is better never to succumb to the temptations of the devil than to try to rid oneself of their effects]
15. Away goes the devil when he finds the door shut against him.
16. It is easy to keep a castle that was never assaulted. [This implies that one cannot claim to have resisted temptation when one has never been tempted]
17. Say to pleasure, 'Gentle Eve, I will none of your apple.'
18. If you can't be good, be careful.

# 170  THRIFT

*Its value*

1. Thrift is a great revenue. [Variants of this proverb substitute "sparing" or "parsimony" for "thrift"]
2. Thrift is the philosopher's stone.
3. No alchemy to saving.
4. Better spare to have of thine own, than ask of other men.
5. A good saver is a good server.
6. Industry is fortune's right hand, and frugality her left.
7. A penny saved is a penny earned.
8. Of saving, comes having.
9. Spare well and have well.
10. Sparing is the first gaining.
11. Frugality is the mother of virtue.
12. A little saving is no sin.
13. He who works begins well; he who economizes ends better.
14. Better spared than ill spent.
15. Better spare at brim than at bottom.
16. It is too late to spare when the bottom is bare.
17. Penny and penny laid up will be many.
18. Little and often fills the purse.
19. A pin a day is a groat a year.
20. Placks and bawbees grow pounds. ["Placks" and "bawbees" were small Scottish coins]
21. Take care of the pence, and the pounds will take care of themselves.
22. Spare when you're young, and spend when you're old.
23. He that saves his dinner will have the more for his supper. ["Dinner" and "supper" here refer to youth and old age]
24. If youth knew what age would crave, it would both get and save.

25. For age and want save while you may: no morning sun lasts a whole day.
26. Save something for the man that rides on the white horse. [A reference to the white hair of old age]
27. Keep something for the sore foot. [The "sore foot" refers to the needs of old age]
28. Keep some till furthermore come.
29. Keep something for a rainy day.

### Its drawbacks

30. You can't take it with you when you die. [An excuse for spending one's money, as savings will be of no use after one's death. The following two proverbs reiterate this idea]
31. Shrouds have no pockets.
32. What we spent we had; what we gave, we have; what we left, we lost.
33. There was a wife that kept her supper for her breakfast, and she died ere day.
34. Better to die a beggar than live a beggar.
35. He who saves for tomorrow saves for the cat.
36. Cats eat what hussies spare. ["Hussies" means "housewives"]
37. Spend, and God will send; spare, and ever bare.
38. The groat is ill saved that shames the master.
39. There is no economy in going to bed early to save candles if the result be twins. [Chinese proverb]
40. Penny wise, pound foolish.

### Against waste

41. Waste not, want not.
42. Waste makes want.
43. Spend and be free, but make no waste.
44. Better shake out the sack than start a full bag.
45. Shameful leaving is worse than shameful eating.
46. Make not orts of good hay. ["Orts" are scraps or leavings]

### Good housekeeping

47. Everything is of use to a housekeeper.
48. Mending and doing without keep the house.
49. Mend your clothes, and you may hold out this year.
50. Patch by patch is good housewifery, but patch upon patch is plain beggary.
51. Think no labour slavery that brings in penny saverly. ["Saverly" means "by saving". The implication is that any task that avoids future expense, such as mending or repairing, is worthwhile]

52. Provision in season makes a rich house. [A reference to the value of buying food when it is in season and therefore at its cheapest]
53. Some savers in a house do well.

See also SPENDING: *Wise spending*

# 171 TIME

## *Its value*

1. Time cures all things.
2. Time is a great healer.
3. Nature, time, and patience are the three great physicians.
4. Time tames the strongest grief.
5. Time works wonders.
6. Patience, time, and money accommodate all things.
7. Time is money.
8. An inch of gold will not buy an inch of time. [Chinese proverb]
9. He that has time, has life.
10. Gain time, gain life.
11. The crutch of time does more than the club of Hercules.
12. With time and art, the leaf of the mulberry-tree becomes satin.
13. Time and straw make medlars ripe.

## *Its effects*

14. Time devours all things.
15. Time is a file that wears and makes no noise.
16. Time undermines us.
17. Time is the rider that breaks youth.
18. Time tries all things.
19. Time will tell.
20. Time tries truth.
21. Time is the father of truth.
22. Truth is time's daughter.

## *Its passing*

23. Time flies. [This proverb is also used in its Latin form, *Tempus fugit*]
24. Time flees away without delay.
25. Time has wings.
26. Time is, time was, and time is past.
27. For the busy man time passes quickly. [Chinese proverb]
28. The sun has stood still, but time never did.
29. Time and tide wait for no man.

30. Time stays not the fool's leisure.

*Losing time*

31. What greater crime than loss of time?
32. Time spent in vice or folly is doubly lost.
33. Lose an hour in the morning and you'll be all day hunting for it.
34. If you lose your time, you cannot get money or gain.
35. Time lost cannot be recalled.
36. Take time when time comes, lest time steal away.

*The appropriate time*

37. There is a time and place for everything.
38. Everything is good in its season.

*The past*

39. Other times, other manners.
40. Now is now, and then was then.
41. It is too late to call back yesterday.
42. Things past cannot be recalled.
43. There are no birds in last year's nests.

*The present*

44. Things present are judged by things past.
45. Today is the scholar of yesterday.
46. The golden age was never the present age.

*The future*

47. The time to come is no more ours than the time past.
48. None knows what will happen to him before sunset.
49. This morning knows not this evening's happenings. [Chinese proverb]
50. He that would know what shall be, must consider what has been.
51. History repeats itself.
52. What has been, may be.
53. Coming events cast their shadows before. [Thomas Campbell (1777–1844) *Lochiel's Warning*]

# 172 TRAVEL

*Its value*

1. Travel broadens the mind.

2. He that travels far, knows much.
3. Much travel is needed to ripen a man's rawness. [Persian proverb]
4. Much travelling teaches how to see. [African proverb]
5. He who does not travel will not know the value of men. [African proverb]

*Its effects*

6. Travellers change climates, not conditions. ["Conditions" here implies "character"]
7. One may change place but not change the mind.
8. If an ass goes a-travelling, he'll not come home a horse. [Some of the numerous variants of this proverb are given below]
9. Who goes a beast to Rome, a beast returns.
10. Send a fool to France and he'll come back a fool.
11. Send a donkey to Paris, he'll return no wiser than he went.
12. Lead a pig to the Rhine, it remains a pig.
13. Travel makes a wise man better, but a fool worse.
14. No man was ever made more healthful by a dangerous sickness, or came home better from a long voyage.
15. Travellers should correct the vice of one country, by the virtue of another.
16. A traveller may lie with authority.
17. Travellers and poets have leave to lie.
18. Don't put tricks upon travellers. [The implication is that travellers know too much to be easily fooled]
19. He that goes far, has many encounters.

*The value of staying at home*

20. There's no place like home.
21. East, west, home's best.
22. Home is home, though it be never so homely.
23. The hare always returns to her form.
24. The bird loves her nest.
25. One's own fire is pleasant.
26. Dry bread at home is better than roast meat abroad.
27. The smoke of a man's own country is better than the fire of another's.
28. Home is where the heart is.
29. He that would be well, needs not go from his own house.
30. Better at home than a mile from it. [Chinese proverb]
31. Far from home, near thy harm.
32. Much spends the traveller more than the abider.
33. A gentleman ought to travel abroad, but dwell at home.
34. Being on sea, sail; being on land, settle.

*The needs of the traveller*

35. To travel through the world, it is necessary to have the mouth of a hog, the legs of a stag, the eyes of a falcon, the ears of an ass, the shoulders of a camel, and the face of an ape, and, overplus, a satchel full of money and patience.
36. The heaviest baggage for a traveller is an empty purse.
37. With Latin, a horse, and money, you may travel the world.
38. Nothing so necessary for travellers as languages.

# 173 TRIAL

*Its necessity*

1. First try and then trust.
2. Prove your friend ere you have need.
3. If you trust before you try, you may repent before you die.
4. All things are good unseyit. ["Unseyit" means "untried"]

*Its methods*

5. The proof of the pudding is in the eating.
6. Gold is tried in the fire.
7. Calamity is the touchstone of a brave mind.
8. You may know by a handful the whole sack.

*Experimenting*

9. Make your experiment on a worthless object.
10. Try your skill in galt first, and then in gold. ["Galt" means "clay"]
11. A surgeon experiments on the heads of orphans.

*Proving*

12. The exception proves the rule.
13. Never try to prove what nobody doubts.
14. That which proves too much, proves nothing.

*Evidence*

15. One reason is as good as fifty.
16. One swallow does not make a summer. [The implication is that a single item of evidence is not sufficient to prove a case]
17. Every picture tells a story.

# 174 TROUBLE-MAKING

*Its sources*

1. He that seeks trouble never misses.
2. Make ado and have ado.
3. Take away fuel, take away flame.

*Against trouble-making*

4. Leave well alone.
5. Let sleeping dogs lie.
6. Wake not a sleeping lion.
7. He who rouses a sleeping tiger exposes himself to danger. [Chinese proverb]
8. It is easier to raise the devil than to lay him.
9. Raise no more devils than you can lay.
10. Kindle not a fire that you cannot extinguish.
11. Rip not up old sores.
12. Put not fire to flax.
13. Pouring oil on the fire is not the way to quench it.

# 175 TRUST

*Its effects*

1. Trust helps many both up and down.
2. Trust makes way for treachery.
3. In trust is treason.
4. Trust is the mother of deceit.
5. Trusting too much to others is the ruin of many.
6. He that trusts much, obliges much.

*Its value*

7. God provides for him that trusts.
8. Trusting often makes fidelity.
9. In trust is truth.

*The need for caution*

10. Better known than trusted.
11. In choosing a wife, and buying a sword, we ought not to trust another.
12. Who trusts to rotten boughs, may fall.
13. Trust not a great weight to a slender thread.

14. First try and then trust.
15. If you trust before you try, you may repent before you die.
16. Try your friend before you trust.
17. When you go to dance, take heed whom you take by the hand.
18. Trust not a new friend or an old enemy.
19. Trust not a woman when she weeps.
20. Never trust a sleeping dog, a swearing Jew, a praying drunkard, or a weeping woman.
21. Three things are not to be trusted: a cow's horn, a dog's tooth, and a horse's hoof.
22. While you trust to the dog, the wolf slips into the sheepfold.
23. If we are bound to forgive an enemy, we are not bound to trust him.
24. He that speaks me fair and loves me not, I'll speak him fair and trust him not.
25. Tell money after your own father. ["Tell" here means "count". The implication is that even one's own parents are not to be trusted]

*Distrust*

26. Remember to distrust.
27. He who trusts not, is not deceived.
28. Wise distrust is the parent of security.
29. If one does not trust enough, one does not meet with trust. [Chinese proverb]
30. Mistrust is an axe at the tree of love.
31. Where there is no trust there is no love.
32. Trust is dead, ill payment killed it.

# 176 TRUTH

*Its value*

1. Truth is God's daughter.
2. Truth has always a sure bottom.
3. Fair fall truth and daylight.
4. Better speak truth rudely, than lie covertly.
5. Truth never grows old.
6. Truthfulness becomes the gentleman.

*Its power*

7. Truth is mighty and will prevail.
8. Truth may walk through the world unarmed. [Arabic proverb]
9. Truth will conquer, falsehood will kill.
10. Though a lie be swift, the truth overtakes it.

11. Truth will out.
12. Truth will come to light.
13. Truth and oil are ever above. [This implies that the truth will always rise above any attempts to conceal it]
14. Truth has no answer. [The implication is that it is futile to argue against the truth]
15. Facts are stubborn things.

## Its straightforwardness

16. Truth is truth.
17. Truth's best ornament is nakedness.
18. The truth shows best being naked.
19. Craft must have clothes, but truth loves to go naked.
20. Truth needs no colours.
21. Truth has no need of rhetoric.
22. The language of truth is simple.
23. Truth needs not the ornament of many words.
24. In many words, the truth goes by.
25. In too much dispute, truth is lost.
26. Truth seeks no corners.
27. Truth may be blamed, but cannot be shamed.
28. Truth fears no trial.

## Its sources

29. Face to face, the truth comes out.
30. Children and fools cannot lie.
31. A fool may sometimes tell the truth.
32. The devil sometimes speaks the truth.
33. Dying men speak true.
34. A good heart cannot lie.
35. There is truth in wine. [This proverb is equally familiar in its Latin form, *In vino veritas*]
36. What everybody says must be true.
37. Many a true word is spoken in jest.
38. What is new cannot be true.
39. Tell a lie and find a truth. [The implication is that an attempt to conceal the truth may have the opposite effect]
40. Time is the father of truth.
41. Truth is time's daughter.
42. In trust is truth.
43. Truth lies at the bottom of a well.
44. Truth often hides in an ugly pool. [Chinese proverb]

*Its dangers*

45. Truth breeds hatred.
46. Four good mothers have four bad daughters: truth, hatred; prosperity, pride; security, peril; familiarity, contempt.
47. Truth finds foes, where it makes none.
48. Truth and roses have thorns about them.
49. Truth has a scratched face.
50. Follow not truth too near the heels, lest it dash out thy teeth. [A warning to historians and biographers]
51. The greater the truth, the greater the libel.
52. Speak the truth and run.
53. He who speaks the truth must have one foot in the stirrup.

*Its unwelcomeness*

54. Truth is a spectre that scares many.
55. The truest jests sound worst in guilty ears.
56. Sooth bourd is no bourd. ["Sooth" means "true"; "bourd" means "jest"]
57. Sooth saws be to lords lothe.
58. The sting of a reproach is in the truth of it.

*Its strangeness*

59. Truth is stranger than fiction. [A variant of this proverb substitutes "fact" for "truth"]

*Telling the truth*

60. Tell the truth and shame the devil.
61. No one was ever ruined by speaking the truth. [Hindi proverb]
62. Hide nothing from thy minister, physician, and lawyer.
63. All truths are not to be told.

# 177 USE

*Its value*

1. The used key is always bright.
2. Iron with use grows bright.
3. Iron not used soon rusts.
4. Use legs and have legs.
5. Drawn wells are seldom dry.

*Usefulness*

6. Keep a thing seven years and you will find a use for it.
7. Lay things by, they may come to use.
8. All's fish that comes to the net. [This and the following proverb imply that everything is of some use]
9. All's grist that comes to the mill.
10. Water is a boon in the desert, but the drowning man curses it.

See also EXPERIENCE: *Its value*

# 178 WAR

*Its dangers*

1. Famine, pestilence, and war are the destruction of a people.
2. War is death's feast.
3. When war begins, then hell opens.
4. Wars bring scars.
5. In war all suffer defeat, even the victors.
6. He that strikes with the sword, shall be beaten with the scabbard.
7. He who lives by the sword dies by the sword.
8. All may begin a war, few can end it.
9. Who preaches war, is the devil's chaplain.
10. Advise none to marry or to go to war.
11. War, hunting, and love, are as full of trouble as pleasure.
12. On painting and fighting look aloof.

*Its rules and tactics*

13. All is fair in love and war.
14. In war, it is not permitted twice to err.
15. He is the best general who makes the fewest mistakes.
16. Cities are taken by the ears. [A reference to the use of propaganda]
17. He that fights and runs away, may live to fight another day.
18. Attack is the best form of defence. [This and the following proverb may be applied to any aggressive situation]
19. Fight fire with fire.

*Attitudes to war*

20. War is sweet to them that know it not.
21. War is the sport of kings.

*Weapons*

22. All the weapons of war will not arm fear.
23. England were but a fling, save for the crooked stick and the greygoose wing. [A reference to the bow and arrow, and the former skill of England's archers in battle]

*The futility of violence*

24. The crutch of time does more than the club of Hercules.
25. Though the left hand conquer the right, no advantage is gained. [Chinese proverb]
26. When all is gone, and nothing left, what avails the dagger with the dudgeon-heft?

See also OCCUPATIONS: *Soldiers*; PEACE: *War and peace*; TALKING: *The tongue as a weapon*

# 179 WEAKNESS

*Its dangers*

1. The weaker goes to the pot.
2. The weakest goes to the wall.
3. The weaker has the worst.
4. The thread breaks where it is weakest.
5. Whether the pitcher strikes the stone, or the stone the pitcher, it is bad for the pitcher. [The implication of this and the next proverb is that the weak always come off worst in disputes with the strong]
6. The earthen pot must keep clear of the brass kettle.

*Its redeeming features*

7. Weak things united become strong.
8. Willows are weak, yet they bind other wood.
9. A mouse may help a lion. [A reference to one of Aesop's fables. The implication is that there are occasions when the weak may help the strong out of difficulties]

*Characteristics of the weak*

10. Weak men had need be witty.
11. Wiles help weak folk.

*Exploitation of the weak*

12. Every one leaps over the dyke where it is lowest. [The implication of

this and the following proverbs is that people tend to take advantage of the weak, who put up the least resistance]
13. Where the hedge is lowest, men may soonest over.
14. A low hedge is easily leaped over.
15. The least boy always carries the greatest fiddle.

## The weakness of mankind

16. Flesh is frail.
17. Men are not angels.
18. Every man has the defects of his qualities.
19. Whatever is made by the hand of man, by the hand of man may be overturned.

# 180 WEALTH

## Its advantages

1. Rich men may have what they will.
2. He that has money has what he wants.
3. A heavy purse makes a light heart.
4. Ready money is a ready medicine.
5. A rich man can do nothing wrong.
6. Rich men's spots are covered with money.
7. There is no companion like the penny.
8. They that have got good store of butter, may lay it thick on their bread.
9. Where there is store of oatmeal, you may put enough in the crock.
10. He that hath the spice, may season as he list. [This and the two preceding proverbs refer to the freedom of the rich to spend as they please]
11. He that has a good harvest may be content with some thistles. [The implication is that the rich can put up with small inconveniences]
12. Fat sorrow is better than lean sorrow. [This implies that it is better to be rich and unhappy than poor and unhappy]
13. Knowledge makes one laugh, but wealth makes one dance.

## Its disadvantages

14. The rich knows not who is his friend.
15. Riches are but the baggage of virtue. [The implication is that riches are an obstacle to virtue]
16. Much coin, much care.
17. Riches bring care and fears.
18. He that has lands, has quarrels.

19. The longest at the fire soonest finds cold. [This implies that those who are most accustomed to wealth and comfort will suffer most in time of hardship]
20. Much money makes a country poor, for it sets a dearer price on everything.
21. Plenty is no dainty. [The implication is that one ceases to appreciate a thing when one has a surfeit of it]
22. Abundance of things engenders disdainfulness.
23. Plenty makes poor.
24. Riches have wings. [A warning that wealth may be short-lived. The following proverbs echo this advice]
25. Ready money will away.
26. Money is round, and rolls away.
27. Riches take away more pleasures than they give. [Chinese proverb]
28. Where wealth is established it is difficult for friendship to find a place.

### Its dangers

29. Money is the root of all evil. [A misquotation from 1 Timothy 6:10. The correct version is "the love of money is the root of all evil"]
30. The abundance of money ruins youth.
31. Abundance, like want, ruins many.
32. As the carl riches he wretches. ["Carl" means "man, fellow"]
33. A rich man's money hangs him oftentimes.
34. Riches serve a wise man but command a fool.
35. When we have gold, we are in fear; when we have none we are in danger.
36. It is easier for a camel to go through the eye of a needle, than for a rich man to enter into the kingdom of God. [Matthew 19:24]
37. A man's wealth is his enemy.
38. Too much money makes one mad.
39. Wealth infatuates as well as beauty. [Chinese proverb]
40. Riches rather enlarge than satisfy appetites.
41. Set a beggar on horseback, and he'll ride to the devil. [A reference to the effects of sudden wealth]

### Its importance

42. A gentleman without an estate is like a pudding without suet.
43. Good blood makes bad puddings without groats or suet. [A reiteration of the sentiments of the preceding proverb]
44. Money makes the man.
45. Money makes the pot boil.
46. Put money in thy purse.
47. Money is often lost for want of money.

48. Wealth is the test of a man's character.
49. Talk is but talk; but 'tis money buys land.
50. It is not what is he, but what has he. [The implication is that a person's wealth is more important than his character]

*Its relative unimportance*

51. The best things in life are free.
52. Money isn't everything.
53. Riches alone make no man happy.
54. The greatest wealth is contentment with a little.
55. He is not rich that possesses much, but he that is content with what he has.
56. He is rich enough that wants nothing.
57. He is rich enough who lacks not bread.
58. Health is better than wealth.
59. Better wit than wealth.
60. Without wisdom, wealth is worthless.
61. A good name is better than riches.
62. Wisest is he who recks not who is rich. ["Reck" means "pay heed to, care about"]
63. Gold is but muck. [A reference to gold's humble origins in the earth]
64. Shrouds have no pockets. [A reminder that wealth is of no importance after death]
65. You can't take it with you when you die.
66. A thousand pounds, and a bottle of hay, is all one thing at doomsday.

*Its sources*

67. Money makes money. [The implication of this and the following six proverbs is that the best source of wealth is wealth itself]
68. Every man bastes the fat hog.
69. He that has plenty of goods shall have more.
70. He that has a goose, will get a goose.
71. Put two pennies in a purse and they will draw together.
72. Money would be gotten if there were money to get it with.
73. Peace makes plenty.
74. By wisdom peace, by peace plenty.
75. Widows are always rich.
76. Where there's muck there's brass. ["Brass" here means "money". This and the next proverb imply that the most lucrative occupations are not necessarily the cleanest]
77. Muck and money go together.
78. Provision in season makes a rich house.

79. Early to bed and early to rise, makes a man healthy, wealthy and wise.
80. He that will be rich before night, may be hanged before noon. [This implies that many sources of rapidly acquired wealth are outside the law]
81. The town for wealth, the country for health.

*Its effects*

82. Wine and wealth change wise men's manners.
83. Plenty breeds pride.
84. Manners and money make a gentleman.
85. Jack would be a gentleman if he had money.
86. A thief passes for a gentleman when stealing has made him rich.
87. Gold dust blinds all eyes.
88. Wealth makes worship.
89. Every one is akin to the rich man.
90. Land was never lost for want of an heir.
91. Rich folk have many friends.
92. He that has a full purse never wanted a friend.
93. Prosperity makes friends, adversity tries them.
94. A rich man's joke is always funny.

*The power of money*

95. Beauty is potent but money is omnipotent.
96. Moyen does mickle, but money does much. ["Moyen" means "influence"]
97. What will not money do?
98. What cannot gold do?
99. Money will do anything.
100. Money will do more than my lord's letter.
101. Money makes a man free everywhere.
102. With Latin, a horse, and money, you may travel the world.
103. Health and money go far.
104. He that has gold may buy land.
105. Gold goes in at any gate except heaven's.
106. An ass laden with gold climbs to the top of the castle.
107. A golden key opens every door.
108. A silver key can open an iron lock.
109. All things are obedient to money.
110. Be it for better, be it for worse, do you after him that bears the purse.
111. Money answereth all things. [Ecclesiastes 10:19]
112. Patience, time, and money accommodate all things.
113. Money is the only monarch.

114. Money governs the world.
115. Money is the ace of trumps.
116. Money makes the mare to go.
117. Money talks.
118. When money speaks the world is silent.
119. Gold is an orator.
120. You may speak with your gold, and make other tongues dumb.
121. Money is the sinews of war.

*Handling wealth*

122. Dally not with women or money.
123. Gear is easier gained than guided. ["Gear" here means "wealth"]
124. Money is a good servant, but a bad master.

*Characteristics of the rich*

125. Poor and liberal, rich and covetous.
126. They that hold the greatest farms, pay the least rent. [The implication is that the richest people show the least gratitude to God for their good fortune]
127. He is wise that is rich.
128. The love of money and the love of learning rarely meet.

See also LOVE: *Love and money*; MARRIAGE: *The dowry*; POVERTY: *Poverty and wealth*

# 181 WEATHER

*Forecasting*

1. If the cock crows on going to bed, he's sure to rise with a watery head. [A forecast of rain]
2. If the cock moult before the hen, we shall have weather thick and thin; but if the hen moult before the cock, we shall have weather hard as a block.
3. When the peacock loudly bawls, soon we'll have both rain and squalls.
4. When black snails on the road you see, then on the morrow rain will be.
5. When the glow-worm lights her lamp, the air is always damp.
6. The gull comes against the rain.
7. If the robin sings in the bush, then the weather will be coarse; but if the robin sings on the barn, then the weather will be warm.
8. The full moon brings fair weather.

9. So many days old the moon is on Michaelmas Day, so many floods after. [Michaelmas Day is September 29th]
10. Near burr, far rain. [The "burr" is the halo that sometimes appears around the moon. According to this proverb, such a halo presages fine weather, but the following two proverbs contradict this forecast]
11. When round the moon there is a brugh, the weather will be cold and rough. ["Brugh" means "halo"]
12. If the moon shows a silver shield, be not afraid to reap your field; but if she rises haloed round, soon we'll tread on deluged ground.
13. Pale moon does rain, red moon does blow: white moon does neither rain nor snow.
14. The farther the sight, the nearer the rain.
15. Sound travelling far and wide, a stormy day will betide.
16. Many haws, many snaws. ["Snaws" are snowstorms]
17. If the oak's before the ash, then you'll only get a splash; if the ash precedes the oak, then you may expect a soak.
18. March in Janiveer, Janiveer in March I fear. ["Janiveer" is January. The implication is that March weather in January presages wintry weather in March]
19. The paleness of the pilot is a sign of a storm.
20. Long foretold, long last; short notice, soon past. [This implies that the duration of a spell of weather depends on the length of time for which it has been predicted by the barometer]
21. Evening red and morning grey help the traveller on his way; evening grey and morning red bring down rain upon his head.
22. Red sky at night, shepherd's delight; red sky in the morning, shepherd's warning. [A variant of this proverb substitutes "sailor" for "shepherd"]

*Wind*

23. The devil is busy in a high wind. [A reference to the damage caused by gales]
24. No weather is ill if the wind be still.
25. If wind follows sun's course, expect fair weather.
26. When the wind veers against the sun, trust it not, for back 'twill run.
27. Where the wind is on Martinmas Eve, there it will be the rest of winter. [Martinmas is November 11th]
28. A windy March and a rainy April make a beautiful May.
29. March winds and April showers bring forth May flowers.
30. March wind kindles the adder and blooms the thorn.
31. March whisker was never a good fisher. [The implication is that a windy March is not favourable to the angler]
32. When the wind is in the north, the skilful fisher goes not forth.
33. The north wind does blow, and we shall have snow.

34. Northern wind brings weather fair.
35. Northerly wind and blubber, brings home the Greenland lubber. [A proverb used by sailors. A "lubber" is a clumsy seaman, but there is also a play on words here if one interprets "Greenland lubber" as "green (i.e. inexperienced) landlubber"]
36. If the wind is north-east, three days without rain, eight days will pass before south wind again.
37. When the wind is in the east, it is neither good for man nor beast.
38. Easterly winds and rain bring cockles here from Spain. ["Cockle" is the name of a disease that turns wheat black and also of a weed that grows in cornfields]
39. When the wind is in the east on Candlemas Day, there it will stick till the second of May. [Candlemas Day is February 2nd]
40. When the wind is in the south, it's in the rain's mouth.
41. When the wind is south it blows your bait into a fish's mouth.
42. A southerly wind and a cloudy sky, proclaim a hunting morning.
43. A southerly wind with showers of rain will bring the wind from west again.
44. When the wind is in the west, the weather is at its best.
45. When the wind is west, the fish bite best.
46. Do business with men when the wind is in the north-west.

*Rain*

47. April showers bring forth May flowers.
48. An April flood carries away the frog and her brood.
49. In April Dove's flood is worth a king's good. [A reference to the river Dove, which runs between Staffordshire and Derbyshire]
50. Some rain, some rest. [A reference to the respite granted to outdoor workers during a shower of rain]
51. More rain, more rest; more water will suit the ducks best.
52. Many rains, many rowans; many rowans, many yawns. [An abundance of rowans, the fruit of the mountain ash, denotes a poor harvest. "Yawns" are light grains of corn]
53. A May flood never did good.
54. After a rainy winter, a plentiful summer.
55. A shower in July, when the corn begins to fill, is worth a plow of oxen, and all belongs there till.
56. A dripping June sets all in tune.
57. When England wrings, Thanet sings. [The Isle of Thanet in Kent has dry, chalky soil that needs plenty of rain]
58. If it rains on Easter Day, there shall be good grass but very bad hay.
59. If on the eighth of June it rain, it foretells a wet harvest men sain.
60. If the first of July it be rainy weather, 'twill rain more or less for four weeks together.

61. St. Swithin's Day, if thou dost rain, for forty days it will remain; St. Swithin's Day, if thou be fair, for forty days 'twill rain na mair. ["Na mair" means "no more". St. Swithin's Day is July 15th]
62. If St. Vitus's Day be rainy weather, it will rain for thirty days together. [St. Vitus's Day is June 15th]
63. Rain from the east: wet two days at least.
64. Rain before seven: fine before eleven.
65. The rain comes scouth when the wind's in the south. ["Scouth" means "heavily"]
66. It rains by planets. [A reference to the former belief that rainfall was governed by the planets]
67. Rain, rain, go away, come again another day. [A popular children's rhyme with many variants]
68. If it rains when the sun is shining, the devil is beating his wife.
69. Bright rain makes fools fain. [The implication is that foolish people believe that a patch of brightness in the sky after a shower of rain presages fine weather]

## Rainbows

70. If two rainbows appear at one time, they presage rain to come.
71. A rainbow at morn, put your hook in the corn; a rainbow at eve, put your head in the sheave.
72. A rainbow in the morning is the shepherd's warning; a rainbow at night is the shepherd's delight. [A variant of this proverb substitutes "sailor" for "shepherd"]

## Thunderstorms

73. Dunder do gally the beans. ["Dunder" is thunder; "gally" means "frighten". The implication is that thunder causes beans to grow quickly]
74. When April blows his horn, it's good both for hay and corn. [A reference to thunder in April]
75. When it thunders in March, it brings sorrow.
76. Winter thunder bodes summer hunger.
77. Winter's thunder and summer's flood never boded Englishman good.
78. Winter's thunder makes old man's wonder. [A reference to the ominous nature of a winter thunderstorm]
79. No tempest, good July, lest corn look ruely.
80. Beware of an oak, it draws the stroke; avoid an ash, it counts the flash; creep under the thorn, it can save you from harm. [A warning against sheltering from lightning under an oak or an ash tree]

255

*Clouds*

81. When Bredon-hill puts on his hat, ye men of the vale beware of that. [Bredon-hill is in Worcestershire. The warning is that when there are clouds around the peak of the hill there will soon be rain or storms in the valley below. The regional variants of this proverb are too numerous to list]

82. If the clouds look as if scratched by a hen, get ready to reef your topsails then.

83. Mackerel sky and mares' tails make lofty ships carry low sails. [A "mackerel sky" is dappled with small white clouds; "mares' tails" are long streaks of cirrus cloud]

84. Red clouds in the east, rain the next day.

85. When it gangs up i' sops, it'll fau down i' drops. [The implication is that small clouds ("sops") gathering around the sides of a mountain are a sign of rain]

86. In the old of the moon, a cloudy morning bodes a fair afternoon.

*Fog*

87. When Tottenham wood is all on fire, then Tottenham street is nought but mire. [The implication is that when fog hangs over Tottenham wood like the smoke from a fire, it is a sign of heavy rain to come]

88. So many mists in March, so many frosts in May.

89. When the mist comes from the hill, then good weather it doth spill; when the mist comes from the sea, then good weather it will be.

*Cold weather*

90. A cold April the barn will fill.

91. A cold May and a windy makes a full barn and a findy. ["Findy" means "substantial"]

92. Cold weather and knaves come out of the north.

93. As the day lengthens, the cold strengthens.

94. There is a good steward abroad when there is a windfrost. [The implication is that there is no need to supervise workmen in cold weather, as they are obliged to work hard in order to keep warm]

*Snow*

95. A snow year, a rich year.

96. Snow for a se'nnight is a mother to the earth, for ever after a stepmother. [A "se'nnight" is a week]

97. Under water, famine; under snow, bread.

98. Widecombe folks are picking their geese, faster, faster, faster. [A saying used by the people of Devon during a snowstorm]

*Frost*

99. A white frost never lasts more than three days.
100. Many frosts and many thowes make many rotten yowes. ["Thowes" are thaws; "yowes" are ewes]
101. The first and last frosts are the worst.
102. He that is surprised with the first frost, feels it all the winter after.
103. Hail brings frost in the tail.

*Sun*

104. On Candlemas Day, if the sun shines clear, the shepherd had rather see his wife on the bier. [Candlemas Day is February 2nd]
105. Remember on St. Vincent's Day, if the sun his beams display, be sure to mark the transient beam, which through the casement sheds a gleam; for 'tis a token bright and clear of prosperous weather all the year. [St. Vincent's Day is January 22nd]
106. A gaudy morning bodes a wet afternoon.
107. The morning sun never lasts a day.
108. A morning sun, and a wine-bred child, and a Latin-bred woman, seldom end well.
109. If red the sun begins his race, expect that rain will flow apace.
110. If the sun goes pale to bed, 'twill rain tomorrow, it is said.
111. If the sun in red should set, the next day surely will be wet; if the sun should set in grey, the next will be a rainy day.
112. When the sun sets in a bank, a westerly wind we shall not want. [The "bank" refers to a bank of dark cloud]
113. When the sun sets bright and clear, an easterly wind you need not fear.
114. The March sun causes dust, and the winds blow it about.
115. The March sun raises, but dissolves not. [The implication is that the March sun is not hot enough to disperse any lingering frosts or snow]

*Mild weather*

116. The Welshman had rather see his dam on the bier, than to see a fair Februeer. [This and the following proverbs warn of the dangers of mild weather in winter]
117. A green Yule makes a fat churchyard.
118. A fair day in winter is the mother of a storm.
119. Summer in winter, and a summer's flood, never boded England good.
120. If Janiveer's calends be summerly gay, 'twill be winterly weather till the calends of May. ["Janiveer" is January. The "calends" of a month are the first day]

*Dry weather*

121. If in February there be no rain, 'tis neither good for hay nor grain.
122. Dry August and warm does harvest no harm.
123. Drought never bred dearth in England.
124. If the twenty-fourth of August be fair and clear, then hope for a prosperous autumn that year.
125. If St. Paul's Day be fair and clear, it will betide a happy year. [St. Paul's Day is January 25th]
126. A peck of March dust, and a shower in May, makes the corn green and the fields gay.
127. A bushel of March dust is worth a king's ransom.
128. March dust and May sun, makes corn white and maids dun.

# 182 WILL

*Its power*

1. Where there's a will there's a way.
2. That which two will, takes effect.
3. You can lead a horse to the water, but you can't make him drink.
4. To bow the body is easy, to bow the will is hard. [Chinese proverb]

*Its inadequacy*

5. Will is no skill.
6. The spirit is willing, but the flesh is weak. [This proverb is based on an extract from Matthew 26:41]

*Its effects*

7. He who wills the end, wills the means.
8. Will buys and money pays.
9. Will is the cause of woe.
10. Will will have will, though will woe win. [The implication is that although wilfulness invariably causes sorrow, the wilful person still insists on having his own way]

*Willingness*

11. Where your will is ready, your feet are light.
12. All things are easy, that are done willingly.
13. It is easy to do what one's own self wills.
14. Nothing is impossible to a willing heart.
15. Fate leads the willing, but drives the stubborn.
16. All lay load on the willing horse.

17. Never spur a willing horse.
18. One volunteer is worth two pressed men.

*Unwillingness*

19. Nothing is easy to the unwilling.
20. He that complies against his will, is of his own opinion still.
21. If the lad go to the well against his will, either the can will break or the water will spill.
22. It is a thrawn faced bairn that is gotten against the father's will. ["Thrawn" means "distorted"]
23. A forced kindness deserves no thanks.

*Stubbornness*

24. Obstinate oxen waste their strength. [Chinese proverb]
25. Swine, women, and bees cannot be turned.
26. A wilful man will have his way.
27. He that will to Cupar, maun to Cupar. [Cupar is a town in Scotland. "Maun" means "must"]
28. None so blind as those who will not see.
29. None so deaf as those who will not hear.
30. Little birds that can sing and won't sing should be made to sing.
31. He that will not go over the stile, must be thrust through the gate.

*Wishes*

32. Mere wishes are silly fishes.
33. Wishes can never fill a sack.
34. If wishes were horses, beggars would ride.
35. If wishes were butter-cakes, beggars might bite.
36. If wishes were thrushes, then beggars would eat birds.
37. Wishers and woulders be no good householders.
38. 'Had I fish' was never good with garlic. [A further illustration of the inadequacy of idle wishes]
39. The wish is father to the thought.
40. We soon believe what we desire.

See also WOMEN: *Their wilfulness*

# 183 WISDOM

*Its sources*

1. The wind in one's face makes one wise. ["The wind in one's face" here implies misfortune or adversity]

2. Trouble brings experience and experience brings wisdom.
3. Experience is the mother of wisdom.
4. From hearing, comes wisdom; from speaking, repentance.
5. A still tongue makes a wise head.
6. Early to bed and early to rise, makes a man healthy, wealthy, and wise.
7. The brains don't lie in the beard.
8. Wisdom goes not always by years.
9. No man is born wise or learned.
10. Wisdom is neither inheritance nor legacy. [The implication is that wisdom can neither be inherited from one's parents nor passed on to one's children]
11. Under a ragged coat lies wisdom.
12. Wisdom sometimes walks in clouted shoes.

### Its value

13. Wisdom is a treasure for all time. [Japanese proverb]
14. Wisdom is more to be envied than riches.
15. Without wisdom, wealth is worthless.
16. Better wit than wealth.
17. Want of wit is worse than want of gear. ["Gear" means "possessions, goods"]
18. He that has money in his purse, cannot want a head for his shoulders. [The implication is that wisdom is of great importance in the handling of money]
19. Wisdom is the least burdensome travelling pack.
20. A wise man is never less alone than when he is alone.
21. Wisdom and virtue are like the two wheels of a cart. [Japanese proverb]
22. Wit and wisdom is good warison. ["Warison" means "provision, store"]
23. Well goes the case when wisdom counsels.
24. He commands enough that obeys a wise man.
25. A wise man never wants a weapon.
26. Wisdom is better than strength.
27. What is not wisdom, is danger.
28. By wisdom peace, by peace plenty.
29. A wise man is a great wonder.
30. An ounce of mother wit is worth a pound of learning.
31. It is good to be merry and wise. [The implication is that merriment should be tempered with wisdom]

### Its unimportance

32. Better be happy than wise.

33. A little wit will serve a fortunate man. [This implies that a man who has good fortune does not need great wisdom]

## Evidence of wisdom

34. It is a great point of wisdom to find out one's own folly.
35. It is wit to pick a lock and steal a horse, but wisdom to let them alone.
36. He that is truly wise and great, lives both too early and too late. [The implication is that a wise man never loses something through arriving too late or too soon]
37. He is wise enough that can keep himself warm.
38. He is a wise man who, when he is well, can keep so.
39. He is wise that has wit enough for his own affairs.
40. He is not wise, who is not wise for himself.
41. He has a good judgment that relies not wholly on his own.
42. He is wise that is ware in time.
43. He is wise that knows when he's well enough.
44. Wisest is he who recks not who is rich. ["Reck" means "pay heed to, care about"]
45. A wise man cares not for what he cannot have.
46. He has wisdom at will, that with an angry heart can hold him still.
47. He was very wise who first gave a reward.
48. What the fool does in the end, the wise man does at the beginning.
49. Honest men marry soon, wise men not at all.
50. The fool wanders, the wise man travels.
51. Riches serve a wise man but command a fool.
52. No wisdom to silence.
53. Wise men silent, fools talk.
54. Wise men have their mouth in their heart, fools their heart in their mouth.
55. A wise head makes a close mouth.
56. He is wise that is honest.
57. Wise is the man who has two loaves, and sells one to buy a lily. [Chinese proverb]

## Characteristics of the wise

58. The wise seek wisdom, a fool has found it.
59. He that is a wise man by day is no fool by night.
60. A wise man changes his mind, a fool never.
61. A wise man needs not blush for changing his purpose.
62. A wise man esteems every place to be his own country. [The implication is that the wise are at ease wherever they are]
63. A wise man may sometimes play the fool.
64. No man can play the fool so well as the wise man.

65. Wise men propose, and fools determine.
66. Reason governs the wise man and cudgels the fool.
67. Fools bite one another, but wise men agree together.

### The fallibility of the wise

68. No man is wise at all times.
69. The wisest man may fall.
70. Wise men are caught in wiles.
71. A wise man commonly has foolish children.
72. If the wise erred not, it would go hard with fools.
73. Great wits have short memories.

See also FOOLISHNESS: *The wisdom of fools*; OLD PEOPLE: *Their wisdom*

## 184 WOMEN

### Their danger

1. Women are the snares of Satan.
2. Women are the devil's nets.
3. A wicked woman and an evil is three halfpence worse than the devil.
4. There is no devil so bad as a she-devil.
5. Women and dogs set men together by the ears.
6. No war without a woman.
7. No mischief but a woman or a priest is at the bottom of it.
8. Weal and women cannot pan, but woe and women can. ["Pan" means "come together". The implication is that women are more often the source of sorrow than of good fortune]
9. Women's counsel is cold. ["Cold" here means "dangerous"]
10. Take heed of a young wench, a prophetess, and a Latin woman.
11. A morning sun, and a wine-bred child, and a Latin-bred woman, seldom end well.
12. Women are like wasps in their anger.
13. Hell hath no fury like a woman scorned. [This proverb is based on a quotation from *The Mourning Bride* by William Congreve (1670–1729)]
14. Women in state affairs are like monkeys in glass-shops.

### Their value

15. All women are good.
16. If a woman were as little as she is good, a pease-cod would make her a gown and a hood. [A "pease-cod" is a pea-pod]

17. Woeful is the household that wants a woman.
18. Women are necessary evils.

### Their capriciousness

19. A woman is a weathercock.
20. A woman's mind and a winter wind change oft.
21. Women are as wavering as the wind.

### Their impulsiveness

22. A woman's thoughts are afterthoughts. [Indian proverb]
23. A woman either loves or hates in extremes.

### Their wilfulness

24. Women must have their wills while they live, because they make none when they die.
25. Women will have their wills.
26. Swine, women, and bees cannot be turned.
27. Forbid a thing, and that women will do.

### Their dissimulation

28. Women naturally deceive, weep and spin.
29. Women may blush to hear what they were not ashamed to do.
30. A maid and a virgin is not all one.
31. Maidens should be meek till they be married.
32. Women are saints in church, angels in the street, and devils at home.

### Their tears

33. Women laugh when they can, and weep when they will.
34. Early rain and a woman's tears are soon over.
35. It is no more pity to see a woman weep, than to see a goose go barefoot.
36. Trust not a woman when she weeps.

### Their lack of wisdom

37. When an ass climbs a ladder, we may find wisdom in women.
38. Women have long hair and short brains.
39. A woman cuts her wisdom teeth when she is dead.
40. A woman's advice is no great thing, but he who won't take it is a fool.

WOMEN

*Their reasoning*

41. Because is a woman's reason.
42. Take the first advice of a woman and not the second. [The implication is that the first advice, based on intuition, will be more reliable than the second, based on inferior reasoning]
43. A woman need but look on her apron-string to find an excuse.
44. Find a woman without an excuse, and find a hare without a meuse. [A "meuse" is a gap in a hedge]

*Their tongue*

45. A woman's sword is her tongue, and she does not let it rust.
46. A woman's strength is in her tongue.
47. Arthur could not tame woman's tongue. [A reference to King Arthur]
48. A woman's tongue wags like a lamb's tail.
49. A woman's tongue is the last thing about her that dies.
50. One tongue is enough for a woman.
51. Women are great talkers.
52. Women will say anything.
53. A woman's answer is never to seek.
54. Women will have the last word.
55. Many women, many words; many geese, many turds.
56. Women and sparrows twitter in company. [Japanese proverb]
57. Where there are women and geese, there wants no noise.
58. Three women make a market. [A reference to the noise generated by three women]
59. Three women, three geese, and three frogs make a market. [A German variant of the preceding proverb]
60. Silence is a woman's best garment.
61. Maidens must be mild and meek, swift to hear and slow to speak.
62. Maidens should be seen, and not heard.
63. The gist of a lady's letter is in the postscript. [This implies that a woman's written communications are as rambling as her speech]
64. A sieve will hold water better than a woman's mouth a secret.
65. A woman conceals what she knows not. [The implication is that the only secrets a woman can keep are those of which she has no knowledge]

*Their needs*

66. Women, priests, and poultry, have never enough.
67. A ship and a woman are ever repairing.
68. Two daughters and a back door are three arrant thieves. [A reference to the expense of bringing up daughters. The "back door" is the

264

means by which dishonest servants dispose of goods stolen from their masters]

## Their duties

69. A woman's place is in the home.
70. Women and hens are lost by gadding.
71. House goes mad when women gad.
72. A woman's work is never done.

## Handling women

73. Dally not with women or money.
74. A woman and a glass are ever in danger.
75. Who has a woman has an eel by the tail.
76. Women and music should never be dated. [The implication is that the age of a woman should neither be asked nor told]
77. Never trust a woman, even if she has borne you seven children. [Japanese proverb]
78. From the evil woman guard yourself, and the good one never trust.
79. Let no woman's painting breed thy stomach's fainting.
80. A woman, a dog, and a walnut-tree, the more you beat them the better they be.
81. All women may be won.
82. Tell a woman she is fair, and she will soon turn fool.
83. A maid that laughs is half taken.
84. A woman kissed is half won.
85. Women resist in order to be conquered.
86. Nineteen nay-says of a maiden are half a grant.
87. Maids say 'Nay' and take it.
88. Saying 'No' a woman shakes her head lengthwise. [Japanese proverb. "Lengthwise" here implies up and down. In other words, a woman nods assent as she says "No"]

## Man and woman

89. Women's instinct is often truer than men's reasoning.
90. Women in mischief are wiser than men.
91. Man is the head, but woman turns it.
92. Men make houses, women make homes.
93. A woman has an eye more than a man.
94. A woman is flax, man is fire, the devil comes and blows the bellows.
95. Woman is the confusion of man.
96. Men get wealth and women keep it.
97. A clever man will build a city, a clever woman will lay it low. [Chinese proverb]

98. A woman is the weaker vessel.
99. A man of straw is worth a woman of gold.
100. Man, woman, and devil, are the three degrees of comparison.
101. A bad woman is worse than a bad man.
102. The female of the species is more deadly than the male. [Rudyard Kipling (1865–1936) *The Female of the Species*]
103. Deeds are males, and words are females.
104. A man is as old as he feels, and a woman as old as she looks.

See also MARRIAGE: 100–128

# 185 WORLD

*Its size*

1. The world is a long journey.
2. The world is a wide place.
3. It's a small world.
4. The world is but a little place, after all. [A variant of the preceding proverb]

*Its perpetual motion*

5. The world turns as a ball.
6. The world goes on wheels.

*Attitudes to the world*

7. The world is like a dancing girl – it dances for a little while to everyone. [Arabic proverb]
8. The world is a net, the more we stir in it, the more we are entangled.
9. The world is bound to no man.
10. The world is a mirror; show thyself in it, and it will reflect thy image. [Arabic proverb]
11. The world is a stage and every man plays his part. [The sentiments of this proverb were familiarized by William Shakespeare in *The Merchant of Venice* and *As You Like It*]
12. The world is a ladder for some to go up and some down.
13. The world is nought.
14. This world is nothing, except it tend to another.
15. It is a good world, but they are ill that are on it.

# 186 WORRY

*Its sources*

1. Riches bring care and fears.
2. Much coin, much care.
3. Little gear, less care. ["Gear" means "possessions"]
4. Little wealth, little care.
5. He that has no ill fortune, is troubled with good. [The implication is that certain people will always find something to worry about]

*Its effects*

6. Care brings grey hair.
7. It is not work that kills, but worry.
8. A poet in adversity can hardly make verses. [This implies that worry prevents the mind from functioning as it should]

*Its futility*

9. Hang care.
10. Care killed the cat.
11. Care is no cure.
12. A pound of care will not pay an ounce of debt.
13. It will be all the same a hundred years hence.

*Sharing one's problems*

14. A trouble shared is a trouble halved. [A variant of this proverb substitutes "problem" for "trouble"]
15. It is good to have company in trouble.

*Against worrying about the future*

16. Sufficient unto the day is the evil thereof. [Matthew 6:34]
17. Don't cross the bridge till you get to it.
18. Take things as they come.
19. Don't cry before you are hurt.
20. Dearths foreseen come not.
21. Our worst misfortunes are those which never befall us.
22. Sorrow is soon enough when it comes.
23. Let your trouble tarry till its own day comes.
24. Don't meet troubles half-way.
25. Never trouble trouble till trouble troubles you.
26. Let the morn come, and the meat with it.

# 187 WORTH

*Its assessment*

1. A man's worth is the worth of his land.
2. A man is valued as he makes himself valuable.
3. Worth has been underrated, ever since wealth has been overrated.
4. The worth of a thing is what it will bring.
5. The worth of a thing is best known by the want of it.
6. Blessings brighten as they take their flight.
7. The cow knows not what her tail is worth till she has lost it.
8. You never miss the water till the well runs dry.
9. If you would know the value of a ducat, try to borrow one.
10. Would you know what money is, go borrow some.
11. What costs little, is less esteemed.
12. The more cost, the more honour.
13. A penny at a pinch is worth a pound.
14. That thing which is rare is dear.

*Everything has some value*

15. All things in their being are good for something.
16. It is a poor dog that is not worth the whistling.
17. Willows are weak, yet they bind other wood.
18. There is no tree but bears some fruit.

# 188 WRITING

*The written word*

1. The pen is mightier than the sword.
2. The calf, the goose, the bee: the world is ruled by these three. ["The calf" refers to parchment, "the goose" to the quill-pen, and "the bee" to sealing-wax]
3. Pen and ink is wit's plough.
4. The pen is the tongue of the hand.
5. The thought has good legs, and the quill a good tongue.
6. Pens may blot, but they cannot blush.
7. The mouth is wind, the pen is a track.
8. Words fly, writings remain. [This proverb is also used in its Latin form, *Littera scripta manet*]
9. Writing destroys the memory.

*Books*

10. Literature is a good staff but a bad crutch. [The warning here is against becoming too dependent on literature]
11. You cannot open a book without learning something. [Chinese proverb]
12. A book that is shut, is but a block.
13. Every book must be chewed to get out its juice. [Chinese proverb]
14. A great book is a great evil.
15. A wicked book is the wickeder because it cannot repent.

*Writers*

16. Like author, like book.
17. The style is the man. [The implication is that the style of writing gives the reader an insight into the personality of the author]
18. Tailors and writers must mind the fashion.

See also FINE ARTS: *Poetry*

# INDEX

Man if he lives a. ...  161:16
Alton   Through the pass of A. ...  58:68
Altrincham   The Mayor of A. ...  58:67
Ambition   A. loses many a man 4:14
   A. makes people diligent 4:1
Ambitious   Every a. man is a captive ...
   4:16
Amend   Some do a. ...  10:37
   The best may a. 97:6
Americans   Good A. ...  133:32
Andrew   St. A. the King ...  117:74
Angels   Men are not a. 179:17
Anger   A. and haste ...  5:4
   A. begins with folly ...  5:14
   A. dies quickly ...  5:20
   A. ends in cruelty 5:8
   A. has no eyes 5:11
   A. is a short madness 5:21
   A. makes a rich man hated ...  5:3
   A. punishes itself 5:5
   A. restrained ...  5:29
   The a. is not warrantable ...  5:22
Anglesey   A. is the mother of Wales 133:81
Angry   An a. man never wants woe 5:2
   He that is a. is seldom at ease 5:1
   He that is a. without a cause ...  5:34
   He who slowly gets a. ...  5:23
   If you be a. ...  5:26
   Two things a man should never be a. at ...
   5:33
   When a man grows a. ...  5:12
   When a man is a. ...  5:15
   When a., count a hundred 5:24
Answer   A soft a. ...  5:28
   Never a. a question ...  8:11
   Such a. as man gives ...  44:18
Ant   The a. had wings ...  4:25
Anvil   When you are an a. ...  28:47
Ape   An a.'s an ape ...  7:43
Apparel   A. makes the man 50:3
Appearances   A. are deceptive 7:1
Appetite   A. comes with eating 82:3
Apple   An a. a day ...  53:59
   Better an a. given ...  75:2
   No good a. ...  18:11
   The a. never falls ...  18:8
Apple-pie   An a. without some cheese ...
   53:50
Apples   The a. on the other side ...  28:41
April   An A. flood ...  181:48
   A. showers ...  181:47
   If they blow in A. ...  117:42
   In A. Dove's flood ...  181:49
   On the first of A., hunt the gowk ...
   117:37

On the first of A., you may send a fool ..
117:36
On the third of A. ...  117:39
When A. blows his horn ...  181:74
Archer   A good a. ...  158:14
Architect   Every man is the a. ...  147:1
Army   An a. marches ...  53:2
   An a. of stags ...  9:15
Arrival   With the a. of the stepmother ...
128:22
Arrow   An a. shot upright ...  44:12
Art   A. has no enemy ...  96:14
   A. improves Nature 119:14
   A. is long ...  107:4
   He who has an a. ...  124:3
   In every a. ...  54:19
   There is an a. even in roasting apples 158:8
Arthur   A. could not tame ...  184:47
   A. himself had but his time 39:10
Ashamed   Never be a. to eat your meat
53:73
Ask   A. and it shall be given you 8:5
   A. a silly question ...  8:10
   A. but enough ...  22:1
   A. much to have a little 22:2
   A. no questions ...  8:12
   Better to a. the way ...  8:4
   He that cannot a. ...  8:1
   You must a. your neighbour ...  121:4
Asks   He that a. faintly ...  8:15
Ass   An a. endures his burden ...  56:8
   An a. laden with gold ...  180:106
   An a. must be tied ...  154:42
   An a. pricked ...  154:41
   Every a. likes to hear ...  69:81
   Every a. thinks himself worthy ...  60:15
   He is an a. ...  69:44
   If an a. goes a-travelling ...  172:8
   If one, two, or three tell you you are an a.
   ...  34:26
   The a. loaded with gold ...  115:19
   The a. that brays most ...  168:4
   When all men say you are an a. ...  34:25
   When an a. climbs a ladder ...  184:37
   When an a. kicks you ...  155:11
   Wherever an a. falls ...  62:23
Atheist   An a. is one point ...  144:49
Atheists   Some are a. only in fair weather
144:42
Attack   A. is the best form ...  178:18
Attorneys   Two a. can live ...  104:44
August   If the twenty-fourth of A. ...
181:124
Aunt   If my a. had been a man ...  108:13
Austerity   There is no a. ...  71:5

Author   Like a. ...   188:16
Authority   A. shows the man 9:10
Autumn   A grassy a. ...   152:12
Avarice   A. hoards itself poor ...   115:1
   A. is the only passion ...   115:22
Avoid   A. a questioner ...   79:35
Away   If a person is a. ...   1:19

# B

Babbling   Much b. ...   168:7
Baby   Don't throw the b. out ...   85:41
Bacchus   B. has drowned ...   51:25
Bachelors   B.' wives and maids' children ...
   3:60
   Two b. drinking to you ...   113:147
   We b. laugh ...   113:32
Back   The b. door ...   33:6
Bacon   He loves b. well ...   53:71
Bad   A b. penny ...   10:36
   B. luck often brings ...   111:25
   No man ever became thoroughly b. ...
   29:21
   Nothing so b. but it might have been worse
   127:6
   Nothing so b. in which there is not some-
   thing of good 127:31
   Where b.'s the best ...   20:8
Bairn   It is a thrawn faced b. ...   182:22
Bait   The b. hides the hook 7:14
Bake   As you b. so shall you eat 147:12
Balance   The b. distinguishes not ...   60:26
Balk   Make not a b. of good ground 126:11
Ball   If the b. does not stick to the wall ...
   42:2
Barber   A b. learns to shave ...   69:41
   One b. shaves another gratis 110:9
Bare   B. walls ...   113:48
   Better a b. foot ...   80:20
Bargain   A good b. ...   22:40
   At a good b. ...   22:14
   Don't b. for fish ...   6:11
   It is an ill b. ...   127:23
Barkers   Great b. ...   168:39
Barking   B. dogs ...   168:38
Barnaby   B. bright ...   117:58
Barter   He is fond of b. ...   46:18
Bartholomew   St. B. brings the cold dew
   117:61
Bashfulness   B. is an enemy ...   8:3
Basket-justice   A b. ...   29:44
Basque   The B. is faithful 133:42
Bastard   B. brood ...   138:18

Bastes   Every man b. the fat hog 180:68
Bathes   He who b. in May ...   117:57
Battle   It is an ill b. ...   46:6
Be   What must b., must be 45:5
Bean   A b. in liberty ...   106:5
   Every b. has its black 97:37
Beans   Sow b. in the mud ...   30:15
Bear   A man may b. ...   56:9
   B. and forbear 56:4
   Call the b. 'uncle' ...   68:10
   He may b. a bull ...   164:2
Beard   A b. well lathered ...   12:15
   If the b. were all ...   7:6
   It is not the b. ...   7:5
Beast   Who goes a b. to Rome ...   172:9
Beat   He that cannot b. the ass ...   147:32
   If you can't b. 'em ...   25:8
   You may b. a horse ...   30:32
Beaten   Better to be b. ...   23:9
Beauty   A thing of b. ...   11:59
   B. and folly ...   11:9
   B. and honesty ...   11:8
   B. draws more than oxen 11:11
   B. fades ...   11:29
   B. is but a blossom 11:30
   B. is eloquent ...   11:13
   B. is in the eye ...   11:35
   B. is no inheritance 11:27
   B. is only one layer 11:2
   B. is only skin-deep 11:1
   B. is potent ...   11:28
   B. may have fair leaves ...   11:3
   B. opens locked doors 11:12
   B.'s sister ...   11:52
   B. without bounty ...   11:21
   B. won't make the pot boil 11:23
Because   B. is a woman's reason 184:41
Bed   As you make your b. ...   147:10
   Better go to b. supperless ...   14:3
   Go to b. with the lamb ...   52:9
   Who goes to b. supperless ...   93:4
Bee   The b. sucks honey ...   127:32
Beef   It is good b. ...   53:37
   Such b. ...   55:11
Been   What has b., may be 171:52
Bees   B. that have honey ...   7:15
   No b., no honey ...   48:17
   When b. are old ...   125:26
   Where b. are, there is honey 48:16
Before   He that looks not b. ...   70:3
Beg   Better b. than steal 136:82
   He learned timely to b. ...   75:18
   Neither b. of him ...   154:26
Beggar   A b. can never be bankrupt 136:18
   A b. pays a benefit ...   88:15
   Every b. is descended ...   60:21

It is better to be a b. ... 136:81
Set a b. on horseback ... 180:41
The b. may sing ... 136:27
Beggars   B.' bags ... 82:28
  B. breed ... 136:102
  B. can't be choosers 80:7
Begin   All may b. a war ... 178:8
  Better never to b. ... 134:8
  Good to b. well ... 134:9
Beginning   A good b. ... 12:11
  An ill b. ... 12:12
  Every b. is hard 12:7
  Everything must have a b. 12:1
  If the b. is good ... 12:10
  Such b. ... 12:13
Begins   He b. to build too soon ... 85:12
  He who b. many things ... 48:54
Begun   Well b. is half done 12:14
Behind   Far b. must follow the faster 103:3
  They are far b. ... 103:11
Beild   There is b. aneath ... 125:17
Being   All things in their b. ... 187:15
Belief   B. is better than investigation 13:8
Believe   B. no tales ... 13:12
  B. nothing of what you hear ... 13:10
  B. well ... 13:5
  To b. in one's dreams ... 159:26
  We soon b. ... 13:1
Believes   He that b. all ... 13:9
Belled   Let aye the b. wether ... 125:9
Bellowing   A b. cow ... 162:27
Bells   B. call others ... 94:17
Belly   A b. full of gluttony ... 76:1
  Better b. burst ... 76:17
  He whose b. is full ... 93:28
  If it were not for the b. ... 76:5
  The b. carries the legs 53:3
  The b. wants ears 93:7
  When the b. is full, the bones ... 53:52
  When the b. is full, the mind ... 112:1
Beloved   To be b. ... 109:12
Bend   Better b. than break 25:9
Benedick   St. B., sow thy pease ... 117:30
Benefits   B. bind 75:38
  B. make a man a slave 75:37
Bengali   If a B. is a man ... 133:8
Bernard   B. did not see everything 97:17
Best   All is for the b. ... 127:9
  B. is best cheap 22:42
  The b. cart ... 97:24
  The b. cloth ... 97:23
  The b. go first 39:62
  The b. is the enemy ... 4:18
  The b. of friends ... 55:8
  The b. of men ... 138:28

The b. things are hard to come by 134:12
The b. things in life ... 180:51
The b. things may be abused 97:19
Bestill   A good b. ... 156:4
Best-laid   The b. schemes ... 97:21
Bet   In a b. there is a fool ... 74:13
Better   Be it for b., be it for worse ... 180:110
  B. sit still ... 4:19
  He that cannot do b. ... 144:83
  If b. were within ... 55:10
Bewails   He that b. himself ... 153:55
Beware   B. of an oak ... 181:80
  B. of breed 15:24
  B. of 'Had I wist' 142:27
  B. of no man ... 153:39
  It is good to b. ... 62:37
Beyond   Every man a little b. himself ... 69:24
Bible   The B. is the religion of Protestants 144:100
Bidden   Do as you're b. ... 123:3
Bigger   The b. the man ... 81:10
  The b. they are ... 81:3
Bind   B. the sack ... 56:12
Birchen   B. twigs break no ribs 49:25
Bird   A b. in the hand ... 135:1
  A b. in the soup ... 135:5
  Every b. loves to hear ... 24:2
  It is an ill b. ... 143:22
  The b. is known by his note ... 168:29
  The b. loves her nest 172:24
Birds   B. are entangled ... 168:1
  B. in their little nests agree 141:31
  B. of a feather ... 157:9
  B. once snared ... 62:25
  Little b. that can sing ... 182:30
  There are no b. ... 171:43
Birth   B. is much ... 15:3
  Great b. is a very poor dish ... 15:31
  Our b. made us mortal ... 39:44
  The b. follows the belly 128:10
Bite   If you cannot b. ... 168:45
Biter   The b. is sometimes bit 44:11
Biting   B. and scratching ... 109:99
Bitten   He that has been b. by a serpent ... 62:26
  Once b. ... 62:21
Bitter   B. pills ... 166:16
Blab   He that is a b. ... 79:32
Black   A b. hen ... 7:40
  A b. plum ... 7:39
  After b. clouds ... 127:18
  B. will take no other hue 18:32
  There's a b. sheep ... 143:9

Black-hearted  If you want to see b. people ... 94:22
Blacks  Two b. do not make a white 10:54
Blames  He that b. would buy 22:5
  Many a one b. his wife ... 147:28
Blate  A b. cat ... 49:21
Bleating  A b. sheep ... 168:5
Bleed  If you b. your nag ... 117:79
Blessed  B. be St. Stephen ... 117:78
  B. is the eye ... 58:22
Blessings  B. brighten ... 187:6
Blind  A b. man may sometimes ... 111:2
  A man should keep from the b. ... 143:20
  A man were better to be half b. ... 80:24
  If the b. lead the blind ... 96:15
  It is a b. goose ... 69:40
  Men are b. ... 153:42
  None so b. ... 182:28
  The b. man's peck ... 22:33
Blindness  There is no b. ... 96:11
Blister  A b. will rise ... 40:12
Blithe  A b. heart ... 84:22
  It is ill to put a b. face ... 162:44
Blockhead  He's a b. that can't make two verses ... 67:9
Blood  All b. is alike ancient 60:10
  B. is thicker ... 143:1
  B. will have blood 148:1
  B. will tell 18:14
  Good b. makes bad puddings ... 15:30
  Like b. ... 113:76
  The b. of the martyrs ... 144:57
  The b. of the soldier ... 124:50
  Where b. has been spilt ... 148:2
  You can't get b. ... 108:25
Blow  A b. that is profitable ... 73:6
Blows  He that b. best ... 44:3
Blue  A b. eye in a Portuguese woman ... 133:45
  B. are the faraway hills 7:27
  B. eyes ... 167:24
  There may be b. ... 47:6
Boast  Great b. ... 24:15
  They can do least who b. loudest 24:13
Boastful  Never be b. ... 24:11
Boil  B. not the pap ... 6:14
  Whether you b. snow ... 55:12
Boiling  To a b. pot ... 129:13
Boisterous  A b. horse ... 49:6
Bold  A b. heart ... 31:7
  Be not too b. with your biggers or betters 37:47
  B. men have generous hearts 31:20
  B. resolution ... 146:1
  He was a b. man ... 53:38
  It is a b. mouse ... 31:30

Nothing so b. as a blind mare 31:31
Bolder  What is b. than a miller's neck-cloth ... 124:29
Bone  The nearer the b. ... 76:6
Bonny  A b. bride is soon buskit ... 11:54
Book  A b. that is shut ... 188:12
  A great b. ... 188:14
  Every b. must be chewed ... 188:13
  You cannot open a b. ... 188:11
  You can't tell a b. ... 7:32
Books  B. and friends ... 72:64
Booted  They that are b. ... 7:12
Born  A man had better ne'er been b. ... 144:65
  As soon as man is b. ... 39:13
  He that is b. a fool ... 69:15
  He that is b. to be hanged ... 45:7
  He that is once b. ... 39:15
  Men know where they were b. ... 39:24
  We are not b. for ourselves 153:20
  Who is b. fair ... 11:56
Borrow  Not so good to b. ... 14:7
Borrowed  A b. loan ... 14:26
  B. garments ... 14:10
  B. thing ... 14:25
Borrower  Neither a b. nor a lender be 14:8
  The b. is servant to the lender 14:21
Borrowing  He that goes a b. ... 14:17
Borrows  He that b. binds himself ... 14:12
  He that b. must pay again ... 14:20
  Who b. to build ... 16:7
Both  You cannot have it b. ways 20:1
Boughs  The b. that bear most ... 81:20
Bound  No man is b. ... 104:51
  They that are b. ... 154:43
Bourbons  The B. learn nothing ... 133:33
Bourd  B. not with Bawty ... 37:49
  They that b. wi' cats ... 37:22
Bow  A b. long bent ... 56:15
  To b. the body is easy ... 182:4
Bows  Every man b. to the bush ... 68:9
Boys  B. will be boys 19:32
  B. will be men 19:42
  He that is manned with b. ... 154:4
  Two b. are half a boy ... 88:10
Brabbling  B. curs ... 141:13
Brag  B. is a good dog ... 24:7
Braggers  Great b. ... 24:14
Brain  If the b. sows not corn ... 114:7
Brains  The b. don't lie ... 125:31
Brave  A b. arm ... 31:17
  A b. man may fall ... 31:19
  A b. man's wounds ... 31:18
  B. men lived ... 64:13
  None but the b. ... 31:9

Some have been thought b. ... 32:19
To a b. and faithful man ... 31:24
Brawling   B. booteth not 141:14
Bread   B. is the staff of life 53:1
Man cannot live by b. alone 53:15
The b. never falls ... 111:23
Break   If things did not b. ... 124:16
You may b. a horse's back ... 164:12
Breaks   A man that b. his word ... 139:13
To him that b. his trust ... 139:14
Breams   He that has b. in his pond ...
53:35
Breath   The first b. ... 39:14
Bred   The best b. ... 15:2
What is b. in the bone ... 18:13
Bredon-hill   When B. puts on his hat ...
181:81
Breeks   Tarry b. ... 110:10
Brevity   B. is the soul of wit 168:77
Brewing   It is a sairy b. ... 17:38
Bribe   A b. will enter ... 29:27
Neither b. ... 29:26
Bricks   You can't make b. ... 108:27
Bride   Happy is the b. the sun shines on ...
113:144
Bridle   It is the b. and spur ... 49:5
Shake a b. over a Yorkshire tike's grave ...
58:29
Bright   B. rain ... 181:69
Look on the b. side 127:1
Brings   He that b. good news ... 122:2
He that b. himself ... 37:21
He that b. up his son to nothing ...
136:61
Broken   A b. friendship ... 72:83
B. bones well set ... 141:20
Broth   Good b. may be made ... 125:22
Brother   The b. had rather see the sister rich
... 115:20
Brown   It is a good thing to eat your b.
bread first 136:19
Bucket   Put not the b. too often in the well
56:17
Buckles   Every man b. his belt ... 47:9
Build   Don't b. the sty ... 6:13
Building   B. and borrowing ... 16:3
B. and marrying ... 16:4
B. is a sweet impoverishing 16:2
B. is a thief 16:1
No good b. ... 12:16
Bullet   Every b. ... 45:8
Bully   A b. is always a coward 32:17
Burden   It is not the b. ... 56:10
Too long b. ... 56:11
Burdens   The greatest b. ... 73:12
Burn   B. not your house ... 116:23

Burns   He that b. most ... 129:5
Burnt   The b. child ... 62:22
Burthen   A b. of one's own choice ...
147:7
Bush   A bad b. ... 80:18
Bushel   A b. of March dust ... 181:127
Busiest   B. men find the most leisure time
48:45
Business   B. before pleasure 22:24
B. is business 22:23
B. is the salt of life 48:9
Do b. with men ... 181:46
Do no b. with a kinsman 143:8
Everybody's b. ... 147:21
Every man knows his own b. best 99:19
Without b., debauchery 48:8
Busy   Ever b. ... 48:49
For the b. man ... 171:27
He that is b. ... 169:9
To be too b. ... 27:5
Who is more b. ... 95:11
Butter   B. is mad twice a year 30:21
B. is once a year ... 30:20
That which will not be b. ... 134:27
Buy   Better b. than borrow 14:1
B. at a fair ... 22:30
B. in the cheapest market ... 22:26
They b. good cheap ... 22:47
To b. dear ... 22:44
When you go to b. ... 22:3
Buyer   Let the b. beware 22:10
The b. needs a hundred eyes ... 22:12
Buyers   There are more foolish b. ... 22:13
Buys   He that b. and sells ... 22:28
Who b. dear and takes up on credit ...
22:25
Bygones   Let b. be bygones 71:17

# C

Caesar   C.'s wife ... 9:14
Cake   You cannot have your c. ... 20:2
Calamity   C. is the touchstone ... 37:18
Calf   C. love, half love ... 109:100
The c., the goose, the bee ... 188:2
They think a c. a muckle beast ... 160:37
Calm   In a c. sea ... 37:19
Camel   It is easier for a c. ... 180:36
The c. never sees its own hump ... 34:13
Can   He c. who believes he can 13:6
Man does what he c. ... 77:74
Those who c., do ... 54:22

Give me a c. for the first seven years ... 49:12
Let not a c. sleep ... 19:39
Put another man's c. in your bosom ... 128:24
The c. is father ... 19:41
The c. says nothing ... 19:22
When the c. is christened ... 88:17
Children  Better c. weep ... 49:10
  C. and chicken ... 19:19
  C. and fools cannot lie 19:21
  C. and fools have merry lives 69:1
  C. and fools must not play ... 69:7
  C. are certain cares ... 19:15
  C. are poor men's riches 19:4
  C. are to be deceived ... 19:16
  C. learn to creep ... 130:40
  C. pick up words ... 19:24
  C. should be seen ... 19:37
  C. suck the mother ... 19:9
  C. when they are little ... 19:13
  He that has c. ... 19:8
  He that has no c. brings. ... 3:61
  He that has no c. knows. ... 19:1
  What c. hear at home ... 19:23
  When c. stand quiet ... 19:38
China  In C. are more tutors ... 133:6
  In C. we have only three religions ... 133:5
Chinaman  A C. is ill only once ... 133:7
Choice  A man has c. to begin love ... 109:38
  No c. amongst stinking fish 20:10
  There's small c. in rotten apples 20:9
Choleric  From a c. man withdraw a little ... 5:10
Choose  C. a wife by your ear ... 113:82
  C. a wife on a Saturday ... 113:83
  C. neither women ... 20:6
  C. not a wife ... 113:81
  C. thy company ... 23:4
  C. your neighbour ... 121:3
  There is nothing to c. between bad tongues ... 79:39
Choosing  In c. a wife ... 113:63
Christian  A complete C. ... 144:50
Christmas  C. comes but once a year 126:2
Church  In c., in an inn ... 60:8
  The c. is an anvil ... 144:60
  What the c. takes not ... 144:63
Churchyard  A piece of c. fits everybody 39:72
Churl  A c.'s feast ... 80:13
Circumstances  C. alter cases 100:16
Cities  C. are taken by the ears 178:16
Citizens  The c. of Cork ... 133:79

City  A great c. ... 161:18
Civility  C. costs nothing 15:6
Clartier  The c. the cosier 21:4
Claw  C. me ... 88:26
Clean  C. and whole ... 21:3
Cleanliness  C. is next to godliness 21:1
Clear  A c. conscience fears not ... 26:14
  A c. conscience is like ... 26:23
  Preserve a c. conscience ... 26:17
Clemency  Sometimes c. is cruelty ... 101:17
Clent  The people of C. ... 58:82
Clergymen  C.'s sons ... 144:74
Clerks  The greatest c. ... 102:25
Clever  A c. man will build a city ... 184:97
Client  A c. twixt his attorney ... 104:37
Climb  He who would c. the ladder ... 130:45
Climbed  He that never c. ... 151:7
Cloak  Have not thy c. to make ... 70:15
  It is good to have a c. for the rain 147:39
Clock  One cannot put back the c. 17:21
Clogs  From c. to clogs ... 136:84
Close  A c. mouth ... 156:5
Clothe  C. thee in war ... 132:8
  C. thee warm ... 53:53
Clothes  C. do not make the man 50:10
  C. make people ... 50:1
  Good c. open all doors 50:5
Cloud  Every c. has a silver lining 127:20
Clouds  All c. bring not rain 7:30
  If the c. look as if scratched by a hen ... 181:82
Cloudy  C. mornings ... 127:17
Clout  Ne'er cast a c. ... 117:55
Clown  Give a c. your finger ... 101:15
Coach  A c. and four ... !04:11
Coat  He who has but one c. ... 105:4
  It is not the gay c. ... 7:7
Cobble  They that can c. and clout ... 124:4
Cobbler  Let the c. stick ... 124:22
Cock  Every c. will crow ... 31:27
  If the c. crows on going to bed ... 181:1
  If the c. moult before the hen ... 181:2
  There's many a good c. ... 7:36
  Who eats his c. alone ... 153:23
Cockers  He that c. his child ... 49:17
Coin  Much c. ... 180:16
  Where c. is not common ... 136:41
Cold  A c. April the barn will fill 181:90
  A c. May and a windy ... 181:91
  C. hands, warm heart 167:20
  C. pudding ... 109:77
  Feed a c. ... 87:37

# COUNSEL

If c. wind reach you through a hole ...
87:24

The c. is Russia's cholera 133:59

Coldest  In the c. flint ...  7:41

Comes  Everything c. to him who waits
130:13

He that c. of a hen ...  18:5

Coming  C. events ...  171:53

Command  C. your man ...  153:33
He is not fit to c. others ...  9:19
The c. of custom ...  104:59

Commands  He c. enough ...  183:24

Commits  He that c. a fault ...  26:12

Commodity  Every c. ...  98:2

Common  C. fame is a liar 79:8
C. fame is seldom to blame 79:1
C. proverb ...  140:7

Companion  A merry c. ...  23:7
There is no c. like the penny 180:7

Company  A man is known by the c. ...
23:11
Good c. upon the road ...  23:6
It is good to have c. in trouble 186:15
Keep c. with good men ...  23:16
Keep good men c. ...  23:3
Keep not ill men c. ...  29:13
The c. makes the feast 23:5

Comparison  It is c. that makes men ...
84:4

Comparisons  C. are odious 100:15

Complains  He c. wrongfully on the sea ...
62:30

Complies  He that c. against his will ...
182:20

Complimentary  One c. letter ...  68:11

Confess  C. and be hanged 89:14

Confide  C. in an aunt ...  79:21

Congruity  C. is the mother of love 109:68

Conquer  Though the left hand c. the right
...  178:25

Conquering  There is no such c. weapon ...
120:3

Conquers  He c. who endures 56:1

Conscience  A good c. is a continual feast
26:22
A good c. is a soft pillow 26:20
A good c. is the best divinity 26:21
A good c. makes an easy couch 26:19
C. does make cowards ...  26:9
C. is a cut-throat 26:2
C. is a thousand witnesses 26:3
Some make a c. ...  94:20
Whose c. is cumbered ...  26:10

Consciences  Men whose c. are clear ...
26:15

Consolation  Great c. may grow ...  140:3

Constancy  The c. of the benefit of the year
...  77:33

Constant  A c. guest ...  92:11
C. dripping ...  134:18

Consulting  Too much c. confounds 3:29

Contempt  C. is the sharpest reproof 27:7
C. pierces ...  27:10
C. will sooner ...  27:6

Contending  It is ill c. with the master ...
37:46

Content  C. is all 28:1
C. is happiness 28:4
C. is more ...  28:3
C. is the philosopher's stone ...  28:5
C. lodges ...  28:10
He who is c. in his poverty ...  28:6
Let every man be c. ...  28:45
No man is c. ...  28:35

Contented  A c. mind ...  28:8
He may well be c. ...  28:11
Who is c. ...  28:9

Contention  C.'s roots are three ...  141:1

Convenience  No c. ...  98:1

Conversation  C. makes one what he is
168:96
C. teaches more ...  168:97

Converses  He that c. not ...  168:99

Cooks  Too many c. ...  88:9

Cool  A c. mouth ...  87:11

Cord  The c. breaks at last ...  56:22

Corn  C. and horn go together 30:5
C. him well ...  131:5
C. is cleansed with wind ...  49:2
If you look at your c. ...  117:56
When the c. is in the shock ...  30:6

Cornish  All C. gentlemen ...  58:37

Cornwall  C. will bear a shower ...  58:39

Corporations  C. have neither bodies ...
147:23

Corrects  He that c. not small faults ...
49:3

Corruption  C. of the best ...  29:23
The c. of one thing ...  29:22

Cost  The more c. ...  187:12

Costs  It c. more to do ill ...  78:50
Nothing c. so much ...  75:39
What c. little ...  187:11

Counsel  Come not to c. uncalled 3:51
C. is irksome ...  3:7
C. is no command 3:10
C. is to be given ...  3:35
C. must be followed ...  3:20
C. over cups ...  3:43
C. will make a man ...  3:14
Give neither c. nor salt ...  3:50
Good c. has no price 3:1

279

Good c. never comes amiss 3:3
Good c. never comes too late 3:2
If the c. be good ... 3:38
Ill c. mars all 3:15
Take c. only ... 3:11
The c. thou wouldst have another keep ...
3:55
We have better c. to give ... 3:56
Counselled He that will not be c. ... 3:19
Counsellor Like c. ... 3:31
Counsellors Though thou hast never so
many c. ... 3:12
Counsels C. in wine ... 3:42
Count C. not four ... 6:10
Don't c. your chickens ... 6:6
Countries All c. stand in need of Britain
... 133:65
So many c., so many customs 104:65
Country In the c. of the blind ... 81:15
Couple Every c. is not a pair 47:7
Courage A man of c. ... 31:16
C. and perseverance ... 31:2
C. and resolution ... 31:1
Course The c. of true love ... 109:50
Court At c., every one for himself 149:27
Far from c., far from care 149:36
He that lives in c. ... 149:33
Long in c. ... 149:37
Whoso will dwell in c. ... 149:28
Courtesy C. is cumbersome ... 15:22
C. is the inseparable companion ... 15:8
Full of c. ... 36:8
Courtiers C. are shod ... 149:32
Covet All c., all lose 82:17
Covetous C. men live drudges ... 115:15
C. men's chests ... 115:8
Over c. was never good 82:14
The c. man is good to none ... 115:18
The c. spends more than the liberal 82:24
Covetousness C. breaks the sack 82:13
C. brings nothing home 82:19
C. is always filling ... 82:4
C. is the father ... 82:8
C. is the root ... 82:12
C. often starves ... 82:10
Cow Bring a c. to the hall ... 18:36
Look to the c. ... 30:28
Many a good c. ... 18:16
The c. knows not ... 187:7
The c. that's first up ... 52:3
Why buy a c. ... 113:25
Coward It is better to be a c. ... 32:12
Put a c. to his mettle ... 32:20
Cowardice C. is afraid ... 32:8
Cowards C. are cruel 32:16

C. die many times ... 32:3
C. die often 32:2
C. run the greatest danger ... 32:1
Many would be c. ... 32:18
Of c. no history ... 32:10
Cowl The c. does not make the monk 7:8
Crab You cannot make a c. walk straight
18:38
Cradle If you rock the c. empty ... 167:27
Craft C. must have clothes ... 176:19
No man is his c.'s master ... 130:38
Crafty A c. knave ... 36:7
To a c. man ... 36:13
Cranes A thousand c. in the air ... 135:3
Crave Nothing c. ... 4:5
Cravers Sore c. ... 131:28
Creaking A c. gate ... 87:31
Credit C. lost ... 64:22
Give c. ... 100:14
He that has lost his c. ... 64:21
Creditors C. have better memories ...
14:19
Creep First c. ... 130:41
Crime C. does not pay 33:20
What greater c. ... 171:31
Crimes C. are made secure ... 33:12
Cripple He that dwells next door to a c. ...
29:15
Croaking The c. raven ... 167:17
Crook There is a c. in the lot ... 2:22
Crooked A c. man should sow beans ...
30:18
C. logs ... 7:37
Crooks Timely c. the tree ... 19:45
Cross Don't c. the bridge ... 186:17
Each c. has its inscription 166:20
No c., no crown 166:8
Crosses C. are ladders ... 166:7
Crow How can a c. sleep soundly ...
169:11
Crowd A c. is not company 161:19
Crown A c. is no cure ... 149:13
Crowns C. have cares 149:8
Cruelty A man of c. ... 35:1
C. deserves no mercy 35:2
C. is a tyrant ... 35:12
C. is more cruel ... 43:11
C. is the first attribute ... 35:3
C. is the strength ... 35:4
Crust A c. is better than no bread 80:9
Crutch The c. of time ... 171:11
Cry Don't c. before you are hurt 186:19
Crying It is no use c. ... 142:5
Cuckold Who is a c. and conceals it ...
155:12

Cuckoo The c. comes in April ... 117:38
  The c. goes to Beaulieu Fair ... 117:40
  When the c. comes, he eats ... 152:6
  When the c. comes to the bare thorn ...
  30:35
Cunning C. surpasses strength 36:1
  Too much c. undoes 36:4
Cupar He that will to C. ... 182:27
Cure A c. for all sorrows ... 162:45
  The c. for old age ... 125:62
  There's no c. for sorrow ... 162:53
Cured What can't be c. ... 56:3
Curiosity C. is endless ... 99:2
  C. is ill manners ... 15:18
  C. killed the cat 99:1
Curses C., like chickens ... 44:14
Custom A bad c. ... 104:64
  C. has the force of law 104:61
  C. is the plague ... 104:62
  C. makes all things easy 62:10
  C. reconciles us ... 83:6
  C. rules the law 104:60
  C. takes the taste ... 65:11
  C. without reason ... 104:63
Customer The c. is always right 22:32
Customs With c. we live well ... 104:58
Cut Better c. the shoe ... 150:8
  C. off a dog's tail ... 18:26
  C. your coat ... 163:19
  Don't c. off your nose ... 148:12
  Don't c. the bough ... 85:40
Cut-purse A c. is a sure trade ... 33:41
Czech Every C. is a musician 133:19

# D

Dainties The d. of the great ... 136:91
  Who d. love ... 163:16
Dallies He that d. with his enemy ...
  37:20
Dally D. not with women ... 184:73
Dam Where the d. leaps over ... 61:13
Dance They that d. ... 147:19
  When you go to d. ... 175:17
Dances He d. well ... 111:32
Danger Better pass a d. once ... 66:12
  D. is next neighbour ... 37:30
  D. itself ... 37:31
  D. makes men devout 37:16
  Nought is never in d. 151:6
  The more d. ... 37:29
  Without d. ... 37:32
Darkest The d. hour ... 127:15

Dart River of D. ... 58:49
Daughter He that would the d. win ...
  109:86
  When the d. is stolen ... 142:32
Daughters Two d. and a back door ...
  184:68
David D. and Chad ... 117:27
  First comes D. ... 117:29
  St. D.'s Day ... 117:26
Dawted D. daughters ... 49:20
Day As the d. lengthens ... 181:93
  Every d. of thy life ... 107:16
  No d. passes ... 162:31
  No d. so clear ... 97:32
  One d. of pleasure ... 84:36
  One may see d. ... 160:19
  The better the d. ... 144:64
  The d. obliterates ... 139:5
Days One of these d. ... 43:24
  So many d. old ... 181:9
Dead A d. bee ... 39:29
  A d. mouse ... 39:37
  A d. wife's the best goods ... 113:128
  D. dogs ... 39:48
  D. men are of no family ... 39:94
  D. men don't bite 39:49
  D. men have no friends 39:96
  D. men tell no tales 39:50
  Let the d. bury their dead 39:98
  The d. are always wrong 39:97
  To d. men and absent ... 39:95
Deadly A d. disease ... 87:44
  The most d. of wild beasts ... 68:15
Deaf A d. husband ... 113:114
  D. men go away ... 147:27
  None so d. ... 182:29
Deal If you can d. with an Armenian ...
  133:61
  If you d. with a fox ... 36:15
  They that d. wi' the devil ... 46:17
Dear D. bought is the honey ... 37:26
  He that could know what would be d. ...
  22:31
  It is a d. collop ... 109:111
Dearer The d. it is the cheaper 22:46
Dearths D. foreseen come not 186:20
Death D. alone can kill hope 91:15
  D. and proverbs ... 140:18
  D. carries a fat tsar ... 39:80
  D. combs us all ... 39:79
  D. defies the doctor 39:18
  D. devours lambs ... 39:68
  D. does not recognize strength 39:20
  D. hath not so ghastly a face ... 39:84
  D. is a dying man's friend 39:45
  D. is a remedy ... 39:38

D. is deaf ... 39:19
D. is sure to all 39:5
D. is the black camel ... 39:8
D. is the end of all 39:27
D. is the great leveller 39:71
D. is the only master ... 39:65
D. is the poor man's ... 39:40
D. keeps no calendar 39:21
D. makes us equal ... 39:78
D. pays all debts 39:42
D. rather frees us ... 39:41
D.'s day ... 39:36
D. sends his challenge ... 125:65
D. surprises us ... 39:23
Look upon d. ... 39:46
The ·d. of a young wolf ... 39:51
The d. of the wolves ... 39:52
When d. is on the tongue ... 39:61
Debt A man in d. ... 14:13
D. is an evil conscience 14:15
D. is the worst poverty 14:4
Out of d. ... 14:35
Debtors D. are liars 14:23
Of ill d., men take oats 14:39
Deceive He that will d. the fox ... 52:16
To d. a deceiver ... 40:25
To d. oneself ... 40:33
Who thinks to d. God ... 40:32
Deceivers D. have full mouths ... 40:39
Deceives He that d. me once ... 62:31
He that once d. ... 40:16
Deceiving D. those that trust us ... 40:21
Deed A good d. is never lost 41:32
An evil d. remains ... 41:42
An ill d. cannot bring honour 41:40
Every d. is to be judged ... 41:28
One good d. atones ... 41:31
The d. comes back ... 44:10
To see a man do a good d. ... 41:33
Deeds By his d. ... 41:4
D. are fruits ... 41:8
D. are males ... 184:103
D. will show themselves ... 41:11
Evil d. are like perfume ... 41:47
Deeply They that too d. loved ... 86:6
Defects Every man has the d. of his quali-
ties 179:18
Deferred What is d. ... 43:17
Delay After a d. ... 43:16
D. is the antidote ... 43:10
That d. is good ... 43:6
Delays D. are dangerous 43:1
D. are not denials 8:18
Delight There is more d. in hope ... 91:8
Deliver D. your words ... 168:79
Demand Where the d. is a jest ... 27:4

Demands He that d. misses not ... 8:7
Denial A civil d. ... 8:17
Depends He who d. on another ... 153:36
Descent The d. to hell ... 144:34
Desert D. and reward ... 44:5
Deserves He d. not the sweet ... 44:22
Desire D. has no rest 4:17
Desires D. are nourished ... 43:7
He that d. but little ... 28:20
Despair D. gives courage ... 31:12
Desperate D. cuts ... 145:12
Destiny A man's d. ... 45:10
D. has four feet ... 45:1
Destroy D. the nests ... 145:14
Devil Away goes the d. ... 169:15
Better keep the d. at the door ... 169:14
Better the d. you know ... 17:10
Give the d. his due 100:13
He that has shipped the d. ... 147:14
He that takes the d. into his boat ...
147:13
He that the d. drives ... 46:8
If the d. find a man idle ... 95:15
Said the d. when flying ... 58:57
The d. always leaves ... 46:5
The d. and the dean ... 144:85
The d. can cite Scripture ... 46:2
The d. dances ... 136:62
The d. finds work ... 95:14
The d. gets up to the belfry ... 29:36
The d. goes shares in gaming 74:1
The d. is a busy bishop ... 46:13
The d. is at home 46:14
The d. is busy ... 181:23
The d. is God's ape 77:67
The d. is in the dice 74:9
The d. is not so black ... 42:14
The d. is subtle ... 46:1
The d. knows many things ... 46:9
The d. looks after his own 111:43
The d. loves no holy water 46:16
The d. lurks ... 46:15
The d. makes his Christmas-pies ... 29:42
The d. never assails a man ... 96:12
The d.'s children ... 111:44
The d. sets his foot ... 117:68
The d.'s meal ... 33:23
The d.'s mouth ... 115:21
The d. sometimes speaks ... 46:4
The d. tempts all ... 169:10
The d. was sick ... 144:40
The d. will not come into Cornwall ...
58:38
The d. will play ... 46:12
The d. wipes his tail ... 136:103
There is a d. in every berry ... 51:26

There is no d. so bad ... 184:4
What is got over the d.'s back ... 112:23
When the d. prays ... 46:3
Where the d. cannot come ... 46:11
**Dicing** D., drabbing and drinking ... 51:30
**Die** All men must d. 39:3
A man can d. ... 39:43
Better d. with honour ... 32:9
Better to d. a beggar ... 170:34
He begins to d. ... 4:11
Never say d. 134:21
They d. well ... 39:86
**Dies** He d. like a beast ... 39:88
Man d. and leave a name ... 118:6
**Difference** The d. is wide ... 141:36
There is a d. between 'Will you buy?' ... 22:9
There is great d. ... 41:19
There is no d. of bloods ... 60:11
There's little d. between a feast and a bellyful 76:19
**Difficult** All things are d. ... 130:39
The d. is done at once ... 108:17
**Diligence** D. is a great teacher 48:5
D. is the mother ... 48:2
D. makes an expert workman 48:4
Without d. ... 48:34
**Diligent** A d. scholar ... 48:11
D. youth ... 19:63
For the d. the week ... 48:58
The d. spinner ... 48:24
**Dimple** A d. in the chin, a devil within 167:23
A d. in the chin, your living comes in ... 167:22
**Ding** You may d. the devil ... 49:29
**Dinner** After d. sit awhile ... 53:51
Better a d. of herbs ... 86:9
If you want your d. ... 53:77
**Dirt** He that deals in d. ... 29:10
He that falls into the d. ... 42:6
He that flings d. at another ... 42:11
Throw d. enough ... 42:1
**Discontent** A man's d. ... 28:31
D. is the first step ... 28:30
**Discontented** A d. man ... 28:32
**Discourse** Sweet d. ... 168:100
**Discreet** D. women ... 168:91
While the d. advise ... 3:16
**Discretion** D. is the better part of valour 31:32
**Disease** A d. known ... 87:34
Whatsoever was the father of a d. ... 53:64
When a d. returns ... 87:42

**Diseases** D. are the price ... 87:21
**Dish** No d. pleases all palates alike 47:16
**Dishes** Many d. ... 53:65
**Disputants** Of two d. ... 141:32
**Dispute** In too much d. ... 141:18
**Disputing** There is no d. a proverb ... 140:9
**Dissemble** Who knows not how to d. ... 94:1
**Distaff** On St. D.'s Day ... 117:5
**Distance** D. lends enchantment ... 7:26
**Distrust** Wise d. ... 175:28
**Divide** D. and rule 141:24
**Divine** D. grace ... 77:46
**Divinity** There's a d. that shapes our ends ... 45:9
**Do** D. as most men do ... 25:12
D. not all you can ... 116:19
D. right ... 26:16
D. what you ought ... 45:4
He that may not d. as he would ... 28:49
If thou thyself canst d. it ... 153:30
It is better to d. well ... 41:13
**Doctor** If the d. cures ... 87:50
One d. makes work ... 87:51
The d. is often ... 87:52
**Doctors** The best d. ... 87:35
**Dog** A good d. ... 44:1
Better to have a d. fawn on you ... 27:17
D. does not eat dog 110:6
Every d. has his day 111:41
Every d. is a lion ... 31:29
Every d. is allowed ... 104:55
Every d. is valiant ... 31:28
Give a d. a bad name ... 42:7
He that keeps another man's d. ... 80:32
If the d. is not at home ... 1:13
If you would wish the d. to follow you ... 154:15
It is an ill d. ... 44:8
It is a poor d. ... 187:16
Never d. barked against the crucifix ... 144:18
One d., one bull 100:20
Only a d. and a Frenchman ... 133:31
The d. bites the stone ... 147:34
The d. that fetches ... 79:37
The d. that is idle ... 95:13
Why keep a d. ... 154:20
**Dogged** It's d. as does it 134:2
**Dogs** D. bark as they are bred 15:23
D. that bark at a distance ... 168:40
D. wag their tails ... 68:8
D. will redd swine 141:37
If you lie down with d. ... 29:16
Many d. may easily worry ... 100:22

Doing  D. is better than saying 41:12
In d. we learn 62:15
Done  Do as you would be d. by 61:10
Whatever man has d. ...  108:5
What's d. cannot be undone 142:1
When a thing is d. ...  3:8
Donkey  Send a d. to Paris ...  172:11
Donkeys  Scabby d. ...  157:11
Door  A d. must either be shut or open 20:4
Every d. may be shut ...  39:9
When one d. shuts ...  127:2
Double  D. charge ...  56:13
He gets a d. victory ...  49:34
Doubt  D. is the key ...  13:21
When in d. ...  146:10
Down  He that is d. ...  2:15
Dowry  A great d. ...  113:53
Draught  Back to the d. ...  87:25
Draw  Never d. your dirk ...  116:21
Drawn  D. wells ...  177:5
Dream  A d. grants ...  159:28
After a d. of a wedding ...  159:21
D. of a funeral ...  159:20
Dreams  D. are lies 159:25
D. go by contraries 159:24
In d. and in love ...  159:29
Dress  D. up a stick ...  50:7
Dressing  Fine d. ...  50:8
Dries  Nothing d. sooner than tears 162:26
Drink  A good d. ...  51:20
Do not d. between meals 51:63
D. as much after an egg ...  51:64
D. less ...  51:57
D. only with the duck 51:55
D. wine, and have the gout ...  51:70
If you d. in your pottage ...  51:69
Those who d. but water ...  51:54
When you d. from the stream ...  80:4
Drinking  D. water ...  51:53
Drinks  He that d. not wine ...  51:71
He who d. a little too much ...  51:68
Dripping  A d. June ...  181:56
Drive  D. your business ...  22:22
Drops  Many d. ...  160:13
Drought  D. never bred dearth ...  181:123
Drowning  A d. man ...  91:14
Drums  Where d. beat ...  104:13
Drunk  Ever d. ...  51:77
Drunkard  A d.'s purse ...  51:13
Let but the d. alone ...  51:12
Drunkards  D. and fools ...  51:3
There are more old d. ...  51:17
Drunken  A d. man is always dry 51:76
D. days ...  51:11
D. folks seldom take harm 51:16

Drunkenness  D. does not produce faults ...  51:6
The best cure for d. ...  51:15
Dry  A d. cough ...  87:32
D. August ...  181:122
D. bread at home ...  172:26
D. feet ...  87:12
Dumb  D. dogs ...  156:35
D. men get no lands 168:21
Dunder  D. do gally the beans 181:73
Dust  While the d. is on your feet ...  22:17
Dwarf  A d. on a giant's shoulders ...  102:19
Dwell  Wherever a man d. ...  97:35
Dying  D. is as natural as living 39:11
D. men speak true 39:60

# E

Eagles  E. do not breed doves 18:3
E. don't catch flies 81:31
Ear  What is told in the e. of a man ...  79:18
Early  E. master ...  163:12
E. rain and a woman's tears ...  184:34
E. sow ...  52:14
E. to bed ...  52:7
E. wed ...  113:90
The e. bird ...  52:1
The e. man never borrows ...  52:13
Ears  It is better to play with the e. ...  168:75
Earth  E. is the best shelter 39:47
Six feet of e. ...  39:75
Earthen  The e. pot ...  179:6
Ease  He is at e. ...  28:13
Easier  E. said than done 41:23
It is e. to commend poverty ...  136:46
Easily  That which is e. done ...  13:3
East  E., west ...  172:21
Too far e. ...  116:38
Easter  At E., let your clothes be new ...  117:34
E. so longed for ...  6:4
When E. Day lies in our Lady's lap ...  117:35
Easterly  E. winds and rain ...  181:38
Easy  All things are e. ...  182:12
E. come ...  163:9
It is e. to bear ...  2:10
It is e. to be wise ...  142:25
It is e. to do ...  182:13
It is e. to keep a castle ...  169:16

Nothing is e. to the unwilling 182:19
Eat   Don't e. the calf ... 6:18
  E. an apple going to bed ... 53:58
  E. at pleasure ... 53:57
  E. to live ... 53:56
  He that will e. the kernel ... 48:37
  We must e. a peck of dirt ... 21:7
Eating   E. and drinking ... 53:22
Eats   He that e. least ... 53:55
  He that e. the king's goose ... 33:17
  He that e. till he is sick ... 76:7
Economy   There is no e. in going to bed
  early ... 170:39
Education   E. begins a gentleman ...
  168:98
  E. polishes good natures ... 54:1
Effect   The e. speaks ... 41:7
Egg   Better an e. in peace ... 132:12
  Better an e. today ... 135:7
  The e. shows the hen ... 3:40
Eggs   Don't put all your e. in one basket
  151:18
  E. and oaths ... 139:2
  He that would have e. ... 98:5
Elbow   E. grease ... 48:13
Elder   When e.'s white ... 30:50
Ell   E. and tell ... 22:16
Elm   Every e. has its man 30:42
Emperor   The e. of Germany ... 133:13
Empty   An e. belly ... 93:5
  An e. purse causes a full heart 136:43
  An e. purse fills the face ... 136:45
  An e. sack ... 136:64
  E. vessels ... 69:75
End   At the e. of the game ... 60:23
  Everything has an e. 55:6
  The e. crowns the work 55:1
  The e. justifies the means 10:49
  The e. makes all equal 39:77
  The e. of passion ... 129:7
Ends   That never e. ill ... 77:18
Endure   He that will not e. labour ...
  48:42
  He that will not e. to itch ... 56:5
Endures   He that e. is not overcome 56:2
Enemies   Better a thousand e. ... 57:9
  If you have no e. ... 57:2
Enemy   An e. may chance ... 57:1
  An e.'s mouth ... 57:6
  An e. to beauty ... 11:58
  Better an open e. ... 72:14
  Better go by your e.'s grave ... 57:11
  Every man is his own worst e. 153:37
  For a flying e. ... 57:13
  His own e. ... 72:55

If you would make an e. ... 105:9
Make your e. your friend 57:12
Nothing worse than a familiar e. 57:8
One e. can do more hurt ... 57:4
One e. is too many ... 57:5
There is no little e. 57:3
Though thy e. seem a mouse ... 57:16
England   E. is a good land ... 58:1
  E. is a little garden ... 58:5
  E. is the paradise of women ... 58:2
  E. is the ringing island 58:3
  E. were but a fling ... 178:23
  When E. wrings ... 181:57
English   An E. summer ... 152:9
  Every E. archer ... 58:14
  The E. are a nation ... 58:8
  The E. are the swearing nation 58:13
  The E. have one hundred religions ...
  58:11
  The E. love ... 133:28
  The E. never know ... 58:16
Englishman   An E. is never happy ...
  133:66
  An E. loves a lord 58:18
  An E.'s word ... 58:12
  A right E. ... 58:17
  It is an E.'s privilege ... 58:19
  One E. can beat ... 58:15
  The E. Italianate ... 133:34
  The E. weeps ... 133:67
  What an E. cares to invent ... 133:54
Enough   E. is as good ... 28:14
  He has e. who is contented ... 28:21
  More than e. ... 28:15
  Of e., men leave 28:16
  There was never e. ... 28:17
Enquire   E. not what boils ... 99:14
Enter   He that will e. into Paradise ...
  144:27
  When you e. into a house ... 5:30
Enters   Nothing e. into a close hand 115:7
Envied   Better be e. ... 136:89
Envies   He who e. admits his inferiority
  59:10
Envious   An e. man waxes lean ... 59:6
  The e. man shall never want woe 59:5
Envy   E. and covetousness ... 59:4
  E. and idleness ... 59:7
  E. eats nothing ... 59:1
  E. envies itself 59:9
  E. never dies 59:3
  E. never enriched any man 59:11
  E. shoots at others ... 59:2
  If e. were a fever ... 59:12
Equal   If all were e. ... 60:3

Ermine  In an e. spots are soon discovered 11:45
Err  To e. is human 97:4
  To e. is human; to forgive, divine 71:7
Errs  Who e. and mends ... 142:38
Escaped  The e. mouse ... 62:29
Essex  E. stiles ... 58:32
Ethiopian  When the E. is white ... 133:29
Evening  E. red and morning grey ... 181:21
  The e. crowns the day 39:32
Every  E. day braw ... 50:16
Evil  Bear with e. ... 91:27
  E. communications ... 29:1
  E. doers are evil dreaders 10:44
  For every e. under the sun ... 145:5
  He that does e. ... 10:20
  Never do e. ... 10:50
  Of an e. crow ... 18:4
  Of e. grain ... 18:12
  Put off the e. hour ... 43:9
  The e. that men do lives after them ... 41:53
  Whoso will no e. do ... 41:46
Evils  Of two e. ... 20:7
  Some e. are cured ... 27:8
  The e. we bring on ourselves ... 147:9
Example  A good e. ... 61:5
  E. is better than precept 61:2
Exception  The e. proves the rule 173:12
Excess  If in e. ... 116:29
Exchange  Fair e. is no robbery 100:18
Excuse  A bad e. ... 147:38
Excuses  Bad e. ... 147:37
  He who e. himself ... 147:36
Expect  We may not e. a good whelp ... 18:1
  What can you e. from a pig ... 18:39
Expectation  E. is better than realization 6:1
Expects  Blessed is he who e. nothing ... 6:26
Experience  E. is a precious gift ... 62:6
  E. is good ... 62:3
  E. is the best teacher 62:13
  E. is the mistress ... 62:19
  E. is the mother ... 62:1
  E. keeps a dear school ... 62:20
  E. must be bought 62:18
  E. without learning ... 62:4
Experiment  Make your e. ... 173:9
Extreme  E. justice ... 100:6
  E. law ... 116:35
  No e. will hold long 116:36
Extremes  E. are dangerous 116:40
  E. meet 116:37

Extremity  Every e. ... 116:34
  Man's e. ... 77:43
Eye  An e. for an eye ... 148:16
  Better e. out ... 150:10
  Better e. sore ... 80:22
  Better to have one e. ... 80:23
  Far from e. ... 1:5
  If thine e. offend thee ... 150:9
  One e. of the master ... 49:36
  The e. is bigger ... 53:19
  The e. of the master ... 49:35
  The e. that sees all things ... 34:15
  What the e. doesn't see ... 96:6
Eyes  Four e. see more than two 88:7
  In the e. of the lover ... 109:4
  Keep your e. open ... 22:11
  Keep your e. wide open ... 113:44
  Many e. are upon ... 149:11
  The e. are the window ... 63:1
Eyewitness  One e. ... 63:5

# F

Face  A good f. is a letter of recommendation 11:14
  A good f. needs no band ... 11:55
  F. to face ... 176:29
  He that looks in a man's f. ... 7:10
  The f. is no index ... 7:9
Facts  F. are stubborn things 176:15
Failed  He is good that f. never 97:8
Failure  F. teaches success 165:10
Faint  F. heart ... 32:7
Fair  A f. day in winter ... 181:118
  A f. death ... 39:91
  A f. face cannot have ... 11:57
  A f. face is half a portion 11:15
  A f. wife and a frontier castle ... 11:50
  A f. woman without virtue ... 11:22
  All is f. ... 109:81
  F. and softly ... 85:50
  F. face, foul heart 11:4
  F. fall truth ... 176:3
  F. is not fair ... 11:36
  F. play's a jewel 100:17
  F. without ... 11:7
  F. words make fools fain 69:71
  In f. weather ... 70:13
  Of f. things the autumn is fair 152:10
  The f. and the foul ... 11:16
  There is many a f. thing ... 11:6
  Who has a f. wife ... 11:48

Fairer  The f. the paper ...  11:46
Fairest  The f. flowers ...  11:31
The f. rose ...  11:32
The f. silk ...  11:44
Faith  F. will move mountains 13:7
Men have greater f. ...  13:4
Put no f. in tale-bearers 79:30
Faithfulness  F. is a sister of love 110:2
Fall  F. not out with a friend ...  72:85
To f. into sin ...  10:35
Fallen  He that is f. ...  88:3
Falls  He that f. today ...  127:10
When one f. ...  147:31
False  A f. friend and a shadow ...  72:32
A f. tongue ...  40:2
F. with one ...  40:38
Two f. knaves ...  10:41
Falsehood  F. never made a fair hinder end 40:18
There is f. in fellowship 40:3
Fame  All f. is dangerous ...  64:8
F. is a magnifying glass 64:5
F. is a thin shadow ...  64:11
F. is but the breath ...  64:10
F. is the perfume ...  64:2
F., like a river ...  64:12
From f. to infamy ...  64:7
Good f. is better than a good face 64:14
Familiarity  F. breeds contempt 65:1
Family  Every f. cooking-pot ...  143:16
The f. that prays together ...  144:99
Famine  A f. in England ...  30:9
After a f. in the stall ...  93:1
All's good in a f. 93:13
F., pestilence, and war ...  178:1
Far  A man f. from his good ...  37:2
F. folk fare best 1:30
F. fowls ...  7:28
He that goes f. ...  172:19
Farm  He that will have his f. full ...  30:34
Fashion  Every man after his f. 47:8
The present f. ...  50:11
What has been the f. ...  50:13
Fasts  He f. enough that has had a bad meal 93:25
He f. enough whose wife scolds ...  93:26
Who f. and does no other good ...  93:24
Fat  A f. belly ...  76:3
F. paunches ...  76:2
F. sorrow ...  180:12
Fate  F. leads the willing ...  45:6
Father  A f.'s goodness ...  128:2
He whose f. is judge ...  128:13
If you live without being a f. ...  19:3
Like f., like son 128:8

One f. is enough ...  128:3
One f. is more ...  128:4
The f. to the bough ...  104:57
Fathers  Our f. which were wondrous wise ...  51:62
Fault  A f. confessed ...  142:39
He has f. of a wife ...  113:66
He may find f. ...  34:22
Like f. ...  44:17
Who is in f. ...  26:11
Faults  Every man has his f. 97:1
Every one's f. are not written ...  34:20
F. are thick ...  109:16
Faulty  The f. stands on his guard 26:5
Favour  F. will as surely perish ...  149:31
Fazarts  To f. ...  32:4
Fear  All f. is bondage 66:10
F. can keep a man out of danger ...  31:4
F. gives wings 66:4
F. has a quick ear 66:5
F. has magnifying eyes 66:6
F. is a great inventor 66:7
F. is one part ...  66:14
F. is stronger ...  66:16
F. is the prison ...  66:11
F. nothing but sin 10:31
F. of death ...  39:81
F. the Greeks ...  75:42
Men f. death ...  39:83
'Twas f. that first ...  66:8
Wise f. begets care 66:15
Fearful  Better a f. end ...  66:13
Fears  He that f. death ...  39:82
He that f. every bush ...  66:22
He that f. every grass ...  66:23
He that f. leaves ...  66:24
He that f. you present ...  1:14
No man f. what he has seen grow 65:8
Who f. to suffer ...  66:9
Feather  A f. in hand ...  135:6
F. by feather ...  134:13
Feathers  Fine f. ...  50:6
February  If in F. there be no rain ...  181:121
Februeer  F. doth cut and shear 117:7
Feed  F. by measure ...  53:54
Feet  All f. tread not ...  47:3
The f. of the avenging deities ...  77:63
Fellow-ruler  He that has a f. ...  9:29
Female  The f. of the species ...  184:102
Fence  There's no f. against ill fortune 111:24
Fences  Good f. ...  121:17
Fern  When f. grows red ...  152:11
When the f. is as high as a spoon ...  30:53

Fetters  No man loves his f. ...  154:35
Fewer  The f. the words ...  144:92
Field  A f. requires three things ...  30:1
Fields  F. have eyes ...  79:23
Fight  F. fire ...  178:19
Fights  He that f. and runs away ...  32:15
Fill  Better f. a man's belly ...  53:20
Filth  The f. under the white snow ...  7:44
Finders  F. keepers ...  135:17
Finding  F.'s keeping 135:18
Fine  F. words dress ill deeds 94:10
Fingers  F. were made before forks ...
  53:68
Finland  F. is the devil's country 133:20
Fire  As f. is kindled by bellows ...  5:16
  F. cannot be hidden ...  18:42
  F. that's closest kept ...  129:15
  Give me f. ...  88:27
  He that can make a f. well ...  141:38
  One's own f. is pleasant 172:25
  Put not f. to flax 174:12
First  F. come ...  52:5
  F. impressions ...  12:5
  F. things first 130:44
  He that comes f. to the hill ...  52:4
  The f. and last frosts ...  181:101
  The f. blow ...  12:6
  The f. day a guest ...  92:14
  The f. degree of folly ...  69:48
  The f. dish is aye best eaten 53:23
  The f. dish pleases all 53:24
  The f. faults ...  71:26
  What we f. learn ...  54:15
Fish  All's f. that comes to the net 177:8
  Big f. ...  81:43
  F. and guests ...  92:13
  F. begins to stink ...  29:20
  F. must swim thrice 51:47
  'Had I f.' ...  182:38
  That f. will soon be caught ...  99:7
  The best f. ...  134:11
  There are as good f. ...  127:3
Fish-guts  Keep your ain f. ...  143:21
Fishing  It is good f. ...  141:23
  It is ill f. before the net 6:12
Fit  All things f. not ...  47:5
Five  F. hours sleeps a traveller ...  159:11
Flatterer  A f.'s throat ...  68:19
  There is no such f. ...  24:5
  When the f. pipes ...  68:20
Flatters  Beware of one who f. unduly ...
  68:16
Flattery  F. sits in the parlour ...  68:1
Flax  Keep f. from fire ...  74:2
Flay  No man can f. a stone 108:22
Flea  If you kill one f. in March ...  117:24

Flee  F. never so fast ...  45:3
Fleech  Better f. the devil ...  68:2
Flesh  F. is frail 179:16
  He that never ate f. ...  96:8
  The f. is aye fairest ...  76:18
Fling  After your f. ...  44:15
  F. at the brod ...  34:27
Flock  He who will have a full f. ...  30:33
Flow  Every f. has its ebb 111:21
Fly  F. that pleasure ...  142:15
  The f. has her spleen ...  160:30
  The f. that plays too long ...  37:23
Flying  No f. from fate 45:2
Foal  How can the f. amble ...  18:6
Foe  No f. to a flatterer 68:18
Follow  F. love ...  109:87
  F. not truth ...  176:50
  It is as hard to f. ...  3:49
  It is good to f. ...  125:7
Follows  He that f. freits ...  167:33
Folly  Both f. and wisdom ...  125:33
  F. and learning ...  69:97
  F. is the product ...  69:22
  If f. were grief ...  69:25
  No f. to being in love 69:11
  The f. of one man ...  69:2
Food  The best f. ...  53:26
Fool  A f. always rushes ...  69:64
  A f. and his money ...  69:68
  A f. at forty ...  69:100
  A f. believes everything 69:69
  A f. knows more in his own house ...
  69:92
  A f. may ask more questions ...  69:93
  A f. may give a wise man counsel 69:89
  A f. may sometimes speak ...  69:90
  A f. may sometimes tell the truth 176:31
  A f. may throw a stone ...  69:94
  A f.'s bell ...  69:78
  A f.'s bolt is soon shot 69:57
  A f.'s bolt may sometimes ...  69:91
  A f.'s tongue ...  69:79
  An easy f. ...  69:70
  Better be a f. than a knave 69:5
  Every man is a f. or a physician 87:61
  Every man is a f. sometimes ...  69:26
  F.'s haste ...  85:43
  He is a f. that forgets himself 69:33
  He is a f. that is not melancholy ...
  162:32
  He is a f. that kisses the maid ...  69:34
  He is a f. that makes a hammer ...  69:35
  He is a f. that marries ...  113:95
  He is a f. that thinks not ...  69:37
  He is a f. who makes his physician ...
  69:38

He is not the f. that the fool is ... 69:36
If the f. knew how to be silent ... 69:85
Make not a f. of thyself ... 69:32
Send a f. to France ... 172:10
Send a f. to the market ... 69:16
The f. asks much ... 69:30
The f. wanders ... 183:50
There's no f. like an old fool 69:99
What the f. does in the end ... 69:49
Foolish  F. tongues ... 69:80
    From a f. judge ... 69:66
    It is a f. sheep ... 69:39
    One cannot do a f. thing ... 69:42
Fools  F. and madmen ... 69:6
    F. are wise as long ... 69:86
    F. are wise men ... 69:98
    F. bite one another ... 183:67
    F. build houses ... 16:6
    F. grow ... 69:20
    F. live poor ... 69:46
    F. may invent fashions ... 50:12
    F. rejoice ... 69:72
    F. rush in ... 69:61
    F. set stools ... 69:95
    F. should not have ... 69:8
    F. will be fools still 69:17
    If all f. had baubles ... 69:28
    If all f. wore feathers ... 69:27
    If f. went not to market ... 69:73
    None but f. and fiddlers ... 53:69
    We have all been f. ... 69:23
    Who has neither f. nor beggars ... 69:29
Foot  Better the f. slip ... 168:15
    One f. is better than two crutches 80:21
    The f. on the cradle ... 113:104
Footprints  F. on the sands of time ...
    48:30
Footsteps  The f. of fortune ... 111:8
Forbid  F. a thing ... 123:11
Forbidden  F. fruit ... 123:12
Force  F. without forecast ... 70:7
    There is great f. hidden ... 101:26
Forced  A f. kindness ... 182:23
Ford  In 'f.', in 'ham' ... 58:79
Forecast  F. is better than work-hard 70:9
Forecasts  He that f. all perils, will never
    sail the sea 32:5
    He that f. all perils, will win no worship
    32:11
Forehead  In the f. and the eye ... 63:2
Foreheets  That which one most f. ...
    123:13
Forenoons  You cannot have two f. ...
    125:58
Forethought  F. is easy ... 70:11
Foretold  Long f., long last ... 181:20

Forewarned  F. is forearmed 70:8
Forewit  One good f. ... 70:1
Forget  Do not f. little kindnesses ... 80:3
Forgive  F. all but thyself 71:20
    F. and forget 71:18
    If we are bound to f. an enemy ... 175:23
Forgiveness  F. from the heart ... 71:9
    F. is perfect ... 71:19
Forgives  He that f. gains the victory 71:4
    He who f. others ... 71:8
Forgiving  F. the unrepentant ... 71:15
Forgotten  Seldom seen, soon f. 1:26
Forth  F. bridles ... 133:73
Fortune  F. can take from us ... 111:30
    F. favours fools 111:35
    F. favours the bold 31:6
    F. favours those ... 111:34
    F. is blind 111:4
    F. is fickle 111:5
    F. is made of glass 111:11
    F. is the mistress ... 111:27
    F. is weary ... 111:10
    F. knocks once ... 111:40
    F., not prudence ... 111:28
    F. to one is mother ... 111:6
    Great f. brings with it ... 111:19
    He that has no ill f. ... 186:5
    If f. torments me ... 91:10
    When f. smiles ... 126:20
Foul  A f. morning ... 127:16
    He that has to do with what is f. ... 29:12
Fouls  No man f. his hands ... 153:17
Four  He that has but f. ... 163:34
Fowler  The f.'s pipe ... 7:25
Fox  A f. should not be of the jury ...
    153:44
    At length the f. ... 36:5
    The f. fares best ... 42:10
    The f. knows much ... 36:12
    The f. may grow grey ... 18:29
    The f. preys farthest ... 36:11
    Though the f. run ... 36:6
    When the f. preaches ... 36:9
France  F. is a meadow ... 133:21
    He that will F. win ... 133:22
    The day of F.'s ruin ... 133:23
Free  He is f. of fruit ... 75:28
    He is f. of horse ... 75:29
Freedom  F. is a fair thing 106:3
Freer  Nothing f. than a gift 75:40
Freezes  He f. who does not burn 129:16
French  Every F. soldier ... 133:24
    The F. would be the best cooks ... 133:25
Frenchman  Have the F. for thy friend ...
    133:26
    The F. is a scoundrel 133:27

# G

Goes  He g. not out of his way ...  51:39
Going  A g. foot ...  48:20
Gold  G. does not belong to the miser ...
115:9
  G. dust blinds all eyes 180:87
  G. goes in at any gate ...  180:105
  G. is an orator 180:119
  G. is but muck 180:63
  G. is tried ...  173:6
  He that has g. ...  180:104
  He who flings g. away ...  163:8
  What cannot g. do 180:98
  When we have g. ...  180:35
Golden  A g. handshake ...  29:41
  A g. key ...  180:107
  G. dreams ...  159:27
  The g. age ...  171:46
  We must not look for a g. life ...  28:51
Golgotha  In G. are skulls ...  39:66
Gone  When all is g. ...  178:26
Good  A g. heart cannot lie 78:37
  A g. heart conquers ill fortune 78:9
  A g. life makes a good death 78:10
  A g. man can no more harm ...  78:38
  All things are g. ...  173:4
  As g. horses draw in carts ...  60:16
  Better a g. cow ...  15:34
  Better g. afar off ...  78:49
  Bode g., and get it 127:5
  Do g.: thou doest it for thyself 41:34
  G. and evil ...  78:45
  G. folks are scarce 78:34
  G. for the liver ...  78:30
  G. is good ...  78:33
  G. is to be sought out ...  78:48
  G. men must die ...  78:40
  G. men suffer much 78:42
  G. people walk on ...  78:43
  G. things are hard 78:31
  He is a silly man that can neither do g. nor
ill 27:16
  He who does no g. ...  10:5
  If one knew how g. it were ...  117:3
  If you can't be g. ...  169:18
  It is a g. goose ...  75:25
  It is a g. horse ...  113:117
  It is g. to be good in your time ...  78:24
  No man so g. ...  138:26
  None so g. ...  78:27
  Nothing but is g. for something 127:30
  Nothing so g. ...  97:20
  Ten g. turns lie dead ...  41:49
  That which is g. for the back ...  78:28
  That which is g. for the head ...  78:29
  The g. die young 39:64
  The g. is the enemy ...  78:32

The g. or ill hap ....  113:62
The only g. Indian ...  57:20
There are two g. men ...  78:35
There is a g. time coming 127:13
There is no such thing as g. small beer ...
53:41
There is nothing either g. or bad ...  114:4
They are aye g. that are away 1:31
Goodman  As the g. says ...  113:110
  When the g. is from home ...  113:97
Goodness  G. is better than beauty 78:6
  G. is not tied to greatness ...  81:13
Goods  A man has no more g. ...  135:24
  G. are theirs ...  135:23
  G. that are much on show ...  65:10
Goose  He that has a g. ...  180:70
Gorse  When the g. is out of bloom ...
30:52
Gospel  With the g. ...  144:48
Gossip  A g. speaks ill of all ...  79:26
  The g. of two women ...  79:12
Gossiping  G. and lying ...  79:6
Gossips  G. are frogs ...  79:27
Got  So g., so gone 163:11
Gout  To the g. ...  87:47
Gown  Look to a g. of gold ...  4:9
  The g. is his that wears it ...  135:22
Grace  G. will last ...  11:33
  The g. of God is enough 77:52
  The g. of God is worth a fair 77:53
Grafting  It is good g. on a good stock
113:68
Grain  G. by grain ...  134:14
  One g. fills not a sack ...  160:9
Grapes  One cannot gather g. of thorns ...
18:10
Grasp  G. all, lose all 82:16
Grass  G. and hay ...  39:2
  G. grows not ...  112:10
  If g. look green ...  117:2
  The g. is always greener ...  28:40
  While the g. grows ...  43:2
Grateful  To a g. man ...  80:2
Gratitude  G. is the least of virtues ...
80:27
  G. preserves old friendships ...  80:1
Graves  G. are of all sizes 39:67
Greases  Who g. his way ...  29:35
Great  A g. man and a great river ...  81:26
  A g. tree ...  81:1
  All things that g. men do ...  81:21
  G. businesses ...  81:40
  G. engines ...  81:41
  G. men have great faults 81:23
  G. men's favours ...  81:27
  G. men's sons ...  81:25

G. oaks ... 81:35
G. persons seldom see ... 81:22
G. things are done ... 31:5
G. trees are good ... 81:16
G. trees keep down ... 81:45
G. weights ... 81:42
G. winds ... 81:2
G. wits have short memories 183:73
If g. men would have care ... 81:33
Some are born g. ... 81:14
The g. and the little ... 81:32
The g. put the little ... 81:44
There would be no g. ones ... 81:34
Greater  G. is he who is above temptation
... 169:13
The g. the man ... 81:24
Greatest  The g. calf ... 160:34
The g. crabs ... 160:35
The g. talkers ... 41:18
The g. vessel ... 81:17
Greedy  G. eaters ... 76:11
G. folks have long arms 82:22
It is hard for a g. eye ... 82:20
The g. man and the gileynour ... 82:21
The g. mouth ... 82:5
Greek  When G. meets Greek ... 60:1
Greeks  The G. only tell the truth ...
133:64
Green  A g. wound is soon healed 52:19
A g. Yule ... 39:56
Grey  G. hairs are death's blossoms 125:66
The g. mare ... 113:103
Grief  G. is lessened ... 162:49
G. pent up ... 162:13
The greater g. ... 162:15
Griefs  All g. with bread ... 162:54
Grieve  Never g. for what you cannot help
142:6
Grieves  He g. sore ... 162:47
Grist  All's g. that comes to the mill 177:9
Groaning  A g. horse ... 113:112
Groat  The g. is ill saved ... 170:38
Groom  Every g. is a king ... 60:18
Grooms  Where g. and householders ...
9:27
Ground  A g. sweat ... 39:39
Growing  A g. moon ... 113:140
A g. youth ... 19:20
Guess  No man can g. in cold blood ...
129:12
Guest  He is an ill g. ... 92:9
The g. of the hospitable ... 92:2
The g. who outstays ... 92:15
Guests  If a man receives no g. at home ...
92:1

Guided  They are well g. ... 77:15
Guilty  A g. conscience feels continual fear
26:4
A g. conscience needs no accuser 26:1
He is g. who is not at home 1:20
Gull  The g. comes against the rain 181:6
Gunner  The g. to his linstock ... 124:23
Gut  G. no fish ... 6:16
Guts  The g. uphold the heart ... 53:5

# H

Habit  H. is a second nature 83:1
Men do more things through h. ... 83:2
Habits  H. are at first cobwebs ... 83:7
Old h. die hard 83:3
Hail  H. brings frost ... 181:103
Hair  H. and hair ... 160:31
No h. so small ... 160:21
Take a h. of the dog ... 145:9
Hale  He should have a h. pow ... 34:12
Half  H. a loaf ... 80:8
H. an egg ... 80:14
H. a word is enough ... 168:84
H. the truth ... 40:7
It is best to take h. in hand ... 131:21
The h. is better ... 116:4
Hall  H. benches are slippery 81:28
Halloo  Do not h. ... 6:20
Halves  Never do things by h. 129:17
Hammer  It is better to be the h. ... 9:2
Hampshire  H. ground ... 58:35
Hand  All is not at h. ... 88:2
Good h. ... 44:7
He that has his h. in the lion's mouth ...
147:15
If thy h. be bad ... 158:10
One h. washes the other 88:20
Put not thy h. ... 99:15
The h. that gave the wound ... 145:8
The h. that gives, gathers 75:9
The h. that rocks the cradle ... 128:12
Handful  A h. of good life ... 78:21
A h. of trade ... 124:6
You may know by a h. ... 173:8
Hands  Many h. make light work 88:4
Handsome  H. is as handsome does 11:20
Hang  H. a thief ... 33:28
He that would h. his dog ... 147:41
Hanged  Better be half h. ... 113:29
He that is h. in May ... 117:50
Hanging  H. and wiving ... 113:38

Hangs  He that h. himself on Sunday ... 144:66

Hap  H. and halfpenny ... 111:18
No man can make his own h. 111:29
Some have the h. ... 111:42

Happiness  All h. is in the mind 84:16
Great h., great danger 84:49
H. is not a horse ... 84:62
With h. comes intelligence ... 84:28

Happy  Better be h. than wise 84:32
Call no man h. ... 39:35
H. is he that chastens himself 84:6
H. is he that is happy ... 84:7
H. is he whose friends ... 84:8
H. is she who marries ... 84:10
H. is that child ... 84:9
H. is the country ... 84:11
H. is the wooing ... 109:93
He is h., that knoweth not ... 84:17
Let him that would be h. for a day ... 84:5
When a man is h. ... 84:29

Hard  It is h. to break a hog ... 83:4
It is h. to make an old mare ... 83:5
Things that are h. to come by ... 134:10

Hard-fought  It's a h. field ... 127:22

Hare  H. is melancholy meat 53:42
The h. always returns ... 172:23

Hares  H. may pull dead lions ... 31:25
If you run after two h. ... 48:55

Harry  King H. robbed the church ... 144:17

Harvest  He that has a good h. ... 180:11

Haste  H. and wisdom ... 69:67
H. comes not alone 85:15
H. is from the devil 85:1
H. is the mother ... 85:21
H. is the sister ... 85:4
H. makes waste 85:16
H. makes waste, and waste makes want ... 113:51
H. trips up ... 85:18
In h. is error 85:20
Make h. slowly 85:24
More h., less speed 85:42
Nothing should be done in h. ... 85:26
Who has no h. in his business ... 130:19

Hasty  A h. man drinks his tea ... 85:44
A h. man never wants woe 85:9
Be not too h. ... 85:28
H. climbers ... 4:20
H. work ... 85:22
The h. bitch ... 85:14
The h. leaps over ... 85:17

Hatch  It is good to have a h. before the door 156:6

Hate  H. not at the first harm 85:29
He that cannot h. ... 86:5
The greatest h. ... 86:7

Hated  He that is h. of his subjects ... 149:20

Hates  One h. not the person ... 10:47

Hatred  H. blasts the crop ... 86:2
H. is blind ... 86:8
H. is worse than murder 86:1
H. with friends ... 86:3

Have  Better to h. than wish 135:8
H. at it ... 134:3
H. is have 135:10
What you h., hold 135:15

Hawks  H. will not pick out ... 110:7

Haws  Many h. ... 181:16

Hay  It is time to cock your h. ... 30:4
Make h. while the sun shines 126:3

Head  Better be the h. ... 4:27
The h. and feet keep warm ... 87:13
When the h. aches ... 149:24

Heads  Two h. are better than one 88:6

Healing  It is ill h. of an old sore 52:20

Health  H. and gaiety ... 87:1
H. and money ... 87:3
H. and wealth ... 87:2
H. is better than wealth 87:5
H. is great riches 87:4
H. is not valued ... 87:9
H. without money ... 136:48
He that wants h. ... 87:8
He who has good h. ... 87:7
The beginning of h. ... 159:2

Healthful  No man was ever made more h. ... 172:14
The h. man ... 3:36

Hear  H. all parties 100:10
H. and see ... 168:71
H. much, speak little 168:70
H. twice ... 168:76

Hearers  Were there no h. ... 79:38

Hearing  From h., comes wisdom ... 168:69
Ill h. ... 114:17

Hears  He that h. much ... 168:72
Who wrong h. ... 114:16

Heart  If your h. is in your prayer ... 144:93
Man's h. is never satisfied ... 28:39
Many a h. is caught ... 109:108
The h.'s letter ... 63:3
Tine h. ... 91:9
What the h. thinks ... 168:65
When the h. is a fire ... 129:4
When the h. is full of lust ... 112:7
Who has not a h. ... 32:24

Heat  If you don't like the h. ... 145:15
There is no h. of affection ... 129:1
Heaven  All of h. and hell ... 144:22
Better go to h. in rags ... 144:19
H. and hell are within ... 144:21
H. takes care of children ... 77:27
If h. drops a date ... 126:8
No coming to h. ... 144:24
There is no going to h. ... 144:29
The way to h. is alike ... 144:32
The way to h. is as ready ... 144:33
Whom H. at his birth ... 69:19
Heaviest  The h. baggage ... 172:36
Heavy  A h. purse ... 180:3
Hedge  A h. between ... 121:16
Where the h. is lowest ... 179:13
Hedgehogs  H. lodge among thorns ...
157:12
Heed  Good take h. does surely speed 3:4
Take h. is a fair thing 3:5
Take h. of an ox before ... 144:84
Take h. of a person marked ... 113:156
Take h. of a young wench ... 184:10
Take h. of mad fools ... 69:9
Take h. of reconciled enemies 57:21
Height  It is h. makes Grantham steeple ...
81:12
Hell  From h., Hull, and Halifax ... 58:56
H. hath no fury ... 184:13
H. is always open 144:37
H. is wherever ... 144:20
The road to h. is paved ... 144:35
Help  A little h. ... 41:14
H., for help in harvest 88:28
One can't h. many ... 88:1
Helping  Three h. one another ... 88:5
Helps  Everything h., quoth the wren ...
160:8
He h. little ... 153:8
He that h. the evil ... 88:11
Hen  If a h. does not prate ... 113:113
Hengsten  H. Down ... 58:46
Henry  H. the Eighth pulled down monks
and their cells ... 144:52
Hens  H. are free ... 75:30
Herb  No h. will cure love 109:80
Hercules  Not even H. ... 164:10
Heresy  H. is the school of pride 144:44
H. may be easier kept out ... 144:45
Heretic  For the same man to be a h. ...
144:47
Hero  No man is a h. ... 65:5
To the real h. ... 31:21
Herring  Every h. must hang ... 147:4
Hesitates  He who h. is lost 146:6
Hide  Don't h. your light ... 24:19

H. nothing from thy minister ... 176:62
High  He who stands h. ... 81:11
Hew not too h. ... 4:23
H. cedars fall ... 81:8
H. places have their precipices 4:21
It is good to be neither too h. ... 116:9
Higher  The h. the ape goes ... 15:21
The h. the hill ... 75:26
The h. the mountain ... 4:22
Highest  The h. branch ... 81:4
The h. tree ... 81:5
Hill  Do on the h. ... 15:19
Himself  Every man for h., and God ...
153:6
Every man for h., and the devil ... 153:5
Every man is nearest h. 153:25
He that is ill to h. ... 153:7
Hindmost  The h. dog ... 130:20
History  H. repeats itself 171:51
Hitch  H. your wagon ... 4:12
Hoards  He that h. up money ... 115:16
Hog  A h. that's bemired ... 29:9
Better my h. dirty home ... 80:25
The h. never looks up ... 80:30
Hogs  He who does not kill h. ... 150:3
Hoist  H. your sail ... 126:5
Hold  H. fast to the words of your ancestors
140:6
They that h. the greatest farms ... 180:126
Hole  A h. in the ice ... 151:8
The h. calls the thief 169:5
Holiday  Every day is h. ... 95:41
Holy  A h. habit ... 7:47
Holyrood  On H. Day ... 117:63
Home  Better at h. ... 172:30
Far from h. ... 172:31
H. is home, as the devil said ... 29:43
H. is home, though it be ... 172:22
H. is where ... 172:28
Homer  H. sometimes nods 97:16
Homo  H. is a common name ... 60:6
Honest  An h. look ... 89:10
An h. man's word ... 89:19
H. men marry soon ... 89:25
No h. man ever repented ... 89:3
You cannot make people h. ... 104:10
Honesty  H. is a fine jewel ... 89:16
H. is ill to thrive by 89:11
H. is praised ... 89:12
H. is the best policy 89:1
H. keeps the crown ... 89:24
H. may be dear bought ... 89:2
Honey  A h. tongue ... 94:12
He that has no h. in his pot ... 136:118
H. catches more flies ... 101:10
It is not with saying 'H., honey,' ... 48:40

Make yourself all h. ... 68:7
Of h. and gall ... 109:52
Too much h. ... 116:28
Honour He that desires h. ... 90:10
He that gives h. to his enemy ... 57:19
H. and ease ... 90:6
H. and profit ... 90:5
H. a physician ... 70:22
H. buys no beef ... 90:3
H. is the reward ... 90:12
H. shows the man 90:2
H. without profit ... 90:4
There is h. among thieves 110:4
Where there is no h. ... 90:7
Honours Great h. ... 90:8
H. change manners 90:1
Hook A h.'s well lost ... 150:4
Hope A good h. ... 91:6
H. deferred ... 91:23
H. for the best 91:24
H. is a good breakfast ... 91:19
H. is but the dream ... 91:18
H. is grief's best music 91:5
H. is the last thing ... 91:13
H. is the poor man's bread 91:1
H. keeps man alive 91:3
H. often deludes ... 91:17
H. springs eternal ... 91:12
H. well ... 91:25
If it were not for h. ... 91:2
There is h. from the mouth of the sea ... 39:31
Too much h. deceives 91:16
Hopers H. go to hell 91:22
Hopes Great h. ... 91:7
He that h. not for good ... 6:27
Hops H. make or break 30:10
Horn A h. spoon ... 136:23
Horns He that has h. in his bosom ... 155:13
Horse A h., a wife, and a sword ... 105:8
A h. that will not carry a saddle ... 95:38
Choose a h. made ... 154:3
Every h. thinks its own pack heaviest 153:53
He that lets his h. ... 113:123
He that seeks a h. or a wife without fault ... 97:43
It is a good h. that never stumbles 97:41
The best h. needs breaking ... 49:4
You can lead a h. to the water ... 182:3
Horseshoe When a fool finds a h. ... 111:12
Host Ask mine h. ... 153:47

Hot A h. May ... 39:57
H. love, hasty vengeance 129:6
H. love is soon cold 129:8
Soon h., soon cold 129:9
Hounds H. and horses ... 154:23
Hour An h. in the morning ... 52:11
At every h. ... 39:22
One h.'s sleep ... 159:10
House A h. divided ... 141:29
A h. is a fine house ... 78:25
A h. well-furnished ... 113:49
Better one h. spoiled ... 113:78
H. goes mad ... 184:71
When h. and land ... 102:16
Housekeepers Fat h. ... 163:14
Howl One must h. with the wolves 25:3
Human H. blood ... 60:9
Humble H. hearts have humble desires 28:22
Humility It is not a sign of h. ... 138:25
Hunchback The h. does not see his own hump ... 34:14
Hundred A h. disorders ... 125:39
Hungarian Do not trust a H. ... 133:52
Where there is a H. ... 133:51
Hungary Outside H. there is no life ... 133:50
Hunger H. and cold ... 93:15
H. breaks stone walls 93:20
H. drives the wolf ... 93:21
H. finds no fault ... 93:8
H. increases the understanding 93:14
H. is good kitchen meat 93:9
H. is sharper ... 93:17
H. is stronger ... 93:18
H. is the best sauce 93:10
H. makes dinners ... 76:20
H. makes hard beans sweet 93:11
They must h. in frost ... 93:3
Hungry A h. horse ... 93:12
A h. man is an angry man 93:16
A h. man is glad ... 93:23
A h. man smells meat ... 93:19
H. dogs ... 93:22
Two h. meals ... 93:27
Hunting H., hawking, and paramours ... 112:13
Hurry H. bequeaths disappointment 85:10
Hurts He that h. another ... 35:8
Husband A good h. makes a good wife 113:96
He is an ill h. ... 113:98
If the h. be not at home ... 113:99
Husbands H. are in heaven ... 113:115

# I

# J

Joan  J. is as good ...  60:25
Jollity  There is no j. ...  84:70
Jolly  Over j. dow not 84:55
Jove  J. laughs ...  109:98
Joy  J. and sorrow ...  84:56
  No j. emanates ...  161:12
  No j. without annoy 84:44
  One j. scatters a hundred griefs 84:34
  The j. of the heart ...  84:23
Judas  Had J. betrayed Christ in Scotland
  ...  133:75
Judge  A good j. conceives quickly ...
  104:45
  A j. knows nothing ...  104:47
  J. not ...  34:3
  Never j. from appearances 7:29
  No one ought to be j. ...  153:43
Judgment  He has a good j. ...  183:41
  He that passes j. as he runs ...  85:7
July  If the first of J. ...  181:60
June  If on the eighth of J. it rain ...
  181:59
Jupiter  Far from J. ...  149:35
Just  A j. war ...  100:5
  Be j. before you are generous 75:15
Justice  In j. is all virtue ...  100:1
  J. will not condemn ...  100:2

# K

Kail  Good k. ...  53:29
  K. spares bread 53:30
Keep  Better k. now ...  135:12
  He that has it and will not k. it ...  136:4
  K. something for the sore foot 170:27
  K. some till furthermore come 170:28
  Who will not k. a penny ...  163:4
Keeps  He k. his road well enough ...
  23:10
Kent  K. and Keer ...  58:48
  Some places of K. ...  58:33
Kettle  The k. calls the pot burnt-arse 34:8
Kick  K. an attorney downstairs ...  104:43
  The k. of the dam ...  49:13
Kid  You can't k. a kidder 40:40
Kill  K. not the goose ...  82:18
Kills  He that k. a man ...  51:27
Kiln  Ill may the k. ...  34:9
Kin  A man cannot bear all his k. ...
  143:18
  It is a poor k. ...  143:12
  It is good to be near of k. to land 143:3

Kind  A k. heart loseth nought ...  101:1
  K. hearts are more than coronets 15:33
  K. hearts are soonest wronged 101:13
Kindle  K. not a fire ...  174:10
Kindly  A k. aver ...  18:40
Kindness  K. cannot be bought ...  101:18
  K. comes of will 101:19
  K. is lost ...  19:17
  K. is the noblest weapon ...  101:6
  K. lies not aye ...  88:22
  One k. is the price of another 88:21
Kindred  Wheresoever you see your k. ...
  143:7
King  A k.'s face ...  149:16
  A k.'s favour ...  149:30
  It is the lot of a k. ...  149:12
  K.'s chaff ...  149:26
  Like k., like people 149:19
  Nearest the k. ...  149:34
  The k. can do no wrong 149:1
  The k. can make a knight ...  15:45
  The k. is dead ...  149:7
  The k. never dies 149:6
  The k.'s cheese ...  149:29
  The k.'s word ...  149:15
  What the k. wills ...  149:4
  When the k. makes a mistake ...  149:23
Kingdoms  K. divided ...  141:30
Kings  K. are out of play 149:18
  K. have long arms 149:2
  K. have many ears ...  149:3
Kinsfolk  Many k. ...  143:4
Kinsman  K. helps kinsman ...  143:2
Kirk  The k. is aye greedy 144:62
Kiss  It is better to k. a knave ...  98:8
  Many k. the child ...  94:6
  Many k. the hand ...  94:5
Kitchen  K. physic ...  87:36
Knave  A k. and a fool ...  69:65
  No k. to the learned knave 102:17
  No k. to the old knave 125:15
  Once a k. ...  18:28
  The more k. ...  111:37
Knavery  K. may serve for a turn ...  89:4
  There is k. in all trades ...  124:35
Knock  K. a carle ...  35:7
Know  He that would k. what shall be ...
  171:50
  He who wants to k. himself ...  121:10
  If you wish to k. a man ...  9:9
  K. thyself 153:48
  One learns to k. oneself ...  79:5
  What you don't k. ...  96:7
  You never k. what you can do ...  48:61
  You should k. a man seven years ...  65:12

Knowledge  K. has bitter roots ...  54:5
  K. is a wild thing ...  102:4
  K. is folly ...  102:28
  K. is no burthen 102:10
  K. is power 102:9
  K. is the mother ...  102:8
  K. makes one laugh ...  102:20
  K. without practice ...  102:21
Known  Better k. than trusted 175:10
  Every man is best k. to himself 153:49
Knows  He k. enough that knows nothing
  ...  156:13
  He that k. little ...  96:18
  He that k. nothing ...  96:4
  No man better k. what good is ...  2:14
  No man k. when he shall die ...  39:25
  None k. what will happen to him ...
  171:48
  The more one k. ...  13:19
  Who k. himself ...  153:50
  Who k. most ...  168:81
  Who k. much ...  166:2
Kythe  K. in your own colours ...  94:24


# L


Labour  A little l. ...  48:15
  L. as long lived ...  48:28
  L. is light ...  109:17
  L. overcomes ...  48:10
Labourer  The l. is worthy ...  44:6
Labours  He that l. and thrives ...  48:21
Labyrinth  If you go into a l. ...  70:19
Lack  Many men l. ...  22:6
Lackey  When a l. comes to hell's door ...
  68:21
Lacking  L. breeds laziness ...  34:2
Lad  L.'s love's a busk of broom ...
  109:102
Ladder  Go down the l. ...  113:79
Lady  On L. Day the latter ...  117:75
  You a l. ...  60:4
Ladybirds  Plenty of l. ...  30:11
Laird  If the l. slight the lady ...  27:13
Lame  The l. tongue ...  168:20
Lament  To l. the dead ...  39:100
Lammas  After L. corn ripens ...  117:60
Lancashire  He that would take a L. man
  ...  58:24
  What L. thinks today ...  58:23
Land  Every l. has its own law 104:66
  He that buys l. ...  51:36
  In the l. of hope ...  91:11

  L. was never lost ...  180:90
  Many a one for l. ...  113:57
  No l. without stones ...  97:26
  The l. is never void ...  3:58
  There is good l. ...  127:24
Lands  He that has l. ...  180:18
Language  That is not good l. ...  168:94
  The l. of truth ...  176:22
  There were no ill l. ...  42:20
Larder  No l. but has its mice 97:36
Last  He that comes l. to the pot ...  103:2
  The l. drop ...  56:20
  The l. straw ...  56:21
  The l. suitor ...  103:13
Late  A l. spring ...  152:2
  Better l. ripe and bear ...  103:9
  Better l. than never 103:8
  It is too l. to call back yesterday 142:2
  It is too l. to grieve ...  142:4
  It is too l. to spare ...  170:16
  L. children ...  128:20
  L. was often lucky 103:10
  Never too l. to learn 103:12
  Never too l. to repent 142:40
  Who comes l. ...  103:1
Late-comers  L. are shent 103:4
Latin  With L., a horse, and money ...
  172:37
Laugh  L. and grow fat 84:26
  L., and the world laughs with you ...
  84:31
  L. at leisure ...  84:58
  L. before breakfast ...  84:59
Laughs  He l. best ...  6:23
  He l. ill ...  84:67
  He who l. last ...  6:24
Laughter  L. is the best medicine 84:35
  L. is the hiccup of a fool 84:3
  L. makes good blood 84:25
Lavishness  L. is not generosity 163:17
Law  Every l. has a loophole 104:12
  Go to l. for a sheep ...  104:29
  L. cannot persuade ...  104:18
  L. governs man ...  104:5
  L. is a bottomless pit 104:20
  L. is a flag ...  29:39
  L. is a lickpenny 104:26
  L. makers ...  104:33
  Much l., but little justice 104:14
  No l. for lying 40:26
  The l. does not concern itself ...  104:49
  The l. grows of sin ...  104:2
  The l. is an ass 104:8
  The l. is not the same ...  104:7
  There's one l. for the rich ...  104:6

Lawful   Many things l. ...   104:19
Laws   Good l. often proceed ...   104:1
 L. catch flies ...   104:9
 The more l. ...   104:21
 We live by l. ...   61:9
Lawsuit   Win your l. ...   104:28
Lawsuits   L. consume time ...   104:27
Lawyer   A good l., an evil neighbour 104:35
 A good l. must be ...   104:38
 A l. never goes ...   104:40
 A l.'s opinion ...   104:30
 He that is his own l. ...   104:41
 The better l. ...   104:36
Lawyers   Few l. die well ...   104:39
 L.' gowns ...   104:31
Lay   L. things by ...   177:7
 Nought l. down ...   37:38
Laziness   L. goes so slowly ...   95:29
Lazy   A l. ox ...   95:36
 A l. sheep ...   95:47
Leak   A small l. ...   163:7
Leal   L. folks never wanted gear 89:21
 L. heart lied never 89:20
Lean   A l. agreement ...   104:25
 A l. fee is a fit reward ...   95:39
 Better a l. jade ...   80:17
 Better a l. peace ...   132:11
 L. liberty ...   106:4
Leap   A l. year is never ...   30:25
 If you l. into a well ...   147:16
Leaps   Every one l. over the dyke ...   179:12
Learn   A man may l. wit ...   54:17
 Better l. by your neighbour's skaith ...   62:35
 If you will l. news ...   122:9
 It is good to l. ...   62:38
 L. in Italy ...   133:16
 L. not and know not 54:2
 L. weeping ...   54:7
 L. young ...   54:10
Learning   L. in one's youth ...   54:12
 L. in the breast of a bad man ...   102:29
 L. is a treasure ...   102:11
 L. is the eye ...   102:13
 L. makes a good man better ...   102:5
 L. makes a man fit company ...   102:12
 L. without wisdom ...   102:22
 Much l. makes men mad 102:30
Learns   He that l. a trade ...   124:9
 Man l. little from success ...   165:11
 Whoso l. young ...   54:11
Learnt   Soon l. ...   54:9
 What's l. in the cradle ...   54:13
Lease   No man has a l. of his life 39:16
Least   L. said soonest mended 168:80

The l. boy ...   179:15
Leave   Better l. than lack 136:90
 He must have l. to speak ...   168:109
 L. is light 15:13
 L. off with an appetite 116:15
 L. well alone 174:4
Leaves   He who l. his house ...   84:18
 He who l. the fame ...   64:6
Lechery   L. and covetousness ...   112:8
Leech   While men go after a l. ...   43:3
Leeches   L. kill with licence 87:54
Leeful   The l. man ...   105:18
Leeks   Eat l. in Lide ...   53:60
Leicestershire   Shake a L. man by the collar ...   58:30
Lend   L. and lose; so play fools 105:19
 L., and lose the loan ...   105:13
 L. money to a bad debtor ...   105:15
 L. never that thing ...   105:3
 L. only that ...   105:2
 L. sitting ...   105:5
 L. your horse ...   105:21
 L. your money ...   105:10
Lending   L. is like throwing away ...   105:17
 L. nurses enmity 105:11
Lends   He that l., gives 105:16
 He that l. his pot ...   105:20
Lent   He has but a short L. ...   14:32
 When I l., I was a friend ...   105:12
Leopard   The l. cannot change his spots 18:31
Lewd   A l. bachelor ...   112:9
Liar   A l. can go round the world ...   40:10
 A l. is not believed ...   40:15
 A l. is worse ...   40:24
 A l. should have a good memory 40:34
 The l. and the murderer ...   40:23
 The l. is sooner caught ...   40:11
Liars   L. begin by imposing ...   40:17
Libertine   A l. life ...   112:11
Liberty   L. is a jewel 106:2
 L. is more worth ...   106:1
 L. is not licence 106:10
 Too much l. ...   106:9
Lice   L. do not bite busy men 48:6
Lie   A l. is the curse of God 40:22
 Better a l. that heals ...   40:29
 Give a l. twenty-four hours' start ...   79:25
 He that will l. ...   40:35
 One l. makes many 40:13
 Tell a l. ...   176:39
 Though a l. be swift ...   176:10
 Though a l. be well drest ...   40:30
 We must not l. down ...   77:36

Lies   He that l. long abed ... 95:31
Life   An ill l. ... 39:87
    L. and misery ... 162:29
    L. begins at forty 107:12
    L. is a pilgrimage 107:14
    L. is a shadow 107:15
    L. is but a span 107:1
    L. is half spent ... 107:2
    L. is just a bowl ... 107:17
    L. is not all beer ... 107:7
    L. is short ... 107:5
    L. is sweet 107:9
    L. means strife 107:13
    L. without a friend ... 72:6
    L. would be too smooth ... 107:8
    Man's l. is like a candle ... 107:3
    Such a l. ... 39:89
    The l. of man ... 107:10
    There is but one way to enter this l. ... 39:53
    While there's l. ... 91:26
Lifeless   He is l. that is faultless 97:2
Light   A l. purse makes a heavy heart 136:44
    Every l. has its shadow 97:30
Light-heeled   A l. mother ... 95:1
Lightning   L. never strikes twice ... 2:32
Like   L. breeds like 157:1
    L. cures like 157:3
    L. to die ... 108:10
    L. will to like 157:8
    No l. is the same 157:6
Likeliest   Do the l. ... 77:11
Likely   L. lies in the mire ... 108:2
Likeness   L. begets love ... 138:20
    L. causes liking 157:5
Likes   Every man l. his own thing best 153:40
Lime   L. makes a rich father ... 30:2
Limerick   L. was ... 133:80
Lion   A man is a l. ... 129:2
    Destroy the l. ... 52:24
    If the l.'s skin cannot ... 164:15
    The l. spares the suppliant 71:14
    Who takes a l. when he is absent ... 31:26
Lip-honour   L. costs little ... 94:3
Listeners   L. never hear good ... 99:3
Literature   L. is a good staff ... 188:10
Litter   The l. is like to the sire and dam 18:7
Little   A l. and good ... 160:38
    A l. bird ... 28:25
    A l. body ... 160:2
    A l. child ... 19:14
    A l. fire ... 160:24
    A l. given seasonably ... 75:35

A l. learning ... 102:32
A l. pot ... 160:43
A l. stone ... 160:27
A l. wind kindles ... 160:6
A l. with quiet ... 28:12
A l. wit will serve ... 183:33
A l. wood ... 28:26
Every l. helps 160:7
He that has l. is the less dirty 136:35
He that has l. shall have less 136:49
L. and often fills the purse 160:16
L. can a long tongue lein 168:13
L. fish are sweet 160:4
L. fishes slip through nets ... 81:9
L. gear ... 136:30
L. Jock ... 136:106
L. sticks kindle the fire ... 160:5
L. things are great ... 28:24
L. things please little minds 69:50
L. wealth ... 136:31
Many a l. makes a mickle 160:10
The l. cannot be great ... 81:39
Live   Everything would fain l. 153:15
    He is unworthy to l. ... 153:22
    He that would l. for aye ... 53:61
    If you would l. ever ... 51:66
    If you would not l. to be old ... 125:60
    Let all l. as they would die 39:90
    L. and learn 62:14
    L. and let live 34:4
    No one can l. on beauty ... 11:24
    One may l. without father or mother ... 144:3
    The longer we l. ... 107:19
    They that l. longest, must die at last 125:61
    They who l. longest, will see most 107:18
    We can l. without our friends ... 121:2
    We l. by laws ... 104:34
    We must l. by the living ... 39:99
Lives   As long l. a merry man ... 84:27
    He l. long ... 78:39
    He that l. ill ... 26:6
    He that l. in hope ... 91:21
    He that l. long ... 166:18
    He that l. not well one year ... 10:8
    He that l. well ... 78:22
    He that l. wickedly ... 10:19
    He who l. by the sword ... 178:7
    Who l. by hope ... 91:20
Living   L. well ... 148:8
    No l. man all things can 97:11
Loan   Give a l. ... 105:14
Lock   No l. will hold ... 29:31
London   L. Bridge was made ... 58:78
Lone   The l. sheep ... 161:15

Long  Be the day never so l. ...  127:37
    He that is l. a giving ...  75:21
    It is a l. lane ...  127:41
    It is not how l. ...  78:23
    L. beards heartless ...  58:21
    L. life has long misery 107:6
    L. looked for comes at last 130:14
    L. mint, little dint 168:44
    Not a l. day ...  48:59
Longer  The l. you look at it ...  146:8
Longest  The l. at the fire ...  180:19
    The l. day has an end 127:38
    The l. night will have an end 127:39
    The l. way round ...  85:46
Longing  Better go away l. ...  116:14
Look  L. before you leap 85:33
    L. to the end 55:3
    L. to thyself ...  153:16
Lookers-on  L. see most ...  153:45
Looks  L. breed love 109:70
Loose  Better hand l. ...  106:6
Lords  Many l. ...  104:3
Lose  A man may l. his goods ...  8:2
    A man may l. more in an hour ...  73:17
    Better l. a jest ...  72:1
    If you l. your time ...  171:34
    L. a leg ...  150:11
    L. an hour in the morning ...  171:33
    What you l. on the swings ...  73:18
    You cannot l. ...  73:24
    You must l. a fly ...  150:2
Losers  Give l. leave to speak 73:28
    L. are always in the wrong 73:27
Loses  He l. his thanks ...  43:14
    He l. indeed ...  73:22
    He l. nothing who keeps God ...  144:6
    He that l. anything ...  73:15
    He that l. his wife ...  113:126
    One never l. by doing a good turn 41:37
    Who l. his liberty ...  106:11
Loss  Better a little l. ...  150:7
    He that is not sensible of his l. ...  73:23
    L. embraces shame 73:21
    No great l. but some small profit 127:28
    One man's l. ...  73:20
    There's no great l. without some gain 73:13
Lost  All is l. that is put into a riven dish 80:33
    All is not l. ...  127:14
    For a l. thing ...  142:9
    He has not l. all ...  91:29
    There is nothing l. by civility 15:7
    What is l. in the hundred ...  73:19
Louse  Better a l. in the pot ...  80:10
Love  As good l. comes ...  109:107
    Greater l. hath no man than this ...  72:54

He that does not l. a woman ...  109:42
He that has l. in his breast ...  109:19
If you l. the boll ...  109:116
In l. is no lack 109:21
In l.'s wars ...  109:79
L. and a cough ...  109:41
L. and business ...  109:31
L. and hate ...  86:4
L. and leprosy ...  109:43
L. and lordship ...  109:123
L. and pease-pottage ...  109:58
L. asks faith ...  109:118
L. begets love 109:71
L. being jealous ...  109:121
L. cannot be compelled 109:37
L. conquers all 109:27
L. covers many infirmities 109:14
L. delights in praise 109:84
L. does much ...  109:124
L. is a fair garden ...  113:134
L. is a flower ...  113:137
L. is a game ...  109:82
L. is as strong ...  109:40
L. is a sweet torment 109:54
L. is blind 109:1
L. is free 109:20
L. is full of fear 109:56
L. is lawless 109:7
L. is never without jealousy 109:122
L. is not found ...  109:75
L. is sweet in the beginning ...  109:53
L. is the fruit ...  109:76
L. is the loadstone ...  109:72
L. is the touchstone ...  109:25
L. is the true reward ...  109:73
L. is without reason 109:6
L. lasts as long ...  109:125
L. laughs at locksmiths 109:34
L. lives in cottages ...  109:128
L. locks no cupboards 109:22
L. makes all hard hearts gentle 109:33
L. makes all men equal 109:30
L. makes a wit ...  109:32
L. makes one fit ...  109:18
L. makes the world ...  109:29
L. me little ...  116:13
L. me, love my dog 109:83
L. needs no teaching 109:74
L. not at the first look 85:30
L. of lads ...  109:101
L. rules his kingdom ...  109:28
L. sees no faults 109:3
L. speaks ...  109:64
L. the babe ...  109:115
L. will creep ...  109:48
L. will find a way 109:35

L. will go through ... 109:36
L. without end ... 109:49
L. without return ... 109:109
L. your friend, but look to yourself 72:30
L. your friend with his fault 72:74
L. your neighbour ... 121:15
Men l. to hear well ... 24:1
Next to l., quietness 109:67
No l. is foul ... 109:5
No l. like the first love 109:103
No l. to a father's 109:114
One cannot l. ... 109:10
One l. expels another 109:105
The l. of money and the love of learning ... 180:128
The l. of the wicked ... 109:59
They l. too much ... 109:60
When l. is greatest ... 109:65
When l. puts in ... 109:57
Where l. fails ... 109:15
Where l. is ... 109:119
Whom we l. best ... 109:66
Loved   Men are best l. ... 1:2
'Tis better to have l. and lost ... 109:26
Lovers   L. are madmen 109:11
L.' quarrels ... 109:96
Loves   Every man as he l. ... 47:20
He that l. the tree ... 109:117
Low   A l. hedge ... 179:14
Lower   The l. millstone grinds ... 60:17
Lowly   L. sit ... 136:32
Loyalty   L. is worth more ... 110:1
Luck   Good l. reaches further ... 111:15
He that would have good l. in horses ... 167:1
Ill l. is good for something 2:16
There is l. in leisure 85:25
There is l. in odd numbers 167:2
You never know your l. 111:7
Lucky   Better be born l. than wise 111:17
It is better to be born l. than rich 111:14
L. at cards ... 167:10
L. at life ... 167:11
L. men need no counsel 111:31
Luke   On St. L.'s Day ... 117:69
St. L. was a saint ... 87:46
Lying   L. rides upon debt's back 40:6

# M

Mackerel   M.'s in season ... 117:41
M. sky and mares' tails ... 181:83

Mad   Every man is m. ... 97:10
For m. words ... 69:87
Maid   A m. and a virgin ... 184:30
A m. marries ... 113:65
A m. oft seen ... 65:9
A m. that laughs ... 184:83
Maiden   A m. with many wooers ... 20:12
Maidens   All are not m. ... 7:4
M. must be mild and meek ... 184:61
M. should be meek ... 184:31
M. should be seen ... 184:62
Maids   M. say 'Nay' ... 184:87
M. want nothing ... 113:15
Main   Look to the m. chance 22:21
Malice   M. hurts itself most 35:9
Malta   M. would be a delightful place ... 133:18
Man   A m. at five ... 19:46
A m. at sixteen ... 19:54
A m. can do no more ... 164:11
A m. is as old as he feels ... 184:104
A m. of straw ... 184:99
As a m. is ... 23:13
Every m.'s man had a man ... 9:28
M. is the head ... 184:91
M. punishes the action ... 41:30
M., woman, and devil ... 184:100
Sike a m. as thou wald be ... 23:14
There is no m. ... 160:28
Whatever is made by the hand of m. ... 179:19
Manchester   What M. says today ... 58:55
Manners   It is not good m. ... 15:15
M. and money ... 15:11
M. make often fortunes 15:10
M. maketh man 15:9
Of evil m. ... 127:26
Many   M. words would have much drink 51:74
March   In M., kill crow ... 117:22
In M., the birds begin to search ... 117:23
M. borrowed from April ... 117:19
M. comes in like a lion ... 117:20
M. comes in with adder heads ... 117:21
M. dust and May sun ... 181:128
M. in Janiveer ... 181:18
M. whisker ... 181:31
M. wind kindles the adder ... 181:30
M. winds and April showers ... 181:29
On the first of M. ... 117:25
The M. sun causes dust ... 181:114
The M. sun raises ... 181:115
Market   He that desires to make a m. of his ware ... 22:20
Markets   Good ware makes quick m. 22:48

MARLS

Marls  He who m. sand ...  30:3
Marriage  An ill m. is a spring ...  113:28
  M. halves our griefs ...  113:35
  M. is a lottery 113:33
  M. is destiny 113:37
  M. is the tomb ...  113:133
  M. makes or mars ...  113:34
  M. rides upon the saddle ...  113:42
  More belongs to m. ...  113:47
  Where there's m. without love ...  113:139
Marriages  At m. and funerals ...  72:43
  M. are made in heaven 113:36
Married  A m. man turns his staff ...  113:13
  A m. woman has nothing ...  113:14
  She is well m. ...  113:130
  The m. man has many cares ...  113:5
Marries  He that m. a widow and two children ...  113:152
  He that m. a widow, will often have ...  113:153
  He that m. ere he be wise ...  113:88
  He that m. for wealth ...  113:54
  He that m. late ...  113:92
  He who m. might be sorry ...  113:4
  The woman who m. many ...  113:151
  Who m. for love ...  113:136
Marry  Before you m. ...  113:46
  It is better to m. a shrew ...  113:69
  It is good to m. late ...  113:91
  It is unlucky to m. for love 113:135
  M. a widow ...  113:155
  M. first, and love will follow 113:138
  M. in haste ...  113:41
  M. in Lent ...  113:141
  M. in May ...  113:142
  M. not an old crony ...  113:56
  M. your daughter and eat fresh fish betimes 113:158
  M. your daughters betimes ...  113:159
  M. your like 113:77
  M. your son ...  113:160
  Never m. a widow ...  113:154
  Never m. for money ...  113:55
  They that m. in green ...  113:143
Martyr  It is better to be a m. ...  144:59
Master  A good m. ...  54:26
  An ill m. ...  54:27
  Every man cannot be a m. 9:21
  He can ill be m. ...  54:25
  He that is m. of himself ...  9:20
  He who is m. of his thirst ...  51:72
  If the m. say the crow is white ...  154:38
  Like m., like man 154:19
  M. easy ...  154:18

One m. in a house is enough 9:24
  The m.'s eye ...  49:37
  The m.'s footsteps ...  49:38
  The most m. ...  113:106
  Where every man is m. ...  9:23
Mastered  No man has ever yet thoroughly m. ...  153:52
Masters  M. should be sometimes blind ...  168:90
Mastery  M. mows the meadows down 9:11
Mastiff  A m. grows the fiercer ...  154:24
  Though the m. be gentle ...  37:50
Matrimony  M. is a school ...  113:21
Matters  It m. not what religion ...  144:13
Matthee  St. M. shut up the bee 117:15
Matthew  St. M. get candlesticks new 117:64
Matthi  St. M. lay candlesticks by 117:16
Matthie  St. M. sends sap ...  117:17
Mattho  St. M., take thy hopper ...  117:18
Maxim  A good m. ...  140:1
Maxims  M. are the condensed good sense ...  140:13
May  A M. cold ...  117:49
  A M. flood ...  181:53
  Every m. be ...  108:6
  He that will not when he m. ...  126:19
  M. birds come cheeping 117:52
  M. makes or mars ...  117:44
  M. never goes out ...  117:53
May-bee  M. was ne'er ...  108:7
May-day  M., pay-day ...  117:48
Meal  A m. without flesh ...  53:34
Mean  The m. is the best 116:6
Measure  He that forsakes m. ...  116:32
  M. is a merry mean 116:5
  M. is medicine 116:3
  M. is treasure 116:2
  There is m. in all things 116:24
Measured  Men are not to be m. ...  160:39
Measures  He that m. not himself ...  116:33
  He that m. oil ...  115:5
Meat  All m. pleases not ...  47:15
  If it wasn't for m. and good drink ...  53:8
  It is better to want m. ...  53:17
  M. and mass ...  53:12
  M. is much ...  53:16
  Much m. ...  53:66
  One man's m. ...  47:14
  The wholesomest m. ...  53:36
  They that have no other m. ...  80:15
  When m. is in ...  53:9
Meats  All m. to be eaten ...  47:17
Medal  Every m. ...  100:12

Meddle M. not with another man's matter 99:11
Meddling Little m. ... 99:17
Medicine There is no m. for fear 66:18
Medicines M. are not meat ... 87:48
Meet M. on the stairs ... 167:28
Melon After m. ... 51:49
Memory A man of great m. ... 102:15
He that has a good m. ... 75:16
Men M. get wealth ... 184:96
M. make houses ... 184:92
M., not walls ... 164:5
So many m., so many opinions 47:10
Mend M. your clothes ... 170:49
One may m. a torn friendship ... 72:84
Mend-fault One m. ... 34:23
Mending M. and doing without ... 170:48
Merchant A m. that gains not, loses 22:27
Mercy M. surpasses justice 71:6
M. to the criminal ... 71:13
Merry All are not m. ... 7:11
A m. heart ... 84:40
Aye be as m. as be can ... 84:38
It is good to be m. and wise 84:66
It is good to be m. at meat 84:72
It is m. in hall ... 84:73
It's m. when maltmen meet 84:74
M. is the feast-making ... 84:52
M. meet ... 84:30
Mettle M. is dangerous ... 129:21
Meum M., tuum, suum ... 135:19
Michaelmas M. chickens ... 117:65
M. rot ... 117:67
The M. moon ... 117:66
Mickle Many a m. makes a muckle 160:11
M. head ... 69:59
M. must a good heart thole 166:19
Might M. is right 164:7
Mile Every m. is two in winter 152:17
Milk M. is white ... 53:32
M. says to wine ... 51:67
Mill He who goes into a m. ... 29:18
The m. cannot grind ... 126:18
The m. gets by going 48:19
The m. that is always going ... 168:107
Miller Put a m., a weaver ... 124:30
The m. is honest ... 124:28
Millers M. and bakers ... 124:26
M. are the last ... 124:25
Mills M. and wives ... 113:17
M. will not grind ... 131:1
The m. of God ... 77:65
Mind A m. enlightened ... 114:5
M. other men ... 153:10
M. your own business 99:10
The m. is the man 114:1

What is a man but his m. 114:2
Minds Great m. think alike 157:7
If m. were alike ... 47:19
Mine What's yours is m. ... 135:21
Mirror The best m. ... 72:58
Mirth M. is the sugar of life 84:41
M. without measure ... 84:65
The m. of the world ... 84:54
Mischief Better a m. ... 98:6
He that m. hatches ... 10:14
M. comes by the pound ... 2:25
M. comes without calling for 10:3
No m. but a woman ... 10:2
The more m., the better sport 10:21
Miser A rich m. is poorer ... 115:17
If a man is a m. ... 115:3
Misery He bears m. best ... 162:39
It is m. enough ... 162:2
M. loves company 162:46
Misfortune M. arrives on horseback ... 2:24
M. comes to all men ... 2:21
M. is not that which can be avoided ... 2:23
M. makes foes ... 2:9
Misfortunes M. come of themselves 2:1
M. find their way ... 2:20
M. hasten age 2:6
M. never come singly 2:27
M. tell us ... 2:13
Our worst m. ... 186:21
Miss A m. is as good ... 165:13
You never m. the water ... 187:8
Mist When the m. comes from the hill ... 181:89
Mistakes He who makes no m. ... 97:12
If you don't make m. ... 97:5
Mistress Where the m. is the master ... 113:107
Mistrust M. is an axe ... 175:30
Mists So many m. in March ... 181:88
Misunderstanding M. brings lies ... 114:14
Mix Never m. your liquor 51:61
Moderation M. in all things 116:1
Modesty M. sets off ... 24:16
Though m. be a virtue ... 24:17
Moist A m. hand ... 167:21
Monday M. for wealth ... 38:1
M. is Sunday's brother ... 38:3
M.'s child ... 38:2
Money A man without m. ... 136:52
He that has m. has what he wants 180:2
He that has m. in his purse ... 183:18
He that has no m. ... 136:25
M. answereth all things 180:111

M. governs the world 180:114
M. is a good servant ... 180:124
M. isn't everything 180:52
M. is often lost ... 180:47
M. is round ... 180:26
M. is the ace of trumps 180:115
M. is the only monarch 180:113
M. is the root ... 180:29
M. is the sinews of love ... 109:126
M. is the sinews of war 180:121
M. makes a man free everywhere 180:101
M. makes marriage 113:58
M. makes money 180:67
M. makes the man 180:44
M. makes the mare to go 180:116
M. makes the pot boil 180:45
M. refused ... 8:24
M. talks 180:117
M. will do anything 180:99
M. will do more ... 180:100
M. would be gotten ... 180:72
Much m. makes a country poor ... 180:20
Of m., wit, and virtue ... 13:11
Put m. in thy purse 180:46
The m. you refuse ... 8:23
Too much m. makes one mad 180:38
What will not m. do 180:97
When m. speaks ... 180:118
Would you know what m. is ... 187:10
Moneyless A m. man ... 136:12
Monk A m. out of his cloister ... 144:82
Moon If the m. shows a silver shield ... 181:12
No m. no man 167:19
The full m. brings fair weather 181:8
When round the m. there is a brugh ... 181:11
When the m.'s in the full ... 69:14
More The m. the merrier ... 84:75
The m. you get ... 82:6
Morn Let the m. come ... 186:26
Morning A m. sun, and a wine-bred child ... 181:108
M. dreams ... 159:23
Some work in the m. ... 52:10
The m. sun never lasts a day 181:107
This m. knows not ... 171:49
Mortal All men are m. 39:1
A man is known to be m. ... 159:8
Most He that does m. at once ... 48:56
Mote You can see a m. in another's eye ... 34:17
Mother A man's m. ... 128:6
A m.'s love is best of all 109:113
A m.'s love never ages 109:112
It is not as thy m. says ... 128:16

Like m., like daughter 128:9
The good m. says not ... 128:17
The m. of mischief ... 141:10
The m. of the coward ... 32:6
The m.'s breath ... 128:18
The m.'s side ... 128:11
Mothering On M. Sunday ... 117:33
Mother-in-law M. and daughter-in-law ... 113:131
The m. remembers not ... 113:132
Mothers Four good m. ... 176:46
Mountain If the m. will not come to Mahomet ... 48:62
Mouse A m. in time ... 134:20
A m. may help ... 179:9
The m. that has but one hole ... 151:19
Well kens the m. ... 1:12
Mouth Into the m. of a bad dog ... 44:25
Keep your m. shut and your ears open 168:73
Keep your m. shut and your eyes open 63:7
The m. is the executioner ... 53:13
The m. is wind ... 188:7
Moyen M. does mickle ... 180:96
Much M. would have more 82:7
Muck M. and money ... 180:77
Where there's m. there's brass 180:76
Mule He who wants a m. without fault ... 97:42
One m. scrubs another 110:8
Murder M. will out 33:18
Music M. has charms ... 67:11
M. helps not ... 67:13
M. is the eye ... 67:12
M. is the food of love 67:10
Musket Take not a m. ... 116:22
Must In things that m. be ... 146:4
Mustard M. is a good sauce ... 84:42
Mutton He loved m. well ... 53:70
Myriad Of the m. vices ... 112:12

# N

Nails N. are not made from good iron ... 124:46
Naked No n. man ... 136:26
Name A good n. is a rich heritage 64:16
A good n. is better than riches 64:15
A good n. is sooner lost than won 64:24
A good n. keeps its lustre ... 64:17
He that has an ill n. ... 42:8
The n. of an honest woman ... 64:20

He that has n. need fear to lose nothing 136:24
If you put n. into your purse ... 48:39
N. comes of nothing 108:28
N. have, nothing crave 136:36
N. is to be got ... 136:5
Where n. is ... 136:21
Nought He that has n. ... 136:50
Novelty N. always appears handsome 17:35
November N. take flail ... 117:71
On the first of N. ... 117:72
Now N. is now ... 171:40
Number Look after n. one 153:2
N. one is the first house ... 153:3
Nurse The n. is valued ... 124:38
The n.'s tongue ... 124:39
Nurses N. put one bit ... 124:36
Nurture N. and good manners ... 15:5
N. is above nature 15:4
Nutmeg If you carry a n. ... 113:146
Nutting If you go n. on Sundays ... 144:67

# O

Oak An o. is not felled ... 130:37
Every o. has been an acorn 81:36
If the o.'s before the ash ... 181:17
Oaks O. may fall ... 81:7
Oats If you cut o. green ... 30:7
O. will mow themselves 30:8
Obedience O. is much more seen ... 123:5
O. is the first duty ... 123:7
O. is the mother ... 123:1
Obedient All things are o. to money 180:109
An o. wife ... 113:108
Obey He that cannot o. ... 123:2
Obstinate O. oxen ... 182:24
Occasion An o. lost ... 126:17
Occupation An o. is as good ... 124:8
Offender The o. never pardons 71:23
Offer To o. much ... 139:17
Office Out of o. ... 9:6
Offspring The o. of those that are very old ... 128:21
Oft O. ettle ... 134:25
Often O. and little eating ... 53:67
Oil Pouring o. on the fire ... 174:13
Old A man must go o. to the court ... 144:28
An o. cart well used ... 125:23

An o. dog barks not ... 125:4
An o. dog bites sore 125:53
An o. fox is not ... 125:11
An o. knave ... 125:14
An o. man in a house ... 125:24
An o. man is a bed ... 125:28
An o. man never wants ... 125:46
An o. man's sayings ... 125:1
An o. man's staff ... 125:64
An o. man who weds ... 113:74
An o. ox makes ... 125:25
An o. ox will find ... 125:49
An o. wise man's shadow ... 125:18
As the o. cock crows ... 125:42
Better be an o. man's darling ... 113:71
He that would be o. long ... 19:55
If the o. dog bark ... 125:3
In the o. of the moon ... 181:86
It is best to be off with the o. love ... 109:106
Never too o. to learn 125:35
None so o. that he hopes not ... 125:72
O. acquaintance ... 72:62
O. age comes stealing on 125:57
O. age doesn't protect ... 125:32
O. age is a hospital ... 125:38
O. age is a malady ... 125:40
O. age is sickness ... 125:37
O. be ... 125:59
O. cattle ... 125:27
O. chains ... 17:28
O. churches ... 125:41
O. customs ... 17:33
O. fish, old oil ... 72:60
O. foxes want no tutors 125:10
O. friends and old wine ... 72:61
O. hate ... 86:10
O. love does not rust 109:45
O. love will not be forgotten 109:44
O. men and travellers ... 125:47
O. men are twice children 125:36
O. men go to death ... 125:69
O. men, when they marry young women ... 113:73
O. shoes ... 17:29
O. sins ... 41:50
O. vessels ... 125:29
O. wives ... 125:48
O. wood is best to burn ... 17:32
O. young ... 19:53
Put an o. cat ... 125:16
She is an o. wife ... 45:11
The o. cow thinks ... 125:56
The o. man has his death ... 125:70
The o. pearl-oyster ... 128:19
Though o. and wise ... 125:34

**P**

When an o. man will not drink ... 125:73
Where o. age is evil ... 125:44
Who leaves the o. way for the new ...
17:27
You cannot put an o. head ... 19:36
Older The o. the bird ... 115:24
Omelette You can't make an o. ... 150:1
Ominous Nothing but what is o. ...
167:32
One By o. and one ... 134:16
O. thing at a time ... 48:57
Onion He who squeezes in between the o.
and the peel ... 29:8
Open An o. door may tempt a saint 169:3
At o. doors dogs come in 169:4
Never o. the door to a little vice ... 10:27
Never o. your pack ... 22:29
O. confession ... 89:7
Opens He who o. his heart ... 4:15
Opera The o. isn't over ... 6:22
Opinion Our own o. ... 153:41
Opinions He that speers all o. ... 3:30
Opportunity O. makes the thief 169:6
O. seldom knocks twice 126:1
Orange The o. that is too hard squeezed ...
56:7
Orts Make not o. of good hay 170:46
Other O. times ... 171:39
Others Do unto o. ... 61:11
Ounce An o. of luck ... 111:16
An o. of mirth ... 84:37
An o. of mother is worth ... 128:5
An o. of mother wit ... 183:30
An o. of vanity ... 24:8
Overhasty O. counsels ... 3:53
Owes He who o., is in all the wrong 14:22
Owl The o. thinks her own young fairest
128:14
Own Every man should take his o. 135:20
Every man will have his o. turn served
153:24
O. is own 135:11
Owt If tha does o. for nowt ... 153:18
Ox An o. is taken by the horns ... 139:12
An o., when he is loose ... 106:7
The o. is never woe ... 30:30
The o. when weariest ... 125:8
Oxford O. for learning ... 58:54
O. is the home of lost causes 58:52
When O. draws knife ... 58:53
Oysters O. are only in season ... 53:63
O. are ungodly ... 53:39

Pace It is the p. that kills 85:2
Padlock A bad p. ... 169:7
Paid Once p., never craved 14:36
Pain Great p. and little gain ... 73:2
It is more p. to do nothing ... 95:12
No p., no cure 87:41
P. is forgotten ... 166:9
P. is gain 166:10
P. is the price ... 166:21
Small p. is eloquent 166:6
Take a p. for a pleasure ... 166:12
There is no p. like the gout ... 166:22
Pains No p., no gains 48:35
Painter A good p. ... 67:4
Painters P. and poets ... 67:5
Painting On p. and fighting ... 67:3
Pair One p. of heels ... 32:14
Pale P. moon does rain ... 181:13
Paleness The p. of the pilot ... 181:19
Pardon P. is the choicest flower ... 71:3
P. makes offenders 71:11
P. one offence ... 71:10
Pardoning P. the bad ... 71:12
Pardons P. and pleasantness ... 71:1
Parents P. are patterns 128:7
Parsley P. fried ... 53:43
P. seed ... 30:54
Parson A house-going p. ... 144:71
Once a p. ... 144:75
The p. always christens ... 153:26
Parsons P. are souls' waggoners 144:76
Partridge If the p. had the woodcock's
thigh ... 30:38
Past P. cure ... 142:7
Things p. cannot be recalled 142:3
Patch P. by patch ... 170:50
Patent There is nothing p. in the New
Testament ... 144:101
Pater 'P. noster' built churches ... 144:53
Path Every p. has a puddle 97:38
Patience Have p. with a friend ... 72:73
He that has p. ... 130:18
Let p. grow ... 130:2
P. is a flower ... 130:3
P. is a plaster ... 130:29
P. is a remedy for every grief 130:28
P. is a virtue 130:1
P. is the best buckler ... 130:4
P. is the key of joy ... 130:7
P. is the knot ... 130:6
P. is the remedy of the world 130:27
P. provoked ... 130:24
P. surpasses learning 130:5

P., time, and money ... 130:17
P. under old injuries ... 130:26
P. with poverty ... 130:31
With p. the mulberry leaf ... 130:21
Patient  Be p. in poverty ... 136:115
P. men win the day 130:11
Paul  If St. P.'s Day be fair and clear ... 181:125
P.'s will not always stand 17:22
Pay  Better to p. and have little ... 14:2
He must p. with his body ... 131:12
He that cannot p. in purse ... 131:13
He that cannot p., let him pray 131:11
If you p. not a servant his wages ... 131:14
If you p. peanuts ... 131:26
P. beforehand and your work ... 131:16
P. beforehand was never well served 131:15
P. what you owe ... 14:33
P. with the same dish ... 14:34
Payer  A good p. ... 131:22
Paymaster  A good p. may build Paul's 131:25
A good p. needs no surety 131:23
A good p. never wants workmen 131:24
An ill p. never wants excuse 131:27
Payment  P. in advance ... 131:17
The best p. ... 131:20
Pays  He that p. last ... 131:19
He who p. the piper ... 131:30
Let him that p. the lawing ... 131:31
Who p. the physician ... 87:39
You p. your money ... 20:11
Peace  He that will not have p. ... 132:6
If you want p. ... 132:7
P. in a thatched hut ... 84:12
P. makes plenty 132:3
Where there is p. ... 132:1
Peaceably  To live p. with all ... 132:2
Peach  The p. will have wine ... 51:48
Peacock  The p. has fair feathers ... 11:5
When the p. loudly bawls ... 181:3
Pearls  Do not cast your p. ... 15:25
Pears  Plant p. for your heirs 30:45
Peas  Sow p. and beans ... 30:17
Pease  Every p. has its veaze ... 53:44
Peck  A p. of March dust ... 181:126
Pedigrees  In good p. ... 143:14
Pedlar  Let every p. carry ... 147:6
Peeps  He who p. through a hole ... 99:4
Peerage  The P. is the Englishman's Bible 15:46
Pen  P. and ink ... 188:3
The p. is mightier ... 188:1
The p. is the tongue ... 188:4
Pence  Take care of the p. ... 170:21

Pennies  Put two p. in a purse ... 180:71
Penniless  P. souls ... 136:59
Penny  A p. at a pinch ... 187:13
A p. saved ... 170:7
Every one has a p. ... 51:38
In for a p. ... 134:28
No p., no pardon 29:37
No p., no paternoster 29:38
P. and penny ... 160:15
P. in purse ... 72:23
P. wise ... 170:40
That p. is well spent ... 163:30
Penny-weight  A p. of love ... 104:15
Pens  P. may blot ... 188:6
People  Like p. ... 144:72
Perfect  P. friendship ... 72:48
P. love ... 109:39
Permanent  There is nothing p. except change 17:24
Perseverance  P. kills the game 134:1
Persuasion  The p. of the fortunate ... 13:23
Petticoats  When p. woo ... 109:95
Physic  If p. do not work ... 87:45
Physician  A p. is an angel ... 87:59
If you have a p. for your friend ... 87:56
No p. like a true friend 72:52
P., heal thyself 34:19
Physicians  P. kill more ... 87:53
Picture  Every p. tells a story 173:17
When a p. leaves the wall ... 167:26
Pictures  P. are the books ... 67:2
There are p. in poems ... 67:6
Pig  Lead a p. to the Rhine ... 172:12
Pigeon  The p. never knows woe ... 30:37
Pigeons  P. and priests ... 144:87
When the p. go a benting ... 30:36
Pigs  P. might fly ... 108:11
P. see the wind 30:27
Pin  A p. a day ... 170:19
See a p. and pick it up ... 167:29
Piss  P. not against the wind 25:7
Pitch  He that touches p. ... 29:11
Pitcher  The p. goes so often ... 56:16
Whether the p. strikes the stone ... 179:5
Pitchers  Little p. have great ears 19:25
Pities  He that p. another ... 88:23
Pitiful  A p. mother ... 49:19
Pity  It is no more p. ... 184:35
P. is akin to love 101:3
Place  There's no p. like home 172:20
Placks  P. and bawbees ... 170:20
Plain  P. dealing is a jewel 89:5
P. dealing is a jewel, but they that use it .. 89:13
P. dealing is best 89:6

P. dealing is dead ... 89:17
P. dealing is praised ... 89:15
Plan  P. the whole year ... 152:4
Play  As good p. for nought ... 131:2
If you p. with fire ... 37:48
It is no p. ... 100:24
It signifies nothing to p. well ... 73:25
No man can p. the fool ... 183:64
P., women, and wine ... 51:32
You may p. with a bull ... 37:24
Playing  No p. with a straw ... 125:13
Plays  He p. best that wins 165:2
He that p. his money ... 74:6
Pleasant  P. hours ... 84:21
Please  He that all men will p. ... 47:24
He that would p. all ... 47:22
It is as hard to p. a knave ... 60:19
P. your eye ... 11:49
You can't p. everyone 47:21
Pleases  When it p. not God ... 77:9
Pleasure  No p. without pain 84:45
No p. without repentance 142:19
P. has a sting ... 84:43
P. is not pleasant ... 84:47
Say to p. ... 169:17
The p. of what we enjoy ... 82:9
There is more p. in loving ... 109:110
Pleasures  The p. of the mighty ... 136:92
Plenty  He that has p. of goods ... 180:69
He who of p. will take no heed ... 136:10
P. breeds pride 180:83
P. is no dainty 180:21
P. makes poor 180:23
Plough  A man must p. ... 28:52
He that by the p. would thrive ... 153:34
P. deep ... 48:23
The p. goes not well ... 49:7
Plunder  The more you p. a Turk ... 133:9
Plymouth  When P. was a vuzzy down ... 58:61
Poacher  An old p. ... 33:30
Pocketful  A p. of right ... 29:40
Poet  A p. in adversity ... 186:8
A p. is born ... 67:8
The p., of all sorts of artificers ... 67:7
Poind  We can p. for debt ... 104:17
Point  P. not at others' spots ... 34:18
Poison  One drop of p. ... 29:5
One p. drives out another 145:10
P. is poison ... 7:24
Poland  P. is the peasant's hell ... 133:53
Policy  P. goes beyond strength 164:17
Pomp  All our p. ... 39:74
Poole  If P. was a fish-pool ... 58:60
Poor  A p. beauty ... 11:26
A p. man gets a poor marriage 113:61

A p. man's cow dies ... 136:95
A p. man's table ... 136:40
A p. man's tale ... 136:108
A p. man wants some things ... 115:13
He is not p. that has little ... 136:73
He is p. that God hates 136:77
It is a hard task to be p. and leal 136:65
It is a p. heart ... 84:71
P. and liberal ... 136:113
P. by condition ... 4:2
P. folk are fain of little 136:20
P. folk fare the best 136:37
P. folks are glad of porridge 136:22
P. folks' friends ... 72:24
P. men go to heaven ... 136:75
P. men have no souls 136:58
P. men seek meat ... 136:98
Put the p. man's penny ... 136:76
The p. man is aye put ... 136:107
The p. man pays for all 136:53
The p. man's shilling ... 136:55
The p. sit on the front benches ... 136:34
The p. suffer ... 136:54
Poorer  The p. one is ... 136:63
Pope  A p. by voice ... 144:80
If you would be p. ... 144:81
Port  Any p. in a storm 37:13
Porter  The p. calls upon God ... 144:43
Portion  Better a p. in a wife ... 113:52
Possessed  P. of happiness ... 84:63
Possession  P. is nine points ... 135:16
Possibilities  P. are infinite 108:3
Possible  All things are p. ... 108:4
Post  The p. of honour ... 90:9
Postern  The p. door ... 33:5
Pot  A p. that belongs to many ... 147:22
The p. calls the kettle black 34:7
Potter  One p. envies another 59:13
Poverty  He that is in p. ... 136:56
P. and anger ... 136:116
P. and wealth ... 136:83
P. breeds strife 136:70
P. does not hurt ... 136:74
P. is an enemy ... 136:11
P. is no disgrace ... 136:47
P. is not a crime 136:79
P. is not a shame ... 136:78
P. is the common fate ... 102:34
P. is the mother of all arts 136:38
P. is the mother of crime 136:60
P. is the mother of health 136:39
P. is the worst guard ... 136:68
P. obstructs ... 136:67
P. parts fellowship 72:26
P. wants many things ... 115:12

311

There is no p. where there is virtue ... 78:7
When p. comes in at the door ... 136:17
Power  Mickle p. makes many enemies 9:5
  P. corrupts 9:8
Powys  P. is the paradise of Wales 133:82
Practice  An ounce of p. .... 62:8
  P. makes perfect 62:9
Practise  P. what you preach 61:1
Praise  A man's p. ... 137:19
  Neither p. nor dispraise thyself ... 137:22
  P. a fair day ... 39:33
  P. by evil men ... 137:9
  P. is always pleasant 137:2
  P. is a spur ... 137:10
  P. is not pudding 137:15
  P. is the reflection ... 137:3
  P. makes good men better ... 137:11
  P. no man ... 39:34
  P. none too much ... 137:8
  P. the child ... 137:12
  P. the Lord ... 144:11
  P. without profit ... 137:17
  P. youth ... 137:5
  Too much p. ... 137:7
Praises  He p. who wishes to sell 22:4
  He that p. himself ... 137:20
  P. fill not the belly 137:16
  Who p. St. Peter ... 137:13
Pray  He that will learn to p. .... 37:35
Prayer  P. should be the key ... 144:96
Prayers  Even the p. of an ant ... 144:94
  P. and provender ... 144:97
  The p. of the wicked ... 144:98
Preaches  He p. well ... 61:6
  He that p. .... 144:77
  Who p. war ... 178:9
Precept  P. begins ... 61:4
Precepts  P. may lead ... 61:3
Present  P. to the eye ... 1:22
  Things p. are judged ... 171:44
Preserve  P. the old ... 17:34
Presumed  Nothing is to be p. on ... 127:7
Pretended  P. holiness ... 94:15
Prettiness  P. dies first 11:34
  P. makes no pottage 11:25
Pretty  P. face ... 11:51
  There's only one p. child ... 128:15
Prevent  You cannot p. the birds of sadness ... 162:28
Prevention  P. is better than cure 70:5
Price  Every man has his p. 29:32
Pricks  It early p. .... 19:43
Pride  P. and grace ... 138:10
  P. and laziness ... 138:11

P. and poverty ... 138:13
P. feels no pain 166:23
P. goes before a fall 138:1
P. goes before, and shame follows after 138:2
P. had rather go ... 138:19
P. increases our enemies ... 138:6
P. is a flower ... 138:5
P. is the sworn enemy ... 138:4
P., joined with many virtues ... 138:7
P. may lurk ... 138:15
P. must be pinched 166:24
P. often wears ... 138:23
P. will spit ... 138:22
P. with pride ... 138:21
The p. of the rich ... 136:93
There are those who despise p. .... 138:24
When p. rides ... 138:3
Pries  He that p. into every cloud ... 99:6
Priest  A p. sees people at their best ... 87:33
  Each p. praises ... 153:46
  Such p. .... 144:73
Prince  He whom a p. hates ... 149:5
  When the p. fiddles ... 149:22
Princes  P. are venison ... 149:17
Prizing  It is ill p. of green barley 6:19
Probabilities  A thousand p. .... 108:1
Procrastination  P. is the thief of time 43:19
Prodigal  The p. robs his heir ... 163:18
  Young p. in a coach ... 163:2
Profit  P. gives no headache 73:7
  Where p. is ... 73:14
Profound  It is p. ignorance ... 96:19
Promise  A man apt to p. .... 139:4
  Men may p. more ... 139:7
  P. is debt 139:11
Promises  He that p. too much ... 139:16
  Many fair p. .... 139:8
  P. are either broken ... 139:3
  P. are like pie-crust ... 139:1
  P. may make friends ... 139:19
Promising  Between p. and performing ... 139:21
Proof  The p. of the pudding ... 173:5
Prophet  A p. is not without honour ... 65:6
Proposes  Man p. ... 77:75
Prospect  P. is often better than possession 6:2
Prosperity  In time of p. .... 72:27
  P. is the blessing ... 144:102
  P. makes friends ... 180:93
Protection  No p. is as sure ... 26:24

Proud  A p. mind ...  138:16
He is a p. tod ...  138:32
I p. and thou proud ...  138:12
It is a p. horse ...  138:31
It is good beating p. folks ...  138:17
Prove  Never try to p. ...  173:13
P. your friend ...  72:69
Proverb  A p. comes not from nothing 140:17
A p. is an ornament ...  140:4
A p. is shorter ...  140:19
A p. is the wit ...  140:16
The p. cannot be bettered 140:5
Though the p. is abandoned ...  140:11
Proverbs  P. are like butterflies ...  140:21
P. are the children ...  140:12
P. are the wisdom ...  140:14
P. cannot be contradicted 140:10
Proves  That which p. too much ...  173:14
Provide  P. for the worst ...  70:12
Providing  P. is preventing 70:6
Provision  P. in season ...  170:52
Public  He that puts on a p. gown ...  9:13
Publicity  Any p. ...  64:9
Publish  We should p. our joys ...  84:64
Pudding  Better some of a p. ...  80:12
Too much p. ...  116:27
Puddings  P. and paramours ...  109:90
Pullet  A p. in the pen ...  135:4
The fine p. ...  19:44
Punctuality  P. is the politeness ...  52:28
P. is the soul ...  52:29
Punishment  P. is lame ...  44:21
Purse  He that shows his p. ...  169:8
Let your p. be your master 163:20
The p. of the patient ...  131:6
Pursuits  P. become habits 102:7

## Q

Quarrel  The q. of lovers ...  109:97
Quarrelling  Q. dogs ...  141:11
Quarrelsome  Q. dogs ...  141:12
Quart  You can't get a q. ...  108:26
Queer  There's nowt so q. ...  47:2
Question  It is not every q. ...  8:13
Like q. ...  8:9
Q. for question ...  8:8
Questions  He that nothing q. ...  13:22
Quey  Q. calves are dear veal 30:31
Quickly  Good and q. ...  85:23
Quiet  A q. conscience ...  26:18

Quietness  Q. is a great treasure 156:17
Quits  He q. his place well ...  72:5

## R

Race  The r. is got by running 48:43
The r. is not to the swift ...  134:6
Ragged  A r. colt ...  19:51
Under a r. coat ...  136:112
Rain  Although it r. ...  70:16
In r. and sunshine ...  144:26
More r., more rest ...  181:51
Near burr, far r. 181:10
R. before seven ...  181:64
R. from the east ...  181:63
R., rain, go away ...  181:67
Some r., some rest 181:50
The r. comes scouth ...  181:65
The r. falls on every roof 60:13
The r. of tears ...  54:6
There is no r. ...  144:54
Rainbow  A r. at morn ...  181:71
A r. in the morning ...  181:72
Rainbows  If two r. appear at one time ... 181:70
Rains  If it r. on Easter Day ...  181:58
If it r. when the sun is shining ...  181:68
It never r. but it pours 2:28
It r. by planets 181:66
Many r., many rowans ...  181:52
Rainy  After a r. winter ...  181:54
Keep something for a r. day 170:29
Raise  It is easier to r. the devil ...  174:8
R. no more devils ...  174:9
Rake  There is little for the r. ...  82:26
Rancour  R. sticks long ...  86:11
Rape  Oft r. rueth 85:5
Rare  That thing which is r. ...  187:14
Rats  R. desert ...  110:14
Raw  R. leather will stretch 19:26
R. pulleyn ...  53:45
Ready  R. money is a ready medicine 180:4
R. money will away 180:25
Reason  A man without r. ...  114:22
Hearken to r. ...  114:21
One r. is as good as fifty 173:15
R. binds the man 114:19
R. governs the wise man ...  114:20
R. lies between ...  116:10
R. rules all things 114:18
Reasons  The r. of the poor ...  136:109
Receiver  The r. is as bad as the thief 33:35

313

Receivers  If there were no r. ...  33:36
Receives  Who r. a gift ...  75:36
Reckless  R. youth ...  19:57
Reckoning  The r. spoils the relish 131:10
Red  A r. cow gives good milk 30:24
  If r. the sun begins his race ...  181:109
  R. clouds in the east ...  181:84
  R. sky at night ...  181:22
  R. wood makes gude spindles 30:41
  To a r. man read thy rede ...  167:25
Redemption  There is no r. from hell 46:10
Reed-player  The r. of your own street ...
  65:7
Reeds  Where there are r. ...  79:3
Reek  R. comes aye down again ...  18:27
Refuse  Never r. a good offer 8:22
  R. a wife ...  113:64
  To r. and to give tardily ...  75:20
Religion  A man without r. ...  144:2
  No r. but can boast ...  144:56
  R., credit ...  144:15
  R. is the rule of life 144:1
Religions  He that is of all r. ...  144:55
Rely  Never r. on love ...  109:51
Remarriage  Frequent r. ...  113:150
Remedy  No r. but patience 130:30
  The best r. against an ill man ...  10:45
  There is a r. for all things ...  145:3
  There is a r. for everything ...  145:4
  There is no r. for fear ...  66:19
  The r. for injuries ...  148:7
  The r. may be worse ...  145:16
Remember  R. man and keep in mind ...
  72:20
  R. to distrust 175:26
  R. you are but a man 138:29
Remembrance  The r. of past sorrows ...
  162:23
Remorse  R. is lust's dessert 142:18
Removals  Three r. ...  17:13
Remove  R. an old tree ...  125:51
Repairs  He that r. not a part ...  52:23
  Who r. not his gutter ...  52:22
Repentance  R. comes too late 142:13
  R. is a bitter physic 142:16
  R. is a pill ...  142:17
  R. is good ...  142:37
  R. is not to be measured ...  142:36
  R. is the loveliest ...  142:35
  R. is the virtue of fools 142:14
Reply  No r. is best 156:15
Reputation  R. is often got ...  64:4
  R. serves to virtue ...  64:19
  Win a good r. ...  64:18
Resolved  The r. mind ...  146:3

Resolves  He that r. to deal ...  89:18
Respect  R. a man ...  27:15
  R. is greater ...  65:2
Respects  He that r. not ...  27:14
Returns  Quick r. ...  22:18
Revenge  He who cannot r. himself ...
  148:15
  R. is a dish ...  148:19
  R. is a morsel ...  148:14
  R. is sweet 148:13
  R. never repairs ...  148:10
  R. of a hundred years ...  148:20
  R., the longer it is delayed ...  148:18
  To take r. ...  148:11
Reward  R. and punishment are the walls
  ...  49:1
Rich  A r. man can do ...  180:5
  A r. man's joke ...  180:94
  A r. man's money ...  180:33
  He is not r. that possesses much ...
  180:55
  He is r. enough that wants nothing 180:56
  He is r. enough who lacks not bread 180:57
  He that will be r. before night ...  180:80
  No one is r. enough ...  121:1
  R. folk have many friends 180:91
  R. men are stewards ...  136:101
  R. men may have ...  180:1
  R. men's spots ...  180:6
  The r. knows not ...  180:14
  The r. man has his ice ...  136:96
  The r. man may dine ...  136:99
  The r. man spends his money ...  136:94
  The r. man thinks of the future ...
  136:100
  They are r. who have true friends 72:51
Riches  It is the r. of the mind ...  114:6
  R. adorn the dwelling ...  78:3
  R. alone ...  180:53
  R. are but the baggage ...  180:15
  R. are like muck ...  75:1
  R. bring care ...  180:17
  R. have made more covetous men ...  82:1
  R. have wings 180:24
  R. rather enlarge ...  180:40
  R. serve a wise man ...  180:34
  R. take away more pleasures ...  180:27
  The r. of Egypt ...  133:3
Ride  Better r. on an ass ...  4:28
  If you can't r. two horses ...  110:13
  When you r. a young colt ...  37:12
Rider  Ill for the r. ...  127:25
Rides  He r. sure ...  97:13
  He that r. ere he be ready ...  85:13
  He who r. a tiger ...  134:29

Riding  Good r. at two anchors ...  151:16
Right  It will all come r. in the wash 127:11
    R. wrongs no man 100:4
Righteous  The r. man sins ...  169:2
Rip  R. not up old sores 174:11
Ripe  Soon r. ...  19:52
Rise  He had need r. betimes that would please everybody 52:18
    He must r. betimes that will cozen the devil 52:17
    Though you r. early ...  52:26
Rises  He that r. first ...  52:6
    He that r. late ...  103:6
    He that r. not early ...  103:5
Rising  R. was a seaport town ...  58:71
    R. was, Lynn is ...  58:70
River  Even the weariest r. ...  127:40
    In a great r. ...  4:24
Rivers  R. need a spring 12:4
Roads  All r. lead to Rome 47:30
Roast  He loves r. meat well ...  53:72
    R. meat does cattle 30:29
Robe  Bode a r. ...  4:10
Robin  If the r. sings in the bush ...  181:7
    The r. and the wren ...  167:9
Robs  He that r. a scholar ...  102:35
Rod  The r. breaks no bones 49:24
Rogue  No r. like to the godly rogue 94:21
Rogues  When r. go in procession ...  46:7
Rolling  A r. stone ...  17:16
Rome  All things are to be bought at R. 133:35
    It is ill sitting at R. ...  25:4
    R. was not built ...  130:35
    When in R. ...  25:1
Room  There's always r. at the top 4:13
Root  No r., no fruit 12:3
Rope  Give a thief enough r. ...  10:48
    Name not a r. ...  168:92
    The r. has never been made ...  114:13
Rose  A r. by any other name ...  118:5
    No r. without a thorn 97:29
Roses  If you lie upon r. ...  19:59
Rotten  The r. apple ...  29:3
Rough  The r. net ...  101:8
Rouk-town  A r.'s seldom a good housewife at home 79:29
Round  At a r. table ...  60:2
Rouses  He who r. a sleeping tiger ...  174:7
Rowan  R. tree and red thread ...  167:16
Royal  There is no r. road ...  54:8
Royet  R. lads ...  19:48
Royston  A R. horse ...  58:63
Rue  Better r. sit ...  17:11

Rued  Never r. the man ...  70:18
Ruined  Many have been r. ...  22:39
    No one was ever r. ...  176:61
Rule  Better to r. ...  9:1
    R. youth well ...  49:11
    This r. in gardening ...  30:14
Ruled  Who will not be r. by the rudder ...  3:25
Ruler  No man can be a good r. ...  9:16
Run  You cannot r. with the hare ...  110:12
Running  A r. horse ...  37:11
Russia  In R. as one must ...  133:57
Russian  R. friendship ...  133:58
    Scratch a R. ...  133:60

# S

Sack  Every one thinks his s. heaviest 153:54
    There comes nought out of the s. ...  18:35
Sad  It is a s. burden ...  162:4
    It is a s. house ...  113:118
Saddle  Put the s. on the right horse 147:35
Sadness  S. and gladness ...  162:5
Safe  A man is s. when alone 161:8
    Better be s. than sorry 151:13
    It is best to be on the s. side 151:14
    It is s. riding ...  151:2
    No s. wading ...  37:5
    S. bind ...  151:12
    The way to be s. ...  151:9
Safer  It is s. to hear ...  3:48
Safest  'Tis s. making peace ...  132:17
Safety  S. lies in solitude 151:11
    S. lies in the middle course 116:8
    There is s. in numbers 151:1
Sage  Set s. in May ...  117:45
Said  It was never ill s. ...  42:21
Sail  He that would s. without danger ...  37:33
    It is hard to s. over the sea ...  108:23
    Make not your s. too big ...  116:16
Sailors  S.' fingers ...  124:40
    S. get money like horses ...  124:43
    S. go round the world ...  124:42
    S. have a port ...  124:41
Saints  All are not s. ...  94:16
    There are more s. in Cornwall ...  58:40
Salisbury  S. Cathedral ...  58:62
    S. Plain ...  58:51
Salmon  S. and sermon ...  117:31

Salt   Help you to s. ...   53:76
  S. beef ...   51:75
  S. seasons all things 53:28
  S. water and absence ...   1:6
Salve   Seek your s. ...   145:7
  There is a s. for every sore 145:2
Same   It will be all the s. ...   186:13
Sands   Many s. ...   160:14
Saturday   A S.'s moon ...   38:11
  S. is the working day ...   144:78
  S.'s new ...   38:12
  S.'s servants ...   38:10
  There is never a S. ...   38:9
Sauce   Make not your s. ...   6:17
  What's s. for the goose ...   100:19
Save   S. a stranger from the sea ...   88:13
  S. a thief from the gallows ...   88:14
  S. something for the man ...   170:26
  S. your breath ...   168:37
Saver   A good s. ...   170:5
Savers   Some s. in a house ...   170:53
Saves   He that s. his dinner ...   170:23
  He who s. for tomorrow ...   170:35
Saving   A little s. ...   170:12
  Of s., comes having 170:8
Saws   Old s. speak truth 140:8
Say   A man may s. too much ...   168:9
  Better s. 'here it is' ...   135:13
  Better s. nothing ...   156:29
  Do as I s. ...   61:7
  Learn to s. before you sing 130:43
  S. as men say ...   25:11
  S. well, and do well ...   41:15
  S. well or be still 168:60
  'They s. so' ...   79:9
Saying   S. and doing ...   41:20
  S. is one thing ...   41:21
  S. 'No' a woman ...   184:88
Says   He who s. what he likes ...   168:8
  Many a one s. well ...   94:11
  What everybody s. must be true 176:36
Scalded   A s. cat ...   62:28
Scare   A good s. is worth more ...   3:13
Scathe   One does the s. ...   147:30
Scatter   S. with one hand ...   163:32
Scholar   Every good s. ...   54:24
  The s. may waur the master 54:28
Scholars   The greatest s. ...   102:24
Science   Much s. ...   102:31
  S. has no enemy ...   96:13
Scold   Who has a s. ...   113:120
Scolds   S. and infants ...   113:111
Score   S. twice before you cut once 85:35
Scorn   S. at first ...   27:9
  S. comes commonly ...   27:3
Scornful   Never was a s. person ...   27:12

Scorpion   There is a s. under every stone 37:8
Scot   A S., a rat ...   133:69
  The S. will not fight ...   133:70
Scotsman   A S. is always wise ...   133:72
Scottish   A S. mist ...   133:74
Scratch   S. my back ...   88:24
  S. my breech ...   88:25
Scratching   By s. and biting ...   141:17
Sea   Being on s., sail ...   172:34
Seaman   A s., if he carries a millstone ...   124:45
Seamen   S. are the nearest to death ...   124:44
Season   Everything is good in its s. 171:38
Second   S. thoughts are best 85:38
  The s. word ...   141:5
Secret   A s. foe ...   57:10
  He that tells a s. ...   79:41
  The s. wall of a town ...   132:5
  Thy s. is thy prisoner ...   79:40
Secure   He that is s. ...   151:10
Seed   Everything has its s. 12:2
Seeing   S. is believing 63:4
Seek   Nothing s. ...   4:6
  S. and ye shall find 4:7
  S. mickle ...   4:8
  S. that which may be found 4:29
  S. till you find ...   134:22
Seem   Be what you would s. to be 94:23
  Things are not always what they s. 7:2
Seill   S. comes not ...   84:14
Sel   S., sel, has half-filled hell 153:21
Seldom   S. is a long man wise ...   160:40
Self   S. do, self have 153:35
Self-praise   S. is no recommendation 137:18
Self-preservation   S. is the first law of nature 153:14
Sell   A man must s. his ware ...   22:19
  Don't s. the skin ...   6:7
  If you s. your purse ...   113:125
  It is no sin to s. dear ...   22:35
  You cannot s. the cow ...   20:3
Separation   S. secures manifest friendship 1:8
September   S. blow soft ...   117:62
Serpent   Whom a s. has bitten ...   62:27
Servant   A good s. must come ...   154:11
  A good s. must have good wages 154:14
  A good s. should have the back of an ass ...   154:9
  A good s. should never be in the way ...   154:8
  An ill s. will never be a good master 154:27
  A s. and a cock ...   154:7
  A s. is known ...   154:10

A s. that is diligent ... 154:12
Choose none for thy s. ... 154:1
If you would have a good s. ... 154:2
One must be a s. ... 154:28
Servants  S. make the worst masters 154:25
S. should put on patience ... 154:39
S. will not be diligent ... 154:17
So many s. ... 154:21
Serve  As long as you s. the tod ... 154:40
No man can s. two masters 110:11
S. a great man ... 154:31
S. a noble disposition ... 154:30
They also s. ... 130:10
You cannot s. God ... 20:5
Served  He that will be s. ... 130:9
He that would be well s., must know ... 154:6
If you would be well s., serve yourself 153:29
Serves  He that s. a good master ... 154:29
He that s. God for money ... 131:32
He that s. well ... 154:13
He who s. God, serves a good master 77:21
He who s. is not free 154:33
Many a man s. ... 154:32
Service  No s. to the king's 149:25
S. is no inheritance 154:36
S. without reward ... 131:4
The first s. a child does ... 19:12
Serving  S. one's own passions ... 129:23
Serving-man  A young s. ... 154:37
Set  S. good against evil 78:47
Seven  Keep a thing s. years ... 177:6
S. hours' sleep ... 159:14
Severity  Sometimes s. is better ... 35:5
Severn  Fix thy pale in S. ... 119:3
Seville  He who has not seen S. ... 133:43
Shadow  Catch not at the s. ... 82:15
Shake  Better s. out the sack ... 170:44
Shaking  After s. hands with a Greek ... 133:63
Shallow  S. streams ... 69:77
Shame  He that has no s., has no conscience 155:8
He who has no s. before the world ... 155:9
He who is without s. ... 155:10
Past s. ... 155:7
S. fades in the morning ... 14:14
S. in a kindred ... 143:17
So long as there is s. ... 155:6
Shameful  S. craving ... 8:16
S. leaving ... 170:45
Share  S. and share alike 100:23
Sharp  All that is s. is short 127:35
A s. stomach ... 93:6

Sharpens  Nothing s. sight ... 59:8
Sharper  The s. the storm ... 127:36
Shaving  It is ill s. against the wool 25:5
Sheaf  One s. of a stook ... 113:70
Shear  S. your sheep in May ... 117:46
Shearer  A bad s. ... 147:25
Sheep  He that has s. ... 30:26
He that makes himself a s. ... 56:26
If one s. leap o'er the dyke ... 61:15
Let every s. hang ... 147:3
One might as well be hanged for a s. ... 10:13
One scabbed s. ... 29:6
One s. follows another 61:14
Sheffield  When S. Park is ploughed and sown ... 58:26
Sheltering  It is good s. ... 125:19
Shift  A good s. may serve long ... 147:40
Ship  A s. and a woman ... 184:67
A s. under sail ... 11:37
Shipwreck  Let another's s. ... 62:39
Shitten  S. luck ... 167:7
Shod  S. in the cradle ... 19:40
Shoe  Every s. fits not ... 47:4
Shoemaker  The s.'s son ... 153:13
Shoots  He that s. oft ... 134:24
Shop  Keep your s. ... 48:18
Short  A s. prayer ... 144:91
S. boughs ... 30:48
S. folk are soon angry 160:41
S. folk's heart ... 160:42
S. pleasure ... 84:46
S. reckonings make long friends 14:37
Shortest  The s. answer ... 41:17
Should  He that does what he s. not ... 33:11
Shoulder  In a s. of veal ... 53:47
One s. of mutton ... 53:21
S. of mutton and English beer ... 58:6
When the s. of mutton is going ... 126:10
Show  S. a good man his error ... 78:44
S. me a liar ... 33:33
S. me the man ... 29:46
Shower  A s. in July ... 181:55
Shrew  Every man can rule a s. ... 3:62
Shrouds  S. have no pockets 180:64
Sick  He that is s. of a fever lurden ... 95:37
That s. man is not to be pitied ... 147:8
Sickness  S. shows us ... 87:28
S. soaks the purse 87:29
The s. of the body ... 87:27
Sides  There are two s. to every question 100:11

Sieve  A s. will hold water ...  184:64
Sight  Out of s. ...  1:21
  The farther the s. ...  181:14
Sign  It is an ill s. ...  36:10
Silence  S. and thinking ...  156:21
  S. catches a mouse 156:18
  S. does seldom harm 156:22
  S. is a woman's best garment 156:16
  S. is golden 156:1
  S. is of the gods 156:2
  S. is the sweet medicine ...  156:3
  S. means consent 156:20
  S. never makes mistakes 156:11
Silent  Beware of a s. man ...  156:33
  He that is s. ...  156:31
Silk  You cannot make a s. purse ...  18:34
Silks  S. and satins ...  163:15
Silly  It is a s. fish ...  62:32
  S. child is soon ylered 54:29
Silver  A s. key ...  180:108
  He that has not s. in his purse ...  136:119
  No s. without its dross 97:27
Simon  S. and Jude ...  117:70
Sin  Every s. brings its punishment ...  10:29
  It is a s. against hospitality ...  92:7
  S. is the root ...  10:9
  S. plucks on sin 10:11
Sing  If you s. before breakfast ...  84:60
  Who can s. so merry a note ...  136:29
Single  S. long ...  113:3
Sings  He that s. on Friday ...  84:61
  Many a man s. ...  113:31
Sinner  The greater the s. ...  10:25
Sins  When all s. grow old ...  115:23
Sits  He s. not sure ...  81:6
  Where MacGregor s. ...  9:12
Six  S. hours' sleep ...  159:13
Sixpence  There is not the thickness of a s. ...  78:46
Skaiths  Better two s. ...  162:36
Skeer  S. your own fire 99:12
Skeleton  Every family has a s. in the cupboard 143:10
Skilfullest  The s. wanting money ...  158:11
Skill  All things require s. ...  53:18
  S. and confidence ...  158:1
  S. is no burden 158:6
  S. will accomplish ...  158:2
  'Tis s., not strength ...  158:3
  Try your s. in galt first ...  173:10
Skin  There is more than one way to s. a cat 47:27
Skirts  Who has s. of straw ...  26:7
Sky  If the s. falls ...  108:12

Slander  S. cannot make ...  42:5
  S. flings stones ...  42:12
  S. is a shipwreck ...  42:4
  S. leaves a score ...  42:3
Slanderer  The s. kills a thousand times ...  42:13
Slave  Give a s. a rod ...  154:22
  He is a s. of the greatest slave ...  153:19
Slavery  Think no labour s. ...  170:51
Sleep  In s. all passes away 159:5
  In s., what difference is there ...  159:6
  S. is a priceless treasure ...  159:3
  S. is better than medicine 159:1
  S. is the brother ...  159:18
  S. is the greatest thief ...  159:9
  S. is the image ...  159:19
  S. is the poor man's treasure 159:4
Sleeping  It is good s. in a whole skin 32:13
  Let s. dogs lie 174:5
  There will be s. enough ...  159:15
Sleeps  He who s. all the morning ...  159:16
  Let him that s. too sound ...  14:16
Sleepy  A s. master ...  49:39
  The s. fox ...  159:17
Slip  There's many a s. ...  6:25
Sloe  When the s. tree is as white as a sheet ...  30:51
Sloth  S. breeds a scab 95:25
  S., like rust ...  95:24
Slothful  The s. is the servant of the counters 95:45
  The s. man is the beggar's brother 95:33
Slow  S. but sure ...  134:4
  S. help ...  88:18
Sluggard  A s. takes an hundred steps ...  95:9
  The s. must be clad in rags 95:34
  The s.'s convenient season ...  95:42
Sluggards  S. are never great scholars 95:46
Slumber  One s. ...  159:7
Small  A s. leak ...  160:26
  Better are s. fish ...  80:11
  From s. beginnings ...  81:38
  He that gives me s. gifts ...  75:33
  It's a s. world 185:3
  Many s. make a great 160:12
  Of a s. spark ...  160:25
  S. birds must have meat 19:11
  S. gifts make friends ...  75:32
  S. is beautiful 160:3
  S. is the seed ...  81:37
  S. rain allays great winds 160:18
  S. rain lays great dust 160:17
  S. riches ...  136:33
  S. sorrows speak ...  162:20

The best things come in s. packages 160:1
Smaller The s. the peas ... 11:47
Smell The best s. is bread ... 53:27
The s. of garlic ... 145:11
Smelt One is not s. ... 29:25
Smith Often a full dexterous s. ... 158:12
Smoke There's no s. without fire 79:2
The s. of a man's own country ... 172:27
Snail The s. slides up the tower at last ... 134:7
Snails When black s. on the road you see ... 181:4
Snake When a s. gets warm on ice ... 133:46
Snite The s. need not ... 34:11
Snow A s. year ... 181:95
S. for a se'nnight ... 181:96
Snowdon S. will yield sufficient pasture ... 133:83
Sober You cannot make people s. ... 51:14
Soberness What s. conceals ... 51:5
Soft S. fire ... 116:12
S. pace goes far 85:49
S. wax will take any impression 19:27
Softly He that goes s. ... 85:52
Ride s. ... 85:51
Sold Pleasing ware is half s. 22:49
Soldiers Old s. never die ... 124:48
S. fight ... 124:51
S. in peace ... 124:49
Solitary A s. man ... 161:17
Solitude S. dulls the thought ... 161:1
S. is often the best society 161:5
S. is the nest ... 161:2
Solomon S. was a wise man ... 108:24
Something S. is better than nothing 80:26
You don't get s. for nothing 48:36
Son A s. is a son ... 19:6
Even the S. of Heaven ... 143:11
Every man is the s. ... 147:2
It is better to have no s. ..., 124:52
Soon He that s. deemeth ... 85:6
S. enough, if well enough 85:27
S. gotten ... 163:10
S. tod ... 167:18
Sooner S. begun ... 52:15
Sooth S. bourd ... 176:56
S. saws ... 176:57
Sore As s. fight wrens as cranes 160:44
Sorrow A hundred pounds of s. ... 142:10
A s. is an itching place ... 162:52
Hang s. ... 162:37
Never lay s. to your heart ... 162:38
Of thy s. be not too sad ... 162:43
One for s. ... 167:31
S. and an evil life ... 162:19

S. comes unsent for 162:34
S. is at parting ... 162:8
S. is born ... 162:6
S. is soon enough ... 186:22
S. kills not ... 162:17
S. makes silence ... 162:21
S. makes websters spin 162:22
S. will pay no debt 142:11
When s. is asleep ... 162:41
Sorrows The s. of the rich ... 136:97
Sorry It is a s. flock ... 113:109
Sound It is a s. head ... 97:9
S. love ... 109:46
S. travelling far and wide ... 181:15
Soup Of s. and love ... 53:31
Southerly A s. wind and a cloudy sky ... 181:42
A s. wind with showers of rain ... 181:43
Sow As you s., so you reap 147:11
S. in the slop ... 30:13
S. or set beans ... 117:10
S. thin and mow thin 115:6
S. with the hand ... 163:31
They that s. the wind ... 10:15
Sows He that s. thistles ... 44:9
He that s., trusts in God ... 77:31
Spain In S., the lawyer ... 133:17
Nothing ill in S. ... 133:40
Spaniard A bad S. ... 133:44
The S. is a bad servant ... 133:41
Spaniels S. that fawn when beaten ... 49:27
Spare Better s. at brim ... 170:15
Better s. to have of thine own ... 170:4
S. the rod ... 49:22
S. to speak ... 168:22
S. well ... 170:9
S. when you're young ... 170:22
Spared Better s. than ill spent 170:14
Sparing S. is the first gaining 170:10
Sparrow Better a s. in the hand ... 135:2
Speak Better s. truth rudely ... 176:4
He cannot s. well ... 168:103
Many s. much ... 168:102
Never s. ill of the dead 168:57
S. and speed ... 168:23
S. fair and think ... 94:2
S. fitly ... 156:30
S. not of a dead man ... 53:74
S. only what is true of the living ... 39:93
S. the truth ... 176:52
S. well of your friend ... 57:14
S. when you are spoken to 15:16
To s. ill of others ... 168:59
To s. of a usurer ... 105:26
When all men s. ... 168:10

You may s. with your gold ... 180:120
Speaks He that s. ill of the mare ... 22:7
  He that s. lavishly ... 79:16
  He that s. me fair ... 94:13
  He that s. sows ... 156:26
  He that s. the thing he should not ... 79:15
  He that s. well ... 168:25
  He who s. much of others ... 79:14
  He who s. the truth ... 176:53
  Of him that s. ill ... 168:61
Speech More have repented s. ... 156:28
  S. is silver ... 156:23
  S. is the picture ... 168:66
Spend If you can s. much ... 163:25
  Know when to s. ... 163:29
  Never s. your money ... 6:9
  S. and be free ... 163:28
  S., and God will send ... 170:37
  S. as you get 163:21
  S. not where you may save ... 163:26
  Who more than he is worth does s. ... 163:5
Spender To a good s. ... 163:27
Spenders Great s. ... 163:33
Spends Much s. the traveller ... 172:32
  Who s. before he thrives ... 163:1
  Who s. more than he should ... 163:3
Spent What we s. we had ... 170:32
Spice He that hath the s. ... 180:10
Spindle Get thy s. and thy distaff ready ... 77:41
Spins She s. well ... 49:15
Spirit The s. is willing ... 182:6
Spit S. on a stone ... 134:17
Spits Who s. against the wind ... 44:13
Spoil Don't s. the ship ... 115:10
Spoils Too much s. ... 116:11
Spoke The highest s. ... 111:9
Spots There are s. even in the sun 97:22
Sprat Every s. now-a-days ... 24:3
  Throw out a s. ... 150:6
Spread Don't s. the cloth ... 6:15
  S. the table ... 53:10
Spring In the s. a young man's fancy ... 152:5
  The s. is not always green 152:3
Spur A s. in the head ... 51:23
  Never s. a willing horse 182:17
  S. a jade a question ... 99:8
Squeaking The s. wheel ... 168:24
Stable It's too late to shut the s. door ... 142:31
Stake Nothing s. ... 37:37
Standing S. pools gather filth 95:8

Stands He s. not surely ... 97:14
Stay He that can s., obtains 130:16
  S. a little ... 122:11
Steal He that will s. an egg ... 33:27
  He that will s. a pin ... 33:26
  If you s. for others ... 33:19
  One man may s. a horse ... 100:9
Steals He that s. honey ... 33:16
Steer S. not after every mariner's direction 3:28
Step S. after step ... 134:15
  The first s. ... 12:8
  The greatest s. ... 12:9
Stepmother Take heed of a s. ... 128:23
Steward There is a good s. abroad ... 181:94
Stick It is easy to find a s. ... 147:42
  The s. is the surest peacemaker 132:16
Sticking S. goes not by strength ... 158:4
Sticks S. and stones ... 168:56
Stile He that will not go over the s. ... 182:31
Still A s. tongue ... 156:8
  Be s., and have thy will 130:15
  S. waters run deep 156:32
  The s. sow ... 7:17
Sting The s. of a reproach ... 176:58
Stinking No man cries s. fish 24:18
Stitch A s. in time ... 52:21
  Don't s. your seam ... 85:36
Stolen S. goods ... 33:22
  S. waters ... 33:14
Stomach Make not thy s. ... 87:49
  To have a s. and lack meat ... 166:3
Stone Never take a s. ... 116:20
  There is a sliddery s. ... 81:29
  The s. that lies not in your gate ... 99:13
  Though s. were changed to gold ... 28:37
Stone-dead S. has no fellow 39:28
Stones Who remove s. ... 37:28
Stools Between two s. ... 146:9
Stoop He that will not s. for a pin ... 138:30
  It is no time to s. ... 142:33
Store They that have got good s. of butter ... 180:8
  Where there is s. of oatmeal ... 180:9
Storm After a s. comes a calm 127:19
Stout Put a s. heart ... 31:10
Stoutest The s. beggar ... 58:73
Straight A s. stick ... 7:38
  S. trees have crooked roots 7:21
Straw Let an ill man lie in thy s. ... 101:14
Straws S. show which way ... 160:23

Stream  The s. stopped ... 129:14
Streets  The s. of London ... 58:77
Strength  S. grows stronger ... 164:1
Stretch  S. your arm ... 163:22
Stretches  Everyone s. his legs ... 163:23
Strife  Better s. than solitude 161:11
  S. never begets ... 141:19
Strike  S. while the iron is hot 126:4
Strikes  He that s. with his tongue ... 168:2
  He that s. with the sword ... 178:6
String  The s. of a man's sack of patience
  ... 130:25
Strings  S. high stretched ... 56:18
Striving  It is ill s. against the stream 25:6
Strokes  Great s. ... 158:5
  Little s. fell great oaks 134:19
Strong  A s. town is not won ... 130:36
  The s. man and the waterfall ... 164:8
Strumpet  Never was s. fair 112:29
Stuarts  All S. are not sib ... 7:13
Studies  A man's s. ... 102:6
  He that s. his content ... 28:34
Stuffing  S. holds out storm 53:4
Stumble  A s. may prevent a fall 98:7
Stumbles  He that s. twice ... 62:33
Stung  It is better to be s. by a nettle ...
  72:15
Style  The s. is the man 188:17
Subject  The s.'s love ... 149:21
Subjects  Although there exist many thou-
  sand s. ... 168:93
Sublime  From the s. to the ridiculous ...
  116:39
Submit  To the man s. ... 92:8
Submitting  The s. to one wrong ... 56:25
Subtlety  S. is better than force 164:18
Succeed  If at first you don't s. ... 134:23
Succeeds  Nothing s. ... 165:1
Success  S. has many friends 165:7
  S. makes a fool seem wise 165:4
Sudden  S. friendship ... 72:67
  S. joy ... 84:50
Suffer  Better s. ill ... 41:41
  If thou s. a calf ... 56:24
  S. the ill ... 98:3
  We must s. much ... 166:17
Sufferance  Of s., comes ease 166:13
Suffered  He that is s. to do more than is
  fitting ... 33:9
Suffering  It is not the s. ... 144:58
  S. does not manifest itself 166:5
  S. is better than care 166:14
  S. is bitter ... 166:15
Suffers  Who s. much ... 166:4
Suffices  That which s. ... 28:18
Sufficient  S. unto the day ... 186:16

Suffolk  S. is the land of churches 58:31
Suit  One s. of law ... 104:22
Summer  Look for s. on the top ... 152:8
  No s., but has its winter 97:33
  S. in winter ... 181:119
  S. is a seemly time 152:7
Sun  Although the s. shine ... 70:17
  If the s. goes pale to bed ... 181:110
  If the s. in red should set ... 181:111
  Let not the s. go down ... 5:32
  No s. without a shadow 97:31
  The s. has stood still ... 171:28
  The s. is never the worse ... 78:41
  The s. shines upon all alike 60:12
  When the s. rises ... 87:38
  When the s. sets bright and clear ...
  181:113
  When the s. sets in a bank ... 181:112
  When the s. sets, the moon rises ... 127:4
  Where the s. enters ... 87:19
Sunday  S.'s wooing ... 144:68
  When S. comes ... 144:69
Sundial  What is the good of a s. ... 24:20
Sup  It is better to s. with a cutty ... 80:16
  No man can s. ... 108:20
Suppers  By s., more have been killed ...
  76:13
Sups  He s. ill ... 19:60
  He who s. with the devil ... 10:46
Surfeits  A man never s. ... 89:8
Surgeon  A good s. must have an eagle's eye
  ... 87:62
  A s. experiments ... 173:11
Surgeons  S. cut ... 87:63
Surprised  He that is s. with the first frost
  ... 181:102
Sussex  S. won't be druv 58:34
Sutton  S. for good mutton ... 58:65
  S. for mutton ... 58:64
Swallow  One s. does not make a summer
  173:16
Swarm  A s. in May ... 117:43
Swear  He that will s. ... 40:36
Sweep  If every man would s. before his
  own door ... 34:21
Sweet  No s. without sweat 48:31
  S. appears sour ... 131:9
  S. are the uses ... 2:17
  S. in the bed ... 95:7
  S. meat ... 44:16
  S. things are bad for the teeth 53:46
  'Tis a s. sorrow ... 113:127
  What is s. in the mouth ... 7:23
Sweet-heart  'S.' and 'Honey-bird' ...
  109:63

Thousand  A t. pounds, and a bottle of hay
... 180:66
In a t. pounds of law ...  104:16
Thread  A t. will tie an honest man ...
89:22
He who holds the t. ...  9:4
The t. breaks ...  179:4
Threatened  There are more men t. than
stricken 168:42
T. folk live long 168:41
Threatens  He t. many ...  35:10
Three  T. dear years ...  124:27
T. may keep a secret ...  79:42
T. things are not to be trusted ...  175:21
T. things cost dear ...  112:18
T. things drive a man out of his house ...
113:119
Thrift  T. is a great revenue 170:1
T. is the philosopher's stone 170:2
Thrive  All things t. ...  167:6
First t. ...  113:45
He that will t. must ask ...  113:101
He that will t., must rise ...  52:8
He who would wish to t. ...  167:14
Thrives  Well t. he ...  77:48
Throw  Don't t. out your dirty water ...
85:39
The best t. of the dice ...  74:11
Thunder  While the t. lasted ...  37:14
Thunders  When it t. in March ...  181:75
When it t., the thief becomes honest 37:15
Thursday  T. come ...  38:4
Tide  The t. must be taken ...  126:12
The t. never goes out so far ...  127:42
Tie  No t. can oblige ...  110:15
Tiger  If you do not enter a t.'s den ...
37:42
Time  He that has t. ...  171:9
It is t. to set in ...  113:93
It is t. to yoke ...  113:94
No t. like the present 43:26
Take t. by the forelock 126:14
Take t. when time comes 126:15
Take t. when time comes, lest time steal
away 171:36
There is a t. and place ...  171:37
There is a t. to speak ...  156:27
The t. to come ...  171:47
Those that make the best use of their t. ...
48:46
T. and straw ...  171:13
T. and tide ...  171:29
T. cures all things 171:1
T. devours ...  171:14
'T. enough' lost the ducks 43:4
T. flees away ...  171:24

T. flies 171:23
T. has wings 171:25
T. is a file ...  171:15
T. is a great healer 171:2
T. is money 171:7
T. is the father ...  171:21
T. is the rider ...  171:17
T. is, time was ...  171:26
T. lost ...  171:35
T., not the mind ...  109:78
T. passes away ...  140:20
T. spent in vice ...  171:32
T. stays not ...  171:30
T. tames ...  171:4
T. tries all things 171:18
T. tries truth 171:20
T. undermines us 171:16
T. will tell 171:19
T. works wonders 171:5
Who will in t. present ...  84:19
With t. and art ...  171:12
Times  Every one puts his fault on the t.
147:29
T. change ...  17:20
Tine  Many t. half-mark whinger ...  115:11
Tired  When a man is t. of London ...
58:75
Tocherless  A t. dame ...  113:59
Tod  The t. never sped better ...  153:27
The t.'s bairns ...  18:2
Today  If t. will not ...  43:8
One hour t. ...  43:21
One t. is worth two tomorrows 43:22
T. a man ...  39:26
T. is the scholar ...  171:45
Toll  When thou dost hear a t. or knell ...
39:17
Tomorrow  Never put off till t. ...  43:20
T. is another day 91:28
T. never comes 43:23
Tongue  A good t. is a good weapon 168:46
A long t. ...  139:22
An ill t. may do much 79:13
If you keep your t. prisoner ...  156:12
It is a good t. that says no ill ...  168:58
Let not thy t. run away ...  168:11
Let not your t. run at rover 168:12
One t. is enough ...  184:50
That t. does lie ...  85:19
The t. breaks bone ...  168:48
The t. is more venomous ...  168:50
The t. is not steel ...  168:52
The t. is the rudder ...  168:26
The t. of experience ...  62:7
The t. of idle persons ...  168:111
The t. stings 168:49

323

The t. talks ... 168:3
Under the t. ... 168:47
Too  T. much of ought ... 116:26
You can have t. much ... 116:25
Toom  T. bags rattle 69:76
T. pokes ... 113:50
Too-too  T. will in two 56:14
Tortoise  The t. wins the race ... 134:5
Tottenham  When T. wood ... 181:87
Touch  T. wood ... 167:15
Town  He that is in a t. ... 117:47
If you see a t. worshipping a calf ... 25:2
There was never a good t. ... 97:34
The t. for wealth ... 180:81
Trade  A t. is better ... 124:12
Every man to his t. 124:24
He that has no good t. ... 124:11
T. is the mother ... 124:5
Who has a t. ... 124:2
Who hath a good t. ... 124:1
Trades  A dozen t. ... 124:14
A man of many t. ... 124:13
Let all t. live 124:17
Tradesmen  T. live upon lack 124:18
Train  T. up a child ... 19:31
Tramp  The more you t. on a turd ... 42:15
T. on a snail ... 35:11
Travel  He who does not t. ... 172:5
It is better to t. hopefully ... 6:5
Much t. is needed ... 172:3
The best way to t. ... 144:7
To t. through the world ... 172:35
T. broadens the mind 172:1
T. makes a wise man better ... 172:13
Traveller  A t. may lie ... 172:16
Travellers  Nothing so necessary for t. ... 172:38
T. and poets ... 172:17
T. change climates ... 172:6
T. should correct ... 172:15
Travelling  Much t. ... 172:4
Travels  He that t. far ... 172:2
He t. fastest ... 161:9
He who t. not by sea ... 37:34
Tre  By T., Pol, and Pen ... 58:80
Tread  When you can t. on nine daisies ... 152:1
Treat  T. a friend ... 72:81
Tree  As a t. falls ... 17:15
A t. often transplanted ... 17:12
He that plants a t. ... 30:39
It is a good t. that has neither knap nor gaw 97:39
There is no t. ... 187:18
The t. that God plants ... 77:7

Trees  Set t. at Allhallontide ... 117:73
Set t. poor ... 30:40
Trencher  T. friends ... 72:57
Tricks  Don't put t. ... 172:18
Tring  T., Wing, and Ivinghoe ... 58:66
Tripe  T.'s good meat ... 53:33
Triumph  Do not t. before the victory 6:21
Trouble  A t. shared ... 186:14
He that seeks t. ... 174:1
Let your t. tarry ... 186:23
Never t. trouble ... 186:25
T. brings experience ... 2:4
Troubles  Don't meet t. half-way 186:24
When t. are few ... 159:31
Trowel  With the t. of patience ... 130:22
True  A t. friend is the best possession 72:50
A t. man and a thief ... 89:23
Many a t. word ... 176:37
T. happiness ... 84:15
T. love kythes ... 109:23
T. love never grows old 109:47
T. praise ... 137:1
Truest  The t. jests ... 176:55
Truly  A t. great man ... 81:19
Trust  If one does not t. enough ... 175:29
If you t. before you try ... 175:15
In t. is treason 175:3
In t. is truth 175:9
Never t. a sleeping dog ... 175:20
Never t. a tailor ... 124:34
Never t. a woman ... 184:77
Put your t. in God ... 144:10
T. a snake before a Jew ... 133:62
T. helps many ... 175:1
T. is dead ... 175:32
T. is the mother ... 175:4
T. makes way ... 175:2
T. not a great weight ... 175:13
T. not a new friend ... 175:18
T. not a woman ... 175:19
Where there is no t. ... 175:31
While you t. to the dog ... 175:22
Trusting  T. often makes fidelity 175:8
T. too much to others ... 175:5
Trusts  He that t. much ... 175:6
He that t. to borrowed ploughs ... 14:11
He who t. not ... 175:27
Who t. to rotten boughs ... 175:12
Truth  The greater the t. ... 176:51
There is t. in wine 51:4
The t. shows best ... 176:18
T. and oil ... 176:13
T. and roses ... 176:48
T. breeds hatred 176:45
T. fears no trial 176:28
T. finds foes ... 176:47

T. has a good face ... 7:35
T. has always a sure bottom 176:2
T. has a scratched face 176:49
T. has no answer 176:14
T. has no need ... 176:21
T. is a spectre ... 176:54
T. is God's daughter 176:1
T. is mighty ... 176:7
T. is stranger ... 176:59
T. is time's daughter 176:41
T. is truth 176:16
T. lies at the bottom ... 176:43
T. may be blamed ... 176:27
T. may walk ... 176:8
T. needs no colours 176:20
T. needs not the ornament ... 176:23
T. never grows old 176:5
T. often hides ... 176:44
T.'s best ornament ... 176:17
T. seeks no corners 176:26
T. will come ... 176:12
T. will conquer ... 176:9
T. will out 176:11

Truthfulness T. becomes the gentleman 176:6
Truths All t. are not to be told 176:63
Try First t. ... 173:1
T. your friend ... 72:70
Tub Every t. must stand ... 147:5
Tubs Put out your t. ... 126:7
Tune There's many a good t. ... 125:21
Turf On the t. all men are equal ... 74:14
Turk Where the T.'s horse once treads ... 133:10
Turkey T., heresy, hops, and beer ... 144:46
Turn One good t. deserves another 88:19
T. about ... 100:25
T. the money in your pocket ... 167:8
Turnips T. like a dry bed ... 30:19
Twelfth At T. Day ... 117:4
Twenty-four There are only t. hours in the day 48:52
Twice If things were to be done t. ... 142:26
Twig As the t. is bent ... 19:29
Two A man cannot be in t. places at once 108:21
It takes t. to make ... 141:4
It takes t. to tango 147:20
Make not t. sorrows ... 162:42
No man can do t. things at once 108:19
That which t. will ... 182:2
T. cats and a mouse ... 141:6

T. dogs strive for a bone ... 141:15
T. in distress ... 162:48
T. is company ... 23:1
T. of a trade ... 124:19
T. sparrows ... 141:7
T. suns ... 141:8
T. things do prolong thy life ... 113:10
T. to one is odds 100:21
Typhoon After a t. there are pears to gather up 127:27
Tyranny The t. of the Turk ... 133:11

# U

Ugly An u. wife ... 113:84
U. women ... 50:9
Unbidden An u. guest knows not ... 92:16
An u. guest must bring ... 92:17
Unborn Better u. than unbred 15:1
Better u. than untaught 54:4
Uncalled Who comes u. ... 92:18
Understanding The u. of an Arab ... 133:12
Understands Who u. ill ... 114:15
Uneasy U. lies the head ... 149:9
Unexpected The u. always happens 6:28
Unhappy An u. man's cart ... 2:31
Union U. is strength 164:3
United U. we stand ... 141:28
Unminded U., unmoaned 1:23
Unpaid U. debts ... 14:31
Unrighteous The u. penny ... 29:2
Unsafely He lives u. ... 37:10
Unseen U., unrued 1:24
Untaught Better u. ... 54:21
Untimeous U. spurring ... 85:3
Use Everything is of u. ... 170:47
Once a u. ... 83:9
U. is all 62:12
U. legs ... 177:4
U. makes mastery 62:11
Used The u. key ... 177:1
Useful A u. trade ... 124:7
Usurers U. are always good husbands 105:24
U. live by the fall of heirs ... 105:25
Usury U. is murder 105:23
Uther-Pendragon Let U. do what he can ... 119:4

**325**

# V

Vain  In v. they rise early ... 52:27
Vainglory  V. blossoms ... 24:6
Valentine  On St. V., all the birds of the air ... 117:11
On St. V.'s Day cast beans in clay ... 117:13
On V.'s Day, will a good goose lay ... 117:14
St. V., set thy hopper by mine 117:12
Valiant  A v. man's look ... 31:14
Valley  He that stays in the v. ... 4:4
Valour  V. delights ... 31:22
V. is born with us ... 31:11
V. is the nobleness ... 31:3
V. would fight ... 31:33
Value  If you would know the v. of a ducat ... 187:9
They that v. not praise ... 137:4
Valued  A man is v. ... 187:2
Variety  V. is charming 17:6
V. is the spice of life 17:4
V. takes away satiety 17:5
Vast  V. chasms can be filled ... 28:38
Vaunter  A v. and a liar ... 24:12
Venom  There is no v. ... 168:51
Venture  Take your v. ... 37:41
V. a small fish ... 150:5
V. not all in one bottom 151:17
Ventured  Nothing v. ... 37:36
Vermilion  Near v. one gets stained pink 29:7
Vice  V. is its own punishment ... 10:16
V. is often clothed ... 78:53
V. makes virtue shine 78:51
Where v. is ... 148:3 .
Victory  It is a great v. ... 132:15
On the day of v. ... 165:6
Victuals  Of all v. ... 51:60
There is more good v. ... 58:7
Village  Better be first in a v. ... 4:26
Vincent  Remember on St. V.'s Day ... 181:105
Vine  Make the v. poor ... 30:49
Take a v. of a good soil ... 113:67
The v. brings forth three grapes ... 51:40
Vinegar  A v. seller ... 124:21
Violent  Nothing that is v. ... 129:10
Viper  No v. so little ... 160:29
Virtue  He that sows v. ... 78:18
There is no v. ... 78:26
The v. of a coward ... 32:23
V. and a trade ... 78:8
V. and happiness ... 78:2

V. and vice ... 78:52
V. flies from the heart ... 131:33
V. has all things ... 78:13
V. is a jewel ... 78:4
V. is found ... 116:7
V. is its own reward 78:14
V. is more important ... 78:15
V. is praised by all ... 78:36
V. is the beauty ... 78:5
V. is the only true nobility 78:16
V. joins man to God 78:1
V. never grows old 78:17
Visits  Long v. ... 92:12
Vitus  If St. V.'s Day be rainy weather ... 181:62
Voice  The v. is the best music 168:27
Volunteer  One v. ... 182:18
Vows  V. made in storms ... 139:6
Voyage  That v. never has luck ... 9:26
Vulgar  The v. will keep no account ... 165:12

# W

Wage  W. will get a page 131:7
Wager  A w. is a fool's argument 74:12
Wages  The w. of sin ... 10:28
Wagon  When the w. of fortune ... 111:20
Wake  W. not a sleeping lion 174:6
Walk  We must learn to w. before we can run 130:42
Walking  It is good w. with a horse ... 151:15
Wallet  We see not what is in the w. behind 34:16
Walls  W. have ears 79:24
Walnut-tree  He who plants a w. ... 30:46
Wame  Lay your w. ... 163:24
Wand  Thraw the w. ... 19:30
Wanswell  All the maids in W. ... 58:74
Want  A thing you don't w. ... 22:37
For w. of a nail ... 160:22
If you w. a thing done, go ... 153:32
If you w. a thing well done ... 153:31
W. of money ... 136:42
Wanton  W. kittens ... 19:49
War  He that makes a good w. ... 132:10
In w. all suffer defeat ... 178:5
In w., it is not permitted ... 178:14
No w. without a woman 184:6
W., hunting, and love ... 178:11
W. is death's feast 178:2
W. is sweet ... 178:20

W. is the sport ... 178:21
W. makes thieves ... 132:13
When w. begins ... 178:3
Warm He that is w. ... 153:28
Warned W. folks may live 168:43
Warning He was slain that had w. ... 3:22
Wars He that is not in the w. ... 37:7
Of all w. ... 132:14
W. bring scars 178:4
Wash Don't w. your dirty linen ... 143:23
W. your hands often ... 87:14
Washing For w. his hands ... 21:2
Waste W. makes want 170:42
W. not, want not 170:41
Watched A w. pot ... 130:34
Water Don't go near the w. ... 37:43
There was aye some w. ... 79:4
Under w., famine ... 181:97
W. drinkers ... 51:56
W. is a boon in the desert ... 177:10
W. is the king ... 51:51
Way Once a w. ... 104:56
The w. to an Englishman's heart ... 53:6
Ways There are many w. to fame 64:3
There are more w. to kill a cat ... 47:28
There are more w. to kill a dog ... 47:29
There are more w. to the wood ... 47:26
Weak Every man has his w. side 97:7
W. men had need be witty 179:10
W. things united ... 179:7
Weaker The w. goes to the pot 179:1
The w. has the worst 179:3
Weakest The w. goes to the wall 179:2
Weal Be it w. or be it woe ... 117:54
No w. without woe 162:24
Wealth A man's w. is his enemy 180:37
Bear w. ... 136:85
If we have not the world's w. ... 136:28
The greatest w. ... 180:54
W. infatuates ... 180:39
W. is best known by want 136:16
W. is the test ... 180:48
W. makes worship 180:88
Where w. is established ... 180:28
Weapon The w. of the brave ... 31:15
Weapons All the w. of war ... 66:17
W. breed peace 132:18
Wear Better to w. out than to rust out 48:12
Better w. out shoes than sheets 48:7
Do not w. out ... 92:10
Weary Never be w. of well doing 41:39
Weasel When the w. and the cat ... 10:6
Weather No w. is ill ... 181:24
Weather-eye Keep your w. open 63:6
Web For a w. begun ... 77:39

Wed Better w. over the mixen ... 113:75
Wedding As your w. ring wears ... 113:11
One w. brings another 113:148
Wedlock W. is a padlock 113:12
Wee Better a w. fire ... 136:87
Weed One ill w. ... 29:4
Weeds The w. overgrow the corn 10:43
W. want no sowing 10:4
Weel W.'s him and wae's him ... 144:86
Weep To w. for joy ... 84:33
Weeping We w. come into the world ... 162:30
Weigh W. justly ... 22:36
Weight W. and measure ... 22:34
Welcome Good will and w. ... 92:3
He that is w. ... 92:4
Such w. ... 92:6
They are w. that bring 75:5
W. is the best dish 92:5
Well All is w. with him ... 121:8
Do w. and have well 41:35
He that does w. ... 41:36
He that would be w. ... 172:29
If the lad go to the w. ... 182:21
That which is w. done ... 48:26
W. is, that well does 41:3
When the w. is full ... 56:19
Where men are w. used ... 101:11
Well-bred A w. youth ... 15:17
Welshman The older the W. ... 133:84
The W. had rather see ... 181:116
The W. keeps nothing ... 133:85
Westminster Who goes to W. for a wife ... 58:76
What It is not w. is he ... 180:50
Wheat Sow w. in dirt ... 30:12
Whip A w. for a fool ... 49:23
Whispered W. words ... 79:19
Whispering Where there is w. ... 79:7
Whistling A w. girl ... 167:13
A w. woman ... 167:12
White A w. wall ... 69:45
He that has a w. horse ... 113:87
W. silver draws black lines 11:10
Whole Our w. life ... 107:11
Whore A w. in a fine dress ... 112:30
A w. repents ... 112:28
Once a w. ... 112:27
Whoredom W. and grace ... 112:31
Whores W. affect not you ... 112:19
W. and rogues ... 112:32
Whoring W. and bawdry ... 112:21
Why Every w. has a wherefore 8:14
Wicked A w. book ... 188:15
A w. man is his own hell 10:17
A w. woman and an evil ... 184:3

It is a w. world ... 10:33
The more w. ... 111:38
Wickedness W. with beauty ... 10:26
Wide He that has a w. therm ... 76:16
Widecombe W. folks are picking their geese ... 181:98
Widow Long a w. ... 155:4
Widows W. are always rich 180:75
Wife A good w. and health ... 113:7
A good w. makes a good husband 113:100
A good w.'s a goodly prize ... 113:9
A man without a w. ... 113:6
A w. is sought for her virtue ... 113:80
He that has a w. has a master 113:105
He that has a w., has strife 113:20
He that has no w. ... 3:63
If you make your w. an ass ... 113:122
Next to no w. ... 113:27
The first w. is matrimony ... 113:149
There is one good w. in the country ... 24:4
There was a w. that kept her supper ... 170:33
The w. is the key ... 113:102
Wae's the w. that wants the tongue ... 113:116
W. and children are bills ... 113:16
Wite yourself if your w. be with bairn 147:17
Wiles Truly at weaving w. ... 133:4
W. help weak folk 36:2
Wilful A w. man ... 182:26
Will If one w. not ... 47:18
Where there's a w. ... 182:1
Where your w. is ready ... 182:11
W. buys ... 182:8
W. is no skill 182:5
W. is the cause ... 182:9
W. will have will ... 182:10
Willing All lay load on the w. horse 182:16
Willow The w. will buy a horse ... 30:43
Willows W. are weak ... 179:8
Wills He who w. the end ... 182:7
Wimble The little w. ... 160:20
Win W. at first ... 73:26
W. gold and wear gold 48:25
W. or lose ... 142:12
You can't w. them all 165:8
You w. some ... 165:9
Wind Come with the w. ... 33:25
Forsaken by the w. ... 134:26
If the w. is north-east ... 181:36
If w. follows sun's course ... 181:25
It is a good w. ... 51:44
It's an ill w. ... 127:21

Take heed of w. that comes in at a hole ... 87:26
The w. in one's face ... 183:1
When the w. is in the east, it is neither good ... 181:37
When the w. is in the east on Candlemas Day ... 181:39
When the w. is in the north ... 181:32
When the w. is in the south, it's in the rain's mouth 181:40
When the w. is in the west, the weather is at its best 181:44
When the w. is south it blows your bait ... 181:41
When the w. is west, the fish bite best 181:45
When the w. veers against the sun ... 181:26
Where the w. is on Martinmas Eve ... 181:27
Windy A w. March ... 181:28
Wine Drink w. in winter ... 51:50
Good w. engenders good blood 51:65
Good w. needs no bush 22:50
Of w. the middle ... 51:46
The best w. ... 125:20
The w. is the master's ... 51:45
When the w. is in ... 51:1
When w. sinks ... 51:9
W. and wealth ... 51:28
W. and wenches ... 51:33
W. and youth ... 51:22
W. does not intoxicate men ... 51:10
W. is a turncoat 51:41
W. is a whetstone ... 51:24
W. is old men's milk 51:42
W. is the best broom ... 51:18
W. is the glass ... 51:8
W. makes all sorts ... 51:43
W. makes old wives wenches 51:21
W. wears no breeches 51:7
You cannot know the w. ... 7:33
Wink W. at small faults 71:21
Winter A good w. ... 152:13
He that passes a w.'s day ... 152:16
W. eats ... 152:14
W. is summer's heir 152:15
W.'s thunder and summer's flood ... 181:77
W.'s thunder makes old man's wonder 181:78
W. thunder bodes summer hunger 181:76
Wisdom By w. peace ... 183:28
He has w. at will ... 183:46
It is a great point of w. ... 183:34
No w. to silence 183:52

What is not w. ... 183:27
W. and virtue ... 183:21
W. goes not always ... 183:8
W. is a treasure ... 183:13
W. is better than strength 183:26
W. is more to be envied ... 183:14
W. is neither inheritance ... 183:10
W. is the least burdensome ... 183:19
W. sometimes walks ... 183:12
Without w., wealth is worthless 183:15
Wise A w. head makes a close mouth 183:55
A w. man cares not ... 183:45
A w. man changes his mind ... 183:60
A w. man commonly has foolish children 183:71
A w. man esteems every place ... 183:62
A w. man is a great wonder 183:29
A w. man is never less alone ... 183:20
A w. man may sometimes play the fool 183:63
A w. man needs not blush ... 183:61
A w. man never wants a weapon 183:25
He is a w. man who, when he is well ... 183:38
He is not w. ... 183:40
He is w. enough that can keep himself warm 183:37
He is w. that has wit enough ... 183:39
He is w. that is honest 183:56
He is w. that is rich 180:127
He is w. that is ware ... 183:42
He is w. that knows when he's well enough 183:43
He is w. who looks ahead 70:2
He seems w. ... 165:5
He that is a w. man by day ... 183:59
He that is truly w. and great ... 183:36
He was very w. who first gave a reward 183:47
If the w. erred not ... 183:72
No man is born w. ... 183:9
No man is w. at all times 183:68
No man so w. but he may be deceived 13:15
None is so w., but the fool overtakes him 69:96
Send a w. man on an errand ... 168:86
The w. forget insults ... 42:16
The w. hand does not all ... 69:82
The w. seek wisdom ... 183:58
W. is the man who has two loaves ... 183:57
W. men are caught in wiles 183:70
W. men have their mouth ... 183:54
W. men learn ... 62:36

W. men make proverbs ... 69:43
W. men propose ... 183:65
W. men silent ... 183:53
W. men wear their horns ... 155:14
Wisest The w. man may fall 183:69
W. is he ... 183:44
Wish The w. is father ... 182:39
Wishers W. and woulders ... 182:37
Wishes If w. were butter-cakes ... 182:35
If w. were horses ... 182:34
If w. were thrushes ... 182:36
Mere w. ... 182:32
W. can never fill a sack 182:33
Wit Better w. than wealth 183:16
It is w. to pick a lock ... 183:35
Want of w. ... 183:17
W. and wisdom ... 183:22
W. without learning ... 102:14
Witham W. pike ... 58:50
Wive It is hard to w. ... 113:18
Wives W. must be had ... 113:40
Wiving In w. and thriving ... 113:43
Woe A man is well or w. ... 114:3
No w. to want 136:57
W. to him that is alone 161:14
W. to the house ... 141:21
W. to the kingdom ... 19:18
Woeful W. is the household ... 184:17
Woes W. unite foes 2:8
Wolf As a w. is like a dog ... 68:17
The w. knows what the ill beast thinks 33:31
The w. may lose his teeth ... 18:30
Who keeps company with the w. ... 29:14
Woman A bad w. ... 184:101
A w., a dog, and a walnut-tree ... 49:26
A w. and a cherry ... 11:53
A w. and a glass ... 184:74
A w. conceals ... 184:65
A w. cuts her wisdom teeth ... 184:39
A w. either loves or hates ... 184:23
A w. has an eye ... 184:93
A w. is a weathercock 184:19
A w. is flax ... 184:94
A w. is the weaker vessel 184:98
A w. kissed ... 184:84
A w. need but look on her apron-string ... 184:43
A w.'s advice is no great thing ... 184:40
A w.'s answer ... 184:53
A w.'s mind and a winter wind ... 184:20
A w.'s place is in the home 184:69
A w.'s strength ... 184:46
A w.'s sword ... 184:45
A w.'s thoughts ... 184:22
A w.'s tongue is the last thing ... 184:49

A w.'s tongue wags ... 184:48
A w.'s work ... 184:72
Find a w. without an excuse ... 184:44
From the evil w. guard yourself ... 184:78
If a w. were as little ... 184:16
Let no w.'s painting ... 184:79
Tell a w. she is fair ... 184:82
The w. that deliberates ... 146:7
Who has a w. has an eel ... 184:75
W. is the confusion ... 184:95
Women   All w. are good 184:15
All w. may be won 184:81
Many w., many words ... 184:55
The more w. look in their glass ... 24:9
Three w. make a market 184:58
Three w., three geese ... 184:59
Weal and w. cannot pan ... 184:8
Where there are w. and geese ... 184:57
W. and dogs ... 184:5
W. and hens ... 184:70
W. and music ... 184:76
W. and sparrows ... 184:56
W. and wine ... 51:34
W. are as wavering ... 184:21
W. are great talkers 184:51
W. are like wasps ... 184:12
W. are necessary evils 184:18
W. are saints in church ... 184:32
W. are the devil's nets 184:2
W. are the snares of Satan 184:1
W. have long hair ... 184:38
W. in mischief ... 184:90
W. in state affairs ... 184:14
W. laugh when they can ... 184:33
W. may blush to hear ... 184:29
W. must have their wills while they live ... 184:24
W. naturally deceive ... 184:28
W., priests, and poultry ... 184:66
W. resist ... 184:85
W.'s counsel is cold 184:9
W.'s instinct ... 184:89
W. will have their wills 184:25
W. will have the last word 184:54
W. will say anything 184:52
Wonder   W. is the daughter of ignorance 96:3
Woo   A man may w. where he will ... 109:92
To w. is a pleasure ... 109:91
Wood   It is a sairy w. ... 143:13
Once w. ... 69:18
W. in a wilderness ... 136:110
Wool   There is no w. so white ... 29:33
Woos   He that w. a maid ... 109:89
Word   A good w. costs no more ... 101:24

A w. and a stone let go ... 168:17
A w. before ... 70:4
A w. spoken ... 142:8
A w. to the wise ... 168:85
From w. to deed ... 41:22
One ill w. asks another 44:19
While the w. is in your mouth ... 168:18
Words   A man of w. ... 41:10
Fair w. and foul deeds ... 41:24
Fair w. and foul play ... 41:25
Fair w. break no bones 101:21
Fair w. fill not the belly 168:31
Fair w. hurt not the mouth 101:22
Fair w. will not make the pot play 168:32
Few w. are best 168:78
Fine w. butter no parsnips 168:30
Flow of w. ... 168:104
Good w. and ill deeds ... 41:26
Good w. anoint us ... 168:64
Good w. are good cheap 101:23
Good w. cool more ... 168:28
Good w. cost nought 101:25
Good w. fill not a sack 168:34
Good w. without deeds ... 41:16
Hard w. break no bones 34:1
He who gives fair w. ... 168:33
Ill w. are bellows ... 168:63
In many w., a lie or two may escape 168:67
In many w., the truth goes by 168:68
Many w., many buffets 168:6
W. and feathers ... 139:9
W. are but wind ... 139:10
W. are but wind, but blows unkind 168:54
W. are mere bubbles of water ... 41:9
W. bind men 168:19
W. cut more than swords 168:53
W. fly ... 188:8
W. have wings ... 168:16
W. may pass ... 168:55
Work   All w. and no play ... 48:50
He who wants the w. badly done ... 131:18
If you won't w. ... 48:41
It is good to w. wisely ... 48:27
It is not w. that kills ... 186:7
Mix w. with leisure ... 48:51
Well to w. and make a fire ... 158:7
W. expands ... 48:47
W. for nought ... 95:2
Workman   A bad w. ... 147:24
The w. is known by his work 48:60
Works   He who w. before dawn ... 52:12
He who w. begins well ... 170:13
World   All the w. loves a lover 109:24
Better be out of the w. ... 50:14
It is a good w. ... 185:15

The w. goes on wheels 185:6
The w. is a ladder ... 185:12
The w. is a long journey 185:1
The w. is a mirror ... 185:10
The w. is a net ... 185:8
The w. is a stage ... 185:11
The w. is a wide place 185:2
The w. is bound ... 185:9
The w. is but a little place ... 185:4
The w. is for him ... 130:12
The w. is full of fools 69:21
The w. is full of knaves 10:34
The w. is like a dancing girl ... 185:7
The w. is nought 185:13
The w. still he keeps ... 14:9
The w. turns as a ball 185:5
The w. will not last alway 17:23
This w. is nothing ... 185:14
This w. is unstable ... 70:24
When all the w. shall be aloft ... 58:25
With all the w. have war ... 58:4
Worm Even a w. will turn 56:6
Worse No man is the w. for knowing ... 153:51
The w. luck now ... 111:26
What is w. than ill luck 2:18
W. things happen ... 28:44
Worst The w. hog ... 44:26
When things are at the w. ... 127:12
Worth A man's w. ... 187:1
He is w. no weal ... 44:24
If a job's w. doing ... 48:1
The w. of a thing is best known ... 187:5
The w. of a thing is what it will bring 187:4
W. has been underrated ... 187:3
Worthier It is a w. thing ... 90:11
Wound An ill w. is cured ... 42:9
The w. that bleeds inwardly ... 162:14
Though the w. be healed ... 62:24
Wounded A w. reputation ... 64:23
Wranglers W. never want words 141:33
Wrath Take heed of the w. of a mighty man ... 5:9
When w. speaks ... 5:13
W. killeth the foolish man 5:6
W. often consumes ... 5:7
Write W. down the advice ... 3:26
Writing By w. you learn to write 62:16
W. destroys ... 188:9
Written It is w. upon a wall in Rome ... 58:69
Wrong All w. will end 127:33
Do w. once ... 41:48
If anything can go w. ... 111:22
No w. without a remedy 104:48

W. has no warrant 10:51
W. laws ... 104:23
W. never comes right 10:52
Wrongs He w. not an old man ... 125:50
Two w. do not make a right 10:53

# Y

Year One y. a nurse ... 124:37
Years The more thy y. ... 125:63
Y. know more ... 125:6
Yellow Y.'s forsaken ... 167:30
Yelping Y. curs ... 141:16
Yorkshire Y. born ... 58:27
Yorkshireman Give a Y. a halter ... 58:28
Young As soon goes the y. lamb's skin ... 39:70
As soon goes the y. sheep ... 39:69
A y. maid married to an old man ... 113:72
A y. man married ... 113:19
A y. man should not marry yet ... 113:89
A y. physician ... 87:55
Of y. men die many ... 125:67
The y. pig grunts ... 125:43
Y. colts will canter 19:34
Y. men may die ... 125:68
Y. men's knocks ... 19:64
Y. men think old men fools ... 125:55
Y. saint ... 19:47
Yourself Y. first ... 153:4
Youth If y. knew what age would crave ... 19:61
What y. is used to ... 54:14
Who that in y. ... 19:65
Y. and age ... 125:54
Y. and white paper ... 19:28
Y. never casts for peril 19:56
Y. will have its course 19:35
Yule Y. is come ... 117:6
Y. is young in Yule even ... 17:39

# Z

Zeal Z. is fit only for wise men ... 129:19
Z., when it is a virtue ... 129:22
Z. without knowledge ... 129:18
Z. without prudence ... 129:20